THE WRITINGS OF

Theodore Roosevelt

THE AMERICAN HERITAGE SERIES

THE AMERICAN HERITAGE SERIES

Under the General Editorship of

LEONARD W. LEVY AND ALFRED YOUNG

THE WRITINGS OF
Theodore Roosevelt

edited by

WILLIAM H. HARBAUGH *A REAL COMIC*

University of Virginia

THE BOBBS - MERRILL COMPANY, INC.

INDIANAPOLIS *and* NEW YORK

FOREWORD

"Teddy" Roosevelt has so often been caricatured as a man of frenetic action—as a cowboy and big game hunter, as a "trust buster" and wielder of the "Big Stick" in foreign affairs—that an anthology representing his "political and social thought" may come as a surprise to some. His reputation has also suffered at the hands of a generation of scholars who found his policies contradictory, his thinking superficial, and his contribution to progressivism solely those of a "moralist."

Professor Harbaugh has perhaps done as much as any scholar to correct these one-sided versions of "T.R." His biography of Roosevelt has already won a place, as the historian Eric Goldman has put it, as "a big lusty volume, vigorous in style, outspoken and combative in its judgments," sympathetic, yet critical, and at all times in command of the historical period. This anthology has been assembled in the same spirit. Roosevelt, Professor Harbaugh points out, was "neither an original nor profound thinker." Yet as the first reform President of the modern era and as the first President to use America's new power on the world scene, he expressed himself frequently and well. The problems on which he broke new ground continue to compel our attention, from the regulation of corporations and social reform, from civil service and conservation to "imperialism" and "power politics."

The anthology covers almost all the issues Roosevelt dealt

with in his own day. Although the focus is on the mature man, the selections also illustrate the changes and contradictions in his thought. Well-known public papers are included, as are important neglected speeches, private letters, and generous excerpts from his autobiography. The result is the fullest one-volume anthology of Roosevelt writings, which, in itself, will help to resolve the question of Roosevelt's "place in history."

This book is one of a series of which the aim is to provide the essential primary sources of the American experience, especially of American thought. The series, when completed, will constitute a documentary library of American history, filling a need long felt among scholars, students, libraries, and general readers for authoritative collections of original materials. Some volumes will illuminate the thought of significant individuals, such as James Madison or Louis Brandeis; some will deal with movements, such as those of the Antifederalists or the Populists; others will be organized around special themes, such as Puritan political thought, or American Catholic thought on social questions. Many volumes will take up the large number of subjects traditionally studied in American history for which, surprisingly, there are no documentary anthologies; others will pioneer in introducing new subjects of increasing importance to scholars and to the contemporary world. The series aspires to maintain the high standards demanded of contemporary editing, providing authentic texts, intelligently and unobtrusively edited. It will also have the distinction of presenting pieces of substantial length that give the full character and flavor of the original. The series will be the most comprehensive and authoritative of its kind.

Leonard W. Levy
Alfred Young

CONTENTS

The Coming of the Spanish-American War

A Defense of the Acquisition of the Philippines

III · THE BURDEN OF EMPIRE

Premature Independence for the Philippines Rejected

The Economic Welfare of the Island Dependencies

The United States' "heel of Achilles"

IV · ROOSEVELT AND LATIN AMERICA

Roosevelt Takes Panama

The Monroe Doctrine

V · ECONOMIC POLICY AND PROBLEMS

Trust Busting Versus Regulation of Corporations

A More Equitable Tax Structure

Tariff Policy

VI · CONSERVATION

The Struggle for an Enlightened Policy

VII · TOWARD THE WELFARE STATE

Organized Labor

X · PROGRESSIVE REFORM

Responsible and Constructive Criticism

Socialism

The Progressive Synthesis

XI · WAR AND PEACE

INTRODUCTION

I

"I have come to the conclusion," Theodore Roosevelt wrote the president of Cornell University in 1900, midway through his two-year term as governor of New York, "that I have mighty little originality of my own. What I do is try to get ideas from men whom I regard as experts along certain lines, and then try to work out those ideas." Sometime later he explained himself further to one of the G.O.P.'s machine bosses: "As for my impulsiveness and my alliance with labor agitators, social philosophers, taxation reformers and the like, . . . I want to be perfectly sane . . . but I do have a good deal of fellow feeling for our less fortunate brother, and I am a good deal puzzled over some of the inequalities in life, as life now exists. . . . All I want to do is cautiously to feel my way to see if we cannot make the general conditions of life a little easier,—a little better."[1]

Flashes of self-revelation like those testify eloquently to Gifford Pinchot's assertion that Roosevelt had "true humility of mind." But they also suggest why he has never been enshrined in the American Pantheon of political philosophers.

---

[1] Except as otherwise noted, all quotations are taken from William Henry Harbaugh, *Power and Responsibility: The Life and Times of Theodore Roosevelt* (New York: Farrar, Straus & Cudahy, 1961).

As he so disarmingly confessed, he was neither an original nor a profound thinker. His works are almost barren of the quest for first principles that gives enduring interest to the writings of the Founding Fathers. They lack the tragic perception that immortalized Lincoln's words or the noble vision that transformed Wilson's substanceless generalities into transcendent realities. And they have none of the metaphysical subtleties that made Calhoun's exposition of a lost and unholy cause so superficially compelling.[2]

Yet, Roosevelt's writings are nonetheless fraught with human interest and practical wisdom. No American President was so widely, and in certain areas, so deeply read as he. No President enjoyed literature more, wrote history as well, or understood nature better. Robert Frost called him one "of our kind," and Van Wyck Brooks considered him "a man of genius." The dean of American historians of the West, Frederick Jackson Turner, termed Roosevelt's four volume *Winning of the West* (1889–1895) "a real service to our history." And the professional naturalist who accompanied him to Africa in 1909 wrote, "I constantly felt while with him that I was in the presence of the foremost naturalist of our time, as indeed I was."

Roosevelt's prose reflected these varied interests and attributes. It is rich in allusions to literary, historical, and natural phenomena; some passages in the historical works and some of the occasional essays are movingly poetic; and the style is vigorously masculine—earthy, pithy, and even when tender, forcibly direct. Nevertheless, it was his political career that gives his writings historical significance. The letters, speeches, and state papers printed here are those of a man who was a dynamic force from his baptism in politics in 1881 to the day of his death in January 1919.

---

[2] For a perceptive statement of this thesis, see Elting E. Morison's introduction to Vol. V, *The Letters of Theodore Roosevelt*, eds. Elting E. Morison and John M. Blum, 8 vols. (Cambridge: Harvard University Press, copyright, 1951–1954 by the President and Fellows of Harvard College.)

Elected to the New York State Assembly at the age of twenty-three as a "Blue-Stocking" Republican, he rose, in his own apt phrase, "like a rocket." In his second term he emerged as the leader of an influential minority of reform-minded Republicans. And despite the death of his mother and young bride early in his third term ("It was a grim and evil fate," he wrote, "but I have never believed it did any good to flinch or yield for any blow, nor does it lighten the blow to cease from working"), he pushed through an imposing body of reform legislation before retiring briefly from politics in 1884.

After spending more than two years in the Dakotas raising cattle and writing history, Roosevelt returned to New York in 1886 to run a hopeless race for mayor against Abram S. Hewitt and Henry George. Then, following a second marriage and a tour of Europe, he lived on Long Island as a gentleman scholar and sportsman until 1889 when he was appointed to the United States Civil Service Commission. During the next six years his energetic and imaginative enforcement of the laws virtually institutionalized civil service, and had he never performed another service for the American nation, that alone would have perpetuated his memory (Documents 47, 48, and 49). As virtually every historian of the movement has written, Roosevelt gave the commission administrative vigor and a sense of mission.

In 1895 Roosevelt again returned to New York City to serve two tumultuous, yet creative, years as president of the Board of Police Commissioners. Then, following his appointment as Assistant Secretary of the Navy in 1897, he tried vainly to persuade the McKinley administration to build a two-ocean fleet. He also worked frenetically for war against Spain; and when it finally came in the spring of 1898, he resigned his post and organized a volunteer cavalry regiment, "The Rough Riders." Discharged that fall as a brevet brigadier-general whose fame was exceeded only by that of Dewey and Hobson, he freely invoked his military image in a successful campaign for the governorship of New York.

Roosevelt's governorship (1899–1901) proved one of the
most distinguished in New York's history to that time—even
the fiercely Democratic New York *World* conceded that "the
controlling purpose and general course of his administration
have been high and good." It also prepared him admirably
for, and in fact proved a microcosm of, his Presidency. As
governor no less than as President, he met bitter opposition by
the conservative leaders of his own party; and as governor
hardly less than as President, he mobilized public opinion so
dramatically that he forced one legislative breakthrough after
another. Such was his challenge to the corporations' domination of the New York state Republican machine, indeed, that
the "Easy Boss," Senator Thomas C. Platt, seized upon an
opportunity to drive him out of the state in 1900 by joining
a full-blown Western movement to nominate him for the vice-
presidency. Elected in the Republican landslide of 1900,
Roosevelt became President on September 14, 1901, following
William McKinley's death of an assassin's bullet.

The youngest man who ever occupied the White House,
Roosevelt was also the first President-reformer of the modern
industrial era—the first to concern himself with the judiciary's
massive property bias, with the maldistribution of wealth, and
with the subversion of the democratic process by businessmen
and their spokesmen in Congress; the first to comprehend the
conservation problem in its multiple facets, the first to set
forth a broad regulatory program for capital, and the first to
encourage, however cautiously, the growth of labor unions. He
was, in fact, the first President who both understood and reacted constructively to the problems created by the rise of a
business civilization. And though his militance prevented him
from being revered, his magnetic leadership and warm human
qualities won him widespread respect and affection. As Stan-
ley M. Isaacs, for years a catalytic force on New York City's
council, wrote four decades after he had marched with Roosevelt's legions in the Bull Moose campaign of 1912, "I doubt

if anyone today can realize the personal inspiration that came from direct contact with T. R. or can appreciate the fervor that animated . . . us. T. R. gave us new goals—faith in our country's ideals . . . and confidence in the ultimate success of justice and sound ideas."

Obviously, no commentary on Roosevelt's personality, no survey of his career or analysis of his thought, can explain the loyalty and devotion he inspired in Isaacs and countless other civic-minded men, including Gifford Pinchot, Felix Frankfurter, and Henry L. Stimson. So great was the range of his interests and the variety of his relationships, in fact, that one is tempted to quote one of Roosevelt's Harvard classmates who wrote that he was *sui generis* and be done with it. But to do that is to beg a question that can be explored, if not resolved. It is also to pass up the pleasures and frustrations of biographical and historical engagement.

For all the strident egotism and occasional ruthlessness that alienated many of his contemporaries and a whole generation of historians, Roosevelt's personality was uniquely appealing. Generous, considerate, and fair-minded, he valued men for what they were worth. "He was different from anybody that I had ever met," his hunting guide and lifelong friend, William W. "Bill" Sewall, recalled. "He didn't look for a brilliant man when he found me." Scores of intimates have remarked on Roosevelt's graciousness and innate courtesy. And even his arch-enemy, Woodrow Wilson, confessed that Roosevelt had "charmed" him. "There is," he said, "a sweetness about him that is very compelling. You can't resist the man."

Charm may explain Roosevelt's hold on tough-minded men's affections, but it hardly accounts for their loyalty or esteem. Here the evidence is conclusive: they believed in his values and purposes even as they disagreed with many of his policies or actions. No one perceived Roosevelt's characteristics more clearly nor described them more graphically than Joseph B. Bishop, a reporter for the New York *Evening Post* during

W.W. replaced Roos.- presidency .

Roosevelt's police commissionership. "What he thinks he says at once, thinks alive," he wrote. "But with it," Bishop continued, "he has great qualities which make him an invaluable public servant—inflexible honesty, absolute fearlessness, and devotion to good government which amounts to religion. We must let him work in his own way for nobody can induce him to change it." Hence Roosevelt's hold on men as divergent in temperament as Elihu Root, who made the decision that drove him to Armageddon in 1912, and William Allen White, the Kansas editor who followed him there.

II

Although Roosevelt's views on public policy developed steadily over the years, most of the assumptions upon which they rested remained constant. As the scion of an old Dutch mercantile family long prominent in New York City's affairs, he was inculcated as a matter of course with a belief in philanthropy, *noblesse oblige,* and civic responsibility. These values were sharpened and reinforced by the example of his father, the consciousness of whom he carried through life. A buoyant, dominant, and energetic man, he combined, in his son's words, "strength and courage with gentleness, tenderness, and great unselfishness." For months after his death in 1878, Theodore had brooded over his loss. "I realize more and more every day," he wrote in his diary, "that I am as much inferior to Father morally and mentally as physically." However, he added in a display of fatalism that lost its religious cast as he grew older, there was nothing to do but "Trust in the Lord and do good!"

The strongest of the elder Roosevelt's influences was on Theodore's moral outlook. For both father and son, morality was the measure of manliness. A man was either honest or dishonest, virtuous or unvirtuous; he was strong or weak, responsible or irresponsible; he had character or he did not have character.

True, Roosevelt softened and even compromised these absolutes in practice. He was forever fascinated by the colorfully wicked—by Western badmen and other asocial types who possessed physical courage if little else. And he usually found it easier to maintain viable relationships with autocratic politicians like Speaker of the House Joseph G. "Uncle Joe" Cannon, for whom power was an end in itself, than with compulsive idealists like Wisconsin's Senator Robert M. La Follette, for whom it was the means to a social end. Yet the point remains: his ultimate belief was in moral absolutes. Neither his understanding of the imperfectibility of man and his institutions nor his avowed commitment to politics as the art of the possible ever changed the ideal.

One of the most important components of Roosevelt's moral system was duty. Man was, or ought to be, a socially responsible being; and as such, his obligations to family, work, and community took precedence over his individualistic drives and wants. If there was a war, the responsible citizen was obliged to fight it. If there was a reform to be enacted, he was constrained to support it. If there was corruption in government, he was bound to expose and destroy it.

This concept of duty is explicit in the opening selection, "The Duties of American Citizenship" (Document 1), and is implicit in most of the selections that follow. Roosevelt was consistently, if not completely, moved by it during his entire career; and on occasions too numerous to list it prompted him to speak out when it was politic to remain silent. As a freshman assemblyman he flouted the G.O.P.'s leadership by charging a Republican-appointed State Supreme Court Justice with collusion. As civil service commissioner a decade later he contributed to President Benjamin Harrison's downfall by openly criticizing the Postmaster General's violations of civil service regulations. And as a military hero in 1898 he lost a decoration he dearly wanted and had surely earned by publicly protesting the War Department's failure to remove troops from the yellow fever zone in Cuba at the end of the Spanish-American War.

Roosevelt's feeling for duty also colored his friendships and influenced the quality of his appointments. Thus his admiration for Elihu Root was based not on Root's conservatism, which he often disapproved, but on Root's acceptance of the burdens of public service. And so with William Howard Taft, Philander C. Knox, and many other conservatives whose disposition to serve society Roosevelt stimulated and utilized.

Of comparable importance was justice. As John Blum has observed, Roosevelt was not ordinarily a compassionate man.[3] He valued individual responsibility and strength of personality too highly to be shaken, as many sensitive men of his generation were, by the plight of the lower classes. But he was an unusually just man in the abstract and, except when personal conflict warped his judgment, when put to the test. Because he was also an intelligent and scientifically-minded man, moreover, he came gradually to conceive of justice in distributive, no less than in retributive, terms. The changes in his attitude toward labor and the underprivileged are revealing of this.

When Roosevelt took his seat in the State Legislature in 1882, he carried most of the prejudices of his class and background with him. He was contemptuous of recent immigrants, particularly Irish-Catholics. He regarded the poor as slothful, the rich as industrious and virtuous. And he subscribed uncritically to the laissez-faire beliefs of his Harvard professors and family friends. For him, as for them, the precepts of political economy were fixed and inviolable; and as late as his third term, he opposed a bill to reduce the working hours of streetcar conductors to twelve per day in the conviction that it was no more possible to alter the iron laws of economics than to repeal the law of gravity.

[3] John Morton Blum, *The Republican Roosevelt* (Cambridge: Harvard University Press, 1954), p. 29.

Yet, at almost the very moment Roosevelt was affirming laissez-faire as a general principle, he was reconsidering its application. The first departure came in his first term in the Assembly when Samuel Gompers engaged his interest in a measure to regulate tenement workshops. As Roosevelt later wrote, "the respectable people I knew were against it; it was contrary to the principles of political economy of the laissez-faire kind; and the business men who spoke to me about it shook their heads and said that it was designed to prevent a man doing as he wished and as he had a right to do with what was his own." Nevertheless, he gave it full and effective support, and thereafter his concern for distributive justice steadily deepened. By 1895, if not before, he was denying that Darwin's law of natural selection applied unqualifiedly to social evolution. The leaders of society, he wrote in a review of Benjamin Kidd's *Social Evolution* (1894), "All . . . came from the classes where the struggle for the bare means of subsistence is less severe . . . than in the class below. In civilized societies the rivalry of natural selection works against progress."[4] As governor in 1899 and 1900, Roosevelt supported numerous measures designed to ease the struggle for existence by state intervention in the economy (Documents 23 and 27). His statements then and later leave no doubt that he believed government should encourage private industry to improve workingmen's conditions of labor. As he said on signing a bill to strengthen the eight-hour day for state employees, it was the duty of the state "to set a good example as an employer of labor both as to the number of hours of labor exacted and as to paying a just and reasonable wage."

While Roosevelt's compulsion for justice was forcing him out of the intellectual strait jacket which bound the social Darwinists, his conservative strain was causing him to affirm

[4] Theodore Roosevelt, "Social Evolution," *The Works of Theodore Roosevelt*, ed. Hermann Hagedorn, Memorial Edition (New York: Charles Scribner's Sons, 1925), XIV, 112.

many traditional values. Few public servants fought corruption as persistently as Roosevelt did. He saw, especially after he began to understand the force of environment, that corruption often reflected the impersonal working of a social, economic, or political system (Documents 36 and 37). But he clung to the belief that only character could prevent the most perfect system from being corrupted. This view pervaded his writings and speeches, determined the quality of his appointments, and caused his refusal to accept socialism as a system in spite of his support of public education and government-owned utilities (Document 57). There were communities where "self-raising is very hard for the time being," he wrote the socialist novelist Upton Sinclair in 1906, but "there are many, many men who lack any intelligence or character and who therefore cannot thus raise themselves." Consequently, he concluded, he deplored the "pathetic belief" of the characters who "preach socialism" in the last chapter of *The Jungle*.

The ideal of justice also had a marked impact upon Roosevelt's attitude toward law. Like most conservatives, he was obsessed with order; and as police commissioner he prosecuted criminals relentlessly. But unlike many men who call themselves conservatives, he insisted that the law should be enforced against rich and poor alike. During his presidency he repeatedly lashed the judiciary for misusing the injunction in labor cases and for failing "to stop the abuses of the criminal rich"; he also flailed juries for not imposing prison sentences on reputable businessmen who had broken the law. And in 1912, after six years of protest against the courts' tendency to disregard the legislatures' will in social and economic cases, he came out for the recall of judicial decisions on the state level (Document 52).

From all this emerged a social philosophy that placed primary emphasis on what may best be termed the commonweal. At once more than voluntarism and less than statism, it conceived that private and public interests should be harmonized and that organizations and their leaders should be encouraged, and if necessary forced, to pursue socially useful ends. This concern for the whole dominated Roosevelt's mature thought; when he preached duty and responsibility, as he so often did, it was in the conviction that there could be no enduring government, no advanced civilization, without it.

The problem, of course, was to avoid thwarting the individual's egoistic, yet potentially creative, thrust. Roosevelt's solution anticipated the mid-twentieth century welfare state. He would use government—local, state, and national—to foster both individual and organizational fulfillment. This meant minimum wage and hours laws and protection of life and limb for workers. It meant public education—mechanical, agricultural, and academic. It meant land reclamation, flood prevention, and constructive utilization of natural resources. It meant active encouragement of labor unions and the regulation of giant corporations. And it meant almost complete acceptance of an evolutionary or open-ended theory of national development.

Perceiving that society was becoming more and more interdependent, Roosevelt concluded that it must constantly reorder its institutions. Far more than any conscious or unconscious desire to aggrandize power, far more than any Germanic bent toward authoritarianism, these views made him a nationalist. Lincoln, not Napoleon or Bismarck, was his hero; a government that responded creatively to the felt needs of the times, his ideal. Succinctly and compellingly, he stated the case for continuous adjustment in his first Annual Message to Congress in December 1901:

> When the Constitution was adopted, at the end of the eighteenth century, no human wisdom could foretell the sweeping changes, alike in industrial and political conditions, which were to take place at the beginning of the twentieth century. At that time it was accepted as a matter of course that the several States were the proper authorities to regulate, so far as was then necessary, the comparatively insignificant and strictly

localized corporate bodies of the day. The conditions are
wholly different and wholly different action is called for.

Despite the regimentation implicit in Roosevelt's concept of
a duty-conscious citizenry and a socially-purposeful government, he was himself less authoritarian than John Adams, more
open-minded than Thomas Jefferson, and less doctrinaire than
Woodrow Wilson. As with most men of action, however, his
thought was often compromised by his deeds. His reading of
history, for example, convinced him of the value of a free
press. He believed, as he explained in an 1883 statement opposing a bill to tighten the newspaper libel law in New York,
that "it is a great deal better to err a little bit on the side of
having too much discussion and having too virulent language
used by the press, rather than to err on the side of having them
not say what they ought to say, especially with reference to
public men and measures." But because he also believed that
"freedom does not mean absence of all restraint," he refused
to regard freedom of speech as an absolute. He often chal-
lenged the right of anarchists and less extreme radicals to
speak out, and as President he once allowed his anger over
an unfair accusation to provoke him into filing libel charges
against two newspapers.

Conversely, personality traits strengthened Roosevelt's experimental bent. His intimates considered him the most advisable of men—Gifford Pinchot said, surely in exaggeration, that
he had "no pride of opinion"—and years before he became
President his tendency to consult experts had become a settled
practice (Document 27). By the time he was governor he was
warning against "attempting to establish invariable rules"; and
both then and later his private conversations, public addresses,
and official messages were so studded with recommendations
for new projects that the phrase, "we should try this to see if
it works," became a virtual refrain. As he put it in a statement
defending public ownership of New York City's water supply,
"In one instance a private corporation may be able to do the

work best. In another the State or city may do it best. In yet a
third, it may be to the advantage of everybody to give free
scope to the power of some individual captain of industry."

III

As much as any other of Roosevelt's works, his historical
writings offer insight into the values and ideals that guided his
public career. Early in the 1880's he published *The Naval
War of 1812*, a work of limited scope, high technical compe-
tence, and superb descriptions of sea battles. Two biographies,
Thomas Hart Benton and *Gouveneur Morris*, followed in 1887
and 1888. Although neither equaled *The Naval War* in scholarship, both illumine Roosevelt's beliefs. In the life of the Missouri Senator he deplored "the short-sighted selfishness of
many of the northeasterners" who opposed Benton's plan to
distribute Western lands to actual settlers at low cost. He
approved Benton's opposition to the Mexican War, terming
the American attitude toward Mexico a "belligerent, or, more
properly speaking, tyrannical way of looking at neighboring
territory." He called slavery "a grossly anachronistic and un-
American form of evil." He held, however, that its eventual
extinction was certain; and he argued that non-abolitionist
political leaders like Lincoln and Seward "did more than all
the professional Abolitionists combined really to bring about
its destruction," adding in a charge not unlike the one he made
against "muck-raking" in 1906 that the abolitionists "belonged
to that class of men that is always engaged in some agitation
or other." He also foreshadowed his attack on free silver in
1896 by endorsing Benton's and Andrew Jackson's stand for
hard money. "A craze for 'soft' or dishonest, money—a green-
back movement, or one for short-weight silver dollars—works
more to the disadvantage of the whole mass of the people,"
he wrote, "than even to that of the Capitalist."
Ironically, the biography of Morris, an arch-conservative of

the era of the American Revolution, brought out more of
Roosevelt's liberal idealism than did the study of Benton. Pre-
dictably, he praised Morris's support of order and "the honest
payment of debts." He also commended him for those attributes "of generous daring and lofty disinterestedness which
we like to associate with the name American." But, and this
was the crux of Roosevelt's brief against Morris and his kind
of conservatism, he "distrusted the mass of the people," denied
the validity of "all generous and unselfish motives," and championed "a system of class representation, leaning toward aristocracy." Morris's trouble, he contended, was that "the force
and subtlety of his reasoning were all marred by his incurable
cynicism and deep-rooted distrust of mankind."

The transcendent theme of both biographies and the four-
volume *Winning of the West* (1889–1895) was national unity.
It was, to repeat, a reasonably tolerant one, for Roosevelt was
not insensitive to the richness of regional differences. Part of
Benton's appeal, in fact, was his ability to blend sectional and
national interests without destroying the former's life force.
But it was nationalism nonetheless; and because of it Roosevelt rejected Jeffersonianism for Hamiltonianism despite his
own disapproval of economic elitism. It was Lincoln, however,
who invoked his uncritical admiration. The Civil War President was, he wrote, "the first who showed how a strong people
might have a strong government and yet remain the freest on
earth."

> He seized—half unwittingly—all that was best and wisest
> in the tradition of Federalism; he was the true successor of the
> Federalist leaders; but he grafted on their system a profound
> belief that the great heart of the nation beat for truth—honor
> —liberty.

Roosevelt's understanding of the Americanizing effect of the
Westward advance also influenced his later attitudes toward
immigration. He most admired the Scotch-Irish pioneers.

"These Irish representatives of the Covenanters were in the West almost what the Puritans were in the Northeast and more than the Cavaliers were in the South," he wrote. "Mingled with the descendents of many other races, they nevertheless formed the kernel of the distinctively and intensely American stock who were the pioneers of our people in their march westward. . . ." But, he continued, a single generation was enough to weld them and the others—the English, Germans, Huguenots, Dutch, and Swedish, into a single people. Long before the revolution they had "lost all remembrance of Europe and all sympathy with things European," he added. "Their iron surroundings made a mould which turned out all alike in the same shape. They resembled one another, and they differed from the rest of the world—even the world of America, and infinitely more, the world of Europe—in dress, in customs, and in mode of life." Furthermore, he concluded in a passage that underlined his grasp of the interaction between heredity and environment, "the influence of heredity was no more plainly perceptible than was the extent of individual variation. . . ." Although Roosevelt later developed misgivings about the power of the environment to Americanize some of the "new" immigrants of his own times rapidly enough to preserve cultural unity, he never changed that analysis fundamentally.

IV

As Roosevelt's biting historical references to abolitionists and reformers suggest, his idealism was often smothered in practice by his harsh conviction that politics was the art of the possible. This was as regrettable as it was inevitable, for it invited charges of insincerity and opportunism by reformers of his own day and by doctrinaire intellectuals of a later day. Perceiving that he understood both the issues and their ideal solutions, they insisted on judging him as a pure intellectual rather than as a political leader of exceptional intellectual interests. And even when they did see him as he actually was, they argued that the gulf between his thought and his deed was greater than it should have been.

To a degree they were right. Roosevelt aspired to greatness, and he was willing to make many of the mean compromises necessary to attain office and hold power. As he once confessed after making a bad appointment, "In politics we have to do a great many things we ought not to do." There were instances, too, when his idealization of gradualism was little more than a rationalization of his vaulting ambition. It is a matter of record that he sometimes rejected the reformers' advanced demands because moderate accomplishment would serve his personal interests better than no accomplishment. Yet even as he trimmed, he emphasized the need for more thorough reforms. And certainly he understood, as the doctrinaire reformers did not, that compromise was often the only constructive course. Resentfully, yet accurately, he unburdened himself to one of his reformer friends after a bitter, but successful, fight to unseat a corrupt state official during his governorship: "You can have no conception of the pressure, political, financial, and every other kind that has been brought to bear upon me to keep him in. . . . If I had done what the *Evening Post* and Dr. Parkhurst and Mr. Godkin and the smaller fry like Jack Chapman wanted [the independent reformers], I would not have had ten votes in the Senate to confirm my man."

The feeling for power that was also one of Roosevelt's dominant characteristics was as much a function of temperament as of mind. Obscure in origin—it may have stemmed from his relationship with his father who was, he once said, "the only man I ever feared"—it nevertheless influenced his actions, colored his value judgments, and suffused his political thought. He took extreme, indeed primitive, satisfaction in the exercise of power, and on a few unhappy occasions he used it abusively. He also defended its possession. "I don't think," he

wrote shortly before he left the Presidency, "that any harm
comes from the concentration of power in one man's hands
provided the holder does not keep it for more than a certain,
definite time, and then returns to the people from whom he
sprang."

Conceiving power as a creative force, Roosevelt sometimes
resented being inhibited by law. Few who knew him would
challenge Blum's statement that he, especially, "may have benefited from the limits on Presidential power which men who
understood the problem in 1787 created."[5] Yet fewer still
would deny that his feeling for power was one of his great
sources of strength, or that his compulsion to use it in the public, rather than his private, interest set him apart from the
Garys, Harrimans, Rockefellers, Morgans, and other authoritarian contemporaries in industry and finance.

The vigorous interplay of his many attributes marked Roosevelt's Presidency. At times his power complex tempered the
basic values of duty, morality, and justice, and occasionally it
overwhelmed them. More often, however, these values were
modified by the realities of the situation and by Roosevelt's
unqualified acceptance of politics as the art of the possible. In
spite of the compromises induced by his urge to achieve, in
spite of two or three wanton violations of democratic procedure, Roosevelt's seven and one-half years as President tended
to disprove rather than confirm Lord Acton's maxim that
power corrupts. Indubitably, the responsibilities of office so-
bered Roosevelt, and on almost all fronts and on almost all
important issues he rose to them. Rarely did he act impul-
sively, though it often appeared that he did, and only in a few
instances did he act arbitrarily. Even his worst blunders owed
more to faulty information than to a capricious attitude toward
power.

[5] Blum, *Republican Roosevelt*, p. 123.

v

Of the domestic issues of Roosevelt's presidency, three afford particular insight into his values and thought: the regulation of business, the conservation of natural resources, and the movement for social justice. The first was the most sensational and the most confusing, for Roosevelt's dramatic resurrection of the Sherman Anti-Trust Act in 1902 (Document 14) created the impression that he favored the indiscriminate destruction of big business. The impression was erroneous. He sought to reform, not destroy, business. Though that segment of the business community that refused to suffer any restraints upon its freedom of action deeply resented him, his main thrust was toward business' long-term welfare hardly less than toward the general public's. Again and again Roosevelt tried to impress this fact upon businessmen, but because he also insisted that they should reform, his effort was largely in vain.

If Roosevelt's thought was too constructive to discount the economic advantages of large-scale organization, it was also too moralistic to condone the inequities that had accompanied big business' rise. Even while he was exciting the popular imagination and expanding the power of the Presidency by attacking the most overweening trusts, he was planning a long-range regulatory program—one that points up his pragmatic, evolutionary cast of mind and his extraordinary respect for facts. Convinced that the first imperative was knowledge, he called for compulsory publicity of corporate earnings in his first Annual Message: "It is no limitation upon property rights or freedom of contract to require that when men receive from government the privilege of doing business under corporate form . . . they shall do so upon absolute truthful representations as to the value of the property in which the capital is to be invested."

A year and one-half later Congress created the Bureau of Corporations within the Department of Commerce and Labor.

Meanwhile Roosevelt intensified his offensive against the trusts in order to demonstrate his independence and to make Congress receptive to thoroughgoing regulation of railways. Partly in response to these pressures, the Hepburn railroad regulation bill (Document 15), the pure food and drug bill, and a meat-packing inspection measure were written into law in 1906. All were criticized as halfway measures, and all embodied compromises, but they were nonetheless significant. Each testified to Roosevelt's command of the political process, ripened his understanding of the regulatory problem, and contributed to the advanced program of the last years of his presidency and the Bull Moose campaign of 1912.

Of all Roosevelt's constructive endeavors, his drive to conserve the nation's natural resources was the most remarkable for sustained intellectual and administrative force. In none other did he fuse his scientific outlook and moralistic view of the public interest so completely; in only one other—foreign policy—did he submerge partisan considerations nearly so decisively; and in few others did he invoke the stewardship concept of his office so effectively. Based on the quasi-socialistic belief that natural resources belong to all the people, this program held no brief for either the rights of the states or the special privileges of private entrepreneurs (Document 54). In theory, it contended that "the fundamental idea of forestry is the perpetuation of forests by use" and that "every stream is a unit from its source to its mouth, and all its uses are interdependent" (Document 22). And in practice, it conflicted with the interests and aspirations of Western monopolies. Indeed, the states' rightists and their allies among the electric power companies were so powerful—Roosevelt called the utilities' monopoly "the most threatening which has ever appeared"—that he failed to marshal even a modicum of congressional support for multi-purpose river valley developments, though he did save what became the heart of the TVA by vetoing a bill that would have opened Muscle Shoals to haphazard private devel-

opment. Certainly Roosevelt's imaginative use of the powers
of his office, including some theretofore dormant ones, had
enduring consequences. Before he left office in March 1909,
one hundred and twenty-five million acres were added to the
forest reserves. Most large lumber companies were converted
to the selective-cutting procedures that assured both the perpetuation and constructive use of timber resources. The number of national parks was doubled, sixteen National Monu-
ments created, and fifty-one wildlife refuges established. Even
his bitter enemy, Senator Robert M. La Follette, wrote, "When
the historian . . . shall speak of Theodore Roosevelt, he is likely
to say . . . that his greatest work was inspiring and actually
beginning a world movement for . . . saving for the human
race the things on which alone a peaceful, progressive, and
happy life can be founded."

At the time, conservation was overshadowed by Roosevelt's
dramatization of the need for social justice, notably in the
treatment of labor. The first breakthrough came in 1902 when,
partly to avoid embarrassment in the fall elections, he intervened in a prolonged anthracite coal strike (Document 24).
Impressed by the miners' reasonableness and repelled by the
operators' arrogance, he used his office as a third force to settle
the strike in the workers' interest. The episode convinced
Roosevelt that big unionism was a necessary counterforce to
big business, and he tried in succeeding years to encourage the
union movement by attacking unfair use of the injunction in
strikes. At heart, however, he feared the power of labor as
much as he feared that of big business; he consequently concluded that the interest of business and labor, and particularly
that of the public, would best be served by compulsory arbitration (Document 25).

Meanwhile Roosevelt's respect for facts deepened his understanding of labor conditions and destroyed those vestiges of
laissez-faire theory that still lingered in his mind. Two matters,
especially, engaged his interest: the courts' tendency to strike

down laws regulating hours of employment and conservatives' contention that employers' liability or workmen's compensation legislation violated freedom of contract. The first provoked the attack on the courts that culminated in his demand for the recall of judicial decisions (Document 52); the second brought forth an early version of the calls for social justice that resounded through the land in 1912. Thus on January 31, 1908, a full year before Herbert Croly published *The Promise of American Life*, the book that was once believed to have converted Roosevelt to progressivism, he defended his standing demand for employers' liability legislation in a message that relegated the survival of the fittest doctrine to limbo. "It is hypocritical baseness," he asserted, "to speak of a girl who works in a factory where the dangerous machinery is unprotected as having the 'right' freely to contract to expose herself to dangers of life and limb. She has no alternative but to suffer want or else to expose herself to such dangers" (Document 31).

To some extent, the instinct for fairness that made Roosevelt an impassioned spokesman for social justice governed his attitude toward religious and ethnic minorities. His support of the open society was far stronger than that of most progressives, including Woodrow Wilson; except for an arbitrary action against three companies of Negro soldiers in 1906, his record was free of prejudice. To be sure, the point should not be pushed too hard; as his attitude toward religious minorities suggests, his policy was more influenced by sophisticated conservatism than liberal positivism. He disapproved, for example, the polygamous practices of the Mormons, and he regarded the Roman Catholic Church's authoritarian structure with distrust. He also believed that parochial education weakened the drive toward the cultural unity he deemed essential to national greatness (Document 45). But he further believed that religious strife was incomparably worse than religious diversity and that cultural unity could best be fostered by tolerating religious pluralism. So he established cordial relations with, and sought the counsel of, Catholic and Jewish leaders. He appointed numerous members of religious minorities to office while police commissioner and governor. And as president he gave preferential treatment to a few Catholics and Jews in order to break down prejudice, dramatize their fitness for high office, and show that the channels of advancement were open (Document 43).

Roosevelt's views on race were even more ambiguous than those on religion. He was too widely and intelligently read in the rise and fall of civilizations to endorse the blatant racism of his times. "A great nation," he observed again and again, "rarely belongs to any one race." But he was also too steeped in biology and kindred subjects to accept uncritically the pure environmentalism of the Reform Darwinists (Documents 36, 37). No single cause, he repeatedly warned, can explain the complex process of social evolution. Forced nevertheless to take a position, he fastened on a pragmatic compromise that put practical considerations above theoretical ones. If a people proved adaptable, they merited full acceptance. If their institutions were backward, their historical conditioning inadequate, society's acceptance was slower and often incomplete. It was this belief that not all peoples could escape their history in one generation that made Roosevelt hold that Negroes should be uplifted before they were integrated (Document 38); that Filipinos should be prepared for self-government before they were granted independence (Document 8); and that the flow of uneducated immigrants into the United States should be restricted (Document 46).

* MY VIEW OF ROSEFIELD —   INCONSISTENTLY
— PRAGMATIC — DOES QUE   VI
SITUATION REQUIRES .

Roosevelt's views on foreign policy lacked the surface consistency of his domestic thought. Pulled first one way and then another by the competing claims of ideals and realities and forced constantly to adjust to a world in flux, he appeared with almost rhythmic regularity as a warhawk and peacemaker or as an ultranationalist and internationalist. Behind these changing stances, however, lay three convictions so unalterable as to constitute principles: (1) self-defense was the first imperative of organized society; (2) the interests of highly civilized ✂ peoples took precedence over those of backward peoples; (3) advanced peoples were morally obligated to support the onward march of civilization. Only in the light of these convictions can Roosevelt's glorification of the warrior be put into proper perspective or the apparent contradictions between his domestic and foreign policies be understood. And even when this is done his thought defies simplification, for at different times and in different situations one or another principle was dominant.

The intrusion of extraneous factors, usually emotional but sometimes political, further complicated matters. Thus, the rationality of Roosevelt's commitment to national security, to take the most obvious example, was obscured by his sometimes uncontrollable passion for military glory. His combative instincts had been reinforced by the tensions of a youthful struggle against ill-health, and he consequently strained from his adolescence to his old age to prove himself by feats of physical daring. More than once in the 1880's and 1890's he called for war in the ill-concealed hope that he might lead troops in battle; and in June 1897, just a little more than three years before he became President of the United States, he wrote, "No qualities called out by a purely peaceful life stand on a level with those stern and virile virtues which move the men of stout heart and strong hand who uphold the honor of their flag in battle."

Yet to cast Roosevelt's idealization of war into a purely psychological mold is to oversimplify both him and the generation of Americans he spoke for. Stripped of their rhetoric and divorced from his own psychic needs, his calls for the heroic stand firmly on the belief that the soldierly virtues of strength, courage, and sacrifice were crucial to the nation's ultimate welfare. It was this conviction that prompted Oliver Wendell Holmes to assert in 1898 that war was "divine" and that "this snug, over-safe corner of the world" needed one in order that the people might "realize that our comfortable routine is no eternal necessity of things . . . and . . . that we may be ready for danger." And it was this same conviction that moved Roosevelt to write when his youngest son was killed in World War I that life embraced more than "the selfish evanescence of the individual" and that unless "men are willing to fight and die for great ideals, including love of country, ideals will vanish, and the world will become one huge sty of materialism."

A similar blend of idealism, romanticism, and realism characterized Roosevelt's thought on imperialism and the Spanish-American War. It is surely true, as he later confided to his military aide, that he went to war in 1898 because it would give him a chance to cut his "little notch on the stick that stands as a measuring rod in every family" (Documents 5, 6). But it is even more true, as the corpus of his writings suggests, that the driving force behind his imperialism was his undeviating conviction that "superior" nations had a right to dominate "inferior" peoples in the interests of higher civilization. "Rome expanded and passed away," he wrote in phrases that would have done justice to Churchill, "but all western Europe, both Americas, Australia and large parts of Asia and Africa to this day continue the history of Rome. . . . Spain expanded and fell, but a whole continent to this day speaks Spanish and is covered with commonwealths of the Spanish tongue and culture. . . . England expanded and England will fall. But think of what she will leave behind her." For Roosevelt the "superior" peoples were those who were capable of governing themselves freely, wisely, and orderly—in a way, in short, that would raise the world-wide level of civilization. Some peoples, notably the Anglo-Americans, possessed this ability in higher degree than others; but, and the point is not irrelevant, their level of attainment was the product of historical rather than of biological factors. As Roosevelt wrote in a review of Charles H. Pearson's *National Life and Character* in 1894, society progresses mainly because of "the transmission of acquired characteristics, a process which in every civilized society operates . . . [against] . . . the baleful law of natural selection. . . ."[6] Upon this reading of social evolution Roosevelt grounded his "right of conquest" theory; and upon it he based its corollary—the duty of conquering nations to prepare subject peoples for self-government as rapidly as their state of development allowed. "I shall endeavor," he said at the start of his exemplary administration of the Philippine Islands, "progressively to increase the share which the Filipinos themselves take in the government of the islands, letting the advance in this direction be rapid or slow precisely in accordance with the capacity which the Filipinos themselves develop for self-restraint, moderation, and ability to combine the enjoyment of liberty with the enforcement of order" (Documents 8, 9).

Roosevelt's realism, and especially his sense of responsibility, softened the application of these principles during his presidency. To be sure, he broke old precedents with almost predictable regularity, acted independently of Congress, and held himself always ready to invoke force in defense of the national interest. But—and this is the measure of his increasing maturity—his conception of the national interest became progressively more enlightened. He abandoned the notion that a far-flung empire was the hallmark of greatness even as he strengthened America's position as a world power. He admitted an oriental country—Japan—into that privileged circle of

[6] Theodore Roosevelt, "National Life and Character," *The Works*, XIV, 249. For a suggestive reappraisal of Roosevelt's views on this and kindred topics, see David H. Burton, "Theodore Roosevelt's Social Darwinism," *Journal of the History of Ideas* (January-March 1965), XXVI, 103-18.

"superior" nations sanctioned to dominate the world. He lost his obsession for glory while maintaining a legitimate, if often hypersensitive, concern with security. And he worked industriously, indeed courageously, to foster world peace. The total performance was not without fault. In 1903 Roosevelt's driving ambition and his belief that inferior nations should not be permitted to retard the advance of civilization combined to prompt him to acquire the Panama Canal Zone under circumstances that left a legacy of ill-will (Document 11). In 1905 he flouted the sensibilities of the Chinese and then threatened them with force on the dubious assumption that they despised "weakness" and should rightfully subordinate their own interests to those of the United States. After he left the presidency, moreover, the shrill belligerency of 1898 returned. In 1916 he virtually urged war against Mexico, and in 1917 he became almost frenzied with desire to lead troops into battle against the Kaiser's legions. But these were the exceptions. On most issues he acted with restraint, sensitivity, and an astute appreciation of the national interest and the limits of American power.

Roosevelt's resolve to defend the United States' strategic interest in Latin America was demonstrated early in his first administration when he persuaded Germany to arbitrate a dispute with Venezuela that it had planned to settle by force. Then, at the request of harassed and misgoverned Santo Domingo, he took control of that nation's customs in a successful effort to avert European intervention for nonpayment of debts. These events confirmed his judgment that most Latin American nations were incapable either of governing or defending themselves effectively; and in May 1905, in what became known as the Roosevelt Corollary to the Monroe Doctrine, he announced that the United States assumed the right to intervene in the internal affairs of Western Hemisphere nations in cases of "brutal wrong-doing" or "impotence" (Document 12).

Meanwhile, Roosevelt's attitude toward the Far East underwent subtle, but important, changes. He had come to the presidency confident that the United States would develop an extensive Oriental trade and determined, in the event, to support the open door policy. Soon after assuming office, however, he perceived that Japan was destined to emerge as a major Far Eastern power, and by 1905 he had concluded that she should be encouraged to serve as a stabilizing force in the Far East. He also decided that the United States' stake in the area would be better served by accepting than by rejecting Japan's new position. For these reasons, fundamentally, he offered his good offices to end the Russo-Japanese War of 1904–1905. Largely because he realized that he lacked the naval power to back up a protest, but partly because he deemed the Koreans inferior to the Japanese, he also acquiesced at this time in Japan's extension of suzerainty over Korea. Two years later he recognized that the Philippines were so indefensible that they constituted the United States' "heel of Achilles" (Document 10), and from then until he left the presidency he and his Secretary of State, Elihu Root, labored hard to maintain Japan's friendship without compromising American interests unduly.

Meanwhile, Roosevelt continued to reassess America's position in the Far East. Before he left office he had begun to resign himself to Japan's special position in Manchuria, and in 1910 he actually advised President Taft to give up commercial ambitions in that area. Pointing out that Japan's main interests were on the continent, he warned that a successful war over Manchuria "would require a fleet as good as that of England, plus an army as good as that of Germany." Then, in an observation that brought his views full circle, he added that although the "'open door' policy in China was an excellent thing . . . , [it] completely disappears as soon as a powerful nation determines to disregard it, and is willing to run the risk of war rather than forego its intention."

During the period of American neutrality in World War I, Roosevelt's emotion-ridden calls for intervention once again distorted the real nature of his thought. Although he had some insight into the war's multiple causation, he also understood the compulsive nature of Prussian militarism and German aspirations for greatness. Fearful of the implications of both, he concluded that a German victory would be inimical to the interests of the United States and, indeed, of the Western world. But instead of emphasizing these issues, he trumpeted for war on the submarine issue alone (Documents 64, 65).

Conversely, Roosevelt's realism dominated, and probably warped, his attitude toward the League of Nations. As one close student of his conduct of foreign affairs has recently observed, Roosevelt as President broke new ground by experimenting with compulsory arbitration, supporting a permanent court of international justice (Document 62), mediating peace between Russia and Japan, and interceding in the Moroccan imbroglio of 1905.[7] He also gave measured approval to the idea of a league to enforce peace in his Nobel Peace Prize address of 1910 (Document 63). But never, not even when gripped by the most idealistic impulses, did he believe that the great power conflicts that wracked the world could be settled by a voluntary association of nations. It was almost foreordained, therefore, that Roosevelt would oppose the League of Nations as Woodrow Wilson conceived it. Viewing it as an addition to, rather than a substitute for, national defense, he endorsed it with reservations while emphasizing the desirability of a universal arbitration treaty with Britain and the need for a firm military alliance of the powers that had won the war (Document 67). Before he could concentrate his full energies on the latter proposals, however, he died in his sleep at Oyster Bay, Long Island, on January 6, 1919.

It is his enduring misfortune that his more grievous verbal and operational excesses are better remembered than his substantial service to world peace and his monumental contribution to progressivism.

[7] Richard W. Leopold, *The Growth of American Foreign Policy* (New York: Alfred A. Knopf, 1962), p. 240.

A ROOSEVELT CHRONOLOGY

1858   October 27: Theodore Roosevelt, Jr. born in New York City, the second child and first son of Theodore Roosevelt, Sr. and Martha Bulloch Roosevelt.

1876   Enters Harvard College after preparation by private tutors.

1878–1879 Interests shift from zoology to history and government.

1880   June: Graduates from Harvard, twenty-first in class of 158. Elected to Phi Beta Kappa.
October 27: Marries Alice Hathaway Lee.

1881   November: Elected to the New York State Assembly. Publishes *The Naval War of 1812*.

1882–1884 Establishes reputation as leader of reform wing of Republican Party in State Legislature.

1884   February: Wife and mother die within a few hours of each other.

1884–1886 Cattle rancher in the Dakota Territory.

1886   November: Defeated in New York City mayoralty election.
December: Marries Edith Kermit Carow.

1887   Publishes *Thomas Hart Benton*.

1888   Publishes *Ranch Life and the Hunting Trail; Essays on Practical Politics; Gouveneur Morris*.

1889	Publishes Volumes I, II of *The Winning of the West*. May: Takes office as member of Civil Service Commission.
1894	Publishes Volume III of *The Winning of the West*.
1895	May: Takes office as member of New York City Police Commission. Publishes Volume IV of *The Winning of the West;* also, *American Ideals*.
1897	April: Takes office as Assistant Secretary of the Navy.
1898	April: Accepts Lieutenant Colonelcy in First U. S. Volunteer Cavalry Regiment (Rough Riders). Summer: Cuban campaign. November: Elected Governor of New York on Republican ticket.
1899	Approves measures to regulate tenement workshops, reorganize Civil Service Commission, improve enforcement of eight-hour law for state employees, and establish tax on corporation franchises.
1900	Publishes *Oliver Cromwell*. Approves measures to establish comprehensive conservation program, open books of corporations to inspection, provide for compulsory education of Indian children, and outlaw segregation in public schools. November: Elected Vice-President of the United States.
1901	September 14: Sworn in as President of the United States one day after the death of President William McKinley.
1902	February: Approves institution of anti-trust proceedings against Northern Securities Company. June: Approves Newlands (Reclamation) Bill.

July: Approves Philippine Civil Government Bill.
October: Anthracite Coal Strike is settled.
December: Venezuelan boundary dispute settled as Germany backs down.

1903   January: Treaty to resolve Alaskan boundary dispute signed by Secretary of State John Hay.
February: Approves Department of Commerce and Labor Bill, providing for creation of Bureau of Corporations. Approves Elkins Anti-rebate Bill.
November: Recognizes Republic of Panama; approves signing of Panama Canal Treaty by Secretary of State John Hay.

1904   May: Roosevelt corollary to Monroe Doctrine promulgated.
November: Elected President by overwhelming majority.

1905   February: Protocol providing for United States control of Santo Domingo's customs houses arranged.
August: Meets with Japanese and Russian envoys aboard Presidential yacht, *Mayflower*, on fifth. Agreement on terms ending Russo-Japanese War reached on twenty-ninth.

1906   April: Indicts muck-rakers.
May: Approves Hepburn Railroad Rate Bill, Pure Food Bill, Agricultural Appropriation Bill, including meat-packing inspection amendment.
November: Orders three companies of Negro soldiers dishonorably discharged for allegedly conspiring to withhold names of soldiers who killed a civilian in Brownsville, Texas.

1907   March: Proclaims twenty-one new forest reserves totaling sixteen million acres.

1907–1908   Series of special messages to Congress calling for workman's compensation, increased control of railroads, national control of corporations, child labor legislation, and the elimination of the abuse of injunctions in labor disputes.

1908   May: Governor's Conference on Conservation. November: William Howard Taft elected President with Roosevelt's support.

1909–1910   Hunting and exploration expedition to Africa; tour of Europe.

1910   May: Accepts Nobel Peace Prize in Christiania, Norway.

June: Returns to United States. Cool to Taft because of his conservatism and political ineptitude.

August-September: Sets forth full-blown progressive program (The New Nationalism) on Western speaking trip. Relations with Taft worsen.

1910–1914   Contributing Editor, *The Outlook.*

1912   February: Announces candidacy for Republican Presidential nomination.

Spring: Defeats Taft by two to one in states having primary elections.

June: His supporters bolt Republican Convention in Chicago, name him at rump convention.

August: Formally nominated by Progressive National Convention.

October: Wounded in assassination attempt.

November: Loses election to Woodrow Wilson.

1913–1914   October: Exploration expedition to South America.

1914   April: Publishes with Edmund Heller, *Life Histories of African Game Animals.*

August: Supports American neutrality in World War I.

Fall: Campaigns for Progressive candidates in congressional elections. Begins to support Allies and to call for preparedness increases.

1915   Leads campaign to increase military forces. Becomes increasingly critical of President Wilson's neutrality policies.

1916	June: Declines Progressive Presidential nomination; comes out for Charles Evans Hughes, the Republican nominee.
1917	April: Request to raise volunteer division for action in France is rejected.
1917–1918	Speaks and writes voluminously in support of war effort.
1918	Fall: Is critical of President Wilson's peace program.
1919	January 6: Dies in sleep at Oyster Bay.

SELECTED BIBLIOGRAPHY

Roosevelt's Works

The Letters of Theodore Roosevelt. Ed. Elting E. Morison and John M. Blum. 8 vols. Cambridge: Harvard University Press, 1951–1954.

No Political Influence Will Help You In The Least; Letters of Theodore Roosevelt. Washington: United States Civil Service Commission, 1958.

Presidential Addresses and State Papers. 8 vols. New York: The Review of Reviews Company, 1910.

Public Papers of Theodore Roosevelt, Governor. 2 vols. Albany: Brandow Printing Company, 1899–1900.

Selections from the Correspondence of Theodore Roosevelt and Henry Cabot Lodge, 1884–1918. Ed. Henry Cabot Lodge. 2 vols. New York: Charles Scribner's Sons, 1925.

Theodore Roosevelt Cyclopedia. Ed. Albert Bushnell Hart and Herbert Ronald Ferleger. New York: Roosevelt Memorial Association, 1941.

Theodore Roosevelt's Letters to His Children. Ed. Joseph B. Bishop. New York: Charles Scribner's Sons, 1919.

The Works of Theodore Roosevelt. Ed. Hermann Hagedorn. 24 vols. Memorial Edition. New York: Charles Scribner's Sons, 1923–1926.

Collateral Reading

Bailey, Thomas A. *Theodore Roosevelt and the Japanese-American Crises*. Palo Alto, Cal.: Stanford University Press, 1934.

Beale, Howard K. *Theodore Roosevelt and the Rise of America to World Power*. Baltimore: The Johns Hopkins University Press, 1956.

Blum, John Morton. *The Republican Roosevelt*. Cambridge: Harvard University Press, 1956.

Chessman, G. Wallace. *Governor Theodore Roosevelt*. Cambridge: Harvard University Press, 1965.

Cutright, Paul Russell. *Theodore Roosevelt the Naturalist*. New York: Harper & Brothers, 1956.

Grantham, Dewey W., Jr. "Theodore Roosevelt in American Historical Writing, 1945–1960," in *Reprint Series in American History*, No. H-89. Indianapolis and New York: Bobbs-Merrill Co. Inc., 1961.

Hagedorn, Hermann. *The Roosevelt Family of Sagamore Hill*. New York: Macmillan Co., 1954.

Harbaugh, William Henry. *The Life and Times of Theodore Roosevelt*. Rev. ed. New York: Collier Books, 1963.

Mowry, George E. *The Era of Theodore Roosevelt*. New York: Harper & Brothers, 1958.

———— *Theodore Roosevelt and the Progressive Movement*. Madison: University of Wisconsin Press, 1946.

O'Gara, Gordon Carpenter. *Theodore Roosevelt and the Rise of the Modern Navy*. Princeton: Princeton University Press, 1943.

Putnam, Carleton. *Theodore Roosevelt: The Formative Years*. New York: Charles Scribner's Sons, 1958.

Pringle, Henry. *Theodore Roosevelt, A Biography*. New York: Harcourt, Brace & Company, 1931.

Wagenknecht, Edward. *The Seven Worlds of Theodore Roosevelt*. New York: Longmans, Green, 1958.

EDITOR'S NOTE

Where documents in this collection have been reprinted from other editions of Roosevelt's works, these works are referred to in the source notes by the following abbreviated titles:

Autobiography: Theodore Roosevelt, *An Autobiography* (New York: Charles Scribner's Sons, 1913; renewal copyright, 1941, Edith K. Carow Roosevelt). Reprinted with the permission of Charles Scribner's Sons. References to page numbers in text pertain to Scribner's 1919 edition.

The Letters: Elting E. Morison and John M. Blum (eds.), *The Letters of Theodore Roosevelt,* 8 vols., (Cambridge: Harvard University Press, copyright, 1951–1954 by the President and Fellows of Harvard College). Reprinted with the permission of Harvard University Press.

Messages and Papers: James D. Richardson (ed.), *A Compilation of Messages and Papers of the Presidents, 1789–1909,* rev. ed., 11 vols. (Bureau of National Literature and Art, 1909).

Presidential Addresses: Theodore Roosevelt, *Presidential Addresses and State Papers,* 8 vols. (New York: The Review of Reviews Company, 1910).

The Works: Hermann Hagedorn (ed.), *The Works of Theodore Roosevelt,* Memorial Edition, 24 vols. (New York: Charles Scribner's Sons, 1925). The essay from *Fear God and Take Your Own Part,* which is included in *The Works,* is reprinted with permission of the Theodore Roosevelt Association.

William H. Harbaugh

March 1966

THE WRITINGS OF
Theodore Roosevelt

I · BASIC CONVICTIONS:
THE FREE CITIZEN

1. · "THE DUTIES OF AMERICAN CITIZENSHIP"

This brief address, delivered when Roosevelt was the thirty-four year old chairman of the United States Civil Service Commission, contains the essence of his values and attitudes: his compulsive sense of duty; his realistic understanding of politics and politicians; his deep belief in reform and his contempt for what he later called "muck-raking." Here, too, is an implicit statement of his concept of *noblesse oblige* and an explicit statement of his conviction that politics is the art of the possible. And here, finally, is his consuming Americanism—an Americanism as intolerant of unbridled individualism as of cultural pluralism.

Of course, in one sense, the first essential for a man's being a good citizen is his possession of the home virtues of which we think when we call a man by the emphatic adjective of manly. No man can be a good citizen who is not a good husband and a good father, who is not honest in his dealings with other men and women, faithful to his friends and fearless in the presence of his foes, who has not got a sound heart, a sound mind, and a sound body; exactly as no amount of attention to civic duties will save a nation if the domestic life is undermined, or there is lack of the rude military virtues which alone can assure a country's position in the world. In a free

Address to the Liberal Club, Buffalo, N. Y., January 26, 1893. From *The Liberal Club, Buffalo [Yearbook], 1892–1893*, pp. 61–82.

republic the ideal citizen must be one willing and able to take arms for the defense of the flag, exactly as the ideal citizen must be the father of many healthy children. A race must be strong and vigorous; it must be a race of good fighters and good breeders, else its wisdom will come to naught and its virtue be ineffective; and no sweetness and delicacy, no love for and appreciation of beauty in art or literature, no capacity for building up material prosperity, can possibly atone for the lack of the great virile virtues.

But this is aside from my subject, for what I wish to talk of is the attitude of the American citizen in civic life. It ought to be axiomatic in this country that every man must devote a reasonable share of his time to doing his duty in the political life of the community. No man has a right to shirk his political duties under whatever plea of pleasure or business; and while such shirking may be pardoned in those of small means, it is entirely unpardonable in those among whom it is most common—in the people whose circumstances give them freedom in the struggle for life. In so far as the community grows to think rightly, it will likewise grow to regard the young man of means who shirks his duty to the State in time of peace as being only one degree worse than the man who thus shirks it in time of war. A great many of our men in business, or of our young men who are bent on enjoying life (as they have a perfect right to do if only they do not sacrifice other things to enjoyment), rather plume themselves upon being good citizens if they even vote; yet voting is the very least of their duties. Nothing worth gaining is ever gained without effort. You can no more have freedom without striving and suffering for it than you can win success as a banker or a lawyer without labor and effort, without self-denial in youth and the display of a ready and alert intelligence in middle age. The people who say that they have not time to attend to politics are simply saying that they are unfit to live in a free community. Their place is under a despotism; or if they are content to do nothing but vote, you can take despotism tempered by an occasional plebescite, like that of the second Napoleon. In one of Lowell's magnificent stanzas about the Civil War he speaks of the fact which his countrymen were then learning, that freedom is not a gift that tarries long in the hands of cowards: nor yet does it tarry long in the hands of the sluggard and the idler, in the hands of the man so much absorbed in the pursuit of pleasure or in the pursuit of gain, or so much wrapped up in his own easy home life as to be unable to take his part in the rough struggle with his fellow men for political supremacy. If freedom is worth having, if the right of self-government is a valuable right, then the one and the other must be retained exactly as our forefathers acquired them, by labor, and especially by labor in organization; that is, in combination with our fellows who have the same interests and the same principles. We should not accept the excuse of the business man who attributed his failure to the fact that his social duties were so pleasant and engrossing that he had no time left for work in his office; nor would we pay much heed to his further statement that he did not like business anyhow because he thought the morals of the business community by no means what they should be, and saw that the great successes were most often won by men of the Jay Gould stamp. It is just the same way with politics. It makes one feel half angry and half amused, and wholly contemptuous, to find men of high business or social standing in the community saying that they really have not got time to go to ward meetings, to organize political clubs, and to take a personal share in all the important details of practical politics; men who further urge against their going the fact that they think the condition of political morality low, and are afraid that they may be required to do what is not right if they go into politics.

The first duty of an American citizen, then, is that he shall work in politics; his second duty is that he shall do that work in a practical manner; and his third is that it shall be done in accord with the highest principles of honor and justice. Of course, it is not possible to define rigidly just the way in which the work shall be made practical. Each man's individual temper and convictions must be taken into account. To a certain extent his work must be done in accordance with his individual beliefs and theories of right and wrong. To a yet greater extent it must be done in combination with others, he yielding or modifying certain of his own theories and beliefs so as to enable him to stand on a common ground with his fellows, who have likewise yielded or modified certain of their theories and beliefs. There is no need of dogmatizing about independence on the one hand or party allegiance on the other. There are occasions when it may be the highest duty of any man to act outside of parties and against the one with which he has himself been hitherto identified; and there may be many more occasions when his highest duty is to sacrifice some of his own cherished opinions for the sake of the success of the party which he on the whole believes to be right. I do not think that the average citizen, at least in one of our great cities, can very well manage to support his own party all the time on every issue, local and otherwise; at any rate if he can do so he has been more fortunately placed than I have been. On the other hand, I am fully convinced that to do the best work people must be organized; and of course an organization is really a party, whether it be a great organization covering the whole nation and numbering its millions of adherents, or an association of citizens in a particular locality, banded together to win a certain specific victory, as, for instance, that of municipal reform. Somebody has said that a racing-yacht, like a good rifle, is a bundle of incompatibilities; that you must get the utmost possible sail power without sacrificing any other quality, and yet that you cannot help sacrificing some other quality if you really do get the utmost sail power; that, in short, you have got to make more or less of a compromise on each in order to acquire the dozen things needful;

but, of course, in making this compromise you must be very careful for the sake of something unimportant not to sacrifice any of the great principles of successful naval architecture. Well, it is about so with a man's political work. He has got to preserve his independence on the one hand; and on the other, unless he wishes to be a wholly ineffective crank, he has got to have some sense of party allegiance and party responsibility, and he has got to realize that in any given exigency it may be a matter of duty to sacrifice one quality, or it may be a matter of duty to sacrifice the other.

If it is difficult to lay down any fixed rules for party action in the abstract; it would, of course, be wholly impossible to lay them down for party action in the concrete, with reference to the organizations of the present day. I think that we ought to be broad-minded enough to recognize the fact that a good citizen, striving with fearlessness, honesty, and common sense to do his best for the nation, can render service to it in many different ways, and by connection with many different organizations. It is well for a man if he is able conscientiously to feel that his views on the great questions of the day, on such questions as the tariff, finance, immigration, the regulation of the liquor traffic, and others like them, are such as to put him in accord with the bulk of those of his fellow citizens who compose one of the greatest parties: but it is perfectly supposable that he may feel so strongly for or against certain principles held by one party, or certain principles held by the other, that he is unable to give his full adherence to either. In such a case I feel that he has no right to plead this lack of agreement with either party as an excuse for refraining from active political work prior to election. It will, of course, bar him from the primaries of the two leading parties, and preclude him from doing his share in organizing their management; but, unless he is very unfortunate, he can surely find a number of men who are in the same position as himself and who agree with him on some specific piece of political work, and they can turn in practically and effectively long before election to try to do this new piece of work in a practical manner.

One seemingly very necessary caution to utter is, that a man who goes into politics should not expect to reform everything right off, with a jump. I know many excellent young men who, when awakened to the fact that they have neglected their political duties, feel an immediate impulse to form themselves into an organization which shall forthwith purify politics everywhere, national, State, and city alike; and I know of a man who having gone round once to a primary, and having, of course, been unable to accomplish anything in a place where he knew no one and could not combine with any one, returned saying it was quite useless for a good citizen to try to accomplish anything in such a manner. . . .

I do wish that more of our good citizens would go into politics, and would do it in the same spirit with which their fathers went into the Federal armies. Begin with the little thing, and do not expect to accomplish anything without an effort. Of course, if you go to a primary just once, never having taken the trouble to know any of the other people who go there, you will find yourself wholly out of place; but if you keep on attending and try to form associations with other men whom you meet at the political gatherings, or whom you can persuade to attend them, you will very soon find yourself a weight. In the same way, if a man feels that the politics of his city, for instance, are very corrupt and wants to reform them, it would be an excellent idea for him to begin with his district. If he joins with other people, who think as he does, to form a club where abstract political virtue will be discussed he may do a great deal of good. We need such clubs: but he must also get to know his own ward or his own district, put himself in communication with the decent people in that district, of whom we may rest assured there will be many, willing and able to do something practical for the procurance of better government. Let him set to work to procure a better assemblyman or better alderman before he tries his hand at making a mayor, a governor, or a president. If he begins at the top he may make a brilliant temporary success, but the chances are a thousand to one that he will only be defeated eventually; and in no event will the good he does stand on the same broad and permanent foundation as if he had begun at the bottom. . . .

But in advising you to be practical and to work hard, I must not for one moment be understood as advising you to abandon one iota of your self-respect and devotion to principle. It is a bad sign for the country to see one class of our citizens sneer at practical politicians, and another at Sunday-school politics. No man can do both effective and decent work in public life unless he is a practical politician on the one hand, and a sturdy believer in Sunday-school politics on the other. He must always strive manfully for the best, and yet, like Abraham Lincoln, must often resign himself to accept the best possible. Of course when a man verges on to the higher ground of statesmanship, when he becomes a leader, he must very often consult with others and defer to their opinion, and must be continually settling in his mind how far he can go in just deference to the wishes and prejudices of others while yet adhering to his own moral standards: but I speak not so much of men of this stamp as I do of the ordinary citizen, who wants to do his duty as a member of the commonwealth in its civic life; and for this man I feel that the one quality which he ought always to hold most essential is that of disinterestedness. If he once begins to feel that he wants office himself, with a willingness to get it at the cost of his convictions, or to keep it when gotten, at the cost of his convictions, his usefulness is gone. Let him make up his mind to do his duty in politics without regard to holding office at all, and let him know that often the men in this country who have done the best work for our public life have not been the men in office. If, on the other hand, he attains public position, let him not strive to plan out for himself a career. I do not think that any man should let himself regard his political career as a means of livelihood, or as his sole occupation in life; for if he does he immediately becomes most seriously handicapped. The moment that he begins to think how such and such an act will affect the voters in his district, or will affect some great political leader who will have an influence over his destiny, he is hampered and his hands are bound. Not only may it be his duty often to disregard the wishes of politicians, but it may be his clear duty at times to disregard the wishes of the people. The voice of the people is not always the voice of God; and when it happens to be the voice of the devil, then it is a man's clear duty to defy its behests. Different political conditions breed different dangers. The demagogue is as unlovely a creature as the courtier, though one is fostered under republican and the other under monarchical institutions. There is every reason why a man should have an honorable ambition to enter public life, and an honorable ambition to stay there when he is in; but he ought to make up his mind that he cares for it only as long as he can stay in it on his own terms, without sacrifice of his own principles; and if he does thus make up his mind he can really accomplish twice as much for the nation, and can reflect a hundredfold greater honor upon himself, in a short term of service, than can the man who grows gray in the public employment at the cost of sacrificing what he believes to be true and honest. And moreover, when a public servant has definitely made up his mind that he will pay no heed to his own future, but will do what he honestly deems best for the community, without regard to how his actions may affect his prospects, not only does he become infinitely more useful as a public servant, but he has a far better time. He is freed from the harassing care which is inevitably the portion of him who is trying to shape his sails to catch every gust of the wind of political favor.

But let me reiterate, that in being virtuous he must not become ineffective, and that he must not excuse himself for shirking his duties by any false plea that he cannot do his duties and retain his self-respect. This is nonsense, he can; and when he urges such a plea it is a mark of mere laziness and self-indulgence. And again, he should beware how he becomes a critic of the actions of others, rather than a doer of deeds himself; and in so far as he does act as a critic (and of course the critic has a great and necessary function) he must beware of indiscriminate censure even more than of indiscriminate praise. The screaming vulgarity of the foolish spread-eagle orator who is continually yelling defiance at Europe, praising everything American, good and bad, and resenting the introduction of any reform because it has previously been tried successfully abroad, is offensive and contemptible to the last degree; but after all it is scarcely as harmful as the peevish, fretful, sneering, and continual faultfinding of the refined, well-educated man, who is always attacking good and bad alike, who genuinely distrusts America, and in the true spirit of servile colonialism considers us inferior to the people across the water. It may be taken for granted that the man who is always sneering at our public life and our public men is a thoroughly bad citizen, and that what little influence he wields in the community is wielded for evil. The public speaker or the editorial writer, who teaches men of education that their proper attitude toward American politics should be one of dislike or indifference, is doing all he can to perpetuate and aggravate the very evils of which he is ostensibly complaining. . . .

Moreover, the very need of denouncing evil makes it all the more wicked to weaken the effect of such denunciations by denouncing also the good. It is the duty of all citizens, irrespective of party, to denounce, and, so far as may be, to punish crimes against the public on the part of politicians or officials. But exactly as the public man who commits a crime against the public is one of the worst of criminals, so, close on his heels in the race for iniquitous distinction, comes the man who falsely charges the public servant with outrageous wrong-doing; whether it is done with foul-mouthed and foolish directness in the vulgar and violent party organ, or with sarcasm, innuendo, and the half-truths that are worse than lies, in some professed organ of independence. Not only should criticism be honest, but it should be intelligent, in order to be effective. I recently read in a religious paper an article railing at the corruption of our public life, in which it was stated incidentally that the lobby was recognized as all-powerful in Washington. This is untrue. There was a day when the lobby was very important at Washington, but its influence in Congress is now very small indeed; and from a pretty intimate acquaintance with several Congresses I am entirely satisfied that there is among the members a very small proportion indeed who are corruptible, in the sense that they will let their action be influenced by money or its equivalent. Congressmen are very often demagogues; they are very often blind partisans; they are often exceedingly shortsighted, narrow-minded, and bigoted; but they are not usually corrupt; and to accuse a narrow-minded demagogue of corruption when he is perfectly honest, is merely to set him more firmly in his evil course and to help him with his constituents, who recognize that the charge is entirely unjust, and in repelling it lose sight of the man's real shortcomings. I have known more than one State legislature, more than one board of aldermen against which the charge of corruption could perfectly legitimately be brought, but it cannot be brought against Congress. Moreover these sweeping charges really do very little good. When I was in the New York legislature, one of the things that I used to mind most was the fact that at the close of every session the papers that affect morality invariably said that that particular legislature was the worst legislature since the days of Tweed.[1]

---

[1] William Marcy Tweed was a Tammany Boss whose corruption was responsible for the Tweed Ring. He was sentenced to jail in 1872 [Ed.].

The statement was not true as a rule; and, in any event, to lump all the members, good and bad, in sweeping condemnation simply hurt the good and helped the bad. Criticism should be fearless, but I again reiterate that it should be honest and should be discriminating. When it is sweeping and unintelligent, and directed against good and bad alike, or against the good and bad qualities of any man alike, it is very harmful. It tends steadily to deteriorate the character of our public men; and it tends to produce a very unwholesome spirit among young men of education, and especially among the young men in our colleges. . . .

. . . Finally, the man who wishes to do his duty as a citizen in our country must be imbued through and through with the spirit of Americanism. I am not saying this as a matter of spread-eagle rhetoric: I am saying it quite soberly as a piece of matter-of-fact, common-sense advice, derived from my own experience of others. Of course, the question of Americanism has several sides. If a man is an educated man, he must show his Americanism by not getting misled into following out and trying to apply all the theories of the political thinkers of other countries, such as Germany and France, to our own entirely different conditions. He must not get a fad, for instance, about responsible government; and above all things he must not, merely because he is intelligent, or a college professor well read in political literature, try to discuss our institutions when he has had no practical knowledge of how they are worked. Again, if he is a wealthy man, a man of means and standing, he must really feel, not merely affect to feel, that no social differences obtain save such as a man can in some way himself make by his own actions. People sometimes ask me if there is not a prejudice against a man of wealth and education in ward politics. I do not think that there is, unless the man in turn shows that he regards the fact of his having wealth and education as giving him a claim to superiority aside from the merit he is able to prove himself to have in actual service. Of course,

if he feels that he ought to have a little better treatment than
a carpenter, a plumber, or a butcher, who happens to stand
beside him, he is going to be thrown out of the race very
quickly, and probably quite roughly; and if he starts in to pa-
tronize and elaborately condescend to these men he will find
that they resent this attitude even more. Do not let him think
about the matter at all. Let him go into the political contest
with no more thought of such matters than a college boy gives
to the social standing of the members of his own and rival
teams in a hotly contested football-match. As soon as he begins
to take an interest in politics (and he will speedily not only
get interested for the sake of politics, but also take a good
healthy interest in playing the game itself—an interest which
is perfectly normal and praiseworthy, and to which only a prig
would object), he will begin to work up the organization in the
way that will be most effective, and he won't care a rap about
who is put to work with him, save in so far as he is a good
fellow and an efficient worker. There was one time that a number of men who think as we do here to-night (one of the
number being myself) got hold of one of the assembly districts
of New York, and ran it in really an ideal way, better than any
other assembly district has ever been run before or since by
either party. We did it by hard work and good organization;
by working practically, and yet by being honest and square in
motive and method: especially did we do it by all turning in
as straight-out Americans without any regard to distinctions of
race origin. Among the many men who did a great deal in
organizing our victories was the son of a Presbyterian clergy-
man, the nephew of a Hebrew rabbi, and two well-known
Catholic gentlemen. We also had a Columbia College professor (the stroke-oar of a university crew), a noted retail butcher,
the editor of a local German paper, various brokers, bankers,
lawyers, bricklayers, and a stone-mason, who was particularly
useful to us, although on questions of theoretic rather than
applied politics he had a decidedly socialistic turn of mind.

Again, questions of race origin, like questions of creed, must not be considered: we wish to do good work, and we are all Americans, pure and simple. In the New York legislature, when it fell my lot to choose a committee—which I always esteemed my most important duty at Albany—no less than three out of the four men I chose were of Irish birth or parentage; and three abler and more fearless and disinterested men never sat in a legislative body; while among my especial political and personal friends in that body was a gentleman from the southern tier of counties, who was, I incidentally found out, a German by birth, but who was just as straight United States as if his ancestors had come over here in the *Mayflower* or in Henry Hudson's yacht. Of course, none of these men of Irish or German birth would have been worth their salt had they continued to act after coming here as Irishmen or Germans, or as anything but plain straight-out Americans. We have not any room here for a divided allegiance. A man has got to be an American and nothing else; and he has no business to be mixing us up with questions of foreign politics, British or Irish, German or French, and no business to try to perpetuate their language and customs in the land of complete religious toleration and equality. If, however, he does become honestly and in good faith an American, then he is entitled to stand precisely as all other Americans stand, and it is the height of unAmericanism to discriminate against him in any way because of creed or birthplace. No spirit can be more thoroughly alien to American institutions than the spirit of the Know-nothings.

In facing the future and in striving, each according to the measure of his individual capacity, to work out the salvation of our land, we should be neither timid pessimists nor foolish optimists. We should recognize the dangers that exist and that threaten us: we should neither overestimate them nor shrink from them, but steadily fronting them should set to work to overcome and beat them down. Grave perils are yet to be en-

countered in the stormy course of the Republic—perils from
political corruption, perils from individual laziness, indolence
and timidity, perils springing from the greed of the unscrupulous rich, and from the anarchic violence of the thriftless
and turbulent poor. There is every reason why we should recognize them, but there is no reason why we should fear them
or doubt our capacity to overcome them, if only each will,
according to the measure of his ability, do his full duty, and
endeavor so to live as to deserve the high praise of being
called a good American citizen.

2. · "NATIONAL UNITY VERSUS CLASS CLEAVAGE"

The main weakness of Roosevelt's social thought was the over-
emphasis it put on character and the short shrift it gave environment. This was partly by design, partly by temperament. Roosevelt
was too sophisticated to believe that all men had equal opportunities; but he was also too Calvinistic to believe that most men could
not improve themselves and their conditions of life by individual
effort. He feared, furthermore, that class conflict grounded on an
environmental interpretation of society would destroy republican
government. Until well into his presidency, accordingly, he was
reluctant to generalize—though he sometimes did—about the impact of deprivation upon the character of the underprivileged and
the influence of vested economic interests upon the attitudes of the
privileged. Instead, he concentrated on exhorting men to conquer
adversity and fulfill their potentials. Both the strength and the
weaknesses of this approach are evident in the remarks that follow.

In speaking on Labor Day at the annual fair of the New
York State Agricultural Association, it is natural to keep espe-

Address at the State Fair, Syracuse, N. Y., September 7, 1903. *Presidential Addresses,* II, 466–81.

cially in mind the two bodies who compose the majority of our people and upon whose welfare depends the welfare of the entire State. If circumstances are such that thrift, energy, industry, and forethought enable the farmer, the tiller of the soil, on the one hand, and the wage-worker, on the other, to keep themselves, their wives, and their children in reasonable comfort, then the State is well off, and we can be assured that the other classes in the community will likewise prosper. On the other hand, if there is in the long run a lack of prosperity among the two classes named, then all other prosperity is sure to be more seeming than real. It has been our profound good fortune as a nation that hitherto, disregarding exceptional periods of depression and the normal and inevitable fluctuations, there has been on the whole from the beginning of our government to the present day a progressive betterment alike in the condition of the tiller of the soil and in the condition of the man who, by his manual skill and labor, supports himself and his family, and endeavors to bring up his children so that they may be at least as well off as, and if possible better off than, he himself has been. There are, of course, exceptions, but as a whole the standard of living among the farmers of our country has risen from generation to generation, and the wealth represented on the farms has steadily increased, while the wages of labor have likewise risen, both as regards the actual money paid and as regards the purchasing power which that money represents.

Side by side with this increase in the prosperity of the wage-worker and the tiller of the soil has gone on a great increase in prosperity among the business men and among certain classes of professional men; and the prosperity of these men has been partly the cause and partly the consequence of the prosperity of farmer and wage-worker. It cannot be too often repeated that in this country, in the long run, we all of us tend to go up or go down together. If the average of well-being is high, it means that the average wage-worker, the average farmer, and the average business man are all alike well off. If the average shrinks, there is not one of these classes which will not feel the shrinkage. Of course, there are always some men who are not affected by good times, just as there are some men who are not affected by bad times. But speaking broadly, it is true that if prosperity comes all of us tend to share more or less therein, and that if adversity comes each of us, to a greater or less extent, feels the tension. Unfortunately, in this world the innocent frequently find themselves obliged to pay some of the penalty for the misdeeds of the guilty; and so if hard times come, whether they be due to our own fault or to our misfortune, whether they be due to some burst of speculative frenzy that has caused a portion of the business world to lose its head—a loss which no legislation can possibly supply—or whether they be due to any lack of wisdom in a portion of the world of labor—in each case the trouble once started is felt more or less in every walk of life.

It is all-essential to the continuance of our healthy national life that we should recognize this community of interest among our people. The welfare of each of us is dependent fundamentally upon the welfare of all of us, and therefore in public life that man is the best representative of each of us who seeks to do good to each by doing good to all; in other words, whose endeavor it is, not to represent any special class and promote merely that class's selfish interests, but to represent all true and honest men of all sections and all classes and to work for their interests by working for our common country.

We can keep our government on a sane and healthy basis, we can make and keep our social system what it should be, only on condition of judging each man, not as a member of a class, but on his worth as a man. It is an infamous thing in our American life, and fundamentally treacherous to our institutions, to apply to any man any test save that of his personal worth, or to draw between two sets of men any distinction save the distinction of conduct, the distinction that marks off

those who do well and wisely from those who do ill and fool-
ishly. There are good citizens and bad citizens in every class
as in every locality, and the attitude of decent people toward
great public and social questions should be determined, not by
the accidental questions of employment or locality, but by
those deep-set principles which represent the innermost souls
of men.

The failure in public and in private life thus to treat each
man on his own merits, the recognition of this government as
being either for the poor as such or for the rich as such, would
prove fatal to our Republic, as such failure and such recognition have always proved fatal in the past to other republics.
A healthy republican government must rest upon individuals,
not upon classes or sections. As soon as it becomes government by a class or by a section it departs from the old American ideal.

It is, of course, the merest truism to say that free institutions
are of avail only to people who possess the high and peculiar
characteristics needed to take advantage of such institutions.
. . . People show themselves just as unfit for liberty whether
they submit to anarchy or to tyranny; and class government,
whether it be the government of a plutocracy or the government of a mob, is equally incompatible with the principles
established in the days of Washington and perpetuated in the
days of Lincoln.

Many qualities are needed by a people which would preserve the power of self-government in fact as well as in name.
Among these qualities are forethought, shrewdness, self-
restraint, the courage which refuses to abandon one's own
rights, and the disinterested and kindly good sense which enables one to do justice to the rights of others. Lack of strength
and lack of courage unfit men for self-government on the one
hand, and on the other, brutal arrogance, envy, in short, any
manifestation of the spirit of selfish disregard, whether of one's
own duties or of the rights of others, are equally fatal.

In the history of mankind many republics have risen, have flourished for a less or greater time, and then have fallen because their citizens lost the power of governing themselves and thereby of governing their state; and in no way has this loss of power been so often and so clearly shown as in the tendency to turn the government into a government primarily for the benefit of one class instead of a government for the benefit of the people as a whole. . . .

. . . The reason why our future is assured lies in the fact that our people are genuinely skilled in and fitted for self-government and therefore will spurn the leadership of those who seek to excite this ferocious and foolish class antagonism. The average American knows not only that he himself intends to do about what is right, but that his average fellow countryman has the same intention and the same power to make his intention effective. He knows, whether he be business man, professional man, farmer, mechanic, employer, or wage-worker, that the welfare of each of these men is bound up with the welfare of all the others; that each is neighbor to the other, is actuated by the same hopes and fears, has fundamentally the same ideals, and that all alike have much the same virtues and the same faults. Our average fellow citizen is a sane and healthy man, who believes in decency and has a wholesome mind. He therefore feels an equal scorn alike for the man of wealth guilty of the mean and base spirit of arrogance toward those who are less well off, and for the man of small means who in turn either feels, or seeks to excite in others the feeling of mean and base envy for those who are better off. The two feelings, envy and arrogance, are but opposite sides of the same shield, but different developments of the same spirit. Fundamentally, the unscrupulous rich man who seeks to exploit and oppress those who are less well off is in spirit not opposed to, but identical with, the unscrupulous poor man who desires to plunder and oppress those who are better off. The courtier and the demagogue are but developments of the same type under different conditions, each manifesting the same servile spirit, the same desire to rise by pandering to base passions; though one panders to power in the shape of a single man and the other to power in the shape of a multitude. So likewise the man who wishes to rise by wronging others must by right be contrasted, not with the man who likewise wishes to do wrong, though to a different set of people, but with the man who wishes to do justice to all people and to wrong none.

The line of cleavage between good and bad citizenship lies, not between the man of wealth who acts squarely by his fellows and the man who seeks each day's wage by that day's work, wronging no one and doing his duty by his neighbor; nor yet does this line of cleavage divide the unscrupulous wealthy man who exploits others in his own interest, from the demagogue, or from the sullen and envious being who wishes to attack all men of property, whether they do well or ill. On the contrary, the line of cleavage between good citizenship and bad citizenship separates the rich man who does well from the rich man who does ill, the poor man of good conduct from the poor man of bad conduct. This line of cleavage lies at right angles to any such arbitrary line of division as that separating one class from another, one locality from another, or men with a certain degree of property from those of a less degree of property.

The good citizen is the man who, whatever his wealth or his poverty, strives manfully to do his duty to himself, to his family, to his neighbor, to the State; who is incapable of the baseness which manifests itself either in arrogance or in envy, but who while demanding justice for himself is no less scrupulous to do justice to others. It is because the average American citizen, rich or poor, is of just this type that we have cause for our profound faith in the future of the Republic.

Ours is a government of liberty, by, through, and under the law. Lawlessness and connivance at lawbreaking—whether the lawbreaking take the form of a crime of greed and cunning or of a crime of violence—are destructive not only of order, but of the true liberties which can only come through order. If alive to their true interests rich and poor alike will set their faces like flint against the spirit which seeks personal advantage by overriding the laws, without regard to whether this spirit shows itself in the form of bodily violence by one set of men or in the form of vulpine cunning by another set of men.

Let the watchwords of all our people be the old familiar watchwords of honesty, decency, fair dealing, and common sense. The qualities denoted by these words are essential to all of us, as we deal with the complex industrial problems of to-day, the problems affecting not merely the accumulation but even more the wise distribution of wealth. We ask no man's permission when we require him to obey the law; neither the permission of the poor man nor yet of the rich man. Least of all can the man of great wealth afford to break the law, even for his own financial advantage; for the law is his prop and support, and it is both foolish and profoundly unpatriotic for him to fail in giving hearty support to those who show that there is in very fact one law, and one law only, alike for the rich and the poor, for the great and the small.

Men sincerely interested in the due protection of property, and men sincerely interested in seeing that the just rights of labor are guaranteed, should alike remember not only that in the long run neither the capitalist nor the wage-worker can be helped in healthy fashion save by helping the other; but also that to require either side to obey the law and do its full duty toward the community is emphatically to that side's real interest.

There is no worse enemy of the wage-worker than the man who condones mob violence in any shape or who preaches class hatred; and surely the slightest acquaintance with our industrial history should teach even the most short-sighted that the times of most suffering for our people as a whole, the times when business is stagnant, and capital suffers from shrinkage and gets no return from its investments, are exactly the times of hardship, and want, and grim disaster among the poor. If all the existing instrumentalities of wealth could be abolished, the first and severest suffering would come among those of us who are least well off at present. The wage-worker is well off only when the rest of the country is well off; and he can best contribute to this general well-being by showing sanity and a firm purpose to do justice to others.

In his turn the capitalist who is really a conservative, the man who has forethought as well as patriotism, should heartily welcome every effort, legislative or otherwise, which has for its object to secure fair dealing by capital, corporate or individual, toward the public and toward the employee. . . .

In other words, legislation to be permanently good for any class must also be good for the nation as a whole, and legislation which does injustice to any class is certain to work harm to the nation. Take our currency system for example. This nation is on a gold basis. The treasury of the public is in excellent condition. Never before has the per capita of circulation been as large as it is this day; and this circulation, moreover, is of money every dollar of which is at par with gold. Now, our having this sound currency system is of benefit to banks, of course, but it is of infinitely more benefit to the people as a whole, because of the healthy effect on business conditions.

In the same way, whatever is advisable in the way of remedial or corrective currency legislation—and nothing revolutionary is advisable under present conditions—must be undertaken only from the standpoint of the business community as a whole, that is, of the American body politic as a whole. Whatever is done, we cannot afford to take any step backward or to cast any doubt upon the certain redemption in standard coin of every circulating note.

Among ourselves we differ in many qualities of body, head, and heart; we are unequally developed, mentally as well as physically. But each of us has the right to ask that he shall be protected from wrong-doing as he does his work and carries his burden through life. No man needs sympathy because he has to work, because he has a burden to carry. Far and away the best prize that life offers is the chance to work hard at work worth doing; and this is a prize open to every man, for there can be no work better worth doing than that done to keep in health and comfort and with reasonable advantages those immediately dependent upon the husband, the father, or the son.

There is no room in our healthy American life for the mere idler, for the man or the woman whose object it is throughout life to shirk the duties which life ought to bring. Life can mean nothing worth meaning, unless its prime aim is the doing of duty, the achievement of results worth achieving. A recent writer has finely said: "After all, the saddest thing that can happen to a man is to carry no burdens. To be bent under too great a load is bad; to be crushed by it is lamentable; but even in that there are possibilities that are glorious. But to carry no load at all—there is nothing in that. No one seems to arrive at any goal really worth reaching in this world who does not come to it heavy laden."

Surely from our own experience each one of us knows that this is true. From the greatest to the smallest, happiness and usefulness are largely found in the same soul, and the joy of life is won in its deepest and truest sense only by those who have not shirked life's burdens. The men whom we most delight to honor in all this land are those who, in the iron years from '61 to '65, bore on their shoulders the burden of saving the Union. They did not choose the easy task. They did not shirk the difficult duty. Deliberately and of their own free will they strove for an ideal, upward and onward across the stony slopes of greatness. They did the hardest work that was then to be done; they bore the heaviest burden that any generation of Americans ever had to bear; and because they did this they have won such proud joy as it has fallen to the lot of no other men to win, and have written their names forevermore on the golden honor roll of the nation. As it is with the soldier, so it is with the civilian. To win success in the business world, to become a first-class mechanic, a successful farmer, an able lawyer or doctor, means that the man has devoted his best energy and power through long years to the achievement of his ends. So it is in the life of the family, upon which in the last analysis the whole welfare of the nation rests. The man or woman who as bread-winner and home-maker, or as wife and mother, has done all that he or she can do, patiently and uncomplainingly, is to be honored; and is to be envied by all those who have never had the good fortune to feel the need and duty of doing such work. The woman who has borne, and who has reared as they should be reared, a family of children, has in the most emphatic manner deserved well of the Republic. Her burden has been heavy, and she has been able to bear it worthily only by the possession of resolution, of good sense, of conscience, and of unselfishness. But if she has borne it well, then to her shall come the supreme blessing, for in the words of the oldest and greatest of books, "Her children shall rise up and call her blessed"; and among the benefactors of the land her place must be with those who have done the best and the hardest work, whether as lawgivers or as soldiers, whether in public or private life.

This is not a soft and easy creed to preach. It is a creed willingly learned only by men and women who, together with the softer virtues, possess also the stronger; who can do, and dare, and die at need, but who while life lasts will never flinch from their allotted task. You farmers, and wage-workers, and business men of this great State, of this mighty and wonderful nation, are gathered together to-day, proud of your State and still prouder of your nation, because your forefathers and predecessors have lived up to just this creed. You have received from their hands a great inheritance, and you will leave an even greater inheritance to your children, and your children's children, provided only that you practise alike in your private and your public lives the strong virtues that have given us as a people greatness in the past. It is not enough to be well-meaning and kindly, but weak; neither is it enough to be strong, unless morality and decency go hand in hand with strength. We must possess the qualities which make us do our duty in our homes and among our neighbors, and in addition we must possess the qualities which are indispensable to the make-up of every great and masterful nation—the qualities of courage and hardihood, of individual initiative and yet of power to combine for a common end, and above all, the resolute determination to permit no man and no set of men to sunder us one from the other by lines of caste or creed or section. We must act upon the motto of all for each and each for all. There must be ever present in our minds the fundamental truth that in a republic such as ours the only safety is to stand neither for nor against any man because he is rich or because he is poor, because he is engaged in one occupation or another, because he works with his brains or because he works with his hands. We must treat each man on his worth and merits as a man. We must see that each is given a square deal, because he is entitled to no more and should receive no less. . . .

II · EMPIRE FOR GLORY

The Imperialistic Thrust

3. · "EXPANSION AND PEACE"

This short essay, written in 1899 to justify the decision to retain the Philippines, faithfully represents many of the values and beliefs that made Roosevelt an expansionist even before the Spanish-American War was fought. Among the more important of these was his conviction that the history of Rome and of England proved that expansion was essential to power, influence, and glory, and hence to the onward march of civilization. Here, however, he argues (1) that wars must often be fought in order to preserve peace and (2) that expansion by civilized powers almost inevitably advances the cause of peace.

It was the gentlest of our poets who wrote:

> "Be bolde! Be bolde! and everywhere, Be bolde";
> Be not too bold! Yet better the excess
> Than the defect; better the more than less.

Longfellow's love of peace was profound; but he was a man, and a wise man, and he knew that cowardice does not promote peace, and that even the great evil of war may be a less evil than cringing to iniquity.

Captain Mahan, than whom there is not in the country a man whom we can more appropriately designate by the fine

Theodore Roosevelt, "Expansion and Peace," *The Independent, LI* (December 21, 1899), 3401–05.

and high praise, "a Christian gentleman," and who is incapable of advocating wrong-doing of any kind, national or individual, gives utterance to the feeling of the great majority of manly and thoughtful men when he denounces the great danger of indiscriminate advocacy of peace at any price, because "it may lead men to tamper with iniquity, to compromise with unrighteousness, soothing their conscience with the belief that war is so entirely wrong that beside it no other tolerated evil is wrong. Witness Armenia and witness Crete. War has been avoided; but what of the national consciences that beheld such iniquity and withheld the hand?"

Peace is a great good; and doubly harmful, therefore, is the attitude of those who advocate it in terms that would make it synonymous with selfish and cowardly shrinking from warring against the existence of evil. The wisest and most farseeing champions of peace will ever remember that, in the first place, to be good it must be righteous, for unrighteous and cowardly peace may be worse than any war; and, in the second place, that it can often be obtained only at the cost of war. Let me take two illustrations:

The great blot upon European international morality in the closing decade of this century has been not a war, but the infamous peace kept by the joint action of the great powers, while Turkey inflicted the last horrors of butchery, torture, and outrage upon the men, women, and children of despairing Armenia. War was avoided; peace was kept; but what a peace! Infinitely greater human misery was inflicted during this peace than in the late wars of Germany with France, of Russia with Turkey; and this misery fell, not on armed men, but upon defenseless women and children, upon the graybeard and the stripling no less than upon the head of the family; and it came, not in the mere form of death or imprisonment, but of tortures upon men, and, above all, upon women, too horrible to relate —tortures of which it is too terrible even to think. Moreover, no good resulted from the bloodshed and misery. Often this is the case in a war, but often it is not the case. The result of the last Turko-Russian war was an immense and permanent increase of happiness for Bulgaria, Servia, Bosnia, and Herzegovina. These provinces became independent or passed under the dominion of Austria, and the advantage that accrued to them because of this expansion of the domain of civilization at the expense of barbarism has been simply incalculable. This expansion produced peace, and put a stop to the ceaseless grinding, bloody tyranny that had desolated the Balkans for so many centuries. There are many excellent people who have praised Tolstoi's fantastic religious doctrines, his fantastic advocacy of peace. The same quality that makes the debauchee and the devotee alternate in certain decadent families, the hysterical development which leads to violent emotional reaction in a morbid nature from vice to virtue, also leads to the creation of Tolstoi's "Kreutzer Sonata"[1] on the one hand, and of his unhealthy peace-mysticism on the other. A sane and healthy mind would be as incapable of the moral degradation of the novel as of the decadent morality of the philosophy. If Tolstoi's countrymen had acted according to his moral theories they would now be extinct, and savages would have taken their place. Unjust war is a terrible sin. It does not nowadays in the aggregate cause anything like the misery that is caused in the aggregate by unjust dealing toward one's neighbors in the commercial and social world; and to condemn all war is just as logical as to condemn all business and all social relations, as to condemn love and marriage because of the frightful misery caused by brutal and unregulated passion. If Russia had acted upon Tolstoi's philosophy, all its people would long ago have disappeared from the face of the earth, and the country would now be occupied by wandering tribes of Tatar barbarians. The Armenian massacres are simply illustrations on

[1] The *Kreutzer Sonata* was a short novel by Tolstoi critical of certain aspects of conventional marriage [Ed.].

a small scale of what would take place on the very largest scale if Tolstoi's principles became universal among civilized people. It is not necessary to point out that the teaching which would produce such a condition of things is fundamentally immoral.

Again, peace may come only through war. There are men in our country who seemingly forget that at the outbreak of the Civil War the great cry raised by the opponents of the war was the cry for peace. One of the most amusing and most biting satires written by the friends of union and liberty during the Civil War was called the "New Gospel of Peace," in derision of this attitude. The men in our own country who, in the name of peace, have been encouraging Aguinaldo[2] and his people to shoot down our soldiers in the Philippines might profit not a little if they would look back to the days of the bloody draft riots, which were deliberately incited in the name of peace and free speech, when the mob killed men and women in the streets and burned orphan children in the asylums as a protest against the war. Four years of bloody struggle with an armed foe, who was helped at every turn by the self-styled advocates of peace, were needed in order to restore the Union; but the result has been that the peace of this continent has been effectually assured. Had the short-sighted advocates of peace for the moment had their way, and secession become an actual fact, nothing could have prevented a repetition in North America of the devastating anarchic warfare that obtained for three quarters of a century in South America after the yoke of Spain was thrown off. We escaped generations of anarchy and bloodshed, because our fathers who upheld Lincoln and followed Grant were men in every sense of the term, with too much common sense to be misled by those who preached that war was always wrong, and with a fund of stern virtue deep in their souls which enabled them to do deeds from which men of over-soft natures would have shrunk appalled.

[2] General Emilio Aguinaldo was the leader of the Filipino guerrillas [Ed.].

Wars between civilized communities are very dreadful, and as nations grow more and more civilized we have every reason, not merely to hope, but to believe that they will grow rarer and rarer. Even with civilized peoples, as was shown by our own experience in 1861, it may be necessary at last to draw the sword rather than to submit to wrong-doing. But a very marked feature in the world-history of the present century has been the growing infrequency of wars between great civilized nations. The Peace Conference at The Hague is but one of the signs of this growth. I am among those who believe that much was accomplished at that conference, and I am proud of the leading position taken in the conference by our delegates. Incidentally I may mention that the testimony is unanimous that they were able to take this leading position chiefly because we had just emerged victorious from our most righteous war with Spain. Scant attention is paid to the weakling or the coward who babbles of peace; but due heed is given to the strong man with sword girt on thigh who preaches peace, not from ignoble motives, not from fear or distrust of his own powers, but from a deep sense of moral obligation.

The growth of peacefulness between nations, however, has been confined strictly to those that are civilized. It can only come when both parties to a possible quarrel feel the same spirit. With a barbarous nation peace is the exceptional condition. On the border between civilization and barbarism war is generally normal because it must be under the conditions of barbarism. Whether the barbarian be the Red Indian on the frontier of the United States, the Afghan on the border of British India, or the Turkoman who confronts the Siberian Cossack, the result is the same. In the long run civilized man finds he can keep the peace only by subduing his barbarian neighbor; for the barbarian will yield only to force, save in instances so exceptional that they may be disregarded. Back of the force must come fair dealing, if the peace is to be permanent. But without force fair dealing usually amounts to nothing. In our history we have had more trouble from the

Indian tribes whom we pampered and petted than from those we wronged; and this has been true in Siberia, Hindustan, and Africa.

Every expansion of civilization makes for peace. In other words, every expansion of a great civilized power means a victory for law, order, and righteousness. This has been the case in every instance of expansion during the present century, whether the expanding power were France or England, Russia or America. In every instance the expansion has been of benefit, not so much to the power nominally benefited, as to the whole world. In every instance the result proved that the expanding power was doing a duty to civilization far greater and more important than could have been done by any stationary power. Take the case of France and Algiers. During the early decades of the present century piracy of the most dreadful description was rife on the Mediterranean, and thousands of civilized men were yearly dragged into slavery by the Moorish pirates. A degrading peace was purchased by the civilized powers by the payment of tribute. Our own country was one among the tributary nations which thus paid blood-money to the Moslem bandits of the sea. We fought occasional battles with them; and so, on a larger scale, did the English. But peace did not follow, because the country was not occupied. Our last payment was made in 1830, and the reason it was the last was because in that year the French conquest of Algiers began. Foolish sentimentalists, like those who wrote little poems in favor of the Mahdists[3] against the English, and who now write little essays in favor of Aguinaldo against the Americans, celebrated the Algerian freebooters as heroes who were striving for liberty against the invading French. But the French continued to do their work; France expanded over Algiers, and the result was that piracy on the Mediterranean came to an end, and Algiers has thriven as never before in its

[3] The Mahdi was the religious leader of a movement directed against Egyptian rule of the Sudan [Ed.].

history. On an even larger scale the same thing is true of England and the Sudan. The expansion of England throughout the Nile valley has been an incalculable gain for civilization. Any one who reads the writings of the Austrian priests and laymen who were prisoners in the Sudan under the Mahdi will realize that when England crushed him and conquered the Sudan she conferred a priceless boon upon humanity and made the civilized world her debtor. Again, the same thing is true of the Russian advance in Asia. As in the Sudan the English conquest is followed by peace, and the endless massacres of the Mahdi are stopped forever, so the Russian conquest of the khanates of central Asia meant the cessation of the barbarous warfare under which Asian civilization had steadily withered away since the days of Jenghiz Khan, and the substitution in its place of the reign of peace and order. All civilization has been the gainer by the Russian advance, as it was the gainer by the advance of France in North Africa; as it has been the gainer by the advance of England in both Asia and Africa, both Canada and Australia. Above all, there has been the greatest possible gain in peace. The rule of law and of order has succeeded to the rule of barbarous and bloody violence. Until the great civilized nations stepped in there was no chance for anything but such bloody violence.

So it has been in the history of our own country. Of course our whole national history has been one of expansion. Under Washington and Adams we expanded westward to the Mississippi; under Jefferson we expanded across the continent to the mouth of the Columbia; under Monroe we expanded into Florida; and then into Texas and California; and finally, largely through the instrumentality of Seward, into Alaska; while under every administration the process of expansion in the great plains and the Rockies has continued with growing rapidity. While we had a frontier the chief feature of frontier life was the endless war between the settlers and the red men. Sometimes the immediate occasion for the war was to be found

DOES CONCEDE WHITES WEREN'T ALWAYS +.

in the conduct of the whites and sometimes in that of the reds, but the ultimate cause was simply that we were in contact with a country held by savages or half-savages. Where we abut on Canada there is no danger of war, nor is there any danger *aguinaldo!* where we abut on the well-settled regions of Mexico. But elsewhere war had to continue until we expanded over the country. Then it was succeeded at once by a peace which has remained unbroken to the present day. In North America, as elsewhere throughout the entire world, the expansion of a civilized nation has invariably meant the growth of the area in which peace is normal throughout the world.

The same will be true of the Philippines. If the men who have counseled national degradation, national dishonor, by urging us to leave the Philippines and put the Aguinaldan oligarchy in control of those islands, could have their way, we should merely turn them over to rapine and bloodshed until some stronger, manlier power stepped in to do the task we had shown ourselves fearful of performing. But, as it is, this country will keep the islands and will establish therein a stable and orderly government, so that one more fair spot of the world's surface shall have been snatched from the forces of darkness. Fundamentally the cause of expansion is the cause of peace.

With civilized powers there is but little danger of our getting into war. In the Pacific, for instance, the great progressive, colonizing nations are England and Germany. With England we have recently begun to feel ties of kindness as well as of kinship, and with her our relations are better than ever before; and so they ought to be with Germany. Recently affairs in Samoa have been straightened out, although there we suffered from the worst of all types of government, one in which three powers had a joint responsibility (the type, by the way, which some of the anti-imperialists actually advocated our introducing in the Philippines, under the pretense of rendering them neutral). This was accomplished very largely because the three nations set good-humoredly to work to come to an agreement which would do justice to all. In the preliminary negotiations the agents of America and Germany were Mr. Tripp and Baron Sternburg. No difficulty can ever arise between Germany and the United States which will not be settled with satisfaction to both, if the negotiations are conducted by such representatives of the two powers as these two men. What is necessary is to approach the subject, not with a desire to get ahead of one another, but to do even and exact justice, and to put into operation a scheme which will work, while scrupulously conserving the honor and interest of all concerned.

Nations that expand and nations that do not expand may both ultimately go down, but the one leaves heirs and a glorious memory, and the other leaves neither. The Roman expanded, and he has left a memory which has profoundly influenced the history of mankind, and he has further left as the heirs of his body, and, above all, of his tongue and culture, the so-called Latin peoples of Europe and America. Similarly to-day it is the great expanding peoples which bequeath to future ages the great memories and material results of their achievements, and the nations which shall have sprung from their loins, England standing as the archetype and best exemplar of all such mighty nations. But the peoples that do not expand leave, and can leave, nothing behind them.

It is only the warlike power of a civilized people that can give peace to the world. The Arab wrecked the civilization of the Mediterranean coasts, the Turk wrecked the civilization of southeastern Europe, and the Tatar desolated from China to Russia and to Persia, setting back the progress of the world for centuries, solely because the civilized nations opposed to them had lost the great fighting qualities, and, in becoming overpeaceful, had lost the power of keeping peace with a strong hand. Their passing away marked the beginning of a period of chaotic barbarian warfare. Those whose memories are not so short as to have forgotten the defeat of the Greeks by the Turks, of the Italians by the Abyssinians, and the feeble campaigns waged by Spain against feeble Morocco, must realize that at the present moment the Mediterranean coasts would be overrun either by the Turks or by the Sudan Mahdists if these warlike barbarians had only to fear those southern European powers which have lost the fighting edge. Such a barbarian conquest would mean endless war; and the fact that nowadays the reverse takes place, and that the barbarians recede or are conquered, with the attendant fact that peace follows their retrogression or conquest, is due solely to the power of the mighty civilized races which have not lost the fighting instinct, and which by their expansion are gradually bringing peace into the red wastes where the barbarian peoples of the world hold sway.

4. · "THE INFLUENCE OF SEA POWER UPON HISTORY"

Few individuals influenced Roosevelt more than Captain Alfred T. Mahan, the great proponent of sea power. Although Roosevelt's views on expansion and the spread of civilization had been formed before he met Mahan or read his writings, Mahan confirmed and amplified them. More than that, he imbued in Roosevelt the belief that successful defense of the continental United States was hardly less dependent on a large battle fleet capable of offensive thrusts than was expansion into the remote reaches of the world.

Captain Mahan has written distinctively the best and most important, and also by far the most interesting, book on naval

Review of Captain Alfred T. Mahan's book, *The Influence of Sea Power Upon History, 1660–1783* (Boston: Little, Brown and Company, 1898) in *The Atlantic Monthly*, LXVI (October 1890), 563–67.

history which has been produced on either side of the water for many a long year. Himself an officer who has seen active service and borne himself with honor under fire, he starts with an advantage that no civilian can possess. On the other hand, he does not show the shortcomings which make the average military man an exasperatingly incompetent military historian. His work is in every respect scholarly, and has not a trace of the pedantry which invariably mars mere self-conscious striving after scholarship. He is thoroughly conversant with his subject, and has prepared himself for it by exhaustive study and research, and he approaches it in, to use an old-fashioned phrase, an entirely philosophical spirit. He subordinates detail to mass-effects, trying always to grasp and make evident the essential features of a situation; and he neither loses sight of nor exaggerates the bearing which the history of past struggles has upon our present problems.

One of his merits is the use of French authorities. For the last three centuries England has been the central and commanding figure in naval history, and, naturally, her writers, followed by our own, have acted blandly on the belief that they themselves wrote the only books on the subject worth reading. As a matter of fact, the French historians and essayists form a school of marked excellence in many ways. It would, for instance, be difficult to match in English such writings as those of Admiral Jurien de la Gravière. Only by a study of the French authors is it possible to arrive at the true facts in the history of the gigantic sea struggle, lasting for over a century, which began at Bantry Bay and Beachy Head and ended at Trafalgar.

In his Introduction, Captain Mahan shows very clearly the practical importance of the study of naval history in the past to those who wish to estimate and use aright the navies of the present. He dwells on the fact that not only are the great principles of strategy much the same as they ever were, but that also many of the underlying principles of the tactics of the past are applicable to the tactics of the present; or, at least, that the tacticians of to-day can with advantage study the battles of the past. He does not fall into the mistake of trying to make forced analogies, but he does prove, for one thing, that the school which professes the mêlée or "never-mind-manoeuvring" principles, no less than the other school, which tends to turn manoeuvring into an end instead of a means, and to develop mere timid tactical trifling, may study the fleet actions and naval campaigns of the last two centuries to good purpose. There are plenty of naval authorities who believe that an encounter between squadrons of modern ironclads, with their accompanying rams and torpedo-boats, can be nothing but a huge bloody scramble, in which each ship fights for its own hand. This belief may be true as an estimate of probabilities; but if it be, it will only show that as yet the nineteenth century does not know how to wield with proper skill the wonderful weapons it has forged. Similarly, the early sea-fights between fleets of sailing-ships were mere mêlées; men knowing nothing more of tactics than that one-sided view of the "shock" principle which consists in running headlong at an adversary —a system whereof the success depends entirely upon the nature of the adversary. But as time went on a change took place, and there arose great admirals, who differed as much from the rough fleet-leaders who preceded them as Alexander differed from Alaric. Sea war grew into an art, and the fleet that conquered had to pay heed to such considerations as unity of action and intelligent direction of force quite as much as to the valor of the seaman and the fighting capacity of the individual ships.

Captain Mahan's effort is to show the tremendous effect which sea power has had upon the development of certain of the great nations of the world, especially at momentous crises of their history. In his introductory chapter he gives one striking illustration, for he shows that it was the sea power of Rome, during the second Punic war, which was one of the chief determining factors in bringing about the failure of Hannibal's campaign in Italy, and the consequent overthrow of Carthage. He makes this point so clear that it is difficult to see how it can be controverted successfully. The second Punic war was one of the all-important world struggles, and has been described again and again by every kind of writer for the past twenty centuries, yet Captain Mahan is the first who has given proper prominence to one of the main causes by which the result was determined. This is a fair example of Captain Mahan's acute historic insight, and it is characteristic of the way his book is written. Hitherto, historians of naval matters, at least so far as English and American writers are concerned, have completely ignored the general strategic bearing of the struggles which they chronicle; they have been for the most part mere annalists, who limited themselves to describing the actual battles and the forces on each side. On the other hand, the general historian sees but dimly how much and in what way the net outcome of a conflict has been influenced by the might of the contestants on the sea, and in consequence pays but vague and unsubstantial heed to the really vital cause by which the result was accomplished. Captain Mahan, however, never loses sight of the deep, underlying causes and of the connection between events. His discussion of the campaigns and battles, of the strategy and tactics, is full and clear, and written in a perfectly scientific and dispassionate spirit. But this is not his greatest merit. He never for a moment loses sight of the relations which the struggles by sea bore to the history of the time; and, for the period which he covers, he shows, as no other writer has done, the exact points and the wonderful extent of the influence of the sea power of the various contending nations upon their ultimate triumph or failure, and upon the futures of the mighty races to which they belonged.

In the first chapter after the Introduction, he discusses the various elements which go to make up sea power, writing always, as elsewhere throughout the book, with especial heed to the circumstances of the United States at the present time. He shows how sea power is affected by the geographical position, physical conformation, extent, and density of population of a country no less than by the character of the people and of the government. He points out the need of adequate fortifications and navy-yards on all the coast, and incidentally specifies the need at some point on the Gulf Coast, preferably the mouth of the Mississippi; and he lays stress on the necessity of a large commercial marine, if we wish the sea population which alone furnishes a secure base for naval power. . . .

. . . One or two of the points which Captain Mahan brings out have a very important bearing on our present condition, especially in view of the increased interest which is felt in the navy and coast defense. There is a popular idea that we could accomplish wonders by privateering—or rather by commerce-destroying, as Captain Mahan calls it. He shows very clearly, on the other hand, that commerce-destroying can never be more than a secondary factor—even though of very considerable importance—in bringing to a conclusion a war with a powerful foe. He shows also that, for the most successful kind of commerce-destroying, there must be a secure base of operations near the line of the enemy's commerce, and some kind of line of battle to fall back on—and the United States possesses neither. Doubtless, in event of a war, we might cause annoyance and loss to an enemy's commerce; but we could not by this method accomplish anything like as much as the people at large, and not a few of our naval officers also, believe. It is beyond all comparison more important to cripple the enemy's fighting-ships than to harass his merchantmen.

Again, as Captain Mahan shows, our experience in the Civil War is worthless as a test of what we could do against a foreign sea power. It is impossible to imagine a more foolish state of mind than that which accepts the belief in our capacity to improvise means of resistance against the sea power of Europe, ready equipped and armed at all points, because we were successful in overcoming with our makeshifts an enemy even more unprepared than we were ourselves. It is true that at the end of four years' warfare we had developed a formidable fleet; but in the event of a European contest, it is not likely that we should be allowed as many weeks before the fatal blow fell. There is a loose popular idea that we could defend ourselves by some kind of patent method, invented on the spur of the moment. This is sheer folly. There is no doubt that American ingenuity could do something, but not enough to prevent the enemy from ruining our coasting-trade and threatening with destruction half our coast towns. Proper forts, with heavy guns, could do much; but our greatest need is the need of a fighting-fleet. Forts alone could not prevent the occupation of any town or territory outside the range of their guns, or the general wasting of the seaboard; while a squadron of heavy battleships, able to sail out and attack the enemy's vessels as they approached, and possessing the great advantage of being near their own base of supplies, would effectually guard a thousand miles of coast. Passive defense, giving the assailant complete choice of the time and place for attack, is always a most dangerous expedient. Our ships should be the best of their kind—this is the first desideratum; but, in addition, there should be plenty of them. We need a large navy, composed not merely of cruisers, but containing also a full proportion of powerful battleships, able to meet those of any other nation. It is not economy—it is niggardly and foolish short-sightedness—to cramp our naval expenditures, while squandering money right and left on everything else, from pensions to public buildings.

In conclusion, it must be said that Captain Mahan's style is clear, simple, and terse. His book is as interesting as it is valuable; and in writing it he has done a real service.

The Coming of the Spanish-American War

5. · INTERVENTION IN CUBA

Roosevelt clearly perceived the Far Eastern implications of war against Spain in 1898; yet his statements on the eve of the crisis emphasized the need to drive Spain from the New World, stop the bloody conflict between Cubans and Spanish, and avenge the destruction of the *Maine*. (Roosevelt never doubted that the Spanish had in fact sunk the *Maine*.) The following letter to Brooks Adams, brother of Henry and author of *The Law of Civilization and Decay*, is typical of many letters Roosevelt wrote at the time.

Washington, March 21, 1898

My dear Adams: . . .

. . . Personally, I feel that it is not too late to intervene in Cuba. What the administration will do I know not. In some points it has followed too closely in Cleveland's footsteps to please me, excellently though it has done on the whole. In the name of humanity and of national self-interest alike, we should have interfered in Cuba two years ago, a year and a half ago, last April, and again last December. The defective imaginations of many good people here, the limited mental horizon of others, and the craven fear and brutal selfishness of the mere money-getters, have combined to prevent us from doing our duty. It has been a case of the offer of the sibylline books over again. Month by month has gone by, each leaving less for us to interfere on behalf of, and increasing the danger that would result from our interference; and yet interfere we must sooner or

Letter to Brooks Adams, March 21, 1898. *The Letters,* I, 797–98.

later. The blood of the Cubans, the blood of women and children who have perished by the hundred thousand in hideous misery, lies at our door; and the blood of the murdered men of the *Maine* calls not for indemnity but for the full measure of atonement which can only come by driving the Spaniard from the New World. I have said this to the President before his Cabinet; I have said it to Judge Day, the real head of the State Department; and to my own chief. I cannot say it publicly, for I am of course merely a minor official in the administration. At least, however, I have borne testimony where I thought it would do good. . . .

6. · "I DON'T EXPECT ANY MILITARY GLORY OUT OF THIS CUBAN WAR."

Roosevelt's decision to resign as Assistant Secretary of War soon after the outbreak of hostilities and to organize the "Rough Riders" was prompted by several considerations. There is little doubt that the call of glory was high among them. Indeed, he later confided to his military aide that he would have left his wife's deathbed "to have answered that call." Yet, as this letter to Paul Dana, editor of the New York *Sun*, suggests, duty was also an impelling motive.

Washington, April 1898.
My dear Dana: . . .
. . . I want to go because I wouldn't feel that I had been entirely true to my beliefs and convictions, and to the ideal I had set for myself if I didn't go. I don't want you to think that I am talking like a prig, for I know perfectly well that one never

Letter to Paul Dana, April 18, 1898. *The Letters*, II, 816–18.

is able to analyze with entire accuracy all of one's motives. But I am entirely certain that I don't expect any military glory out of this Cuban war, more than what is implied in the honorable performance of duty. For two years I have consistently preached the doctrine of a resolute foreign policy, and of readiness to accept the arbitrament of the sword if necessary; and I have alway intended to act up to my preaching if occasion arose. Now the occasion has arisen, and I ought to meet it. I have had, as you know, a perfect horror of the ideas which are perhaps most clearly crystalized in the editorials of papers like the *Evening Post;* that is, of the ideas of the peace-at-any-price theorists on the one side, the timid and scholarly men in whom refinement and culture have been developed at the expense of all the virile qualities; and a horror even greater of the big moneyed men in whose minds money and material prosperity have finally dwarfed everything else. I don't think this nation needs any incitement to development on the money-making side, and if we who have preached the doctrine fail to put our words into effect when the time comes, our preaching will lose much of its force. For two years I have been urging that we put Spain out of Cuba, and if there ever was a righteous war it will be this; and if, owing to the unfortunate delay in beginning it, we see our men dying of yellow fever in Cuba I should hate to be comfortably at home in Washington, although I have as much dislike of death as anyone could have, and take as keen enjoyment in life.

Moreover, an additional reason for my going is the fact that though I have a wife and six children, they are not dependent upon my exertions for support. I am not a rich man, and my children will have to work; but they will be well educated and comfortably brought up, and inasmuch as I have never been in a money-making pursuit my loss would not very materially affect their income.

I have written you thus at length, and with what may seem too great frankness, because I was really very much touched by the editorial, and because I want you to believe that whether I am right or not, I am at least acting conscientiously and in pursuance of convictions which I have held for many years, and which I should feel rather ashamed to abandon at this time.

A Defense of the Acquisition of the Philippines

should be provided to keep p's. armed —

7. · "THE PROPHESIES OF MR. BRYAN"

Unlike the anti-imperialists, Roosevelt refused to regard overseas expansion as fundamentally different from the continental expansion that had peopled the nation. As the Republican vice-presidential candidate in 1900, Roosevelt campaigned widely and energetically against the Democratic presidential nominee, William Jennings Bryan, while President McKinley issued homilies from the front porch of his home in Canton, Ohio. In this excerpt from one of Roosevelt's campaign speeches, he draws several specious parallels between the purchase of continental territories and the purchase of the Philippines. At the same time, he exposes the cant in the Democrats' espousal of the "consent of the governed" doctrine with a telling allusion to Southern Democrats' treatment of American Negroes.

. . . There is not the least little danger of imperialism and there is not a dividing line of any kind to be drawn between our methods of expansion in 1898 and 1899 and the methods of expansion under which we acquired Michigan, Illinois, Florida, Louisiana, Minnesota, Missouri, Oregon, California,

A campaign speech at Detroit, Michigan, September 7, 1900. *The Works*, XVI, 573–75.

Hawaii, and Alaska. Mr. Bryan has recently spoken of us as having purchased the Filipinos at two dollars and fifty cents a head, treating it as analogous to buying slaves at one thousand dollars a head. It seems impossible that such a statement could be made unless as a jest. Mr. Bryan must know that the Philippines were paid for precisely as Florida, Louisiana, California, and Alaska were paid for. The Filipinos were no more purchased than were the individual dwellers in New Orleans, St. Augustine, Sante Fé and Sitka. If the Filipinos were purchased at so much a head by President Mc-Kinley, then the inhabitants of Louisiana were so purchased by Jefferson, and the Christianized half-castes of Alaska were so purchased by Seward. When in 1776 the United States declared itself a nation, Illinois, Indiana, and Michigan formed a part of Canada. Illinois and Indiana were acquired by conquest during the Revolution. Many of the inhabitants did not want to become a part of the United States, any more than did the people of Quebec; but they were conquered and brought in. Detroit, however, was held by the British for many years after the Revolutionary War ended, and was only surrendered in consequence of Jay's treaty, for what was in effect a money equivalent. The Indian aboriginal inhabitants of these States were not consulted in the treaty, nor were the white inhabitants of French extraction. The author of the Declaration of Independence, being of sane and healthy mind, did not push the doctrine of "the consent of the governed" to a conclusion that would have resulted in our great Commonwealth being confined to the east of the Alleghanies, while this mighty West, in which I am now speaking, would have been left as a hunting-ground for savages and a dwelling-place for fur-traders. ALSO SAVAGES.

Mr. Bryan and his associates cannot say enough about the "consent of the governed" doctrine as applying to the Philippines. They dwell upon the fact that "no man is good enough to govern another." In North Carolina, and other Southern

States, we see before our eyes the process of the disfranchise-
ment of the negro. We see before our eyes the black man
governed without his consent by the white man. Be it remembered too, that the men thus disfranchised have always
been Mr. Bryan's fellow citizens, most of them born as free as
he was born. If our opponents are sincere they must necessarily denounce what has been done in North Carolina with
even more bitterness than they have shown in denouncing
what has been done in the Philippines. They say that in the
Philippines one man is not entitled to govern another, even
when the one does so only to protect the other from the rule
of a savage oligarchy until he grows able to protect himself.
It is a matter of astonishment that such doctrine can be either
uttered or listened to without laughter, when it is spoken by
and to men who go to their candidate pledging him the votes
of their States, because in these States these very men do
govern other men without their consent. Until our opponents
have removed the beam from their own eye, by applying
their "consent of the governed" doctrine at home, let them
hold their peace about the Tagal[1] bandits to whom their
words give fresh heart to shoot down our soldiers in the Far
Eastern archipelago. *NONSENSE.*

The policy of expansion is America's historic policy. We
have annexed the Philippines exactly as we have annexed *WHY.*
Hawaii, New Mexico, and Alaska. They are now part of
American territory and we have no more right to give them
up than we have the right to restore Hawaii to the Kanaka
Queen or to abandon Alaska to the Esquimaux. There is not
a particle of difference between the cases. We cannot go back,
first for the sake of the islands themselves, and next for the
sake of our own honor. The men who are making speeches on
the unrighteousness of our expanding in the Philippines

---

[1] The Tagalogs were a people of central Luzon in the Philippines
[Ed.].

DON'T.

might with as much justification incite the Sioux and the Apache tribes to outbreak against us, on the ground that we have no right to retain South Dakota or Arizona. The policy of the Kansas City platform is a policy of economic disaster and financial dishonor at home and of unworthy shrinking from duty abroad; and we appeal to all honest, far-seeing, brave, and patriotic men, North or South, East or West, whatever their political affiliations may have been in the past, to stand with us now against the men who would bring such shame and misery upon our country, and to support us as we uphold the cause of honesty and of industrial well-being at home and the honor of the American flag in the face of all the peoples of the earth.

III · THE BURDEN OF EMPIRE

Premature Independence for the
Philippines Rejected

8. · "THE FILIPINOS ARE NOT READY FOR INDEPENDENCE."

During the first year of his presidency, Roosevelt was subjected
to heavy pressure to set a specific date for granting independence
to the Philippines. Much of it came from Democrats. Some, like
Bryan, feared that colonialism would subvert American democratic
values; others wanted to disengage for racist or economic reasons.
Roosevelt inclined to agree that independence was a desirable goal.
But as this letter to Senator George F. Hoar, a high-minded Republican anti-imperialist from Massachusetts, reveals, he felt too
strongly the responsibility to prepare the Filipinos for independence
to act prematurely.

Personal   Washington, June 16, 1902
My dear Senator Hoar: It would be but a poor-spirited man
who would resent such a letter as yours or fail to be moved
as I am moved both by the spirit which prompts it and by its
references to me individually.

Mr. Andrew Carnegie has just written me in terms not
wholly unlike the sentences you quote.

When I used the sentence containing the word indepen-

Letter to George Frisbie Hoar, June 16, 1902. *The Letters,* III,
276–77.

dence I was thinking of our conversation. As you know, I went carefully over with Judge Taft[1] the advisability of definitely stating what you desire. I told Judge Taft that I was entirely willing to take the position which as I understood you wished—that is, that when and if the Filipinos attained a degree and capacity for self-government which in our judgment made it reasonably probable they could stand by themselves, then we should leave it to them to decide whether or not they would be independent of us or continue knit to us by some form less of dependence than of interdependence. Governor Taft earnestly advised me not to make such an announcement. He said that it would in its effects simply produce a feeling of unrest among the Filipinos, that it would change their attitude from that of desiring to secure peaceful self-government under our laws into one of agitation for immediate independence and would inevitably do great and serious damage, encouraging our enemies to work for independence in the immediate future and making our friends afraid that we would desert them, and thereby checking and perhaps reversing the present steady movement towards orderly liberty. Now, my dear Senator, you are the last man who would ask me to do something which might be fraught with disaster to the people of the Philippines, with the idea of straightening my own record in the future. I do not think that the people of the Philippines would believe in or would care for a promise which might very well apply not to them but to their descendants a generation or two generations hence.

You speak of the Mexican war and of what followed, and you please me by saying that you have read my life of Benton. You doubtless remember that I all along took a different view of the Mexican war from that taken by most Republicans of inherited antislavery feeling. It seems to me that my present

------

[1] William Howard Taft, U. S. Circuit Judge, 1892–1900; Civil Governor of the Philippines, 1901–1904; President of the U. S., 1909–1913 [Ed.].

position should be compared rather with the attitude of the early Republican leaders towards slavery, in contradistinction to the attitude of the Wendell Phillips[2] and Garrison abolitionists. Lincoln absolutely declined to announce that he was an abolitionist or that slavery should be destroyed in the States where it existed. He even declined to announce that he favored its abolition in the District of Columbia, saying merely that he believed that Congress had the right to abolish it, but should exercise that right only when the people of the District were altogether willing. His great effort was to prevent the extension of slavery; not to abolish it. Now, it seems to me that Lincoln in these matters showed not abandonment of a high ideal, but great common sense. I do not think he was less moral than Wendell Phillips or Garrison; I believe he was more practical.

I am striving my best, doubtless with many shortcomings, but, as I am sure you believe, with sincerity and earnestness, to hasten the day when we shall need no more force in the Philippines than is needed in New York. I am encouraging in every way the growth of the conditions which now make for self-government in the Philippines and which, if the Filipino people can take advantage of them, will assuredly put them where some day we shall say that if they desire independence they shall have it. But I cannot be certain when that day will be, and of course there is always the possibility that they may themselves behave in such fashion as to put it off indefinitely. Now I do not want to make a promise which may not be kept. Above all things, I want for myself and for the nation that there shall be good faith. Senator Hoar, I honor you and revere you. I think you are animated by as lofty a spirit of patriotism and of devotion to and belief in mankind as any man I have ever met in public life. I hate to seem in your eyes to be falling short of my duty on a great question. I ask

[2] Reformer, orator, and staunch supporter of William Lloyd Garrison [Ed.].

you to believe that after much painful thought, after much groping and some uncertainty as to where my duty lay, I am now doing it as light has been given me to see it.

The Economic Welfare of the Island Dependencies

9. • "INTRODUCING BOTH LIBERTY AND ORDER"

Unlike many Republicans who had called loudly for expansion at the turn of the century, Roosevelt shouldered the burden of empire as willingly as he wore the glory. His seven and one-half years as President were marked by the same attitude of *noblesse oblige* toward the new dependencies as characterized his policies toward factory workers. Here he reviews the progress already made in the Philippines, Puerto Rico, and Hawaii, then calls on Congress to enact additional laws to promote their political and economic welfare.

THE PHILIPPINES

I most earnestly hope that the bill to provide a lower tariff for or else absolute free trade in Philippine products will become a law. No harm will come to any American industry; and while there will be some small but real material benefit to the Filipinos, the main benefit will come by the showing made as to our purpose to do all in our power for their welfare. So far our action in the Philippines has been abundantly justified, not mainly and indeed not primarily because of the added dignity it has given us as a nation by proving that we are capable honorably and efficiently to bear the international burdens which a mighty people should bear, but even more

An excerpt from Roosevelt's Annual Message to Congress, 1906. *Messages and Papers*, XI, 1208–10.

because of the immense benefit that has come to the people of the Philippine Islands. In these islands we are steadily introducing both liberty and order, to a greater degree than their people have ever before known. We have secured justice. We have provided an efficient police force, and have put down ladronism. Only in the islands of Leyte and Samar is the authority of our government resisted and this by wild mountain tribes under the superstitious inspiration of fakirs and pseudoreligious leaders. We are constantly increasing the measure of liberty accorded the islanders, and next spring, if conditions warrant, we shall take a great stride forward in testing their capacity for self-government by summoning the first Filipino legislative assembly; and the way in which they stand this test will largely determine whether the self-government thus granted will be increased or decreased; for if we have erred at all in the Philippines it has been in proceeding too rapidly in the direction of granting a large measure of self-government. We are building roads. We have, for the immeasurable good of the people, arranged for the building of railroads. Let us also see to it that they are given free access to our markets. This nation owes no more imperative duty to itself and mankind than the duty of managing the affairs of all the islands under the American flag—the Philippines, Porto Rico, and Hawaii—so as to make it evident that it is in every way to their advantage that the flag should fly over them.

PORTO RICO

American citizenship should be conferred on the citizens of Porto Rico. The harbor of San Juan in Porto Rico should be dredged and improved. The expenses of the Federal court of Porto Rico should be met from the Federal Treasury. The administration of the affairs of Porto Rico, together with those of the Philippines, Hawaii, and our other insular possessions, should all be directed under one executive department; by preference the Department of State or the Department of War.

HAWAII

The needs of Hawaii are peculiar; every aid should be given the islands; and our efforts should be unceasing to develop them along the lines of a community of small freeholders, not of great planters with coolie-tilled estates. Situated as this Territory is, in the middle of the Pacific, there are duties imposed upon this small community which do not fall in like degree or manner upon any other American community. This warrants our treating it differently from the way in which we treat Territories contiguous to or surrounded by sister Territories or other States, and justifies the setting aside of a portion of our revenues to be expended for educational and internal improvements therein. Hawaii is now making an effort to secure immigration fit in the end to assume the duties and burdens of full American citizenship, and whenever the leaders in the various industries of those islands finally adopt our ideals and heartily join our administration in endeavoring to develop a middle class of substantial citizens, a way will then be found to deal with the commercial and industrial problems which now appear to them so serious. The best Americanism is that which aims for stability and permanency of prosperous citizenship, rather than immediate returns on large masses of capital. - HE IS BEING SINCERE .

The United States' "heel of Achilles"

10. · INDEPENDENCE FOR THE PHILIPPINES RECONSIDERED

Worried by the failure of both Congress and the American people to rise to the full responsibilities of empire and world power, Roosevelt began to conclude after Japan's spectacular victory

Letter to William Howard Taft, August 21, 1907. *The Letters*, V, 761–62.

against Russia in 1905 that the United States was overextended in the Far East. He agreed in that year to recognize Japanese suzerainty over Korea because, as he told Secretary of State John Hay, the Koreans "couldn't possibly strike one blow in their own defense." And by 1907, if not before, he had also concluded that Japan could seize and retain the Philippines at will. In August of that year he wrote Secretary of War William H. Taft that the Philippines were "our heel of Achilles" and that they should be given independence at an early date partly in order to "remove a temptation from Japan's way."

Oyster Bay, August 21, 1907

Dear Will: . . .

There is just one point as to which I feel uneasy, and that is the Philippine question. We have continually to accommodate ourselves to conditions as they actually are and not as we would wish them to be. I wish our people were prepared permanently, in a duty-loving spirit, and looking forward to a couple of generations of continuous manifestation of this spirit, to assume the control of the Philippine Islands for the good of the Filipinos. But as a matter of fact I gravely question whether this is the case. Even in the West Indies, which are right under us here at home, and where anything that happens is brought home close to us, and where we are at an enormous advantage compared with foreign powers in dealing with any situation, it is exceedingly difficult to get this people to take a proper view of any emergency that arises. In Cuba last year while we carried our people with us, there was a week or two when things trembled in the balance, because on the one hand certain extremists wished us to announce that we would forthwith seize and hold Cuba for our own profit, while a larger number of people objected to our interfering at all. It took me two years to get through the Santo Domingan treaty—a treaty which was of undiluted benefit to this country,—simply because the people as a whole would not bother

their heads about the situation. I have never gotten them up
to the point of taking even a tepid interest in Castro's[1] outrageous iniquity in treating American interests in Venezuela;
and this is all where the Monroe Doctrine applies and where
in consequence the average American has something in the
way of traditional national action to which appeal can be
made as a precedent. As regards the Philippines all is different. In the excitement of the Spanish War people wanted to
take the islands. They had an idea they would be a valuable
possession. Now they think that they are of no value, and I
am bound to say that in the physical sense I don't see where
they are of any value to us or where they are likely to be of
any value. It has been everything for the islands and everything for our own national character that we should have
taken them and have administered them with the really lofty
and disinterested efficiency that has been shown. But it is impossible for instance to awaken any public interest in favor of
giving them tariff advantages; it is very difficult to awaken
any public interest in providing any adequate defense of the
islands; and though if attacked our people would certainly
defend them at no matter what cost in warfare, the result
would in the end be such utter disgust that at the first opportunity the islands would be cut adrift or handed over to anyone. Mind you I am not saying what I think our people *ought*
to feel, but what I fear they *do* feel—just as in connection
with the Californians and Japanese, while I partly altered my
own convictions on the subject, I partly simply had to recognize that the convictions of the great mass of our people on
the Pacific Slope were unalterable.

   This leads me up to saying that I think we shall have to be
prepared for giving the islands independence of a more or less
complete type much sooner than I think advisable from their
own standpoint, or than I would think advisable if this coun-

[1] Cipriano Castro, dictator of Venezuela, 1899–1909 [Ed.].

try were prepared to look ahead fifty years and to build the navy and erect the fortifications which in my judgment it should. The Philippines form our heel of Achilles. They are all that makes the present situation with Japan dangerous. I think that in some way and with some phraseology that you think wise you should state to them that if they handle themselves wisely in their legislative assembly we shall at the earliest possible moment give them a nearly complete independence. Root used the expression a couple of years ago of saying that our aim was to put them in the position of Cuba. Just at the moment Cuba's position is not that in which I hope to see the Philippine Islands; and it may be that you can as you suggest better use the simile of Canada and Australia, saying that they will have as complete self-government as Canada and Australia have. My point is that we must very seriously consider both domestic and foreign conditions as regards the retention of the islands. To have Hale[2] at the head of the naval committee is a bad thing anyhow, but to have him at the head of the committee while the possession of the Philippines renders us vulnerable in Asia for lack of a great fleet is a veritable national calamity. To keep the islands without treating them generously and at the same time without adequately fortifying them and without building up a navy second only to that of Great Britain, would be disastrous in the extreme. Yet there is danger of just this being done. It is the islands themselves and not us that have benefited by the connection, save of course, as we benefit and as all people benefit by doing well a piece of duty that ought to be done. I do not believe our people will permanently accept the Philippines simply as an unremunerative and indeed expensive duty. I think that to have some pretty clear avowal of our intention not to permanently keep them and to give them independence would remove a

[2] Eugene Hale, Republican senator from Maine, 1881–1911, and Chairman of the Senate Committee on Naval Affairs [Ed.].

temptation from Japan's way and would render our task at home easier. Personally I should be glad to see the islands made independent, with perhaps some kind of international guarantee for the preservation of order, or with some warning on our part that if they did not keep order we would have to interfere again; this among other reasons because I would rather see this nation fight all her life than to see her give them up to Japan or any other nation under duress.

I am more and more pleased with the fact that the fleet has been ordered to the Pacific. It is good from every standpoint. There will be difficulties of all kinds in connection with getting it there; and it is only by the actual experience of these difficulties that we shall be able to force the creatures of the Hale type into providing what the navy actually needs.

Good luck go with you!

IV · ROOSEVELT AND LATIN AMERICA

Roosevelt Takes Panama

11. · AN AUTOBIOGRAPHICAL DEFENSE

This labored, self-righteous account of the United States' acquisition of the Panama Canal Zone is good autobiography and inconclusive history. It is good autobiography because of the light it casts on the principals' motives and rationalizations. It makes clear, for example, that Roosevelt conceived an interocean highway as a boon to civilization. But it is inconclusive history because of its omissions, distortions, and failure to discuss other possibilities. Thus there is no intimation of the intrigues and backstage maneuvers that both inspired and assured the success of the revolution in Panama. There is no indication that the Colombian President's power was seriously circumscribed by internal factors. And there is no suggestion that a decision to buy new rights from Colombia on the same terms the United States bought the old rights from the French stockholders might have resolved matters without leaving a legacy of ill-will. THE OTHER ALTERNATIVE.

By far the most important action I took in foreign affairs during the time I was President related to the Panama Canal. Here again there was much accusation about my having acted in an "unconstitutional" manner—a position which can be upheld only if Jefferson's action in acquiring Louisiana be also

Autobiography, pp. 512–27.

treated as unconstitutional; and at different stages of the affair believers in a do-nothing policy denounced me as having "usurped authority"—which meant, that when nobody else could or would exercise efficient authority, I exercised it.

During the nearly four hundred years that had elapsed since Balboa crossed the Isthmus, there had been a good deal of talk about building an Isthmus Canal, and there had been various discussions of the subject and negotiations about it in Washington for the previous half-century. So far it had all resulted merely in conversation; and the time had come when unless somebody was prepared to act with decision we would have to resign ourselves to at least half a century of further conversation. Under the Hay-Pauncefote Treaty signed shortly after I became President, and thanks to our negotiations with the French Panama Company, the United States at last acquired a possession, so far as Europe was concerned, which warranted her in immediately undertaking the task. It remained to decide where the canal should be, whether along the line already pioneered by the French company in Panama, or in Nicaragua. Panama belonged to the Republic of Colombia. Nicaragua bid eagerly for the privilege of having the United States build the canal through her territory. As long as it was doubtful which route we would decide upon, Colombia extended every promise of friendly co-operation: at the Pan-American Congress in Mexico her delegate joined in the unanimous vote which requested the United States forthwith to build the canal; and at her eager request we negotiated the Hay-Herran Treaty with her, which gave us the right to build the canal across Panama. A board of experts sent to the Isthmus had reported that this route was better than the Nicaragua route, and that it would be well to build the canal over it provided we could purchase the rights of the French Company for forty million dollars; but that otherwise they would advise taking the Nicaragua route. Ever since 1846 we had had a treaty with the power then in control of the Isthmus, the Republic of New Granada, the predecessor of the Republic of Colombia and of the present Republic of Panama, by which treaty the United States was guaranteed free and open right of way across the Isthmus of Panama by any mode of communication that might be constructed, while in return our government guaranteed the perfect neutrality of the Isthmus with a view to the preservation of free transit.

For nearly fifty years we had asserted the right to prevent the closing of this highway of commerce. . . .

. . . We had again and again been forced to intervene to protect the transit across the Isthmus, and the intervention was frequently at the request of Colombia herself. The effort to build a canal by private capital had been made under De Lesseps and had resulted in lamentable failure. Every serious proposal to build the canal in such manner had been abandoned. The United States had repeatedly announced that we would not permit it to be built or controlled by any Old World government. Colombia was utterly impotent to build it herself. Under these circumstances it had become a matter of imperative obligation that we should build it ourselves without further delay.

I took final action in 1903. During the preceding fifty-three years the governments of New Granada and of its successor, Colombia, had been in a constant state of flux; and the state of Panama had sometimes been treated as almost independent, in a loose Federal league, and sometimes as the mere property of the government at Bogota; and there had been innumerable appeals to arms, sometimes for adequate, sometimes for inadequate, reasons. . . .

. . . Only the active interference of the United States had enabled her [Colombia] to preserve so much as a semblance of sovereignty. Had it not been for the exercise by the United States of the police power in her interest, her connection with the Isthmus would have been sundered long before it was. In 1856, in 1860, in 1873, in 1885, in 1901, and again in 1902, sailors and marines from United States war-ships were forced to land in order to patrol the Isthmus, to protect life and property, and to see that the transit across the Isthmus was kept open. In 1861, in 1862, in 1885, and in 1900, the Colombian Government asked that the United States Government would land troops to protect Colombian interests and maintain order on the Isthmus. The people of Panama during the preceding twenty years had three times sought to establish their independence by revolution or secession—in 1885, in 1895, and in 1899. . . .

. . . When the government in nominal control of the Isthmus continually besought American interference to protect the "rights" it could not itself protect, and permitted our government to transport Colombian troops unarmed, under protection of our own armed men, while the Colombian arms and ammunition came in a separate train, it is obvious that the Colombian "sovereignty" was of such a character as to warrant our insisting that inasmuch as it only existed because of our protection there should be in requital a sense of the obligations that the acceptance of this protection implied.

Meanwhile Colombia was under a dictatorship. In 1898 M. A. Sanclamente was elected president, and J. M. Maroquin vice-president, of the Republic of Colombia. On July 31, 1900, the vice-president, Maroquin, executed a *coup d'état* by seizing the person of the president, Sanclamente, and imprisoning him at a place a few miles out of Bogota. Maroquin thereupon declared himself possessed of the executive power because of "the absence of the president"—a delightful touch of unconscious humor. He then issued a decree that public order was disturbed, and, upon that ground, assumed to himself legislative power under another provision of the constitution; that is, having himself disturbed the public order, he alleged the disturbance as a justification for seizing absolute power. Thenceforth Maroquin, without the aid of any legislative body, ruled as a dictator, combining the supreme executive, legislative, civil, and military authorities, in the so-called Republic of Colombia. The "absence" of Sanclamente from the capital became permanent by his death in prison in the year 1902. When the people of Panama declared their independence in November, 1903, no congress had sat in Colombia since the year 1898, except the special congress called by Maroquin to reject the canal treaty, and which did reject it by a unanimous vote, and adjourned without legislating on any other subject. The constitution of 1886 had taken away from Panama the power of self-government and vested it in Colombia. The *coup d'état* of Maroquin took away from Colombia herself the power of government and vested it in an irresponsible dictator.

Consideration of the above facts ought to be enough to show any human being that we were not dealing with normal conditions on the Isthmus and in Colombia. We were dealing with the government of an irresponsible alien dictator, and with a condition of affairs on the Isthmus itself which was marked by one uninterrupted series of outbreaks and revolutions. As for the "consent-of-the-governed" theory, that absolutely justified our action; the people on the Isthmus were the "governed"; they were governed by Colombia, without their consent, and they unanimously repudiated the Colombian Government, and demanded that the United States build the canal.

I had done everything possible, personally and through Secretary Hay, to persuade the Colombian Government to keep faith. Under the Hay-Pauncefote Treaty, it was explicitly provided that the United States should build the canal, should control, police, and protect it, and keep it open to the vessels of all nations on equal terms. We had assumed the position of guarantor of the canal, including, of course, the building of the canal, and of its peaceful use by all the world. The enterprise was recognized everywhere as responding to an international need. It was a mere travesty on justice to treat the

government in possession of the Isthmus as having the right—
which Secretary Cass forty-five years before had so emphatically repudiated—to close the gates of intercourse on one of
the great highways of the world. When we submitted to Colombia the Hay-Herran Treaty, it had been settled that the
time for delay, the time for permitting any government of
antisocial character, or of imperfect development, to bar the
work, had passed. The United States had assumed in connection with the canal certain responsibilities not only to its
own people, but to the civilized world which imperatively
demanded that there should be no further delay in beginning the work. The Hay-Herran Treaty, if it erred at all, erred
in being overgenerous toward Colombia. The people of Panama were delighted with the treaty, and the president of Colombia, who embodied in his own person the entire government of Colombia, had authorized the treaty to be made. But
after the treaty had been made the Colombia Government
thought it had the matter in its own hands; and the further
thought, equally wicked and foolish, came into the heads of
the people in control at Bogota that they would seize the
French Company at the end of another year and take for
themselves the forty million dollars which the United States
had agreed to pay the Panama Canal Company.

President Maroquin, through his minister, had agreed to
the Hay-Herran Treaty in January, 1903. He had the absolute
power of an unconstitutional dictator to keep his promise or
break it. He determined to break it. To furnish himself an
excuse for breaking it he devised the plan of summoning a
congress especially called to reject the canal treaty. This the
congress—a congress of mere puppets—did, without a dissenting vote; and the puppets adjourned forthwith without
legislating on any other subject. The fact that this was a mere
sham, and that the president had entire power to confirm his
own treaty and act on it if he desired, was shown as soon as
the revolution took place, for on November 6 General Reyes,
of Colombia, addressed the American minister at Bogota, on

behalf of President Maroquin, saying that "if the government of the United States would land troops and restore the Colombian sovereignty" the Colombian president would "declare martial law; and, by virtue of vested constitutional authority, when public order is disturbed, would approve by decree the ratification of the canal treaty as signed; or, if the government of the United States prefers, would call an extra session of the congress—with new and friendly members—next May to approve the treaty." This, of course, is proof positive that the Colombian dictator had used his congress as a mere shield, and a sham shield at that, and it shows how utterly useless it would have been further to trust his good faith in the matter.

When, in August, 1903, I became convinced that Colombia intended to repudiate the treaty made the preceding January, under cover of securing its rejection by the Colombian legislature, I began carefully to consider what should be done. By my direction, Secretary Hay, personally and through the minister at Bogota, repeatedly warned Colombia that grave consequences might follow her rejection of the treaty. The possibility of ratification did not wholly pass away until the close of the session of the Colombian congress on the last day of October. There would then be two possibilities. One was that Panama would remain quiet. In that case I was prepared to recommend to Congress that we should at once occupy the Isthmus anyhow, and proceed to dig the canal; and I had drawn out a draft of my message to this effect. But from the information I received, I deemed it likely that there would be a revolution in Panama as soon as the Colombian congress adjourned without ratifying the treaty, for the entire population of Panama felt that the immediate building of the canal was of vital concern to their well-being. Correspondents of the different newspapers on the Isthmus had sent to their respective papers widely published forecasts indicating that there would be a revolution in such event.

Moreover, on October 16, at the request of Lieutenant-General Young, Captain Humphrey, and Lieutenant Murphy, two army officers who had returned from the Isthmus, saw me and told me that there would unquestionably be a revolution on the Isthmus, that the people were unanimous in their criticism of the Bogota Government and their disgust over the failure of that government to ratify the treaty; and that the revolution would probably take place immediately after the adjournment of the Colombian congress. They did not believe that it would be before October 20, but they were confident that it would certainly come at the end of October or immediately afterward, when the Colombian congress had adjourned. Accordingly I directed the Navy Department to station various ships within easy reach of the Isthmus, to be ready to act in the event of need arising.

These ships were barely in time. On November 3 the revolution occurred. Practically everybody on the Isthmus, including all the Colombian troops that were already stationed there, joined in the revolution, and there was no bloodshed. But on that same day four hundred new Colombian troops were landed at Colon. Fortunately, the gunboat *Nashville*, under Commander Hubbard, reached Colon almost immediately afterward, and when the commander of the Colombian forces threatened the lives and property of the American citizens, including women and children, in Colon, Commander Hubbard landed a few score sailors and marines to protect them. By a mixture of firmness and tact he not only prevented any assault on our citizens, but persuaded the Colombian commander to re-embark his troops for Cartagena. On the Pacific side a Colombian gunboat shelled the city of Panama, with the result of killing one Chinaman—the only life lost in the whole affair.

No one connected with the American Government had any part in preparing, inciting, or encouraging the revolution, and except for the reports of our military and naval officers, which I forwarded to Congress, no one connected with the government had any previous knowledge concerning the proposed revolution, except such as was accessible to any person who read the newspapers and kept abreast of current questions and current affairs. By the unanimous action of its people, and without the firing of a shot, the state of Panama declared themselves an independent republic. The time for hesitation on our part had passed.

My belief then was, and the events that have occurred since have more than justified it, that from the standpoint of the United States it was imperative, not only for civil but for military reasons, that there should be the immediate establishment of easy and speedy communication by sea between the Atlantic and the Pacific. These reasons were not of convenience only, but of vital necessity, and did not admit of indefinite delay. The action of Colombia had shown not only that the delay would be indefinite, but that she intended to confiscate the property and rights of the French Panama Canal Company. The report of the Panama Canal Committee of the Colombian senate on October 14, 1903, on the proposed treaty with the United States, proposed that all consideration of the matter should be postponed until October 31, 1904, when the next Colombian congress would have convened, because by that time the new Congress would be in condition to determine whether through lapse of time the French Company had not forfeited its property and rights. "When that time arrives," the report significantly declared, "the Republic, without any impediment, will be able to contract and will be in more clear, more definite and more advantageous possession, both legally and materially." The naked meaning of this was that Colombia proposed to wait a year, and then enforce a forfeiture of the rights and property of the French Panama Company, so as to secure the forty million dollars our government had authorized as payment to this company. If we had sat supine, this would doubtless have meant that France would have interfered to protect the company, and we should

[handwritten marginal note: XPEDIENCY OVER MORALITY]

then have had on the Isthmus, not the company, but France; and the gravest international complications might have ensued. Every consideration of international morality and expediency, of duty to the Panama people, and of satisfaction of our own national interests and honor, bade us take immediate action. I recognized Panama forthwith on behalf of the United States, and practically all the countries of the world immediately followed suit. The State Department immediately negotiated a canal treaty with the new republic. One of the foremost men in securing the independence of Panama, and the treaty which authorized the United States forthwith to build the canal, was M. Philippe Bunau-Varilla, an eminent French engineer formerly associated with De Lesseps and then living on the Isthmus; his services to civilization were notable, and deserve the fullest recognition.

From the beginning to the end our course was straightforward and in absolute accord with the highest of standards of international morality. Criticism of it can come only from misinformation, or else from a sentimentality which represents both mental weakness and a moral twist. To have acted otherwise than I did would have been on my part betrayal of the interests of the United States, indifference to the interests of Panama, and recreancy to the interests of the world at large. Colombia had forfeited every claim to consideration; indeed, this is not stating the case strongly enough: she had so acted that yielding to her would have meant on our part that culpable form of weakness which stands on a level with wickedness. As for me personally, if I had hesitated to act, and had not in advance discounted the clamor of those Americans who have made a fetich of disloyalty to their country, I should have esteemed myself as deserving a place in Dante's inferno beside the faint-hearted cleric who was guilty of *il gran rifiuto*. The facts I have given above are mere bald statements from the record. They show that from the beginning there had been acceptance of our right to insist on free transit, in whatever form was best, across the Isthmus; and that toward the end there had been a no less universal feeling that it was our duty to the world to provide this transit in the shape of a canal—the resolution of the Pan-American Congress was practically a mandate to this effect. Colombia was then under a one-man government, a dictatorship, founded on usurpation of absolute and irresponsible power. She eagerly pressed us to enter into an agreement with her, as long as there was any chance of our going to the alternative route through Nicaragua. When she thought we were committed, she refused to fulfil the agreement, with the avowed hope of seizing the French company's property for nothing and thereby holding us up. This was a bit of pure bandit morality. It would have achieved its purpose had I possessed as weak moral fibre as those of my critics who announced that I ought to have confined my action to feeble scolding and temporizing until the opportunity for action passed. I did not lift my finger to incite the revolutionists. The right simile to use is totally different. I simply ceased to stamp out the different revolutionary fuses that were already burning. When Colombia committed flagrant wrong against us, I considered it no part of my duty to aid and abet her in her wrong-doing at our expense, and also at the expense of Panama, of the French company, and of the world generally. There had been fifty years of continuous bloodshed and civil strife in Panama; because of my action Panama has now known ten years of such peace and prosperity as she never before saw during the four centuries of her existence—for in Panama, as in Cuba and Santo Domingo, it was the action of the American people, against the outcries of the professed apostles of peace, which alone brought peace. We gave to the people of Panama self-government, and freed them from subjection to alien oppressors. We did our best to get Colombia to let us treat her with a more than generous justice; we exercised patience to beyond the verge of proper forbearance. When we did act and recognize Pan-

WAR To
BRING
PAX.

ama, Colombia at once acknowledged her own guilt by promptly offering to do what we had demanded, and what she had protested it was not in her power to do. But the offer came too late. What we would gladly have done before, it had by that time become impossible for us honorably to do; for it would have necessitated our abandoning the people of Panama, our friends, and turning them over to their and our foes, who would have wreaked vengeance on them precisely because they had shown friendship to us. Colombia was solely responsible for her own humiliation; and she had not then, and has not now, one shadow of claim upon us, moral or legal; all the wrong that was done was done by her. If, as representing the American people, I had not acted precisely as I did, I would have been an unfaithful or incompetent representative; and inaction at that crisis would have meant not only indefinite delay in building the canal, but also practical admission on our part that we were not fit to play the part on the Isthmus which we had arrogated to ourselves. I acted on my own responsibility in the Panama matter. John Hay spoke of this action as follows: "The action of the President in the Panama matter is not only in the strictest accordance with the principles of justice and equity, and in line with all the best precedents of our public policy, but it was the only course he could have taken in compliance with our treaty rights and obligations."

I deeply regretted, and now deeply regret, the fact that the Colombian Government rendered it imperative for me to take the action I took; but I had no alternative, consistent with the full performance of my duty to my own people, and to the nations of mankind. . . . I am well aware that the Colombian people have many fine traits; that there is among them a circle of high-bred men and women which would reflect honor on the social life of any country; and that there has been an intellectual and literary development within this small circle which partially atones for the stagnation and illiteracy of the mass of the people; and I also know that even the illiterate

[margin handwritten note: ONLY A CIRCLE / - RACIST IMPLICATIONS.]

[bottom handwritten note: UPHOLDS FEUDAL ARISTOCRACY.]

mass possesses many sterling qualities. But unfortunately in international matters every nation must be judged by the action of its government. The good people in Colombia apparently made no effort, certainly no successful effort, to cause the government to act with reasonable good faith toward the United States; and Colombia had to take the consequences. If Brazil, or the Argentine, or Chile, had been in possession of the Isthmus, doubtless the canal would have been built under the governmental control of the nation thus controlling the Isthmus, with the hearty acquiescence of the United States and of all other powers. But in the actual fact the canal would not have been built at all save for the action I took. If men choose to say that it would have been better not to build it, than to build it as the result of such action, their position, although foolish, is compatible with belief in their wrongheaded sincerity. But it is hypocrisy, alike odious and contemptible, for any man to say both that we ought to have built the canal and that we ought not to have acted in the way we did act. . . .

The Monroe Doctrine

12. · THE ROOSEVELT COROLLARY

The Monroe Doctrine was one of Roosevelt's fundamental articles of faith. He had no desire to acquire additional territory once the Panama matter was settled, but he was almost obsessively fearful that European powers might extend their holdings in Latin America or establish new ones. This, he believed, would jeopardize defense of the Canal Zone in time of war. The issue first came to a head in January 1904, when the Santo Dominican government

T.R. to Elihu Root, May 20, 1904. New York *Tribune*, May 21, 1904, p. 1.

requested the United States to assume control of its finances in order to avert possible intervention by Germany, Italy, and Spain for nonpayment of debts. Roosevelt wrote privately that he had "about the same desire to annex . . . [Santo Domingo] as a gorged boa constrictor might have to swallow a porcupine wrong-end to." But he reluctantly agreed to take charge of Santo Domingo's customs houses. Bolstered by the success of the venture, he rejected suggestions that an international organization be created to handle future disputes over the collection of debts. Instead, he had former Secretary of War Elihu Root read the letter printed below at a Cuban Anniversary dinner in New York; he then repeated its essence in his Annual Message of 1904. In so doing, Roosevelt formalized a policy that could have been implemented quietly through normal diplomatic channels had he followed his own maxim, "Speak softly and carry a big stick."

Washington, May 20, 1904

My dear Mr. Root: Through you I want to send my heartiest greetings to those gathered to celebrate the second anniversary of the Republic of Cuba. I wish that it were possible to be present with you in person. I rejoice in what Cuba has done and especially in the way in which for the last two years her people have shown their desire and ability to accept in a serious spirit the responsibilities that accompany freedom. Such determination is vital, for those unable or unwilling to shoulder the responsibility of using their liberty aright can never in the long run preserve such liberty.

As for the United States, it must ever be a source of joy and gratification to good American citizens that they were enabled to play the part they did as regards Cuba. We freed Cuba from tyranny; we then stayed in the island until we had established civil order and laid the foundations for self-government and prosperity; we then made the island independent, and have since benefited her inhabitants by making closer the commercial relations between us. I hail what had been done in Cuba not merely for its own sake, but as showing the purpose and desire of this nation toward all the nations south of us. It is not true that the United States has any land hunger or entertains any projects as regards other nations, save such as are for their welfare. *HE IS SINCERE ?*

All that we desire is to see all neighboring countries stable, orderly and prosperous. Any country whose people conduct themselves well can count upon our hearty friendliness. If a nation shows that it knows how to act with decency in industrial and political matters, if it keeps order and pays its obligations, then it need fear no interference from the United States. Brutal wrongdoing, or an impotence which results in a general loosening of the ties of civilized society, may finally require intervention by some civilized nation, and in the Western Hemisphere the United States cannot ignore this duty; but it remains true that our interests, and those of our southern neighbors, are in reality identical. All that we ask is that they shall govern themselves well, and be prosperous and orderly. Where this is the case they will find only helpfulness from us.

WITH ACQUIESCENCE TO U.S. ?

To-night you are gathered together to greet a young nation which has shown hitherto just these needed qualities; and I congratulate not only Cuba but also the United States upon the showing which Cuba has made.

13. · "THE UNITED STATES AND THE SOUTH AMERICAN REPUBLICS"

Both the Monroe Doctrine and the problems created by the instability of many Latin American republics continued to weigh heavily on Roosevelt after he left the presidency. Here, in a speech that has been generally overlooked, he expands his personal conception of the doctrine by (1) predicting that its enforcement would ultimately devolve upon the Latin American nations themselves and (2) asserting that Argentina, Brazil, and Chile were already acting as its guardians.

I appreciate very deeply this farewell dinner given to me on the eve of my departure for South America. I am going in response to the invitations of certain learned bodies in the three great republics, the three prosperous and progressive commonwealths of Brazil, the Argentine, and Chile. I gladly accepted the invitations when once I understood that I was asked because these great democracies wished to hear my views on democracy, and in addition wished to hear me, as a private citizen who once held a position of prominence in this Republic, speak of the questions that peculiarly concern all the peoples of the western hemisphere. . . .

It is continually growing less and less possible for any great civilized nation to live purely for and by itself. Exactly as steam and electricity and the extraordinary agencies of modern industrialism have rendered more complex and more intimate the relations of all the individuals within each nation, so the same causes have rendered more complex and more intimate the relations of the various civilized nations with one another. In the western hemisphere each nation has been in the past so busy developing the new resources of its own new soil that it has tended to let the representatives of Old World peoples have complete charge of what these resources produced in the way of commodities in international business. This period is now drawing to a close. We are no longer content to see all the international business of all the American commonwealths transacted through European hands. In particular we feel that there should be closer business and economic relations between our own great business Republic, our great industrial Republic, of the United States, and the repub-

Address to a group of Progressive Party friends, New York, October 3, 1912. *The Works*, XVIII, 391–403.

lics that have been growing so fast in prosperity and stability
and power in South America. . . .

. . . As all inhabitable parts of the globe are now known,
this is pre-eminently the time for us to gain, and not release,
wherever we can, a commercial footing on a "live-and-let-
live" basis; a footing that will furnish an outlet for the most
characteristic trait of our American men, namely, executive
and organizing ability in business. There is no better or more
worth-while field for this than in Latin America and the Far
East. Other nations are already keenly alive to their need for
commercial outlets. Already we are behind the European
countries in our trade and commerce with the countries to the
south of us. The latest figures I have been able to obtain show
that in 1911 the sales of Mexico, the West Indies, Central
and South America to the outside world aggregated over one
billion three hundred million dollars; while the sales of the
outside world to those countries aggregated about one billion
two hundred million dollars, a credit balance to those countries of over one hundred million dollars. And yet in the same
year the sales of those countries to the United States aggregated over four hundred and fifty million dollars, while the
sales of the United States to them aggregated only two hundred and ninety million dollars, a balance against the United
States of one hundred and sixty million dollars. There are
many reasons why this condition should be changed, and
pre-eminent among them is the importance of more permanent
employment and better wages for those actually engaged in
raising and making the wares that we have for sale.

Our relations with the other republics of this hemisphere
must necessarily be both political and economic. As, in the
years now opening, they will certainly be closer than ever
before, it is eminently desirable that they should be on a better
basis than ever before. Let me speak of the economic relations
first. Fortunately, the time has gone by when it was believed
that a business transaction was normally beneficial to one

party and detrimental to the other. Exactly as no private business is healthy unless on the average both parties to the transaction are benefited, so no international business can ever be on a really flourishing basis unless it is to the advantage of both the nations engaged.

We wish to open the countries of South America to our business, we wish to create a market for the products of our business men, the farmers, and wage-workers in South America. This cannot be done at all unless it is to the advantage of the various peoples of South America to have such products. It cannot be made a striking success unless the South Americans find that it is very much to *their* advantage to deal with us, and unless they so thrive and prosper that it will be greatly to *our* advantage to extend our dealings with them. In private life a man's only customers who are worth anything are those who can pay for what they get, and his best customers are those whose prosperity increases so that they can get a great deal; in other words it is self-evidently to the advantage of every business man to have a prosperous community with which to do business.

In just the same way it is to the advantage of us as a nation to see the nations with which we do business thrive, prosper, and enormously to increase their material well-being, and therefore their wish and their ability to enter into business relations with us. If we are decent people we ought in any event to be glad to see prosperity come to our neighbors. But in addition to this, if we possess an intelligent appreciation of our own material self-interest, we shall rejoice for our own sakes at the marvellous economic and political growth in such nations as the three I have mentioned and am about to visit, Brazil, the Argentine, and Chile. We could not be useful to them if we were not ourselves prosperous, and their usefulness to us in return is largely conditioned upon their prosperity. The material well-being of both sides is helped by any increase of material well-being on either side.

Don't misunderstand me. I am the last man who would preach the doctrine, and this is the last audience that would tolerate the doctrine, that material prosperity is or can ever be the be-all or end-all of national life, or that international relations should be based only on material considerations. But it is absolutely necessary that there should be a foundation of material prosperity in order to achieve greatness, national or international. Sane and healthy material prosperity in a man's neighbors benefits the man; and prosperity in neighboring countries benefits the country that deals with them. We Progressives preach within our own nation the doctrine of social consciousness, the doctrine that in the long run each of us is helped to go up if all of us are helped to go up. So likewise we preach the doctrine of an international social consciousness, the doctrine that teaches us, not in a spirit of sentimentalism but with cool-headed sanity, to understand that in the long run it is good for each nation of mankind to see the other nations of mankind go up and not down. We no more believe in weakness in dealing with international offenders than in dealing with criminals within our own limits. We no more intend to do away with the American navy and abandon the fortification of the Panama Canal, than we intend to do away with the New York police. But we do intend to do all we can to help all the nations of mankind, including our own, to rise, away from barbarism and savagery and the brutalities of physical violence, toward an orderly self-respecting and law-abiding civilization, to which brutality and fraud are as alien as weakness, and where justice and fair dealing are accepted ideals not only as among the individuals within the nation but in dealing with all other nations. . . .

. . . I ask your especial attention to the Monroe Doctrine. That doctrine has been formulated for some eighty years, and although unformulated it was to a certain extent appreciated and acted upon for eight or ten years previously, that is, ever since the time when the Latin-American colonies began to assert their independence. The central thesis of the doctrine is that this hemisphere shall no longer be treated as a region in which Old World powers shall seek territorial aggrandizement. There are certain necessary implications in this doctrine; such as, for example, that Old World powers shall not be permitted to enter on a course of action which will be likely to lead to territorial aggrandizement on their part; and that New World powers shall not be upheld in wrong-doing which will provoke and justify such territorial aggrandizement. But these are mere necessary details of the application of the theory with which we need not at the moment concern ourselves.

The main thesis was that there should be no territorial aggrandizement on this continent at the expense or to the jeopardy of any American commonwealth by Old World powers; this doctrine being advanced both in our interest, in the interest of our own safety and protection, and also in the interest of the other peoples of this hemisphere. Now no such doctrine, no such policy is worth the paper on which it is written unless there is ability to back it up. The one efficient guaranty of the Monroe Doctrine in the past has been the more or less general acceptance abroad of the belief that the American people were willing and able to back it up. If the United States stopped building up its navy, the Monroe Doctrine would be the emptiest of empty phrases. At the time that the doctrine was promulgated the only power on the western hemisphere to which foreign nations paid any heed at all was the United States. As soon as the United States became involved in Civil War, so that its power in the face of other nations vanished and became for the time being a negligible quantity, all respect for the Monroe Doctrine also vanished. European powers invaded and took possession of American soil, and finally they actually set up a foreign empire just south of us, an empire that fell as soon as the United States again became an undivided nation.

In the past then, it was an absolute necessity that the United

States should treat the Monroe Doctrine as being within its special custodianship and to be invoked by it as regards all sections of the continent. As rapidly, however, as the other nations on this continent achieve political and social stability, and the economic prosperity that goes hand in hand with such stability and power, the need for treating our country as the sole and special guardian of the Monroe Doctrine just to that extent decreases. I believe that the century that is opening will see South America, will see Latin America, so grow in power and prosperity as to make this growth the central feature in the growth of the world in the twentieth century, precisely as the growth of North America was the central feature in the growth of the civilized world during the nineteenth century. As the several countries of Latin America thus grow in orderly strength and well-being, they will themselves naturally and inevitably assume for themselves the guardianship of the doctrine; and if, and so long as, this orderly growth continues, our responsibility for the doctrine and the need for exercising the responsibility will gradually, step by step, cease until we either share it with many others or the need for its assertion altogether vanishes. As yet such result is not within the ken of our vision for large portions of the territory in question; including for instance the lands and waters through which the Panama Canal and its approaches run, where our interests are vital, and can be defended only by a power of the first class.

But already this result has in my judgment actually come to pass in the southern half of South America. Brazil, the Argentine, Chile, have achieved positions of such assured material and political progress, of such political stability and power and economic prosperity, and have shown by their actions in reference to one another such power of efficient and unified effort for a just and common end, that in my judgment it is safe to say that there is no further need for the United States to concern itself about asserting the Monroe Doctrine so far as these powers are concerned. Their progress in all ways has been so great that they neither invite attack by wrong-doing to others and by disorder, nor yet invite it by inability to defend themselves. Under these conditions, the enforcement of the principle of the Monroe Doctrine as far as they are concerned can be safely left to their own initiative and interest; and in this matter as in all other matters henceforth the dealings of this country with them should be merely those of an equal dealing with equals who are able to guard their own interests and who are desirous of dealing honorably with all men. In short, as regards these three great commonwealths our attitude should be substantially what it is as regards the great Canadian commonwealth north of us. In the utterly, the well-nigh impossible event of any one of them being attacked by some outside power, and in jeopardy of conquest, the United States with all its strength would stand ready to offer its aid, but with no thought of further interference than is implied in such action. *7 FEAR IS FROM INTERNAL FACTIONS.*

I ask you, my hearers, to remember that such a policy as I have outlined must rest on a basis not only of good intentions and sincerity but also of strength. There is no mental attitude more mischievous than the confounding of folly and weakness with virtue. I have spoken above of the Panama Canal, and of the enormous benefits its building, now so nearly accomplished, will confer upon us and upon the nations of mankind. Remember that the Canal could not have been built if I and those about me ten years ago had paid heed to the counsels of folly and weakness masquerading as virtue. What this country wished was to see that Canal built. It did not interfere as long as there was a chance that it would be built by outside effort in such shape that it would not be in any way under the control of any non-American power. If any of the three countries I have already mentioned in this speech, if Chile, if the Argentine, if Brazil, had possessed the Isthmus, the Canal would undoubtedly have been built under the direction of the government owning the Isthmus, and with a hearty Godspeed from the United States. In the actual event I was finally faced by the alternative of seeing the building of the Canal indefinitely postponed, or else of having America, in the interest of the people of Panama through whose territory the Canal was to pass, in our own interest, and in the interest of the nations of mankind, take hold and build it. . . .

. . . The United States has but one request to make of each of its neighbors, the request that that neighbor shall prosper; for such prosperity can only come on a basis of order, of stability, of just regard for the rights of others, and of power to insist upon one's own rights. In the long run anarchy reduces a country to impotence both abroad and at home, impotence to do justice to the strangers within its borders, and impotence to protect itself from aggression. No such condition can permanently endure in countries which are obviously within the sphere of action of the United States. The United States is disinterestedly anxious to see its neighbors do well. All it asks of them is that they do well, that they themselves show the qualities which will enable them to grow and to prosper. But this much it must ask, and with less than this it cannot permanently be contented. . . .

T.R,
MEET
HEMINGWAY

V · ECONOMIC POLICY AND PROBLEMS

Trust Busting Versus Regulation of Corporations

14. · RESURRECTION OF THE SHERMAN ANTI-TRUST LAW

The most explosive, and in a sense the most ironic, single action of Roosevelt's presidency was his resurrection of the Sherman Anti-trust Law in February 1902 by the institution of proceedings against the Northern Securities Company, a railroad trust organized by J. P. Morgan, E. H. Harriman, and others. Convinced by his experience as governor of New York that the federal government would have to act energetically because of the incapacity of the states to deal effectively with industrial and communications giants, he set forth the assumptions upon which his policy toward large corporations was to be based in his first Annual Message to Congress. They were: (1) corporations existed by the grace of society and not vice versa; (2) full publicity of corporate activities was the first requisite for intelligent supervision; (3) all corporations engaged in interstate commerce should be regulated; and (4) the federal government should be the regulatory body. Before Congress could consider this program, however, Roosevelt invoked the Sherman law against the Northern Securities combine. Although the reasons for this apparent reversal of policy—it was actually an amplification—are not wholly clear, its symbolic importance is beyond dispute. As Roosevelt suggests in his *Autobiography*, it dramatized the need both to control big business and to destroy anti-social monopolies (as distinguished from large, but legitimate, corporations); and as he does not suggest, it served notice on business and

Autobiography, pp. 423–32.

Congress alike that he would use the vast powers of the presidential office to achieve his objectives.

One of the vital questions with which as President I had to deal was the attitude of the nation toward the great corporations. Men who understand and practise the deep underlying philosophy of the Lincoln school of American political thought are necessarily Hamiltonian in their belief in a strong and efficient National Government and Jeffersonian in their belief in the people as the ultimate authority, and in the welfare of the people as the end of government. The men who first applied the extreme democratic theory in American life were, like Jefferson, ultraindividualists, for at that time what was demanded by our people was the largest liberty for the individual. During the century that had elapsed since Jefferson became President the need had been exactly reversed. There had been in our country a riot of individualistic materialism, under which complete freedom for the individual—that ancient license which President Wilson a century after the term was excusable has called the "New" Freedom—turned out in practice to mean perfect freedom for the strong to wrong the weak. The total absence of governmental control had led to a portentous growth in the financial and industrial world both of natural individuals and of artificial individuals—that is, corporations. In no other country in the world had such enormous fortunes been gained. In no other country in the world was such power held by the men who had gained these fortunes; and these men almost always worked through, and by means of, the giant corporations which they controlled. The power of the mighty industrial overlords of the country had increased with giant strides, while the methods of controlling them, or checking abuses by them on the part of the people, through the government, remained archaic and therefore practically impotent. The courts, not unnaturally, but most regrettably, and

to the grave detriment of the people and of their own standing, had for a quarter of a century been on the whole the
agents of reaction, and by conflicting decisions which, however, in their sum, were hostile to the interests of the people,
had left both the nation and the several States well-nigh
impotent to deal with the great business combinations. Sometimes they forbade the nation to interfere, because such interference trespassed on the rights of the States; sometimes they
forbade the States to interfere (and often they were wise in
this), because to do so would trespass on the rights of the
nation; but always, or well-nigh always, their action was negative action against the interests of the people, ingeniously devised to limit their power against wrong, instead of affirmative
action giving to the people power to right wrong. They had
rendered these decisions sometimes as upholders of property
rights against human rights, being especially zealous in securing the rights of the very men who were most competent to
take care of themselves; and sometimes in the name of liberty,
in the name of the so-called "new freedom," in reality the old,
old "freedom," which secured to the powerful the freedom to
prey on the poor and the helpless.

One of the main troubles was the fact that the men who saw
the evils and who tried to remedy them attempted to work in
two wholly different ways, and the great majority of them in
a way that offered little promise of real betterment. They tried
(by the Sherman-law method) to bolster up an individualism
already proved to be both futile and mischievous; to remedy
by more individualism the concentration that was the inevitable result of the already existing individualism. They saw the
evil done by the big combinations, and sought to remedy it by
destroying them and restoring the country to the economic
conditions of the middle of the nineteenth century. This was
a hopeless effort, and those who went into it, although they
regarded themselves as radical progressives, really represented
a form of sincere rural toryism. They confounded monopolies

with big business combinations, and in the effort to prohibit both alike, instead of where possible prohibiting one and drastically controlling the other, they succeeded merely in preventing any effective control of either.

On the other hand, a few men recognized that corporations and combinations had become indispensable in the business world, that it was folly to try to prohibit them, but that it was also folly to leave them without thoroughgoing control. These men realized that the doctrines of the old *laissez-faire* economists, of the believers in unlimited competition, unlimited individualism, were in the actual state of affairs false and mischievous. They realized that the government must now interfere to protect labor, to subordinate the big corporation to the public welfare, and to shackle cunning and fraud exactly as centuries before it had interfered to shackle the physical force which does wrong by violence.

The big reactionaries of the business world and their allies and instruments among politicians and newspaper editors took advantage of this division of opinion, and especially of the fact that most of their opponents were on the wrong path; and fought to keep matters absolutely unchanged. These men demanded for themselves an immunity from governmental control which, if granted, would have been as wicked and as foolish as immunity to the barons of the twelfth century. Many of them were evil men. Many others were just as good men as were some of these same barons; but they were as utterly unable as any mediaeval castle-owner to understand what the public interest really was. There have been aristocracies which have played a great and beneficent part at stages in the growth of mankind; but we had come to the stage where for our people what was needed was a real democracy; and of all forms of tyranny the least attractive and the most vulgar is the tyranny of mere wealth, the tyranny of a plutocracy.

When I became President, the question as to the *method* by which the United States Government was to control the corporations was not yet important. The absolutely vital question was whether the government had power to control them at all. This question had not yet been decided in favor of the United States Government. It was useless to discuss methods of controlling big business by the National Government until it was definitely settled that the National Government had the power to control it. A decision of the Supreme Court had, with seeming definiteness, settled that the National Government had not the power.

This decision I caused to be annulled by the court that had rendered it; and the present power of the National Government to deal effectively with the trusts is due solely to the success of the Administration in securing this reversal of its former decision by the Supreme Court.

The Constitution was formed very largely because it had become imperative to give to some central authority the power to regulate and control interstate commerce. At that time when corporations were in their infancy and big combinations unknown, there was no difficulty in exercising the power granted. In theory, the right of the nation to exercise this power continued unquestioned. But changing conditions obscured the matter in the sight of the people as a whole; and the conscious and the unconscious advocates of an unlimited and uncontrollable capitalism gradually secured the whittling away of the national power to exercise this theoretical right of control until it practically vanished. After the Civil War, with the portentous growth of industrial combinations in this country, came a period of reactionary decisions by the courts which, as regards corporations, culminated in what is known as the Knight case.

The Sherman antitrust law was enacted in 1890 because the formation of the Tobacco Trust and the Sugar Trust, the only two great trusts then in the country (aside from the Standard Oil Trust, which was a gradual growth), had awakened a popular demand for legislation to destroy monopoly and curb industrial combinations. This demand the antitrust law was intended to satisfy. The administrations of Mr. Harrison and Mr. Cleveland evidently construed this law as prohibiting such combinations in the future, not as condemning those which had been formed prior to its enactment. In 1895, however, the Sugar Trust, whose output originally was about fifty-five per cent of all sugar produced in the United States, obtained control of three other companies in Philadelphia by exchanging its stock for theirs, and thus increased its business until it controlled ninety-eight per cent of the entire product. Under Cleveland, the government brought proceedings against the Sugar Trust, invoking the antitrust law, to set aside the acquisition of these corporations. The test case was on the absorption of the Knight Company. The Supreme Court of the United States, with but one dissenting vote, held adversely to the government. . . . The effect of this decision was not merely the absolute nullification of the antitrust law, so far as industrial corporations were concerned, but was also in effect a declaration that, under the Constitution the National Government could pass no law really effective for the destruction or control of such combinations.

This decision left the National Government, that is, the people of the nation, practically helpless to deal with the large combinations of modern business. The courts in other cases asserted the power of the Federal Government to enforce the antitrust law so far as transportation rates by railways engaged in interstate commerce were concerned. But so long as the trusts were free to control the production of commodities without interference from the general government, they were well content to let the transportation of commodities take care of itself—especially as the law against rebates was at that time a dead letter; and the court by its decision in the Knight case had interdicted any interference by the President or by Congress with the production of commodities. It was on the authority of this case that practically all the big trusts in the

United States, excepting those already mentioned, were formed. Usually they were organized as "holding" companies, each one acquiring control of its constituent corporations by exchanging its stock for theirs, an operation which the Supreme Court had thus decided could not be prohibited, controlled, regulated, or even questioned by the Federal Government.

Such was the condition of our laws when I acceded to the presidency. Just before my accession, a small group of financiers, desiring to profit by the governmental impotence to which we had been reduced by the Knight decision, had arranged to take control of practically the entire railway system in the Northwest—possibly as the first step toward controlling the entire railway system of the country. This control of the northwestern railway systems was to be effected by organizing a new "holding" company, and exchanging its stock against the stock of the various corporations engaged in railway transportation throughout that vast territory, exactly as the Sugar Trust had acquired control of the Knight company and other concerns. This company was called the Northern Securities Company. Not long after I became President, on the advice of the attorney-general, Mr. Knox, and through him, I ordered proceedings to be instituted for the dissolution of the company. As far as could be told by their utterances at the time, among all the great lawyers in the United States Mr. Knox was the only one who believed that this action could be sustained. The defense was based expressly on the ground that the Supreme Court in the Knight case had explicitly sanctioned the formation of such a company as the Northern Securities Company. . . .

. . . It was necessary to reverse the Knight case in the interests of the people against monopoly and privilege just as it had been necessary to reverse the Dred Scott case in the interest of the people against slavery and privilege; just as later it became necessary to reverse the New York Bakeshop case in the interest of the people against that form of monopolistic privilege which put human rights below property rights where wage-workers were concerned.

By a vote of five to four the Supreme Court reversed its decision in the Knight case, and in the Northern Securities case sustained the government. The power to deal with industrial monopoly and suppress it and to control and regulate combinations, of which the Knight case had deprived the Federal Government, was thus restored to it by the Northern Securities case. After this later decision was rendered, suits were brought by my direction against the American Tobacco Company and the Standard Oil Company. Both were adjudged criminal conspiracies, and their dissolution ordered. The Knight case was finally overthrown. The vicious doctrine it embodied no longer remains as an obstacle to obstruct the pathway of justice when it assails monopoly. Messrs. Knox, Moody, and Bonaparte, who successively occupied the position of attorney-general under me, were profound lawyers and fearless and able men; and they completely established the newer and more wholesome doctrine under which the Federal Government may now deal with monopolistic combinations and conspiracies.

The decisions rendered in these various cases brought under my direction constitute the entire authority upon which any action must rest that seeks through the exercise of national power to curb monopolistic control. The men who organized and directed the Northern Securities Company were also the controlling forces in the Steel Corporation, which has since been prosecuted under the act. . . .

From the standpoint of giving complete control to the National Government over big corporations engaged in interstate business, it would be impossible to overestimate the importance of the Northern Securities decision and of the decisions afterward rendered in line with it in connection with the other trusts whose dissolution was ordered. The success of the Northern Securities case definitely established the power of the government to deal with all great corporations. Without this success the National Government must have remained in the impotence to which it had been reduced by the Knight decision as regards the most important of its internal functions. But our success in establishing the power of the National Government to curb monopolies did not establish the right method of exercising that power. We had gained the power. We had not devised the proper method of exercising it.

. . . I at once began to urge upon Congress the need of laws supplementing the antitrust law—for this law struck at all big business, good and bad, alike, and as the event proved was very inefficient in checking bad big business, and yet was a constant threat against decent business men. I strongly urged the inauguration of a system of thoroughgoing and drastic governmental regulation and control over all big business combinations engaged in interstate industry.

Here I was able to accomplish only a small part of what I desired to accomplish. I was opposed both by the foolish radicals who desired to break up all big business, with the impossible ideal of returning to mid-nineteenth-century industrial conditions; and also by the great privileged interests themselves, who used these ordinarily—but sometimes not entirely —well-meaning "stool-pigeon progressives" to further their own cause. The worst representatives of big business encouraged the outcry for the total abolition of big business, because they knew that they could not be hurt in this way, and that such an outcry distracted the attention of the public from the really efficient method of controlling and supervising them, in just but masterly fashion, which was advocated by the sane representatives of reform. However, we succeeded in making a good beginning by securing the passage of a law creating the Department of Commerce and Labor, and with it the erection of the Bureau of Corporations. The first head of the Department of Commerce and Labor was Mr. Cortelyou, later secretary of the treasury. He was succeeded by Mr. Oscar Straus. The first head of the Bureau of Corporations was Mr. Garfield, who was succeeded by Mr. Herbert Knox Smith. No four better public servants from the standpoint of the people as a whole could have been found. . . .

15. · FOR MORE THOROUGH-GOING REGULATION

Even while the attack on the Northern Securities Company and numerous other combinations was earning Roosevelt the sobriquet "trust-buster," he was pushing Congress to enact his regulatory program. By the fall of 1906 he had signed a number of regulatory measures into law. Some, such as the Elkins anti-rebate bill of 1903, had been so broadly endorsed by business that passage was hardly more than a formality. Others, such as the pure food and drug bill of 1906, had been bitterly fought by the industries concerned and by conservatives in the Senate. Still others, notably the Hepburn bill to strengthen the Interstate Commerce Commission, had been resisted so effectively that he had been forced to accept compromise provisions. Partly because of this opposition and partly because of his deepening understanding of the implications of concentrated industrial power, Roosevelt's approach became increasingly comprehensive as his tenure in office lengthened. He refused, furthermore, to be deterred by charges that he was fostering socialism. A progressive conservative to the core, he saw that unregulated capitalism would eventually destroy individualism while creating such an industrial feudalism as would make government ownership

From the Annual Message to Congress, 1906. *Messages and Papers,* XI, 1196–1200.

mandatory. Hence, in part, the increasing tempo of his program for federal action.

The present Congress has taken long strides in the direction of securing proper supervision and control by the National Government over corporations engaged in interstate business —and the enormous majority of corporations of any size are engaged in interstate business. The passage of the railway-rate bill, and only to a less degree the passage of the pure-food bill, and the provision for increasing and rendering more effective national control over the beef-packing industry, mark an important advance in the proper direction. In the short session it will perhaps be difficult to do much further along this line; and it may be best to wait until the laws have been in operation for a number of months before endeavoring to increase their scope, because only operation will show with exactness their merits and their shortcomings and thus give opportunity to define what further remedial legislation is needed. Yet in my judgment it will in the end be advisable in connection with the packing-house-inspection law to provide for putting a date on the label and for charging the cost of inspection to the packers. All these laws have already justified their enactment. The interstate commerce law, for instance, has rather amusingly falsified the predictions, both of those who asserted that it would ruin the railroads and of those who asserted that it did not go far enough and would accomplish nothing. During the last five months the railroads have shown increased earnings and some of them unusual dividends; while during the same period the mere taking effect of the law has produced an unprecedented, a hitherto unheard-of, number of voluntary reductions in freights and fares by the railroads. Since the founding of the commission there has never been a time of equal length in which anything like so many reduced tariffs have been put into effect. On August 27, for instance, two days before the new law went into effect, the commission received notices of over 5,000 separate tariffs which represented reductions from previous rates.

It must not be supposed, however, that with the passage of these laws it will be possible to stop progress along the line of increasing the power of the National Government over the use of capital in interstate commerce. For example, there will ultimately be need of enlarging the powers of the Interstate Commerce Commission along several different lines, so as to give it a larger and more efficient control over the railroads.

It cannot too often be repeated that experience has conclusively shown the impossibility of securing by the actions of nearly half a hundred different State legislatures anything but ineffective chaos in the way of dealing with the great corporations which do not operate exclusively within the limits of any one State. In some method, whether by a national license law or in other fashion, we must exercise, and that at an early date, a far more complete control than at present over these great corporations—a control that will among other things prevent the evils of excessive overcapitalization, and that will compel the disclosure by each big corporation of its stockholders and of its properties and business, whether owned directly or through subsidiary or affiliated corporations. This will tend to put a stop to the securing of inordinate profits by favored individuals at the expense whether of the general public, the stockholders, or the wage-workers. Our effort should be not so much to prevent consolidation as such, but so to supervise and control it as to see that it results in no harm to the people. The reactionary or ultraconservative apologists for the misuse of wealth assail the effort to secure such control as a step toward socialism. As a matter of fact it is these reactionaries and ultra-conservatives who are themselves most potent in increasing socialistic feeling. One of the most efficient methods of averting the consequences of a dangerous agitation, which is eighty per cent wrong, is to remedy the twenty per cent of evil as to which the agitation is well founded. The best way to avert the very undesirable move for the government ownership of railways is to secure by the government on behalf of the people as a whole such adequate control and regulation of the great interstate common carriers as will do away with the evils which give rise to the agitation against them. So the proper antidote to the dangerous and wicked agitation against the men of wealth as such is to secure by proper legislation and executive action the abolition of the grave abuses which actually do obtain in connection with the business use of wealth under our present system—or rather no system—of failure to exercise any adequate control at all. Some persons speak as if the exercise of such governmental control would do away with the freedom of individual initiative and dwarf individual effort. This is not a fact. It would be a veritable calamity to fail to put a premium upon individual initiative, individual capacity and effort; upon the energy, character, and foresight which it is so important to encourage in the individual. But as a matter of fact the deadening and degrading effect of pure socialism, and especially of its extreme form, communism, and the destruction of individual character which they would bring about, are in part achieved by the wholly unregulated competition which results in a single individual or corporation rising at the expense of all others until his or its rise effectually checks all competition and reduces former competitors to a position of utter inferiority and subordination.

In enacting and enforcing such legislation as this Congress already has to its credit, we are working on a coherent plan, with the steady endeavor to secure the needed reform by the joint action of the moderate men, the plain men who do not wish anything hysterical or dangerous, but who do intend to deal in resolute common-sense fashion with the real and great evils of the present system. The reactionaries and the violent extremists show symptoms of joining hands against us. Both assert, for instance, that, if logical, we should go to government ownership of railroads and the like; the reactionaries, because on such an issue they think the people would stand with them, while the extremists care rather to preach discontent and agitation than to achieve solid results. As a matter of fact, our position is as remote from that of the Bourbon reactionary as from that of the impracticable or sinister visionary. We hold that the government should not conduct the business of the nation, but that it should exercise such supervision as will insure its being conducted in the interest of the nation. Our aim is, so far as may be, to secure, for all decent, hard-working men, equality of opportunity and equality of burden.

The actual working of our laws has shown that the effort to prohibit all combination, good or bad, is noxious where it is not ineffective. Combination of capital like combination of labor is a necessary element of our present industrial system. It is not possible completely to prevent it; and if it were possible, such complete prevention would do damage to the body politic. What we need is not vainly to try to prevent all combination, but to secure such rigorous and adequate control and supervision of the combinations as to prevent their injuring the public, or existing in such form as inevitably to threaten injury—for the mere fact that a combination has secured practically complete control of a necessary of life would under any circumstances show that such combination was to be presumed to be adverse to the public interest. It is unfortunate that our present laws should forbid all combinations, instead of sharply discriminating between those combinations which do good and those combinations which do evil. Rebates, for instance, are as often due to the pressure of big shippers (as was shown in the investigation of the Standard Oil Company and as has been shown since by the investigation of the tobacco and sugar trusts) as to the initiative of big railroads. Often railroads would like to combine for the purpose of preventing a big shipper from maintaining improper advantages at the expense of small shippers and of the general public. Such a combination, instead of being forbidden by law, should be favored. In other words, it should be permitted to railroads to make agreements, provided these agreements were sanctioned by the Interstate Commerce Commission and were published. With these two conditions complied with it is impossible to see what harm such a combination could do to the public at large. It is a public evil to have on the statute-books a law incapable of full enforcement because both judges and juries realize that its full enforcement would destroy the business of the country; for the result is to make decent railroad men violators of the law against their will, and to put a premium on the behavior of the wilful wrong-doers. Such a result in turn tends to throw the decent man and the wilful wrong-doer into close association, and in the end to drag down the former to the latter's level; for the man who becomes a lawbreaker in one way unhappily tends to lose all respect for law and to be willing to break it in many ways. No more scathing condemnation could be visited upon a law than is contained in the words of the Interstate Commerce Commission when, in commenting upon the fact that the numerous joint traffic associations do technically violate the law, they say: "The decision of the United States Supreme Court in the Trans-Missouri case and the Joint Traffic Association case has produced no practical effect upon the railway operations of the country. Such associations, in fact, exist now as they did before these decisions, and with the same general effect. In justice to all parties, we ought probably to add that it is difficult to see how our interstate railways could be operated with due regard to the interest of the shipper and the railway without concerted action of the kind afforded through these associations."

This means that the law as construed by the Supreme Court is such that the business of the country cannot be conducted without breaking it. I recommend that you give careful and

early consideration to this subject, and if you find the opinion
of the Interstate Commerce Commission justified, that you
amend the law so as to obviate the evil disclosed.

16. · A DEFENSE OF POLICY

The sweeping character of Roosevelt's regulatory program
fiercely antagonized many of the most powerful business elements
in the nation. When structural weaknesses and other factors combined to produce a financial panic in 1907, they blamed their
troubles on the President's "anti-business" policies and statements.
Roosevelt cooperated in measures to end the panic, but he refused
to modify his policies. In the letter to Attorney General Charles J.
Bonaparte printed below, he accurately and passionately describes
business' counterattack on himself and his administration; he also
reveals the sense of justice that was rapidly transforming his concept of the regulatory state into that of the welfare state. (See
Chapter VII.)

Washington, January 2, 1908
My dear Bonaparte: I must congratulate you on your admirable speech at Chicago. You said the very things it was good to
say at this time. What you said bore especial weight because
it represented what you had done. You have shown by what
you have actually accomplished that the law is enforced
against the wealthiest corporation, and the richest and most
powerful manager or manipulator of that corporation, just as
resolutely and fearlessly as against the humblest citizen. The

Letter to Charles J. Bonaparte, January 2, 1908. *The Letters*, VI,
883–90.

Department of Justice is now in very fact the Department of Justice, and justice is meted out with an even hand to great and small, rich and poor, weak and strong. Those who have denounced you and the action of the Department of Justice are either misled, or else are the very wrongdoers, and the agents of the very wrongdoers, who have for so many years gone scot-free and flouted the laws with impunity. Above all, you are to be congratulated upon the bitterness felt and exprest towards you by the representatives and agents of the great law-defying corporations of immense wealth, who, until within the last half dozen years, have treated themselves and have expected others to treat them as being beyond and above all possible check from law.

It was time to say something, for the representatives of predatory wealth, of wealth accumulated on a giant scale by iniquity, by wrongdoing in many forms, by plain swindling, by oppressing wageworkers, by manipulating securities, by unfair and unwholesome competition, and by stockjobbing, in short by conduct abhorrent to every man of ordinary decent conscience, have during the last few months made it evident that they are banded together to work for a reaction, to endeavor to overthrow and discredit all who honestly administer the law, and to secure a return to the days when every unscrupulous wrongdoer could do what he wisht unchecked, provided he had enough money. They attack you because they know your honesty and fearlessness, and dread them. The enormous sums of money these men have at their control enable them to carry on an effective campaign. They find their tools in a portion of the public press including especially certain of the great New York newspapers. They find their agents in some men in public life—now and then occupying, or having occupied, positions as high as Senator or Governor—in some men in the pulpit, and most melancholy of all, in a few men on the bench. By gifts to colleges and universities they are occasionally able to subsidize in their own interest some head of an educational body, who, save only a judge, should of all men be most careful to keep his skirts clear from the taint of such corruption. There are ample material rewards for those who serve with fidelity the Mammon of unrighteousness, but they are dearly paid for by that institution of learning whose head, by example and precept, teaches the scholars who sit under him that there is one law for the rich and another for the poor. The amount of money the representatives of the great monied interests are willing to spend can be gauged by their recent publication broadcast thruout the papers of the country from the Atlantic to the Pacific of huge advertisements, attacking with envenomed bitterness the Administration's policy of warring against successful dishonesty, advertisements that must have cost enormous sums of money. This advertisement, as also a pamphlet called "The Roosevelt Panic," and one or two similar books and pamphlets, are written especially in the interest of the Standard Oil and Harriman combinations, but also defend all the individuals and corporations of great wealth that have been guilty of wrongdoing. From the railroad rate law to the pure food law, every measure for honesty in business that has been pressed during the last six years, has been opposed by these men, on its passage and in its administration, with every resource that bitter and unscrupulous craft could suggest, and the command of almost unlimited money secure. These men do not themselves speak or write; they hire others to do their bidding. Their spirit and purpose are made clear alike by the editorials of the papers owned in, or whose policy is dictated by, Wall Street, and by the speeches of the public men who, as Senators, Governors, or Mayors, have served these their masters to the cost of the plain people. At one time one of their writers or speakers attacks the rate law as the cause of the panic; he is, whether in public life or not, usually a clever corporation lawyer, and he is not so foolish a being as to believe in the truth of what he says; he has too closely represented the railroads not to know well that the Hepburn

Rate Bill has helped every honest railroad, and has hurt only
the railroads that regarded themselves as above the law. At
another time, one of them assails the Administration for not
imprisoning people under the Sherman Antitrust Law; for de-
clining to make what he well knows, in view of the actual
attitude of juries (as shown in the Tobacco Trust cases and in
San Francisco in one or two of the cases brought against corrupt businessmen) would have been the futile endeavor to
imprison defendants, whom we are actually able to fine. He
raises the usual clamor, raised by all who object to the enforcement of the law, that we are fining corporations instead of
putting the heads of the corporations in jail; and he states that
this does not really harm the chief offenders. Were this statement true he himself would not be found attacking us. The
extraordinary violence of the assault upon our policy contained
in speeches like these, in the articles in the subsidized press,
in such huge advertisements and pamphlets as those above
referred to, and the enormous sums of money spent in these
various ways, give a fairly accurate measure of the anger and
terror which our actions have caused the corrupt men of vast
wealth to feel in the very marrow of their being.

The man thus attacking us is usually, like so many of his
fellows, either a great lawyer, or a paid editor who takes his
commands from the financiers and his arguments from their
attorneys. If the former, he has defended many malefactors
and he knows well that, thanks to the advice of lawyers like
himself, a certain kind of modern corporation has been turned
into an admirable instrument by which to render it well-nigh
impossible to get at the real guilty man, so that in most cases
the only way of punishing the wrong is by fining the corporation or by proceeding personally against some of the minor
agents. These lawyers and their employers are the men mainly
responsible for this state of things, and their responsibility is
shared with the legislators who ingeniously oppose the passing
of just and effective laws, and with those judges whose one

aim seems to be to construe such laws so that they cannot be executed. Nothing is sillier than this outcry on behalf of the "innocent stockholders" in the corporations. We are besought to pity the Standard Oil Company for a fine relatively far less great than the fines every day inflicted in the police courts upon multitudes of pushcart peddlers and other petty offenders, whose woes never extort one word from the men whose withers are wrung by the woes of the mighty. The stockholders have the control of the corporation in their own hands. The corporation officials are elected by those holding the majority of the stock and can keep office only by having behind them the good will of these majority stockholders. They are not entitled to the slightest pity if they deliberately choose to resign into the hands of great wrongdoers the control of the corporations in which they own the stock. Of course innocent people have become involved in these big corporations and suffer because of the misdeeds of their criminal associates. Let these innocent people be careful not to invest in corporations where those in control are not men of probity, men who respect the laws; above all let them avoid the men who make it their one effort to evade or defy the laws. But if these honest innocent people are in the majority in any corporation they can immediately resume control and throw out of the directory the men who misrepresent them. Does any man for a moment suppose that the majority stockholders of the Standard Oil are others than Mr. Rockefeller and his associates themselves and the beneficiaries of their wrongdoing? When the stock is watered so that the innocent investors suffer, a grave wrong is indeed done to these innocent investors as well as to the public; but the public men, lawyers and editors, to whom I refer, do not under these circumstances express sympathy for the innocent; on the contrary they are the first to protest with frantic vehemence against our efforts by law to put a stop to overcapitalization and stock-watering. The apologists of successful dishonesty always declaim against any effort to punish or prevent it on the ground that such effort will "unsettle business." It is they who by their acts have unsettled business; and the very men raising this cry spend hundreds of thousands of dollars in securing, by speech, editorial, book or pamphlet, the defense by misstatement of what they have done; and yet when we correct their misstatements by telling the truth, they declaim gainst us for breaking silence, lest "values be unsettled"! They have hurt honest businessmen, honest workingmen, honest farmers; and now they clamor against the truth being told.

The keynote of all these attacks upon the effort to secure honesty in business and in politics, is exprest in a recent speech in which the speaker stated that prosperity had been checked by the effort for the "moral regeneration of the business world," an effort which he denounced as "unnatural, unwarranted and injurious" and for which he stated the panic was the penalty. The morality of such a plea is precisely as great as if made on behalf of the men caught in a gambling establishment when that gambling establishment is raided by the police. If such words mean anything they mean that those sentiments they represent stand against the effort to bring about a moral regeneration of business which will prevent a repetition of the insurance, banking and street railroad scandals in New York; repetition of the Chicago and Alton deal; a repetition of the combination between certain professional politicians, certain professional labor leaders and certain big financiers from the disgrace of which San Francisco has just been rescued; a repetition of the successful efforts by the Standard Oil people to crush out every competitor, to overawe the common carriers, and to establish a monopoly which treats the public with the contempt which the public deserves so long as it permits men like the public men of whom I speak to represent it in politics, men like the heads of colleges to whom I refer to educate its youth. The outcry against stopping dishonest practices among the very wealthy is precisely similar to the outcry raised against every effort for cleanliness and decency in city government because, forsooth, it will "hurt business." The same outcry is made against the Department of Justice for prosecuting the heads of colossal corporations that is made against the men who in San Francisco are prosecuting with impartial severity the wrongdoers among businessmen, public officials, and labor leaders alike. The principle is the same in the two cases. Just as the blackmailer and the bribe-giver stand on the same evil eminence of infamy, so the man who makes an enormous fortune by corrupting Legislatures and municipalities and fleecing his stockholders and the public stands on a level with the creature who fattens on the blood money of the gambling house, the saloon and the brothel. Moreover both kinds of corruption in the last analysis are far more intimately connected than would at first sight appear; the wrongdoing is at bottom the same. Corrupt business and corrupt politics act and react, with ever increasing debasement, one on the other; the rebate-taker, the franchise-trafficker, the manipulator of securities, the purveyor and protector of vice, the blackmailing ward boss, the ballot-box-stuffer, the dema-gogue, the mob leader, the hired bully and man-killer, all alike work at the same web of corruption, and all alike should be abhorred by honest men.

The "business" which is hurt by the movement for honesty is the kind of business which, in the long run, it pays the country to have hurt. It is the kind of business which has tended to make the very name "high finance" a term of scandal to which all honest American men of business should join in putting an end. One of the special pleaders for business dis-honesty, in a recent speech, in denouncing the Administration for enforcing the law against the huge and corrupt corpora-tions which have defied the law, also denounced it for endeav-oring to secure a far-reaching law making employers liable for injuries to their employees. It is meet and fit that the apolo-gists for corrupt wealth should oppose every effort to relieve weak and helpless people from crushing misfortune brought upon them by injury in the business from which they gain a bare livelihood and their employers fortunes. It is hypocritical baseness to speak of a girl who works in a factory where the dangerous machinery is unprotected as having the "right" freely to contract to expose herself to dangers to life and limb. She has no alternative but to suffer want or else to expose herself to such dangers, and when she loses a hand or is otherwise maimed or disfigured for life it is a moral wrong that the burden of the risk necessarily incidental to the business should be placed with crushing weight upon her weak shoulders and the man who has profited by her work escape scot-free. This is what our opponents advocate, and it is proper that they should advocate it, for it rounds out their advocacy of those most dangerous members of the criminal class, the criminals of vast wealth, the men who can afford best to pay for such championship in the press and on the stump.

It is difficult to speak about the judges, for it behooves us all to treat with the utmost respect the high office of judge; and our judges as a whole are brave and upright men. But there is need that those who go wrong should not be allowed to feel that there is no condemnation of their wrongdoing. A judge who on the bench either truckles to the mob or bows down before a corporation; or who, having left the bench to become a corporation lawyer, seeks to aid his clients by denouncing as enemies of property all those who seek to stop the abuses of the criminal rich; such a man performs an even worse service to the body politic than the Legislator or Executive who goes wrong. In no way can respect for the courts be so quickly undermined as by teaching the public thru the action of a judge himself that there is reason for the loss of such respect. The judge who by word or deed makes it plain that the corrupt corporation, the law-defying corporation, the law-defying rich man, has in him a sure and trustworthy ally, the judge who by misuse of the process of injunction makes it plain that in him the wageworker has a determined and unscrupulous enemy, the judge who when he decides in an employer's liability or a tenement house factory case shows that he has neither sympathy for nor understanding of those fellow citizens of his who most need his sympathy and understanding; these judges work as much evil as if they pandered to the mob, as if they shrank from sternly repressing violence and disorder. The judge who does his full duty well stands higher, and renders a better service to the people, than any other public servant; he is entitled to greater respect; and if he is a true servant of the people, if he is upright, wise and fearless he will unhesitatingly disregard even the wishes of the people if they conflict with the eternal principles of right as against wrong. He must serve the people; but he must serve his conscience first. All honor to such a judge; and all honor cannot be rendered him if it is rendered equally to his brethren who fall immeasurably below the high ideals for which he stands. There should be a sharp discrimination against such judges. They claim immunity from criticism, and the claim is heatedly advanced by men and newspapers like those of whom I speak. Most certainly they can claim immunity from untruthful criticism; and their champions, the newspapers and the public men I have mentioned, exquisitely illustrate by their own actions mendacious criticism in its most flagrant and iniquitous form.

But no servant of the people has a right to expect to be free from just and honest criticism. It is the newspapers and the public men whose thoughts and deeds show them to be most alien to honesty and truth who themselves loudly object to truthful and honest criticism of their fellow servants of the great monied interests.

We have no quarrel with the individuals, whether public men, lawyers or editors, to whom I refer. These men derive their sole power from the great, sinister offenders who stand behind them. They are but puppets who move as the strings are pulled by those who control the enormous masses of corporate wealth which if itself left uncontrolled threatens dire evil to the Republic. It is not the puppets, but the strong, cunning men and the mighty forces working for evil behind, and to a certain extent thru, the puppets, with whom we have to deal. We seek to control law-defying wealth, in the first place to prevent its doing evil, and in the next place to avoid the vindictive and dreadful radicalism which if left uncontrolled it is certain in the end to arouse. Sweeping attacks upon all property, upon all men of means, without regard to whether they do well or ill, would sound the death knell of the Republic; and such attacks become inevitable if decent citizens permit rich men whose lives are corrupt and evil to domineer in swollen pride, unchecked and unhindered, over the destinies of this country. We act in no vindictive spirit, and we are no respecters of persons. If a labor union does what is wrong we oppose it as fearlessly as we oppose a corporation that does wrong; and we stand with equal stoutness for the rights of the man of wealth and for the rights of the wageworkers; just as much so for one as for the other. We seek to stop wrongdoing; and we desire to punish the wrong-doer only so far as is necessary in order to achieve this end. We are the staunch upholders of every honest man, whether businessman or wageworker.

I do not for a moment believe that our actions have brought on business distress; so far as this is due to local and not world-wide causes, and to the actions of any particular individuals, it is due to the speculative folly and flagrant dishonesty of a few men of great wealth, who now seek to shield themselves from the effects of their own wrongdoings by ascribing its results to the actions of those who have sought to put a stop to the wrongdoing. But if it were true that to cut out rottenness from the body politic meant a momentary check to an unhealthy-seeming prosperity, I should not for one moment hesitate to put the knife to the cancer. On behalf of all our people, on behalf no less of the honest man of means than of the honest man who earns each day's livelihood by that day's sweat of his brow, it is necessary to insist upon honesty in business and politics alike, in all walks of life, in big things and in little things; upon just and fair dealing as between man and man. We are striving for the right in the spirit of Abraham Lincoln when he said:

> Fondly do we hope—fervently do we pray—that this mighty scourge [of war] may speedily pass away. Yet, if God wills that it continue until all the wealth piled by the bondsmen's two hundred and fifty years of unrequited toil shall be sunk, and until every drop of blood drawn with the lash shall be paid by another drawn with the sword, as was said three thousand years ago, so still it must be said, "The judgments of the Lord are true and righteous altogether."
> With malice toward none; with charity for all; with firmness in the right, as God gives us to see the right, let us strive on to finish the work we are in.

17. · THE INADEQUACY OF THE SHERMAN ANTI-TRUST LAW

Debate over the most effective means to control the trusts continued through the administration of William Howard Taft and reached a crescendo during the presidential campaign of 1912. Taft, Woodrow Wilson, and probably a majority of Progressive Party leaders from the Middle West favored dissolution. But Roosevelt held to the regulatory position he had consistently occupied. To the distress of the Midwesterners, who incorrectly believed he had been mesmerized by the Morgan partner, George W. Perkins,

From Roosevelt's address to the Progressive Party National Convention in Chicago, August 6, 1912. *New York Times*, August 7, 1912, pp. 8–9.

he vigorously attacked dissolution and defended regulation in his moving address, "A Confession of Faith," to the 1912 national convention of the Progressive Party.

Again and again while I was President, from 1902 to 1908, I pointed out that under the antitrust law alone it was neither possible to put a stop to business abuses nor possible to secure the highest efficiency in the service rendered by business to the general public. The antitrust law must be kept on our statute-books, and, as hereafter shown, must be rendered more effective in the cases where it is applied. But to treat the antitrust law as an adequate, or as by itself a wise, measure of relief and betterment is a sign not of progress, but of Toryism and reaction. It has been of benefit so far as it has implied the recognition of a real and great evil, and the at least sporadic application of the principle that all men alike must obey the law. But as a sole remedy, universally applicable, it has in actual practice completely broken down; as now applied it works more mischief than benefit. It represents the waste of effort—always damaging to a community—which arises from the attempt to meet new conditions by the application of outworn remedies instead of fearlessly and in common-sense fashion facing the new conditions and devising the new remedies which alone can work effectively for good. The antitrust law, if interpreted as the Baltimore platform demands it shall be interpreted, would apply to every agency by which not merely industrial but agricultural business is carried on in this country; under such an interpretation it ought in theory to be applied universally, in which case practically all industries would stop; as a matter of fact, it is utterly out of the question to enforce it universally; and when enforced sporadically, it causes continual unrest, puts the country at a disadvantage with its trade competitors in international commerce, hopelessly puzzles honest business men and honest farmers as to what their rights are, and yet, as has just been shown in the cases of the Standard Oil and the Tobacco Trusts, it is no real check on the great trusts at which it was in theory aimed, and indeed operates to their benefit. Moreover, if we are to compete with other nations in the markets of the world as well as to develop our own material civilization at home, we must utilize those forms of industrial organization that are indispensable to the highest industrial productivity and efficiency.

An important volume entitled "Concentration and Control" has just been issued by President Charles R. Van Hise, of the University of Wisconsin. The University of Wisconsin has been more influential than any other agency in making Wisconsin what it has become, a laboratory for wise social and industrial experiment in the betterment of conditions. President Van Hise is one of those thoroughgoing but sane and intelligent radicals from whom much of leadership is to be expected in such a matter. The subtitle of his book shows that his endeavor is to turn the attention of his countrymen toward practically solving the trust problem of the United States. In his preface he states that his aim is to suggest a way to gain the economic advantages of the concentration of industry and at the same time to guard the interests of the public, and to assist in the rule of enlightenment, reason, fair play, mutual consideration, and toleration. In sum, he shows that unrestrained competition as an economic principle has become too destructive to be permitted to exist and that the small men must be allowed to co-operate under penalty of succumbing before their big competitors; and yet such co-operation, vitally necessary to the small man, is criminal under the present law. . . .

. . . In his main thesis President Van Hise is unquestionably right. The Democratic platform offers nothing in the way of remedy for present industrial conditions except, first, the enforcement of the antitrust law in a fashion which, if words mean anything, means bringing business to a standstill; and, second, the insistence upon an archaic construction of the

States'-rights doctrine in thus dealing with interstate commerce —an insistence which, in the first place, is the most flagrant possible violation of the Constitution to which the members of the Baltimore Convention assert their devotion, and which, in the next place, nullifies and makes an empty pretense of their first statement. The proposals of the platform are so conflicting and so absurd that it is hard to imagine how any attempt could be made in good faith to carry them out; but, if such attempt were sincerely made, it could only produce industrial chaos. Were such an attempt made, every man who acts honestly would have something to fear, and yet no great adroit criminal able to command the advice of the best corporation lawyers would have much to fear.

What is needed is action directly the reverse of that thus confusedly indicated. We Progressives stand for the rights of the people. When these rights can best be secured by insistence upon States' rights, then we are for States' rights; when they can best be secured by insistence upon national rights, then we are for national rights. Interstate commerce can be effectively controlled only by the nation. The States cannot control it under the Constitution, and to amend the Constitution by giving them control of it would amount to a dissolution of the government. The worst of the big trusts have always endeavored to keep alive the feeling in favor of having the States themselves, and not the nation, attempt to do this work, because they know that in the long run such effort would be ineffective. There is no surer way to prevent all successful effort to deal with the trusts than to insist that they be dealt with by the States rather than by the nation, or to create a conflict between the States and the nation on the subject. The well-meaning ignorant man who advances such a proposition does as much damage as if he were hired by the trusts themselves, for he is playing the game of every big crooked corporation in the country. The only effective way in which to regulate the trusts is through the exercise of the collective power of our people as a whole through the governmental agencies established by the Constitution for this very purpose. Grave injustice is done by the Congress when it fails to give the National Government complete power in this matter; and still graver injustice by the Federal courts when they endeavor in any way to pare down the right of the people collectively to act in this matter as they deem wise; such conduct does itself tend to cause the creation of a twilight zone in which neither the nation nor the States have power. Fortunately, the Federal courts have more and more of recent years tended to adopt the true doctrine, which is that all these matters are to be settled by the people themselves, and that the conscience of the people, and not the preferences of any servants of the people, is to be the standard in deciding what action shall be taken by the people. As Lincoln phrased it: "The [question] of national power and State rights as a principle is no other than the principle of generality and locality. Whatever concerns the whole should be confided to the whole—to the general government; while whatever concerns only the State should be left exclusively to the State."

It is utterly hopeless to attempt to control the trusts merely by the antitrust law, or by any law the same in principle, no matter what the modifications may be in detail. In the first place, these great corporations cannot possibly be controlled merely by a succession of lawsuits. The administrative branch of the government must exercise such control. The preposterous failure of the Commerce Court has shown that only damage comes from the effort to substitute judicial for administrative control of great corporations. In the next place, a loosely drawn law which promises to do everything would reduce business to complete ruin if it were not also so drawn as to accomplish almost nothing.

As construed by the Democratic platform, the antitrust law would, if it could be enforced, abolish all business of any size or any efficiency. The promise thus to apply and construe the law would undoubtedly be broken, but the mere fitful effort thus to apply it would do no good whatever, would accomplish wide-spread harm, and would bring all trust legislation into contempt. Contrast what has actually been accomplished under the interstate commerce law with what has actually been accomplished under the antitrust law. The first has, on the whole, worked in a highly efficient manner and achieved real and great results; and it promises to achieve even greater results (although I firmly believe that if the power of the commissioners grows greater, it will be necessary to make them and their superior, the President, even more completely responsible to the people for their acts). The second has occasionally done good, has usually accomplished nothing, but generally left the worst conditions wholly unchanged, and has been responsible for a considerable amount of downright and positive evil. . . .

A More Equitable Tax Structure

18. · THE GRADUATED INCOME AND INHERITANCE TAXES

One of Roosevelt's most controversial actions as governor of New York had been his support of a Democratic-sponsored bill to impose a tax on corporate franchises. It was, he explained, "a matter of plain decency and honesty." During his presidency his interest in taxation continued to grow, and by 1906 he had become a strong proponent of the steeply graduated inheritance tax. This commitment was animated both by his realization that the government would soon need new sources of revenue and his fear of the antidemocratic and morally corrosive effects of swollen fortunes. As he

From the Annual Message to Congress, 1906. *Messages and Papers,* XI, 1200–02.

once said of huge inheritances, "They rarely do good and they often do harm to those who inherit them." Roosevelt was less certain of the efficacy of a graduated income tax, for he wished to distinguish between fortunes "gained as an incident to performing great services to the community . . . and those gained in evil fashion by keeping just within the limits of mere law honesty." He knew, however, that it was impracticable to make the distinction. So in 1906 he also came out for the income tax. His first recommendations to Congress were more moderate than his actual beliefs, for his design was to encourage Congress to act, not to provoke it to resist.

The question of taxation is difficult in any country, but it is especially difficult in ours with its Federal system of government. Some taxes should on every ground be levied in a small district for use in that district. Thus the taxation of real estate is peculiarly one for the immediate locality in which the real estate is found. Again, there is no more legitimate tax for any State than a tax on the franchises conferred by that State upon street railroads and similar corporations which operate wholly within the State boundaries, sometimes in one and sometimes in several municipalities or other minor divisions of the State. But there are many kinds of taxes which can only be levied by the general government so as to produce the best results, because, among other reasons, the attempt to impose them in one particular State too often results merely in driving the corporation or individual affected to some other locality or other State. The National Government has long derived its chief revenue from a tariff on imports and from an internal or excise tax. In addition to these there is every reason why, when next our system of taxation is revised, the National Government should impose a graduated inheritance tax, and, if possible, a graduated income tax. The man of great wealth owes a peculiar obligation to the State, because he derives special advantages from the mere existence of government. Not only should he recognize this obligation in the way he leads his daily life and in the way he earns and spends his money, but it should also be recognized by the way in which he pays for the protection the State gives him. On the one hand, it is desirable that he should assume his full and proper share of the burden of taxation; on the other hand, it is quite as necessary that in this kind of taxation, where the men who vote the tax pay but little of it, there should be clear recognition of the danger of inaugurating any such system save in a spirit of entire justice and moderation. Whenever we, as a people, undertake to remodel our taxation system along the lines suggested, we must make it clear beyond peradventure that our aim is to distribute the burden of supporting the government more equitably than at present; that we intend to treat rich man and poor man on a basis of absolute equality, and that we regard it as equally fatal to true democracy to do or permit injustice to the one as to do or permit injustice to the other.

I am well aware that such a subject as this needs long and careful study in order that the people may become familiar with what is proposed to be done, may clearly see the necessity of proceeding with wisdom and self-restraint, and may make up their minds just how far they are willing to go in the matter; while only trained legislators can work out the project in necessary detail. But I feel that in the near future our national legislators should enact a law providing for a graduated inheritance tax by which a steadily increasing rate of duty should be put upon all moneys or other valuables coming by gift, bequest, or devise to any individual or corporation. It may be well to make the tax heavy in proportion as the individual benefited is remote of kin. In any event, in my judgment the pro rata of the tax should increase very heavily with the increase of the amount left to any one individual after a certain point has been reached. It is most desirable to encourage thrift and ambition, and a potent source of thrift and ambition is the desire on the part of the bread-winner to leave his children well off. This object can be attained by making the tax very small on moderate amounts of property left; because the prime object should be to put a constantly increasing burden on the inheritance of those swollen fortunes which it is certainly of no benefit to this country to perpetuate.

There can be no question of the ethical propriety of the government thus determining the conditions upon which any gift or inheritance should be received. Exactly how far the inheritance tax would, as an incident, have the effect of limiting the transmission by devise or gift of the enormous fortunes in question it is not necessary at present to discuss. It is wise that progress in this direction should be gradual. At first a permanent national inheritance tax, while it might be more substantial than any such tax has hitherto been, need not approximate, either in amount or in the extent of the increase by graduation, to what such a tax should ultimately be.

This species of tax has again and again been imposed although only temporarily, by the National Government. It was first imposed by the act of July 6, 1797, when the makers of the Constitution were alive and at the head of affairs. It was a graduated tax; though small in amount, the rate was increased with the amount left to any individual, exceptions being made in the case of certain close kin. A similar tax was again imposed by the act of July 1, 1862; a minimum sum of $1,000 in personal property being excepted from taxation, the tax then becoming progressive according to the remoteness of kin. The war-revenue act of June 13, 1898, provided for an inheritance tax on any sum exceeding the value of $10,000, the rate of the tax increasing both in accordance with the amounts left and in accordance with the legatee's remoteness of kin. The Supreme Court has held that the succession tax imposed at the time of the Civil War was not a direct tax but an impost or excise which was both constitutional and valid. More recently the court, in an opinion delivered by Mr. Justice White, which contained an exceedingly able and elaborate discussion of the powers of the Congress to impose death duties, sustained the constitutionality of the inheritance-tax feature of the war-revenue act of 1898.

In its incidents, and apart from the main purpose of raising revenue, an income tax stands on an entirely different footing from an inheritance tax; because it involves no question of the perpetuation of fortunes swollen to an unhealthy size. The question is in its essence a question of the proper adjustment of burdens to benefits. As the law now stands it is undoubtedly difficult to devise a national income tax which shall be constitutional. But whether it is absolutely impossible is another question; and if possible it is most certainly desirable. The first purely income-tax law was passed by the Congress in 1861, but the most important law dealing with the subject was that of 1894. This the court held to be unconstitutional.

The question is undoubtedly very intricate, delicate, and troublesome. The decision of the court was only reached by one majority. It is the law of the land, and of course is accepted as such and loyally obeyed by all good citizens. Nevertheless, the hestitation evidently felt by the court as a whole in coming to a conclusion, when considered together with the previous decisions on the subject, may perhaps indicate the possibility of devising a constitutional income-tax law which shall substantially accomplish the results aimed at. The difficulty of amending the Constitution is so great that only real necessity can justify a resort thereto. Every effort should be made in dealing with this subject, as with the subject of the proper control by the National Government over the use of corporate wealth in interstate business, to devise legislation which without such action shall attain the desired end; but if this fails, there will ultimately be no alternative to a constitutional amendment.

Tariff Policy

19. · A POLITICAL DEFENSE

Although the manifest conservatism of the Republican leaders in Congress repeatedly forced Roosevelt to compromise, he usually won acceptance of a portion of his recommendations. Only rarely prior to 1907 did Congress repulse the President completely, and almost never did he fail to strengthen the gathering progressive movement by taking the issue to the people when it did. One of the rare exceptions was the tariff. Far more than the following statement indicates, Roosevelt understood the desirability of tariff reform. But he also understood that the manufacturers who constituted the G.O.P.'s financial backbone would under no circumstances approve a general reduction of rates. He further saw that to raise the issue seriously would be to jeopardize passage of other parts of his program, notably the regulation of corporations. Reluctantly, therefore, he decided after a few false starts to defer to the Old Guard's sensibilities. As this portion of his letter accepting the 1904 Republican presidential nomination shows, however, his moralism was so strident that he could not justify the decision on pragmatic political grounds.

Oyster Bay, L. I.,
September 12, 1904

My dear Sir:

. . . When we take up the great question of the tariff we are at once confronted by the doubt as to whether our opponents do or do not mean what they say. They say that "protection is

From a letter to Joseph G. Cannon, September 12, 1904. *Official Proceedings of the Thirteenth Republican National Convention* (Minneapolis, 1904), pp. 195–218.

robbery," and promise to carry themselves accordingly if they are given power. Yet prominent persons among them assert that they do not really mean this and that if they come into power they will adopt our policy as regards the tariff; while others seem anxious to prove that it is safe to give them partial power, because the power would be only partial and therefore they would not be able to do mischief. The last is certainly a curious plea to advance on behalf of a party seeking to obtain control of the Government.

At the outset it is worth while to say a word as to the attempt to identify the question of tariff revision or tariff reduction with a solution of the trust question. This is always a sign of desire to avoid any real effort to deal adequately with the trust question. In speaking on this point at Minneapolis, on April 4, 1903, I said:

"The question of tariff revision, speaking broadly, stands wholly apart from the question of dealing with the trusts. No change in tariff duties can have any substantial effect in solving the so-called trust problem. Certain great trusts or great corporations are wholly unaffected by the tariff. Almost all the others that are of any importance have as a matter of fact numbers of smaller American competitors; and of course a change in the tariff which would work injury to the large corporation would work not merely injury but destruction to its smaller competitors; and equally of course such a change would mean disaster to all the wage-workers connected with either the large or the small corporations. From the standpoint of those interested in the solution of the trust problem such a change would therefore merely mean that the trust was relieved of the competition of its weaker American competitors, and thrown only into competition with foreign competitors; and that the first effort to meet this new competition would be made by cutting down wages, and would therefore be primarily at the cost of labor. In the case of some of our greatest trusts such a change might confer upon them a positive benefit. Speaking broadly, it is evident that the changes in the tariff will affect the trusts for weal or for woe simply as they affect the whole country. The tariff affects trusts only as it affects all other interests. It makes all these interests, large or small, profitable; and its benefits can be taken from the large only under penalty of taking them from the small also."

There is little for me to add to this. It is but ten years since the last attempt was made, by means of lowering the tariff, to prevent some people from prospering too much. The attempt was entirely successful. The tariff law of that year was among the causes which in that year and for some time afterward effectually prevented anybody from prospering too much, and labor from prospering at all. Undoubtedly it would be possible at the present time to prevent any of the trusts from remaining prosperous by the simple expedient of making such a sweeping change in the tariff as to paralyze the industries of the country. The trusts would cease to prosper; but their smaller competitors would be ruined, and the wage-workers would starve, while it would not pay the farmer to haul his produce to market. The evils connected with the trusts can be reached only by rational effort, step by step, along the lines taken by Congress and the Executive during the past three years. If a tariff law is passed under which the country prospers, as the country has prospered under the present tariff law, then all classes will share in the prosperity. If a tariff law is passed aimed at preventing the prosperity of some of our people, it is as certain as anything can be that this aim will be achieved only by cutting down the prosperity of all of our people. . . .

. . . It is a matter of regret that the protective-tariff policy, which, during the last forty-odd years, has become part of the very fibre of the country, is not now accepted as definitely established. Surely we have a right to say that it has passed beyond the domain of theory, and a right to expect that not only its original advocates but those who at one time distrusted it on theoretic grounds should now acquiesce in the results that have been proved over and over again by actual experience. These forty-odd years have been the most prosperous years this Nation has ever seen; more prosperous years than any other nation has ever seen. Beyond question this prosperity could not have come if the American people had not possessed the necessary thrift, energy, and business intelligence to turn their vast material resources to account. But it is no less true that it is our economic policy as regards the tariff and finance which has enabled us as a nation to make such good use of the individual capacities of our citizens, and the natural resources of our country. Every class of our people is benefited by the protective tariff. During the last few years the merchant has seen the export trade of this country grow faster than ever in our previous history. The manufacturer could not keep his factory running if it were not for the protective tariff. The wage-worker would do well to remember that if protection is "robbery," and is to be punished accordingly, he will be the first to pay the penalty; for either he will be turned adrift entirely, or his wages will be cut down to the starvation point. As conclusively shown by the bulletins of the Bureau of Labor, the purchasing power of the average wage received by the wage-worker has grown faster than the cost of living, and this in spite of the continual shortening of working hours. The accumulated savings of the working men of the country, as shown by the deposits in the savings-banks, have increased by leaps and bounds. At no time in the history of this or any other country has there been an era so productive of material benefit alike to working man and employer as during the seven years that have just passed.

The farmer has been benefited quite as much as the manufacturer, the merchant, and the wage-worker. The most welcome and impressive fact established by the last census is the wide and even distribution of wealth among all classes of our countrymen. The chief agencies in producing this distribution are shown by the census to be the development of manufactures, and the application of new inventions to universal use. The result has been an increasing interdependence of agriculture and manufactures. Agriculture is now, as it always has been, the basis of civilization. The six million farms of the United States, operated by men who as a class, are steadfast, single-minded, and industrious, form the basis of all the other achievements of the American people and are more fruitful than all their other resources. The men on those six million farms receive from the protective tariff what they most need, and that is the best of all possible markets. All other classes depend upon the farmer, but the farmer in turn depends upon the market they furnish him for his produce. The annual output of our agricultural products is nearly four billions of dollars. Their increase in value has been prodigious, although agriculture has languished in most other countries; and the main factor in this increase is the corresponding increase of our manufacturing industries. American farmers have prospered because the growth of their market has kept pace with the growth of their farms. The additional market continually furnished for agricultural products by domestic manufacturers has been far in excess of the outlet to other lands. An export trade in farm products is necessary to dispose of our surplus; and the export trade of our farmers, both in animal products and in plant products, has very largely increased. Without the enlarged home market to keep this surplus down, we should have to reduce production or else feed the world at less than the cost of production. In the forty years ending in 1900 the total value of farm property increased twelve and a half billions of dollars; the farmer gaining even more during this period than the manufacturer. Long ago overproduction would have checked the marvellous development of our national agriculture, but for the steadily increasing demand of American manufacturers for farm products required as raw materials for steadily expanding industries. The farmer has become dependent upon the manufacturer to utilize that portion of his produce which does not go directly to food-supply. . . .

20. · A CALL FOR SCIENTIFIC REVISION

After he left the presidency, and particularly after he bolted from the Republican party, Roosevelt tended to view the tariff more objectively. When he did so, he found that "certain interests have been improperly favored by overprotection" and that "the tariff should be revised." But by then he had concluded that Congress was subject to too much pressure from thousands of special interests to enact a scientific law—one that would uphold the protectionist principle without raising the schedules excessively—unaided by experts. So in this and other speeches he vigorously recommended creation of a tariff commission authorized to make specific recommendations.

I believe in a protective tariff, but I believe in it as a principle, approached from the standpoint of the interests of the whole people, and not as a bundle of preferences to be given to favored individuals. In my opinion, the American people favor the principle of a protective tariff, but they desire such a tariff to be established primarily in the interests of the wageworker and the consumer. The chief opposition to our tariff at the present moment comes from the general conviction that certain interests have been improperly favored by overprotection. I agree with this view. The commercial and industrial experience of this country has demonstrated the wisdom of the protective policy, but it has also demonstrated that in the ap-

From Roosevelt's address to the Progressive Party National Convention at Chicago, August 6, 1912. *New York Times*, August 7, 1912.

plication of that policy certain clearly recognized abuses have developed. It is not merely the tariff that should be revised, but the method of tariff-making and of tariff administration. Wherever nowadays an industry is to be protected it should be on the theory that such protection will serve to keep up the wages and the standard of living of the wage-worker in that industry with full regard for the interest of the consumer. To accomplish this the tariff to be levied should as nearly as is scientifically possible approximate the differential between the cost of production at home and abroad. This differential is chiefly, if not wholly, in labor cost. No duty should be permitted to stand as regards any industry unless the workers receive their full share of the benefits of that duty. In other words, there is no warrant for protection unless a legitimate share of the benefits gets into the pay-envelope of the wage-worker.

The practice of undertaking a general revision of all the schedules at one time and of securing information as to conditions in the different industries and as to rates of duty desired chiefly from those engaged in the industries, who themselves benefit directly from the rates they propose, has been demonstrated to be not only iniquitous but futile. It has afforded opportunity for practically all of the abuses which have crept into our tariff-making and our tariff administration. The day of the log-rolling tariff must end. The progressive thought of the country has recognized this fact for several years, and the time has come when all genuine Progressives should insist upon a thorough and radical change in the method of tariff-making.

The first step should be the creation of a permanent commission of non-partisan experts whose business shall be to study scientifically all phases of tariff-making and of tariff effects. This commission should be large enough to cover all the different and widely varying branches of American industry. It should have ample powers to enable it to secure exact and reliable information. It should have authority to examine closely all correlated subjects, such as the effect of any given duty on the consumers of the article on which the duty is levied; that is, it should directly consider the question as to what any duty costs the people in the price of living. It should examine into the wages and conditions of labor and life of the workmen in any industry, so as to insure our refusing protection to any industry unless the showing as regards the share labor receives therefrom is satisfactory. This commission would be wholly different from the present unsatisfactory Tariff Board, which was created under a provision of law which failed to give it the powers indispensable if it was to do the work it should do.

It will be well for us to study the experience of Germany in considering this question. The German tariff commission has proved conclusively the efficiency and wisdom of this method of handling tariff questions. The reports of a permanent, expert, and non-partisan tariff commission would at once strike a most powerful blow against the chief iniquity of the old log-rolling method of tariff-making. One of the principal difficulties with the old method has been that it was impossible for the public generally, and especially for those members of Congress not directly connected with the committees handling a tariff bill, to secure anything like adequate and impartial information on the particular subjects under consideration.

The reports of such a tariff commission would at once correct this evil and furnish to the general public full, complete, and disinterested information on every subject treated in a tariff bill. With such reports it would no longer be possible to construct a tariff bill in secret or to jam it through either House of Congress without the fullest and most illuminating discussion. The path of the tariff "joker" would be rendered infinitely difficult.

As a further means of disrupting the old crooked, log-rolling method of tariff-making, all future revisions of the tariff should be made schedule by schedule as changing conditions may require. Thus a great obstacle will be thrown in the way of the trading of votes which has marked so scandalously the enactment of every tariff bill of recent years. The tariff commission should render reports at the call of Congress or of either branch of Congress and to the President. Under the Constitution, Congress is the tariff-making power. It should not be the purpose in creating a tariff commission to take anything away from this power of Congress, but rather to afford a wise means of giving to Congress the widest and most scientific assistance possible, and of furnishing it and the public with the fullest disinterested information. Only by this means can the tariff be taken out of politics. The creation of such a permanent tariff commission, and the adoption of the policy of schedule by schedule revision, will do more to accomplish this highly desired object than any other means yet devised.

The Democratic platform declares for a tariff for revenue only, asserting that a protective tariff is unconstitutional. To say that a protective tariff is unconstitutional, as the Democratic platform insists, is only excusable on a theory of the Constitution which would make it unconstitutional to legislate in any shape or way for the betterment of social and industrial conditions. The abolition of the protective tariff or the substitution for it of a tariff for revenue only, as proposed by the Democratic platform, would plunge this country into the most wide-spread industrial depression we have yet seen, and this depression would continue for an indefinite period. There is no hope from the standpoint of our people from action such as the Democrats propose. The one and only chance to secure stable and favorable business conditions in this country, while at the same time guaranteeing fair play to farmer, consumer, business man, and wage-worker, lies in the creation of such a commission as I herein advocate. Only by such a commission and only by such activities of the commission will it be possible for us to get a reasonably quick revision of the tariff schedule by schedule—revision which shall be downward and not upward, and at the same time secure a square deal not merely to the manufacturer, but to the wage-worker and to the general consumer. . . .

. . . The welfare of the tiller of the soil is as important as the welfare of the wage-worker himself, and we must sedulously guard both. The farmer, the producer of the necessities of life, can himself live only if he raises these necessities for a profit. On the other hand, the consumer who must have that farmer's product in order to live, must be allowed to purchase it at the lowest cost that can give the farmer his profit, and everything possible must be done to eliminate any middleman whose function does not tend to increase the cheapness of distribution of the product; and, moreover, everything must be done to stop all speculating, all gambling with the bread-basket which has even the slightest deleterious effect upon the producer and consumer. There must be legislation which will bring about a closer business relationship between the farmer and the consumer. Recently experts in the agricultural department have figured that nearly fifty per cent of the price for agricultural products paid by the consumer goes into the pockets, not of the farmer, but of various middlemen; and it is probable that over half of what is thus paid to middlemen is needless, can be saved by wise business methods (introduced through both law and custom), and can therefore be returned to the farmer and the consumer.

Through the proposed interstate industrial commission we can effectively do away with any arbitrary control by combinations of the necessities of life. Furthermore, the governments of the nation and of the several States must combine in doing everything they can to make the farmer's business profitable, so that he shall get more out of the soil, and enjoy better business facilities for marketing what he thus gets. In this manner his return will be increased while the price to the consumer is diminished. The elimination of the middleman by agricultural exchanges and by the use of improved business methods generally, the development of good roads, the reclamation of arid lands and swamplands, the improvement in the productivity of farms, the encouragement of all agencies which tend to bring people back to the soil and to make country life more interesting as well as more profitable—all these movements will help not only the farmer but the man who consumes the farmer's products.

There is urgent need of non-partisan expert examination into any tariff schedule which seems to increase the cost of living, and, unless the increase thus caused is more than countervailed by the benefit to the class of the community which actually receives the protection, it must of course mean that that particular duty must be reduced. The system of levying a tariff for the protection and encouragement of American industry so as to secure higher wages and better conditions of life for American laborers must never be perverted so as to operate for the impoverishment of those whom it was intended to benefit. But, in any event, the effect of the tariff on the cost of living is slight; any householder can satisfy himself of this fact by considering the increase in price of articles, like milk and eggs, where the influence of both the tariff and the trusts is negligible. No conditions have been shown which warrant us in believing that the abolition of the protective tariff as a whole would bring any substantial benefit to the consumer, while it would certainly cause unheard-of immediate disaster to all wage-workers, all business men, and all farmers, and in all probability would permanently lower the standard of living here. In order to show the utter futility of the belief that the abolition of the tariff and the establishment of free trade would remedy the condition complained of, all that is necessary is to look at the course of industrial events in England and in Germany during the last thirty years, the former under free trade, the latter under a protective system. During these thirty years it is a matter of common knowledge that

Germany has forged ahead relatively to England, and this not only as regards the employers, but as regards the wage-earners—in short, as regards all members of the industrial classes. Doubtless, many causes have combined to produce this result; it is not to be ascribed to the tariff alone, but, on the other hand, it is evident that it could not have come about if a protective tariff were even a chief cause among many other causes of the high cost of living.

It is also asserted that the trusts are responsible for the high cost of living. I have no question that, as regards certain trusts, this is true. I also have no question that it will continue to be true just as long as the country confines itself to acting as the Baltimore platform demands that we act. This demand is, in effect, for the States and National Government to make the futile attempt to exercise forty-nine sovereign and conflicting authorities in the effort jointly to suppress the trusts, while at the same time the National Government refuses to exercise proper control over them. There will be no diminution in the cost of trust-made articles so long as our government attempts the impossible task of restoring the flintlock conditions of business sixty years ago by trusting only to a succession of lawsuits under the antitrust law—a method which it has been definitely shown usually results to the benefit of any big business concern which really ought to be dissolved, but which causes disturbance and distress to multitudes of smaller concerns. Trusts which increase production—unless they do it wastefully, as in certain forms of mining and lumbering—cannot permanently increase the cost of living; it is the trusts which limit production, or which, without limiting production, take advantage of the lack of governmental control, and eliminate competition by combining to control the market, that cause an increase in the cost of living. There should be established at once, as I have elsewhere said, under the National Government an interstate industrial commission, which should exercise full supervision over the big industrial concerns doing an interstate business into which an element of monopoly enters. Where these concerns deal with the necessaries of life the commission should not shrink, if the necessity is proved, of going to the extent of exercising regulatory control over the conditions that create or determine monopoly prices.

By such action we shall certainly be able to remove the element of contributory causation on the part of the trusts and the tariff toward the high cost of living. There will remain many other elements. Wrong taxation, including failure to tax swollen inheritances and unused land and other natural resources held for speculative purposes, is one of these elements. The modern tendency to leave the country for the town is another element; and exhaustion of the soil and poor methods of raising and marketing the products of the soil make up another element, as I have already shown. Another element is that of waste and extravagance, individual and national. No laws which the wit of man can devise will avail to make the community prosperous if the average individual lives in such fashion that his expenditure always exceeds his income.

National extravagance—that is, the expenditure of money which is not warranted—we can ourselves control, and to some degree we can help in doing away with the extravagance caused by international rivalries. . . .

Aid to Farmers

21. · AGRICULTURAL EDUCATION

This letter to Herbert Myrick, president of the Orange Judd Company and editor of a chain of farm weeklies, is especially illu-

Letter to Herbert Myrick, September 10, 1908. *The Letters*, VI, 1224–29.

minating. First, it shows Roosevelt's informed concern about rural isolation—a concern that led him to appoint one of the most notable fact-finding bodies of that time, The Commission on Country Life. Secondly, it underlines his practical approach to agricultural education and homestead legislation. Thirdly, it emphasizes his appreciation of the need for scientific management. And finally, it gives a suggestive insight into his attitude toward federal-state relationships at that time. In calling for federal aid to agricultural high schools or vocational schools, for example, he conceives that Washington should supply expertise and set guidelines but that state and local officials should exercise control.

Oyster Bay, L. I.,
September 10, 1908

My dear Mr. Myrick: As unfortunately it is not in my power to be present at the dedication of your building at Springfield, I avail myself of this opportunity not only to wish you well on this occasion, but also to say a few words on the question of national co-operation in technical education, especially in agricultural education—a matter which I have so much at heart and for which your papers have so stoutly battled.

It is a matter of real gratification to all of us that you should be able now to dedicate your great building, for the Orange Judd agricultural papers have been managed so as to combine intelligent championship of the needs of the farm with successful handling of the enterprise itself as a business proposition. You have practically applied the principle of co-operation. Only once has your business been forced to reduce compensation—in the year 1894. I was both pleased and interested to know that on that occasion dividends were first reduced; then salaries, beginning with the head of the concern; and, finally, wages, but that the women were spared when the readjustment of wages began. Shortly after, wages were restored, then salaries, and finally, dividends. This recognizes the human element, the helpful idea, the principle of doing as one would be done by; the principle of genuine co-operation, a co-operation which in your case included agricultural labor, capital, and domestic economy. Such work can never be done in a merely sentimental spirit. It must represent sound, practical common sense, but it must also represent mutual confidence, helpfulness and service. I am glad to be told that in your case the result has proven profitable, alike to the coworker and the co-owner. It seems to me peculiarly valuable that a lesson like this should be taught by practical example to those engaged in farm work, as well as to those engaged in other occupations —and also to those whose work is in the homes. Self-help is the best help and makes the best citizenship; but the highest type of self-help is that which is combined with the right kind of helpfulness to others.

Now, in striving for co-operation between the National and State Governments and the farmers, for the uplifting of farm life, I am striving for exactly this principle, the principle of combining self-help with mutual helpfulness. Of course the prime thing to be done for the farmer, as for everyone else, is to help him to help himself. If he won't help himself, if he lies down on others and tries to make them carry him, we can rest assured that neither Nation, State, nor neighbors can permanently benefit him. Nevertheless, a helping hand is often of great service when extended even to those most capable of helping themselves. The individual, the community, the State, each must give an example of self-help; but groups of individuals and of States—and the largest group of all, the Nation— may all co-operate with advantage for their common interests. Perhaps this is especially true in trying to secure the conservation of our forests and waters, the protection of our streams from pollution, and the like. It is for this reason that I wish to see the Nation not only establish forest reserves wherever possible all thru the western States and Territories, but join in making the White Mountain region a forest reserve, just as it proposes to do with the Appalachian region.

We have been in the past, and we are yet, a people with

whom agriculture has been the most important business. There never has been in history any movement comparable to the wonderful westward march of the hard-working American pioneer farmers, and of those who came after them, who have overspread this continent, who are now filling its remotest corners, and thanks to whom there are uninterrupted stretches of farm land from sea to sea, from the Gulf to the watershed of the Arctic Ocean. The rough wilderness has been subdued by those who in their veins blend in a common stream the blood of so many nations of the Old World. Thru that most wise economic statute, the homestead law, we have been enabled to develop the family farm, the most important and the most American of all our institutions; for our greatness as a people rests in no small degree upon the fact that instead of having here in the country districts a population of peasants on minute holdings, or else of tenants who work for large landowners, we have everywhere, as the typical American farm a medium-sized farm, tilled mainly or in large part by the owner himself and his sons.

But now that the more desirable areas of our public land have been settled, the homestead law does not meet the new conditions, and we adhere best to its spirit when we try to modify the system of landownership in such a way as to insure continuous progress and uplift so that the American farmer may not only obtain material prosperity, but on it build a high type of civilization. Important tho the city is, and fortunate tho it is that our cities have grown as they have done, it is still more important that the family farm, where the homemaking and the outdoor business are combined into a unit, should continue to grow. In every great crisis of our Government, and in all the slow, steady work between the crises which alone enables us to meet them when they do arise, it is the farming folk, the people of the country districts, who have shown themselves to be the backbone of the Nation.

Now, when I ask that the Nation co-operate with the States

and with the farmers themselves for the steady growth and uplift of farm life, I am not so much asking that the State help the people as I am that it shall provide free opportunity for the people to continue their upward course thru self-help and associated effort.

The farms of America are worth some thirty billions of dollars, and their annual produce amounts to about eight billions. For this present year, 1908, the crops as a whole promise the largest aggregate in quantity, quality, and value ever produced in our history. This means that the six millions and over of farm families, more than thirty millions of farm people, are in a good position already; but I wish this position to be made sure and better.

The farm no longer produces the domestic manufactures of two generations ago, but merely the raw products of food and clothing; for the great improvements in agricultural production and in transportation have rendered it possible for one man on the farm now to produce food and clothing for three, whereas formerly it needed two to perform such a feat for themselves and a third. Thus with every improvement in crop and livestock production, an increased number of people are set free to work in other fashion for the building up of the permanent wealth of all of us, and for adding to the daily well-being, and meeting the intellectual and spiritual needs, of all of us.

It would be a very great wrong to allow our country people, who have prospered so much, whose welfare has meant so much for the Nation in the past, in any way to fall off from their former position. There is no need whatever for this happening. With wise care of our natural resources, our forests will grow better each year, our rivers more available for navigation, while the soil of our farms will improve with wise use instead of deteriorating. While as a Nation we are growing wealthier and wealthier, we should see that the schools and the roads—in short, all of what may be called the rural realty

—should be improved. Here, as everywhere else, our prime object should be the development of the highest type of average citizen. Therefore, we should especially devote ourselves to the things that are of interest to the average citizen. The country school is therefore of even more importance than the higher college, thoroly alive tho we all should be to the vitalizing force which these higher colleges represent. There must be improvement in farm management; this is even now being brought about, partly by the work of the demonstration farmers, employed mostly at public expense, and partly by the joint action of the farmers themselves. So far as it is possible, we should strive for a common sense co-operation in institutions which shall do what the isolated farms cannot well do by themselves. As an example we can refer to the experiments recently carried on, by private individuals, and by the National Department of Agriculture, and by the State experiment stations, to show the extraordinary possibilities in improving the breeds of our food plants and of our animals.

In all of this we have to grapple with one fact which has made both the strength and the weakness of the American farmer, and that is, his isolation. This isolation implies a lack both of the pleasure and of the inspiration which come from closer contact between people, and from a well-developed organization for social pleasures, for religious life, for education. On the other hand, it is to this isolation more than to anything else that we owe the strength of character so typical of the American farmer, who lives under a peculiarly individualistic system in the management alike of the farm and of the farm home. The successfully managed family farm gives to the father, the mother, and the children better opportunities for useful work and for a happy life than any other occupation. Our object must be so far as practicable to do away with the disadvantages which are due to the isolation of the family farm, while conserving its many and great advantages. We wish to keep at its highest point the peculiarly American quality of individual efficiency, while at the same time bringing about that co-operation which indicates capacity in the mass. Both qualities can be used to increase the industrial and ethical proficiency of our people, for there is much the individual can only do for himself, and there is much also which must be done by all combined because the individual cannot do it. Our aim must be to supplement individualism on the farm and in the home with an associated effort in those country matters that require organized working together.

Moreover, we must not forget that there is a new phase of the matter of transportation, which is the problem of country homes for city workers. Cheap transportation, which has strengthened so much the tendency to city growth, is now helping to scatter the population of large cities for home purposes thru the adjacent country. As we come nearer the healthy ideal of a universal eight-hour day, and a closer association between employer and employee, there will be growth in the opportunity for city people to enjoy suburban homes.

Therefore we have to deal now, and will have to deal in the future, with a nation of families on the land; and our system of public education should be so broadened in its scope as to include not merely the traditional cultural studies, excellent and indispensable in their way, but also instruction relative to the farm, the trades, and the home. Our immediate purpose is to take the first steps in providing for the ninety-five per cent who are not now trained for a vocation, advantages corresponding to those enjoyed by the relatively few who are trained in the professional and technical schools. Industrial training, training which will fit a girl to do work in the home, which will fit a boy to work in the shop if in a city, to work on a farm if in the country, is the most important of all training aside from that which develops character; and it is a grave reproach to us as a nation that we have permitted our training to lead the children away from the farm and shop instead of toward them. We should try to provide the many with training in their professions, just as the few, the doctors, the ministers, the lawyers, are trained for their professions. In other words, the school system should be aimed primarily to fit the scholar for actual life rather than for a university. The exceptional individual, of the highest culture and most efficient training possible, is an important asset for the State. He should be encouraged and his development promoted; but this should not be done at the expense of all the other individuals who can do their work best on the farms and in the workshops; it is for the benefit of these individuals that our school system should be primarily shaped.

I thoroly believe that our people approve of the higher education; but I also believe that they are growing more and more to demand a reform in secondary schools which shall fit the ordinary scholar for the actual work of life. Therefore I believe that the National Government should take an active part in securing better educational methods. . . . I feel that the Nation should by making appropriations put a premium upon industrial, and especially agricultural, training in the State schools; the States themselves being required in these schools to contribute what is necessary for the ordinary training, and the expenditures for the National Government to be under the supervision of the Department of Agriculture. Teachers must be trained, or their teaching will not be adequate; and these teachers must then give vocational training to the scholars in the ordinary schools. The Nation would simply co-operate with the State or city or town, and what it thus gives would be applied to industrial, technical, agricultural training. The growth in the consolidated rural school which has in so many instances supplanted the old-time district school, offers the chance to do the best possible service by means of such a system as that outlined above. Where possible, the secondary agricultural schools should be in farm communities rather than in towns, and the training should be of the most practical character and such as will not only fit the scholars to do their part in farm work, but also fit them to enjoy in the fullest degree the pleasures and opportunities of country life. We should do everything that we can to give well-trained leaders to each country community. The United States Department of Agriculture would preserve an intimate relation to all these proposed agricultural high schools, as well as the branch stations connected with them, for the work that the Department does is steadily becoming of more and more consequence to the farmers.

All this simply means that the Nation ought to co-operate with the State to help the people help themselves thru better educational facilities, the schools being left wholly and directly under the control of the people thru their local authorities, but suggestion and general oversight as well as improvement being supplied by the experts employed by the nation, so that the children and the young men and girls in the smaller towns and in the country may have the educational facilities now only to be obtained in wealthier communities. This would merely be putting into effect that cardinal American doctrine of furnishing a reasonable equality of opportunity, of education and chance of development, to all our children, wherever they live and whatever may be their station in life. Such a federal co-operation in technical education will help in many ways. It will mean much for our country life, for the life of the family farm, for the life of those city workers who seek landed homes in the country near the city in which they work. It will mean much along the lines of the great policy of the conservation of the natural resources of our land. Finally, it will mean much to the Nation of the future, because it will represent the effort to give exact justice, and an equal opportunity for development, to each of the boys and girls who in the future are to make up the Nation.

VI • CONSERVATION

The Struggle for an Enlightened Policy

22. "THE NATURAL RESOURCES OF THE NATION"

This straight-forward and generally accurate account of Roosevelt's conservation policies illumines the values and ideas that inspired him and his great subordinate, Gifford Pinchot. Among the most important were: (1) indiscriminate exploitation of natural resources was morally wrong and should be stopped by government action; (2) the nation's natural resources belonged to all the people and the President was their steward; (3) the government should reclaim arid land; (4) forests could be both preserved and efficiently used by selective cutting; (5) river systems should be regarded as single units and developed as same; (6) the federal government should pursue a publicity campaign to familiarize state and local governments with scientific conservation procedures.

RECLAMATION

. . . The first work I took up when I became President was the work of reclamation. Immediately after I had come to Washington, after the assassination of President McKinley, while staying at the house of my sister, Mrs. Cowles, before going into the White House, [Frederick H.] Newell and [Gifford] Pinchot called upon me and laid before me their plans for national irrigation of the arid lands of the West, and for the

Autobiography, pp. 394–421.

consolidation of the forest work of the government in the Bureau of Forestry.

At that time a narrowly legalistic point of view toward natural resources obtained in the departments, and controlled the governmental administrative machinery. Through the General Land Office and other government bureaus, the public resources were being handled and disposed of in accordance with the small considerations of petty legal formalities, instead of for the large purposes of constructive development, and the habit of deciding, whenever possible, in favor of private interests against the public welfare was firmly fixed. It was as little customary to favor the bona-fide settler and home-builder, as against the strict construction of the law, as it was to use the law in thwarting the operations of the land-grabbers. A technical compliance with the letter of the law was all that was required.

The idea that our natural resources were inexhaustible still obtained, and there was as yet no real knowledge of their extent and condition. The relation of the conservation of natural resources to the problems of national welfare and national efficiency had not yet dawned on the public mind. The reclamation of arid public lands in the West was still a matter for private enterprise alone; and our magnificent river system, with its superb possibilities for public usefulness, was dealt with by the National Government not as a unit, but as a disconnected series of pork-barrel problems, whose only real interest was in their effect on the re-election or defeat of a congressman here and there—a theory which, I regret to say, still obtains.

The place of the farmer in the national economy was still regarded solely as that of a grower of food to be eaten by others, while the human needs and interests of himself and his wife and children still remained wholly outside the recognition of the government.

All the forests which belonged to the United States were held and administered in one department, and all the foresters in government employ were in another department. Forests and foresters had nothing whatever to do with each other. The national forests in the West (then called forest reserves) were wholly inadequate in area to meet the purposes for which they were created, while the need for forest protection in the East had not yet begun to enter the public mind.

Such was the condition of things when Newell and Pinchot called on me. I was a warm believer in reclamation and in forestry, and, after listening to my two guests, I asked them to prepare material on the subject for me to use in my first message to Congress, of December 3, 1901. This message laid the foundation for the development of irrigation and forestry during the next seven and one-half years. It set forth the new attitude toward the natural resources in the words: "The forest and water problems are perhaps the most vital internal problems of the United States."

On the day the message was read, a committee of Western senators and congressmen was organized to prepare a reclamation bill in accordance with the recommendations. By far the most effective of the senators in drafting and pushing the bill, which became known by his name, was Newlands. The draft of the bill was worked over by me and others at several conferences and revised in important particulars; my active interference was necessary to prevent it from being made unworkable by an undue insistence upon States' rights, in accordance with the efforts of Mr. Mondell and other congressmen, who consistently fought for local and private interests as against the interests of the people as a whole.

On June 17, 1902, the Reclamation Act was passed. It set aside the proceeds of the disposal of public lands for the purpose of reclaiming the waste areas of the arid West by irrigating lands otherwise worthless, and thus creating new homes upon the land. The money so appropriated was to be repaid to the government by the settlers, and to be used again as a revolving fund continuously available for the work.

The impatience of the Western people to see immediate

results from the Reclamation Act was so great that red tape was disregarded, and the work was pushed forward at a rate previously unknown in government affairs. Later, as in almost all such cases, there followed the criticisms of alleged illegality and haste which are so easy to make after results have been accomplished and the need for the measures without which nothing could have been done has gone by. These criticisms were in character precisely the same as that made about the acquisition of Panama, the settlement of the anthracite-coal strike, the suits against the big trusts, the stopping of the panic of 1907 by the action of the Executive concerning the Tennessee Coal and Iron Company; and, in short, about most of the best work done during my administration.

With the reclamation work, as with much other work under me, the men in charge were given to understand that they must get into the water if they would learn to swim; and, furthermore, they learned to know that if they acted honestly, and boldly and fearlessly accepted responsibility, I would stand by them to the limit. In this, as in every other case, in the end the boldness of the action fully justified itself.

Every item of the whole great plan of reclamation now in effect was undertaken between 1902 and 1906. By the spring of 1909 the work was an assured success, and the government had become fully committed to its continuance. The work of reclamation was at first under the United States Geological Survey, of which Charles D. Walcott was at that time director. In the spring of 1908 the United States Reclamation Service was established to carry it on, under the direction of Frederick Hayes Newell, to whom the inception of the plan was due. Newell's single-minded devotion to this great task, the constructive imagination which enabled him to conceive it, and the executive power and high character through which he and his assistant, Arthur P. Davis, built up a model service—all these have made him a model servant. The final proof of his merit is supplied by the character and records of the men who later assailed him.

Although the gross expenditure under the Reclamation Act is not yet as large as that for the Panama Canal, the engineering obstacles to be overcome have been almost as great, and the political impediments many times greater. The reclamation work had to be carried on at widely separated points, remote from railroads, under the most difficult pioneer conditions. The twenty-eight projects begun in the years 1902 to 1906 contemplated the irrigation of more than three million acres and the watering of more than thirty thousand farms. Many of the dams required for this huge task are higher than any previously built anywhere in the world. They feed main-line canals over seven thousand miles in total length, and involve minor constructions, such as culverts and bridges, tens of thousands in number.

What the Reclamation Act has done for the country is by no means limited to its material accomplishment. This act and the results flowing from it have helped powerfully to prove to the nation that it can handle its own resources and exercise direct and businesslike control over them. The population which the Reclamation Act has brought into the arid West, while comparatively small when compared with that in the more closely inhabited East, has been a most effective contribution to the national life, for it has gone far to transform the social aspect of the West, making for the stability of the institutions upon which the welfare of the whole country rests: it has substituted actual home-makers, who have settled on the land with their families, for huge, migratory bands of sheep herded by the hired shepherds of absentee owners. . . .

FORESTRY

. . . When I became President, the Bureau of Forestry (since 1905 the United States Forest Service) was a small but growing organization, under Gifford Pinchot, occupied mainly with laying the foundation of American forestry by scientific study of the forests, and with the promotion of forestry on private lands. It contained all the trained foresters in the government service, but had charge of no public timber-land whatsoever. The government forest reserves of that day were in the care of a division in the General Land Office, under the management of clerks wholly without knowledge of forestry, few if any of whom had ever seen a foot of the timber-lands for which they were responsible. Thus the reserves were neither well protected nor well used. There were no foresters among the men who had charge of the national forests, and no government forests in charge of the government foresters.

In my first message to Congress I strongly recommended the consolidation of the forest work in the hands of the trained men of the Bureau of Forestry. This recommendation was repeated in other messages, but Congress did not give effect to it until three years later. In the meantime, by thorough study of the Western public timber-lands, the groundwork was laid for the responsibilities which were to fall upon the Bureau of Forestry when the care of the national forests came to be transferred to it. It was evident that trained American foresters would be needed in considerable numbers, and a forest school was established at Yale to supply them.

In 1901, at my suggestion as President, the secretary of the interior, Mr. Hitchcock, made a formal request for technical advice from the Bureau of Forestry in handling the national forests, and an extensive examination of their condition and needs was accordingly taken up. The same year a study was begun of the proposed Appalachian national forest, the plan of which, already formulated at that time, has since been carried out. A year later experimental planting on the national forests was also begun, and studies preparatory to the application of practical forestry to the Indian reservations were undertaken. In 1903, so rapidly did the public work of the Bureau of Forestry increase, that the examination of land for new forest reserves was added to the study of those already created, the forest-lands of the various States were studied, and co-operation with several of them in the examination and handling of their forest-lands was undertaken. While these practical tasks were pushed forward, a technical knowledge of American forests was rapidly accumulated. The special knowledge gained was made public in printed bulletins; and at the same time the bureau undertook, through the newspaper and periodical press, to make all the people of the United States acquainted with the needs and the purposes of practical forestry. It is doubtful whether there has ever been elsewhere under the government such effective publicity—publicity purely in the interest of the people—at so low a cost. Before the educational work of the forest service was stopped by the Taft administration, it was securing the publication of facts about forestry in fifty million copies of newspapers a month at a total expense of six thousand dollars a year. Not one cent has ever been paid by the forest service to any publication of any kind for the printing of this material. It was given out freely, and published without cost because it was news. Without this publicity the forest service could not have survived the attacks made upon it by the representatives of the great special interests in Congress; nor could forestry in America have made the rapid progress it has.

The result of all the work outlined above was to bring together in the Bureau of Forestry, by the end of 1904, the only body of forest experts under the government, and practically all of the first-hand information about the public forests which was then in existence. In 1905, the obvious foolishness of continuing to separate the foresters and the forests, reinforced by the action of the First National Forest Congress, held in Washington, brought about the Act of February 1, 1905, which transferred the national forests from the care of the Interior Department to the Department of Agriculture, and resulted in the creation of the present United States Forest Service.

The men upon whom the responsibility of handling some sixty million acres of national forest-lands was thus thrown were ready for the work, both in the office and in the field, because they had been preparing for it for more than five years. Without delay they proceeded, under the leadership of Pinchot, to apply to the new work the principles they had already formulated. One of these was to open all the resources of the national forests to regulated use. Another was that of putting every part of the land to that use in which it would best serve the public. Following this principle, the Act of June 11, 1906, was drawn, and its passage was secured from Congress. This law throws open to settlement all land in the national forests that is found, on examination, to be chiefly valuable for agriculture. Hitherto all such land had been closed to the settler.

The principles thus formulated and applied may be summed up in the statement that the rights of the public to the natural resources outweigh private rights, and must be given its first consideration. Until that time, in dealing with the national forests, and the public lands generally, private rights had almost uniformly been allowed to overbalance public rights. The change we made was right, and was vitally necessary; but, of course, it created bitter opposition from private interests.

One of the principles whose application was the source of much hostility was this: It is better for the government to help a poor man to make a living for his family than to help a rich man make more profit for his company. This principle was too sound to be fought openly. It is the kind of principle to which politicians delight to pay unctuous homage in words. But we translated the words into deeds; and when they found that this was the case, many rich men, especially sheep-owners, were stirred to hostility, and they used the congressmen they controlled to assault us—getting most aid from certain demagogues, who were equally glad improperly to denounce rich men in public and improperly to serve them in private. The forest service established and enforced regulations which favored the settler as against the large stock-owner; required that necessary reductions in the stock grazed on any national forest should bear first on the big man, before the few head of the small man, upon which the living of his family depended, were reduced; and made grazing in the national forests a help, instead of a hindrance, to permanent settlement. As a result, the small settlers and their families became, on the whole, the best friends the forest service has; although in places their ignorance was played on by demagogues to influence them against the policy that was primarily for their own interest.

Another principle which led to the bitterest antagonism of all was this—whoever (except a bona-fide settler) takes public property for private profit should pay for what he gets. In the effort to apply this principle, the forest service obtained a decision from the attorney-general that it was legal to make the men who grazed sheep and cattle on the national forests pay for what they got. Accordingly, in the summer of 1906, for the first time, such a charge was made; and, in the face of the bitterest opposition, it was collected. . . .

. . . The idea that the Executive is the steward of the public welfare was first formulated and given practical effect in the forest service by its law officer, George Woodruff. The laws were often insufficient, and it became well-nigh impossible to get them amended in the public interest when once the representatives of privilege in Congress grasped the fact that I would sign no amendment that contained anything not in the public interest. It was necessary to use what law was already in existence, and then further to supplement it by Executive action. The practice of examining every claim to public land before passing it into private ownership offers a good example of the policy in question. This practice, which has since become general, was first applied in the national forests. Enormous areas of valuable public timber-land were thereby saved from fraudulent acquisition; more than two hundred and fifty thousand acres were thus saved in a single case.

This theory of stewardship in the interest of the public was well illustrated by the establishment of a water-power policy. Until the forest service changed the plan, water-powers on the navigable streams, on the public domain, and in the national forests were given away for nothing, and substantially without question, to whoever asked for them. At last, under the principle that public property should be paid for and should not be permanently granted away when such permanent grant is avoidable, the forest service established the policy of regulating the use of power in the national forests in the public interest and making a charge for value received. This was the beginning of the water-power policy now substantially accepted by the public, and doubtless soon to be enacted into law. But there was at the outset violent opposition to it on the part of the water-power companies, and such representatives of their views in Congress as Messrs. Tawney and Bede.

Many bills were introduced in Congress aimed, in one way or another, at relieving the power companies of control and payment. When these bills reached me I refused to sign them; and the injury to the public interest which would follow their passage was brought sharply to public attention in my message of February 26, 1908. The bills made no further progress.

Under the same principle of stewardship, railroads, and other corporations, which applied for and were given rights in the national forests, were regulated in the use of those rights. In short, the public resources in charge of the forest service were handled frankly and openly for the public welfare under the clear-cut and clearly set forth principle that the public rights come first and private interest second.

The natural result of this new attitude was the assertion in every form by the representatives of special interests that the forest service was exceeding its legal powers and thwarting the intention of Congress. Suits were begun wherever the chance arose. It is worth recording that, in spite of the novelty and complexity of the legal questions it had to face, no court of last resort has ever decided against the forest service. This statement includes two unanimous decisions by the Supreme Court of the United States (U. S. *vs.* Grimaud, 220 U. S., 506, and Light *vs.* U. S., 220 U. S., 523).

In its administration of the national forests, the forest service found that valuable coal-lands were in danger of passing into private ownership without adequate money return to the government and without safeguard against monopoly; and that existing legislation was insufficient to prevent this. When this condition was brought to my attention I withdrew from all forms of entry about sixty-eight million acres of coal-land in the United States, including Alaska. The refusal of Congress to act in the public interest was solely responsible for keeping these lands from entry.

CONSERVATION

The conservation movement was a direct outgrowth of the forest movement. It was nothing more than the application to our other natural resources of the principles which had been worked out in connection with the forests. Without the basis of public sentiment which had been built up for the protection of the forests, and without the example of public foresight in the protection of this, one of the great natural resources, the conservation movement would have been impossible. The first formal step was the creation of the Inland Waterways Commission, appointed on March 14, 1907. In my letter appointing the commission, I called attention to the value of our streams as great natural resources, and to the need for a progressive plan for their development and control, and said: "It is not possible to properly frame so large a plan as this for the control of our rivers without taking account of the orderly development of other natural resources. Therefore I ask that the Inland Waterways Commission shall consider the relations of the streams to the use of all the great permanent natural resources and their conservation for the making and maintenance of prosperous homes."

Over a year later, writing on the report of the commission, I said:

"The preliminary report of the Inland Waterways Commission was excellent in every way. It outlines a general plan of waterway improvement which when adopted will give assurance that the improvements will yield practical results in the way of increased navigation and water transportation. In every essential feature the plan recommended by the commission is new. In the principle of co-ordinating all uses of the waters and treating each waterway system as a unit; in the principle of correlating water traffic with rail and other land traffic; in the principle of expert initiation of projects in accordance with commercial foresight and the needs of a growing country; and in the principle of co-operation between the States and the Federal Government in the administration and use of waterways, etc.; the general plan proposed by the commission is new, and at the same time sane and simple. The plan deserves unqualified support. I regret that it has not yet been adopted by Congress, but I am confident that ultimately it will be adopted."

The most striking incident in the history of the commission was the trip down the Mississippi River in October, 1907, when, as President of the United States, I was the chief guest. This excursion, with the meetings which were held and the wide public attention it attracted, gave the development of our inland waterways a new standing in public estimation. During the trip a letter was prepared and presented to me asking me to summon a conference on the conservation of natural resources. My intention to call such a conference was publicly announced at a great meeting at Memphis, Tenn.

In the November following I wrote to each of the governors of the several States and to the presidents of various important national societies concerned with natural resources, inviting them to attend the conference, which took place May 13 to 15, 1908, in the East Room of the White House. It is doubtful whether, except in time of war, any new idea of like importance has ever been presented to a nation and accepted by it with such effectiveness and rapidity, as was the case with this conservation movement when it was introduced to the American people by the conference of governors. The first result was the unanimous declaration of the governors of all the States and Territories upon the subject of conservation, a document which ought to be hung in every schoolhouse throughout the land. A further result was the appointment of thirty-six State conservation commissions and, on June 8, 1908, of the National Conservation Commission. The task of this commission was to prepare an inventory, the first ever made for any nation, of all the natural resources which underlay its property. The making of this inventory was made possible by an Executive order which placed the resources of the government departments at the command of the commission, and made possible the organization of subsidiary committees by which the actual facts for the inventory were prepared and digested. Gifford Pinchot was made chairman of the commission.

The report of the National Conservation Commission was not only the first inventory of our resources, but was unique in the history of government in the amount and variety of information brought together. It was completed in six months. It laid squarely before the American people the essential facts regarding our natural resources, when facts were greatly needed as the basis for constructive action. This report was presented to the Joint Conservation Congress in December, at which there were present governors of twenty States, representatives of twenty-two State conservation commissions, and representatives of sixty national organizations previously represented at the White House conference. The report was unanimously approved, and transmitted to me, January 11, 1909. On January 22, 1909, I transmitted the report of the National Conservation Commission to Congress with a special message, in which it was accurately described as "one of the most fundamentally important documents ever laid before the American people." . . .

. . . Among the most difficult topics considered by the Public Lands Commission was that of the mineral-land laws. This subject was referred by the commission to the American Institute of Mining Engineers, which reported upon it through a committee. This committee made the very important recommendation, among others, "that the government of the United States should retain title to all minerals, including coal and oil, in the lands of unceded territory, and lease the same to individuals or corporations at a fixed rental." The necessity for this action has since come to be very generally recognized. Another recommendation, since partly carried into effect, was for the separation of the surface and the minerals in lands containing coal and oil.

Our land laws have of recent years proved inefficient; yet the land laws themselves have not been so much to blame as the lax, unintelligent, and often corrupt administration of these laws. The appointment on March 4, 1907, of James R. Garfield as secretary of the interior led to a new era in the interpretation and enforcement of the laws governing the public lands. His administration of the Interior Department was beyond comparison the best we have ever had. It was based primarily on the conception that it is as much the duty of public-land officials to help the honest settler get title to his claim as it is to prevent the looting of the public lands. The essential fact about public-land frauds is not merely that public property is stolen, but that every claim fraudulently acquired stands in the way of the making of a home or a livelihood by an honest man.

As the study of the public-land laws proceeded and their administration improved, a public-land policy was formulated in which the saving of the resources on the public domain for public use became the leading principle. There followed the withdrawal of coal-lands as already described, of oil-lands and phosphate-lands, and finally, just at the end of the Administration, of water-power sites on the public domain. These withdrawals were made by the Executive in order to afford to

Congress the necessary opportunity to pass wise laws dealing with their use and disposal; and the great crooked special interests fought them with incredible bitterness.

COMMISSION ON COUNTRY LIFE

. . . After long discussion a plan for a country-life commission was laid before me and approved. The appointment of the commission followed in August, 1908. In the letter of appointment the reasons for creating the commission were set forth as follows: "I doubt if any other nation can bear comparison with our own in the amount of attention given by the government, both Federal and State, to agricultural matters. But practically the whole of this effort has hitherto been directed toward increasing the production of crops. Our attention has been concentrated almost exclusively on getting better farming. In the beginning this was unquestionably the right thing to do. The farmer must first of all grow good crops in order to support himself and his family. But when this has been secured, the effort for better farming should cease to stand alone, and should be accompanied by the effort for better business and better living on the farm. It is at least important that the farmer should get the largest possible return in money, comfort, and social advantages from the crops he grows, as that he should get the largest possible return in crops from the land he farms. Agriculture is not the whole of country life. The great rural interests are human interests, and good crops are of little value to the farmer unless they open the door to a good kind of life on the farm."

The commission on country life did work of capital importance. By means of a widely circulated set of questions the commission informed itself upon the status of country life throughout the nation. Its trip through the East, South, and West brought it into contact with large numbers of practical farmers and their wives, secured for the commissioners a most valuable body of first-hand information, and laid the foundation for the remarkable awakening of interest in country life which has since taken place throughout the nation. . . .

BUREAU OF CORPORATIONS

. . . The work of the Bureau of Corporations, under Herbert Knox Smith, formed an important part of the conservation movement almost from the beginning. Mr. Smith was a member of the Inland Waterways Commission and of the National Conservation Commission and his bureau prepared material of importance for the reports of both. The investigation of standing timber in the United States by the Bureau of Corporations furnished for the first time a positive knowledge of the facts. Over nine hundred counties in timbered regions were covered by the bureau, and the work took five years. The most important facts ascertained were that forty years ago three-fourths of the standing timber in the United States was publicly owned, while at the date of the report four-fifths of the timber in the country was in private hands. The concentration of private ownership had developed to such an amazing extent that about two hundred holders owned nearly one-half of all privately owned timber in the United States; and of this the three greatest holders, the Southern Pacific Railway, the Northern Pacific Railway, and the Weyerhaeuser Timber Company, held over ten per cent. Of this work, Mr. Smith says:

"It was important, indeed, to know the facts so that we could take proper action toward saving the timber still left to the public. But of far more importance was the light that this history (and the history of our other resources) throws on the basic attitude, tradition and governmental beliefs of the American people. The whole standpoint of the people toward the proper aim of government, toward the relation of property to the citizen, and the relation of property to the government, were brought out first by this conservation work."

The work of the Bureau of Corporations as to water-power was equally striking. In addition to bringing the concentration of water-power control first prominently to public attention, through material furnished for my message in my veto of the James River dam bill, the work of the bureau showed that ten great interests and their allies held nearly sixty per cent of the developed water-power of the United States. Says Commissioner Smith: "Perhaps the most important thing in the whole work was its clear demonstration of the fact that the only effective place to control water-power in the public interest is at the power sites; that as to powers now owned by the public it is absolutely essential that the public shall retain title. . . . The only way in which the public can get back to itself the margin of natural advantage in the water-power site is to rent that site at a rental which, added to the cost of power production there, will make the total cost of water-power about the same as fuel-power, and then let the two sell at the same price, *i. e.*, the price of fuel-power.". . .

BEAUTY AND NATIONAL PARKS

. . . The things accomplished that have been enumerated above were of immediate consequence to the economic well-being of our people. In addition certain things were done of which the economic bearing was more remote, but which bore directly upon our welfare, because they add to the beauty of living and therefore to the joy of life. Securing a great artist, Saint-Gaudens, to give us the most beautiful coinage since the decay of Hellenistic Greece was one such act. In this case I had power myself to direct the Mint to employ Saint-Gaudens. The first, and most beautiful, of his coins were issued in thousands before Congress assembled or could intervene; and a great and permanent improvement was made in the beauty of the coinage. In the same way, on the advice and suggestion of Frank Millet, we got some really capital medals by sculptors of the first rank. Similarly, the new buildings in Washington were erected and placed in proper relation to one another, on plans provided by the best architects and landscape-architects. I also appointed a Fine Arts Council, an unpaid body of the best architects, painters, and sculptors in the country, to advise the government as to the erection and decoration of all new buildings. The "pork-barrel" senators and congressmen felt for this body an instinctive, and perhaps from their standpoint a natural, hostility; and my successor a couple of months after taking office revoked the appointment and disbanded the council.

Even more important was the taking of steps to preserve from destruction beautiful and wonderful wild creatures whose existence was threatened by greed and wantonness. During the seven and a half years closing on March 4, 1909, more was accomplished for the protection of wild life in the United States than during all the previous years, excepting only the creation of the Yellowstone National Park. The record includes the creation of five national parks—Crater Lake, Oregon; Wind Cave, South Dakota; Platt, Oklahoma; Sully Hill, North Dakota, and Mesa Verde, Colorado; four big-game refuges in Oklahoma, Arizona, Montana, and Washington; fifty-one bird reservations; and the enactment of laws for the protection of wild life in Alaska, the District of Columbia, and on national bird reserves. . . .

VII • TOWARD THE WELFARE STATE

Organized Labor

23. • TENEMENT WORKSHOPS

Roosevelt's youthful attachment to laissez-faire and uncritical acceptance of the survival-of-the-fittest theory made him somewhat slower to respond to the needs of labor than to the movement for good government. Yet, as this moving account of his first contact with labor as a freshman state legislator in 1882 indicates, his basic decency and instinct for fairness gradually impelled him to take an active and constructive interest in labor's problems.

. . . In the America of that day, and especially among the people whom I knew, the successful business man was regarded by everybody as pre-eminently *the* good citizen. The orthodox books on political economy, not only in America but in England, were written for his especial glorification. The tangible rewards came to him, the admiration of his fellow citizens of the respectable type was apt to be his, and the severe newspaper moralists who were never tired of denouncing politicians and political methods were wont to hold up "business methods" as the ideal which we were to strive to introduce into political life. Herbert Croly, in "The Promise of American Life," has set forth the reasons why our individualistic democracy—which taught that each man was to rely exclusively on himself, was in no way to be interfered with by

Autobiography, pp. 77–82.

others, and was to devote himself to his own personal welfare —necessarily produced the type of business man who sincerely believed, as did the rest of the community, that the individual who amassed a big fortune was the man who was the best and most typical American.

In the legislature the problems with which I dealt were mainly problems of honesty and decency and of legislative and administrative efficiency. They represented the effort, the wise, the vitally necessary effort, to get efficient and honest government. But as yet I understood little of the effort which was already beginning, for the most part under very bad leadership, to secure a more genuine social and industrial justice. Nor was I especially to blame for this. The good citizens I then knew best, even when themselves men of limited means— men like my colleague Billy O'Neill, and my backwoods friends Sewall and Dow—were no more awake than I was to the changing needs the changing times were bringing. Their outlook was as narrow as my own, and, within its limits, as fundamentally sound.

I wish to dwell on the soundness of our outlook on life, even though as yet it was not broad enough. We were no respecters of persons. Where our vision was developed to a degree that enabled us to see crookedness, we opposed it whether in great or small. As a matter of fact, we found that it needed much more courage to stand up *openly* against labor men when they were wrong than against capitalists when they were wrong. The sins against labor are usually committed, and the improper services to capitalists are usually rendered, behind closed doors. Very often the man with the moral courage to speak in the open against labor when it is wrong is the only man anxious to do effective work for labor when labor is right.

The only kinds of courage and honesty which are permanently useful to good institutions anywhere are those shown by men who decide all cases with impartial justice on grounds of conduct and not on grounds of class. We found that in the long run the men who in public blatantly insisted that labor was never wrong were the very men who in private could not be trusted to stand for labor when it was right. We grew heartily to distrust the reformer who never denounced wickedness unless it was embodied in a rich man. Human nature does not change; and that type of "reformer" is as noxious now as he ever was. The loud-mouthed upholder of popular rights who attacks wickedness only when it is allied with wealth, and who never publicly assails any misdeed, no matter how flagrant, if committed nominally in the interest of labor, has either a warped mind or a tainted soul, and should be trusted by no honest man. It was largely the indignant and contemptuous dislike aroused in our minds by the demagogues of this class which then prevented those of us whose instincts at bottom were sound from going as far as we ought to have gone along the lines of governmental control of corporations and governmental interference on behalf of labor.

I did, however, have one exceedingly useful experience. A bill was introduced by the Cigarmakers' Union to prohibit the manufacture of cigars in tenement-houses. I was appointed one of a committee of three to investigate conditions in the tenement-houses and see if legislation should be had. Of my two colleagues on the committee, one took no interest in the measure and privately said he did not think it was right, but that he had to vote for it because the labor-unions were strong in his district and he was pledged to support the bill. The other, a sporting Tammany man who afterward abandoned politics for the race-track, was a very good fellow. He told me frankly that he had to be against the bill because certain interests which were all-powerful and with which he had dealings required him to be against it, but that I was a free agent, and that if I would look into the matter he believed I would favor the legislation. As a matter of fact, I had supposed I would be against the legislation, and I rather think that I was put on the committee with that idea, for the respectable people I knew were against it; it was contrary to the principles of political economy of the *laissez-faire* kind; and the business men who spoke to me about it shook their heads and said that it was designed to prevent a man doing as he wished and as he had a right to do with what was his own.

However, my first visits to the tenement-house districts in question made me feel that, whatever the theories might be, as a matter of practical common sense I could not conscientiously vote for the continuance of the conditions which I saw. These conditions rendered it impossible for the families of the tenement-house workers to live so that the children might grow up fitted for the exacting duties of American citizenship. I visited the tenement-houses once with my colleagues of the committee, once with some of the labor-union representatives, and once or twice by myself. In a few of the tenement-houses there were suites of rooms ample in number where the work on the tobacco was done in rooms not occupied for cooking or sleeping or living. In the overwhelming majority of cases, however, there were one, two, or three room apartments, and the work of manufacturing the tobacco by men, women, and children went on day and night in the eating, living, and sleeping rooms—sometimes in one room. I have always remembered one room in which two families were living. On my inquiry as to who the third adult male was I was told that he was a boarder with one of the families. There were several children, three men, and two women in this room. The tobacco was stowed about everywhere, alongside the foul bedding, and in a corner where there were scraps of food. The men, women, and children in this room worked by day and far on into the evening, and they slept and ate there. They were Bohemians, unable to speak English, except that one of the children knew enough to act as interpreter.

Instead of opposing the bill I ardently championed it. It was a poorly drawn measure, and the governor, Grover Cleveland, was at first doubtful about signing it. The Cigarmakers' Union then asked me to appear before the governor and argue for it. I accordingly did so, acting as spokesman for the battered, undersized foreigners who represented the Union and the workers. The governor signed the bill. Afterward this tenement-house cigar legislation was declared invalid by the court of appeals in the Jacobs decision. Jacobs was one of the rare tenement-house manufacturers of cigars who occupied quite a suite of rooms, so that in his case the living conditions were altogether exceptional. What the reason was which influenced those bringing the suit to select the exceptional instead of the average worker I do not know; of course such action was precisely the action which those most interested in having the law broken down were anxious to see taken. The court of appeals declared the law unconstitutional, and in their decision the judges reprobated the law as an assault upon the "hallowed" influences of "home." It was this case which first waked me to a dim and partial understanding of the fact that the courts were not necessarily the best judges of what should be done to better social and industrial conditions. The judges who rendered this decision were well-meaning men. They knew nothing whatever of tenement-house conditions; they knew nothing whatever of the needs, or of the life and labor, of three-fourths of their fellow citizens in great cities. They knew legalism, but not life. Their choice of the words "hallowed" and "home," as applicable to the revolting conditions attending the manufacture of cigars in tenement-houses, showed that they had no idea what it was that they were deciding. Imagine the "hallowed" associations of a "home" consisting of one room where two families, one of them with a boarder, live, eat, and work! This decision completely blocked tenement-house reform legislation in New York for a score of years, and hampers it to this day. It was one of the most serious setbacks which the cause of industrial and social progress and reform ever received.

I had been brought up to hold the courts in especial reverence. The people with whom I was most intimate were apt to praise the courts for just such decisions as this, and to speak of them as bulwarks against disorder and barriers against demagogic legislation. These were the same people with whom the judges who rendered these decisions were apt to foregather at social clubs, or dinners, or in private life. Very naturally they all tended to look at things from the same standpoint. Of course it took more than one experience such as this Tenement Cigar Case to shake me out of the attitude in which I was brought up. But various decisions, not only of the New York court but of certain other State courts and even of the United States Supreme Court, during the quarter of a century following the passage of this tenement-house legislation, did at last thoroughly wake me to the actual fact. I grew to realize that all that Abraham Lincoln had said about the Dred Scott decision could be said with equal truth and justice about the numerous decisions which in our own day were erected as bars across the path of social reform, and which brought to naught so much of the effort to secure justice and fair dealing for working men and working women, and for plain citizens generally.

24. · THE CASE FOR UNIONS

The great anthracite coal strike of 1902 proved a watershed in Roosevelt's labor thought. It made him realize that the conditions he had observed in New York's tenements in the 1880's were more general than unique; that relations between employers and employees were worse than he had believed; that property rights

Autobiography, pp. 461–63, 470–72.

were too often put above human rights; and that labor unions offered the workingman more hope of betterment, even, than individual effort. The following selection from his autobiography briefly treats all four of these concepts.

By the time I became President I had grown to feel with deep intensity of conviction that governmental agencies must find their justification largely in the way in which they are used for the practical betterment of living and working conditions among the mass of the people. I felt that the fight was really for the abolition of privilege; and one of the first stages in the battle was necessarily to fight for the rights of the working man. For this reason I felt most strongly that all that the government could do in the interest of labor should be done. The Federal Government can rarely act with the directness that the State governments act. It can, however, do a good deal. My purpose was to make the National Government itself a model employer of labor, the effort being to make the per diem employee just as much as the Cabinet officer regard himself as one of the partners employed in the service of the public, proud of his work, eager to do it in the best possible manner, and confident of just treatment. Our aim was also to secure good laws wherever the National Government had power, notably in the Territories, in the District of Columbia, and in connection with interstate commerce. I found the eight-hour law a mere farce, the departments rarely enforcing it with any degree of efficiency. This I remedied by executive action. Unfortunately, thoroughly efficient government servants often proved to be the prime offenders so far as the enforcement of the eight-hour law was concerned, because in their zeal to get good work done for the government they became harsh taskmasters, and declined to consider the needs of their fellow employees who served under them. The more I had studied the subject the more strongly I had become convinced that an eight-hour day under the conditions of labor in the United States was all that could, with wisdom and propriety, be required either by the government or by private employers; that more than this meant, on the average, a decrease in the qualities that tell for good citizenship. I finally solved the problem, as far as government employees were concerned, by calling in Charles P. Neill, the head of the Labor Bureau; and, acting on his advice, I speedily made the eight-hour law really effective. Any man who shirked his work, who dawdled and idled, received no mercy; slackness is even worse than harshness; for exactly as in battle mercy to the coward is cruelty to the brave man, so in civil life slackness toward the vicious and idle is harshness toward the honest and hard-working.

We passed a good law protecting the lives and health of miners in the Territories, and other laws providing for the supervision of employment agencies in the District of Columbia, and protecting the health of motormen and conductors on street-railways in the District. We practically started the Bureau of Mines. We provided for safeguarding factory employees in the District against accidents, and for the restriction of child labor therein. We passed a workmen's compensation law for the protection of government employees; a law which did not go as far as I wished, but which was the best I could get, and which committed the government to the right policy. We provided for an investigation of woman and child labor in the United States. We incorporated the National Child-Labor Committee. Where we had most difficulty was with the railway companies engaged in interstate business. We passed an act improving safety appliances on railway-trains without much opposition, but we had more trouble with acts regulating the hours of labor of railway employees and making those railways which were engaged in interstate commerce liable for injuries to or the death of their employees while on duty. One important step in connection with these latter laws was taken by Attorney-General Moody when, on behalf of the government, he intervened in the case of a wronged employee. It is unjust that a law which has been declared public policy by the representatives of the people should be submitted to the possibility of nullification because the government leaves the enforcement of it to the private initiative of poor people who have just suffered some crushing accident. It should be the business of the government to enforce laws of this kind, and to appear in court to argue for their constitutionality and proper enforcement. Thanks to Moody, the government assumed this position. The first employers' liability law affecting interstate railroads was declared unconstitutional. We got through another, which stood the test of the courts. . . .

. . . The great anthracite strike of 1902 left an indelible impress upon the people of the United States. It showed clearly to all wise and far-seeing men that the labor problem in this country had entered upon a new phase. Industry had grown. Great financial corporations, doing a nation-wide and even a world-wide business, had taken the place of the smaller concerns of an earlier time. The old familiar, intimate relations between employer and employee were passing. A few generations before, the boss had known every man in his shop; he called his men Bill, Tom, Dick, John; he inquired after their wives and babies; he swapped jokes and stories and perhaps a bit of tobacco with them. In the small establishment there had been a friendly human relationship between employer and employee.

There was no such relation between the great railway magnates, who controlled the anthracite industry, and the one hundred and fifty thousand men who worked in their mines, or the half-million women and children who were dependent upon these miners for their daily bread. Very few of these mine-workers had ever seen, for instance, the president of the Reading Railroad. Had they seen him many of them could not have spoken to him, for tens of thousands of the mine-workers were recent immigrants who did not understand the language which he spoke and who spoke a language which he could not understand.

Again, a few generations ago an American workman could have saved money, gone West and taken up a homestead. Now the free lands were gone. In earlier days a man who began with pick and shovel might have come to own a mine. That outlet too was now closed, as regards the immense majority, and few, if any, of the one hundred and fifty thousand mine-workers could ever aspire to enter the small circle of men who held in their grasp the great anthracite industry. The majority of the men who earned wages in the coal industry, if they wished to progress at all, were compelled to progress not by ceasing to be wage-earners, but by improving the conditions under which all the wage-earners in all the industries of the country lived and worked, as well, of course, as improving their own individual efficiency.

Another change which had come about as a result of the foregoing was a crass inequality in the bargaining relation between the employer and the individual employee standing alone. The great coal-mining and coal-carrying companies, which employed their tens of thousands, could easily dispense with the services of any particular miner. The miner, on the other hand, however expert, could not dispense with the companies. He needed a job; his wife and children would starve if he did not get one. What the miner had to sell—his labor—was a perishable commodity; the labor of to-day—if not sold to-day—was lost forever. Moreover, his labor was not like most commodities—a mere thing; it was part of a living, breathing human being. The workman saw, and all citizens who gave earnest thought to the matter saw, that the labor problem was not only an economic, but also a moral, a human problem. Individually the miners were impotent when they sought to enter a wage contract with the great companies; they could make fair terms only by uniting into trade-unions to bargain collectively. The men were forced to co-operate to secure not only their economic, but their simple human rights. They, like other workmen, were compelled by the very conditions under which they lived to unite in unions of their industry or trade, and these unions were bound to grow in size, in strength, and in power for good and evil as the industries in which the men were employed grew larger and larger.

A democracy can be such in fact only if there is some rough approximation to similarity in stature among the men composing it. One of us can deal in our private lives with the grocer or the butcher or the carpenter or the chicken-raiser, or if we are the grocer or carpenter or butcher or farmer, we can deal with our customers, because *we are all of about the same size.* Therefore a simple and poor society can exist as a democracy on a basis of sheer individualism. But a rich and complex industrial society cannot so exist; for some individuals, and especially those artificial individuals called corporations, become so very big that the ordinary individual is utterly dwarfed beside them, and cannot deal with them on terms of equality. It therefore becomes necessary for these ordinary individuals to combine in their turn, first in order to act in their collective capacity through that biggest of all combinations called the government, and second, to act, also in their own self-defense, through private combinations, such as farmers' associations and trade-unions.

This the great coal operators did not see. They did not see that their property rights, which they so stoutly defended, were of the same texture as were the human rights, which they so blindly and hotly denied. They did not see that the power which they exercised by representing their stockholders was of the same texture as the power which the union leaders demanded of representing the workmen, who had democratically elected them. They did not see that the right to use one's property as one will can be maintained only so long as it is consistent with the maintenance of certain fundamental human rights, of the rights to life, liberty, and the pursuit of happiness. . . .

25. · FEDERAL ARBITRATION OF LABOR DISPUTES

Roosevelt's intervention in the anthracite strike of 1902 also convinced him that the public's stake in industrial disputes was so critical that a federal arbitration commission should be established. Although he did not demand that the commission's findings be made legally binding, he did argue persuasively that by forcing negotiation it would almost certainly reduce the incidence of costly strikes.

The commission appointed by the President October 16, 1902, at the request of both the anthracite-coal operators and miners, to inquire into, consider, and pass upon the questions in controversy in connection with the strike in the anthracite regions of Pennsylvania and the causes out of which the controversy arose, in their report, findings, and award expressed the belief "that the State and Federal governments should provide the machinery for what may be called the compulsory investigation of controversies between employers and employees when they arise." This expression of belief is deserving of the favorable consideration of the Congress and the enactment of its provisions into law. A bill has already been introduced to this end.

Records show that during the twenty years from January 1, 1881, to December 31, 1900, there were strikes affecting 117,509 establishments, and 6,105,694 employees were thrown

From the Annual Message to Congress, 1906. *Messages and Papers*, XI, 1194–95.

out of employment. During the same period there were 1,005 lockouts, involving nearly 10,000 establishments, throwing over one million people out of employment. These strikes and lockouts involved an estimated loss to employees of $307,000,000 and to employers of $143,000,000, a total of $450,000,000. The public suffered directly and indirectly probably as great additional loss. But the money loss, great as it was, did not measure the anguish and suffering endured by the wives and children of employees whose pay stopped when their work stopped, or the disastrous effect of the strike or lockout upon the business of employers, or the increase in the cost of products and the inconvenience and loss to the public.

Many of these strikes and lockouts would not have occurred had the parties to the dispute been required to appear before an unprejudiced body representing the nation and, face to face, state the reasons for their contention. In most instances the dispute would doubtless be found to be due to a misunderstanding by each of the other's rights, aggravated by an unwillingness of either party to accept as true the statements of the other as to the justice or injustice of the matters in dispute. The exercise of a judicial spirit by a disinterested body representing the Federal Government, such as would be provided by a commission on conciliation and arbitration, would tend to create an atmosphere of friendliness and conciliation between contending parties; and the giving each side an equal opportunity to present fully its case in the presence of the other would prevent many disputes from developing into serious strikes or lockouts, and, in other cases, would enable the commission to persuade the opposing parties to come to terms.

In this age of great corporate and labor combinations, neither employers nor employees should be left completely at the mercy of the stronger party to a dispute, regardless of the righteousness of their respective claims. The proposed measure would be in the line of securing recognition of the fact that in many strikes the public has itself an interest which cannot wisely be disregarded; an interest not merely of general convenience, for the question of a just and proper public policy must also be considered. In all legislation of this kind it is well to advance cautiously, testing each step by the actual results; the step proposed can surely be safely taken, for the decisions of the commission would not bind the parties in legal fashion, and yet would give a chance for public opinion to crystallize and thus to exert its full force for the right.

26. · THE CASE FOR COLLECTIVE BARGAINING

Although Theodore Roosevelt was more sympathetic to organized labor than any president before Franklin D. Roosevelt, neither the American Federation of Labor nor its leader, Samuel Gompers, trusted him completely. One reason for this was Roosevelt's failure to accept labor's program uncritically. He vehemently opposed the secondary boycott, and in spite of his repeated criticisms of the courts' abuse of the injunction, he refused to recommend its complete abolition. A second reason was labor's growing disenchantment with the tendency of the Congressional wing of the Republican party to serve as an adjunct of the National Association of Manufacturers. And a third, and probably most important, reason was Roosevelt's disposition to attack the malpractices of unions with the same force he attacked those of business. Nevertheless, as this and numerous other statements prove, Roosevelt understood the importance of unions as a countervailing force to big business and, accordingly, encouraged their growth.

One of the prime objects which the Progressives have in view in seeking to secure the highest governmental efficiency

Theodore Roosevelt, "Nationalism and the Working Man," *The Outlook*, XCVII (February 4, 1911), 253–56.

of both the National and the State Governments is to safeguard and guarantee the vital interests of the wage-workers. We believe in property rights; normally and in the long run property rights and human rights coincide; but where they are at variance we are for human rights first and for property rights second. Lincoln phrased it in one of his homely anecdotes when he said, "We are for both the man and the dollar; but if we must choose between them, we put the man above the dollar"; and in a more formal speech, when he said: "Labor is the superior of capital, and deserves much the higher consideration." . . .

. . . At the outset let me make clear one point. I have no sympathy with any limitation of efficiency, no sympathy with any provision which seeks to reduce the work of the high-grade man to the level of the low-grade man. The very fact that I so emphatically believe in the high dignity of manual labor, and desire to do all in my power to raise its position as compared with merely mental labor, gives the reason why I feel we should welcome high skill in manual labor, extreme efficiency therein, just as we recognize skill and efficiency in any form of mental labor. Unless there is pride in efficiency in any line of work that work will never stand high in the popular estimation. If all that a man desires is to get through his job with the minimum of effort and skill on his part, then he will never have, because he will never deserve, the respect of his fellows. . . .

. . . In order to raise the status, not of the exceptional people, but of the great mass of those who work with their hands under modern industrial conditions, it is imperative that there should be more than merely individual action. The old plea that collective action by all the people through the State, or by some of them through a union or other association, is necessarily hostile to individual growth has been demonstrated to be false. On the contrary, in the world of labor as in the world of business, the advent of the giant corporation and the very wealthy employer has meant that the absence of all governmental supervision implies the emergence of a very few exceptionally powerful men at the head and the stamping out of all individual initiative and power lower down. Unrestricted individualism in violence during the dark ages merely produced a class of brutal and competent individual fighters at the top, resting on a broad foundation of abject serfs below. Unrestricted individualism in the modern industrial world produces results very little better, and in the end means the complete atrophy of all power of real individual initiative, real individual capacity for self-help, in the great mass of the workers.

There must, therefore, be collective action. This need of collective action is in part supplied by the unions, which, although they have on certain points been guilty of grave shortcomings, have nevertheless on the whole rendered inestimable service to the working man. In addition, there must be collective action through the government, the agent of all of us.

Probably the chief obstacle in the way of taking such wise collective action lies in the mental attitude of those who still adhere to the doctrinaire theory of eighteenth-century individualism, and treat as a cardinal virtue the right to absolute liberty of contract—and of course, carried out logically, the theory of absolute liberty of contract simply means the legalization of all kinds of slavery. It is essential that the nation and the State should be able to forbid the exercise of that kind of pseudoliberty which means the abridgment of real liberty. There has been a steady growth in these matters, and views which a century ago the courts accepted as almost axiomatic are now upset in decision after decision. The Supreme Court of the United States on January 3 last stated the case as regards liberty of contract as follows: "There is no such thing as absolute freedom of contract. The power of government extends to the denial of liberty of contract to the extent of forbidding or regulating every contract which is reasonably calculated to injuriously affect the public interest." The decision goes on to state that the power of the United States is absolute as regards regulating commerce between the States. . . .

. . . Wages and other most important conditions of employment must remain largely outside of governmental control and be left for adjustment by free contract between employer and employee, with the important proviso that there should be legislation to prevent the conditions that compel men and women to accept wages that represent less than will insure a decent living. But the question of contract between employer and employee should not be left to individual action, for under modern industrial conditions the individual is often too weak to guard his own rights as against a strongly organized body or a great capitalist. In the present state of society, and until we advance much farther than at present along lines of genuine altruism, there must be effective and organized collective action by the wage-workers in great industrial enterprises. They must act jointly through the process of collective bargaining. Only thus can they be put upon a plane of economic equality with their corporate employers. Capital is organized, and the laborer can secure proper liberty and proper treatment only if labor organizes also. It is, I trust, unnecessary to say that the most emphatic recognition of this need does not mean any condonation of whatever is evil in the practices of labor organizations. Labor organizations are like other organizations, like organizations of capitalists; sometimes they act very well, and sometimes they act very badly. We should consistently favor them when they act well, and as fearlessly oppose them when they act badly. I wish to see labor organizations powerful; and the minute that any organization becomes powerful it becomes powerful for evil as well as for good; and when organized labor becomes sufficiently powerful the State will have to regulate the collective use of

labor just as it must regulate the collective use of capital.
Therefore the very success of the effort we are making to increase the power of labor means that among labor leaders and
among other citizens there must be increased vigilance and
courage in unhesitatingly rebuking anything that labor does
that is wrong.

Wages and Hours

27. · THE HOURS OF DRUG CLERKS

By the time Roosevelt became governor of New York in 1899
his belief in laissez-faire had largely given way to a kind of pos-
itivist empiricism. One evidence of this was a reversal of his attitude
toward government regulation of working hours. In this letter to
Jacob Riis, the Danish-born reformer and newspaperman whose
writings of slums markedly influenced Roosevelt, he expresses no
reservations about the state's power to regulate hours; his sole question is the efficacy of the bill at issue.

Albany, May 11, 1899
Dear Jake: I am very much puzzled over the Drug Clerks'
Shorter Hour bill. You and Seth Low[1] and Reynolds[2] are for

Letter to Jacob Riis, May 11, 1899. *The Letters,* II, 1010.
[1] Educator, civic leader, and Mayor of New York, 1902–1904 [Ed.].
[2] James Bronson Reynolds, lawyer, social worker, and civic reformer
[Ed.].

it and I have had some touching letters from drug clerks who want it enacted into law. On the other hand, I have received a larger number of protests also from drug clerks who insist that in its present state it would be a positive detriment to them and would knock out their day off, while the smaller east and west side druggists who keep but one clerk say it would mean absolute ruin, and claim that in their occupation the hours of the drug clerk have to be long for the same reason that the doctor's hours are long. The labor unions are pressing for the bill, but I think that this simply means that they go for anything that calls for shorter hours, and I was by no means impressed with the advocates of the bill who appeared here. What I am anxious to do is whatever will really benefit the druggist clerks in the smaller shops (those of the larger class are all right as it is), without working needless ruin upon the owners of the small shops. Is the separate bed room feature not a hardship?

I wish you would take the bill, of which I enclose a copy, and if you have the time, would go to some small druggists anywhere, it does not make any difference where, on the East Side, and find out if you can what some of the clerks and some of the small druggists really think about it, and what they believe its effects really would be.

28. · FOR A GENERAL EIGHT-HOUR DAY

As president, Roosevelt enforced with conviction the existing statute for an eight-hour day for federal employees. He also called

From the Annual Message to Congress, 1906. *Messages and Papers*, XI, 1193.

on Congress to extend the eight-hour day to railroad employees and to set in motion the forces that would make the eight-hour day almost universal in American industry. The following statement from his Annual Message of 1906 is typical of his numerous recommendations.

I call your attention to the need of passing the bill limiting the number of hours of employment of railroad employees. The measure is a very moderate one and I can conceive of no serious objection to it. Indeed, so far as it is in our power, it should be our aim steadily to reduce the number of hours of labor, with as a goal the general introduction of an eight-hour day. There are industries in which it is not possible that the hours of labor should be reduced; just as there are communities not far enough advanced for such a movement to be for their good, or, if in the tropics, so situated that there is no analogy between their needs and ours in this matter. On the Isthmus of Panama, for instance, the conditions are in every way so different from what they are here that an eight-hour day would be absurd; just as it is absurd, so far as the Isthmus is concerned, where white labor cannot be employed, to bother as to whether the necessary work is done by alien black men or by alien yellow men. But the wage-workers of the United States are of so high a grade that alike from the merely industrial standpoint and from the civic standpoint it should be our object to do what we can in the direction of securing the general observance of an eight-hour day. Until recently the eight-hour law on our Federal statute-books has been very scantily observed. Now, however, largely through the instrumentality of the Bureau of Labor, it is being rigidly enforced, and I shall speedily be able to say whether or not there is need of further legislation in reference thereto; for our purpose is to see it obeyed in spirit no less than in letter. Half-holidays during summer should be established for government employees; it is as desirable for wage-workers who toil with their hands as for salaried officials whose labor is mental that there should be a reasonable amount of holiday.

29. · THE ABOLITION OF CHILD LABOR

On no single issue was the hold of the manufacturing interests on Republican congressmen more evident than in their failure to support Roosevelt's modest recommendations, as given below, for the abolition of child labor in the District of Columbia. Characteristically, Roosevelt overcame his frustrations by appointing an investigatory commission whose findings helped prepare the way for national legislation during the Wilson administration.

The Congress at its last session wisely provided for a truant court for the District of Columbia; a marked step in advance on the path of properly caring for the children. Let me again urge that the Congress provide for a thorough investigation of the conditions of child labor and of the labor of women in the United States. More and more our people are growing to recognize the fact that the questions which are not merely of industrial but of social importance outweigh all others; and these two questions most emphatically come in the category of those which affect in the most far-reaching way the home life of the nation. The horrors incident to the employment of young children in factories or at work anywhere are a blot on

From the Annual Message to Congress, 1906. *Messages and Papers*, XI, 1194.

our civilization. It is true that each State must ultimately settle the question in its own way; but a thorough official investigation of the matter, with the results published broadcast, would greatly help toward arousing the public conscience and securing unity of State action in the matter. There is, however, one law on the subject which should be enacted immediately, because there is no need for an investigation in reference thereto, and the failure to enact it is discreditable to the National Government. A drastic and thoroughgoing child-labor law should be enacted for the District of Columbia and the Territories.

30. · "THE MINIMUM WAGE"

Roosevelt's basic assumptions about the labor movement were largely formed by 1907. Through the last two years of his presidency and especially during the Bull Moose Campaign of 1912, however, he continued to expand their application. In the selection printed below, first delivered as a speech at Spokane, Washington, on September 9, 1912, he defends a minimum wage law for women on the following grounds: (1) an inadequate wage is an inducement to crime and vice; (2) an exploitative society must sooner or later fall; and (3) the human needs of working men and women have precedence over the rights of property or capital.

Mr. [Woodrow] Wilson has distinctly stated in his speech of acceptance that he does not regard the Democratic platform as a programme. We Progressives are more fortunate. For we regard our platform as a very practical programme, and we

Theodore Roosevelt, "The Minimum Wage," *The Outlook,* CII (September 28, 1912), 159–160.

intend to put it into effect if the people give us the power. Mr. Wilson, while expressing general approval of the Progressive platform, has made specific mention only of those parts which he condemns. Among the things which he condemns is our minimum-wage plank.

As reported, he states that he opposes this plank because he thinks that employers, if such a law were enacted, would reduce the wages of all their employees to the minimum prescribed by law. Such a fear is so groundless that I do not believe it would be expressed by any man who has studied the conditions of life and work at first-hand among the workers. The objection is purely academic; it is formed in the schoolroom; it will not have any weight with men who know what life actually is. Those employers who now pay their lowest-paid employees a starvation wage prove by that very fact that they are paying to all their employees the very least that they can get them to take. They have already brought them down as far as possible; if it were possible for them to reduce the wages of their higher-paid employees, they would do so. It is a wholly needless apprehension that they have let any wages stay up by an oversight and would reduce them to a minimum only in case the minimum for the poorest paid were raised by law above the starvation point.

The minimum-wage plank is peculiarly in harmony with the general spirit of the Progressive platform. The portions of that platform dealing with social and industrial justice are meant especially to help the men and women who are wage-workers in industrial pursuits. The promises of the platform are specific and reasonable. They are promises which can be kept, and which will be kept if power is given to the Progressives. We stand, in the nation and in the several States, for the abolition of child labor; for the reduction of hours of labor for women in industry to eight a day; for workmen's compensation laws; for laws guarding the health of workers in factories, and protecting them against accidents to life and limb; for laws securing proper conditions of life to wage-workers; for laws providing that in continuous industry there shall be one day's rest in seven, and three eight-hour shifts a day; and for a law establishing a minimum wage for women workers. No proposals such as these are to be found in the platforms of either of the old parties; and no such platform, we believe, would be or could be enacted into law by either of the old parties. The Progressive proposal regarding a minimum wage is not an ultraradical one. It is both modest and conservative. We do not at the moment take up the question of a minimum wage generally; we know that in all matters like this it is necessary to proceed slowly so that we may test each experiment, and then, if the test is successful, proceed further along the same line. The men and women who framed this plank and who advocate it have studied the conditions of life and labor among girls and women in industry and know the dreadful suffering and misery, know the crime and vice, that are produced by a wage that is insufficient to enable the girl or woman to keep body and soul together in surroundings of ordinary decency. Any man who goes to the night session of such a court as the Jefferson Market Women's Night Court in New York City, and who follows up some of the cases brought before that court, will soon learn for himself just what misery and immorality are produced among women when they receive less than a living wage. We are faced with the actual fact of doing away with heart-breaking misery which now exists in the concrete, and we are not to be frightened from our purpose by suggestions of a purely academic kind, however well meant they may be, as to highly improbable possibilities. We intend to put a stop to the misery which now actually exists, and we believe that the minimum-wage plank is a humane, practical, and effective method of attacking that misery.

We shall sedulously safeguard the rights of property and protect it from all injustice. But we hold with Lincoln that labor deserves higher consideration than capital. Therefore we hold that labor has a right to the means of life—that there must be a living wage. I doubt whether the protection of the workers from the evils of overwork, unemployment, sweat-shop wages, and child labor will really enhance the cost of production; but, in any event, I would rather see the cost of production enhanced than see it kept low by underpaid labor, physically and morally unhealthy and socially unstable. For, as the great scientist Huxley has pointed out, a society based on such labor, whatever temporary success it obtains, must in the end fall, through hideous misery and degradation, to utter ruin.

I believe that Mr. Wilson, whose sincerity of conviction in this matter I do not for a moment question, and the other worthy and respectable men who in the name of conservatism oppose the minimum-wage plank, are misled by the fact that they get their information from study of the laws laid down by political economists who wrote when all social and industrial conditions were utterly different from what they have now become. Under present industrial conditions, to leave wages in all cases to free competition must sometimes mean that under the pressure of the competition the freedom left to the laborer is only the freedom to starve outright or else to starve slowly by accepting a wage insufficient to sustain life as it should be sustained. We in this democracy must shackle force and cunning and fraud alike, and we must not permit the weak to remain at the mercy of the strong who are also brutal.

The men and women who are broken by the hard strain of modern industry, and are driven lower and ever lower until they accept wages which will not allow them to be decently fed and clothed or comfortably housed, cannot render to the community the services which should be demanded of all American citizens. Idleness is a curse and hard, reasonable work a blessing. But wearing overwork, long continued, destroys the body and the soul, and underpayment will achieve the same end and more rapidly.

It is bad enough to exploit men, but it is inhuman to exploit women in such fashion as to force them to sell their labor power at a wage which reduces them to a condition incompatible with the public welfare. I am not at the present time going beyond what the platform of the Progressive party has announced; whether ultimately we shall or shall not do so is for the future to decide. But most emphatically I am standing for the announcements in that platform, and in my judgment one of the best things in it is the declaration for a minimum wage for women workers.

Social Security

31. · EMPLOYERS' LIABILITY

One of the most significant breakthroughs in Roosevelt's labor thought while president was his abandonment of the old fellow-servant rule of liability, which placed the responsibility for accidents on the individual or his fellow workers rather than on the employer, for the new concept of employers' liability and workmen's compensation. His understanding of the modern industrial system convinced him that most workingmen had "no alternative but to suffer want" or expose themselves to sometimes fatal hazards, and from 1906 on he gave impassioned support to proposals to shift the risks of employment from the employee to the employer. As he asserted in his Annual Message of 1907, "The practice of putting the entire burden of loss of life or limb upon the victim or the vic-

From the Annual Message to Congress, 1907. *Messages and Papers*, XI, 1245–46.

tim's family is a form of social injustice in which the United States stands in unenviable prominence."

The National Government should be a model employer. It should demand the highest quality of service from each of its employees and it should care for all of them properly in return. Congress should adopt legislation providing limited but definite compensation for accidents to all workmen within the scope of the Federal power, including employees of navy-yards and arsenals. In other words, a model employers' liability act, far-reaching and thoroughgoing, should be enacted which should apply to all positions, public and private, over which the National Government has jurisdiction. . . .

. . . The number of accidents to wage-workers, including those that are preventable and those that are not, has become appalling in the mechanical, manufacturing, and transportation operations of the day. It works grim hardship to the ordinary wage-worker and his family to have the effect of such an accident fall solely upon him; and, on the other hand, there are whole classes of attorneys who exist only by inciting men who may or may not have been wronged to undertake suits for negligence. As a matter of fact a suit for negligence is generally an inadequate remedy for the person injured, while it often causes altogether disproportionate annoyance to the employer. The law should be made such that the payment for accidents by the employer would be automatic instead of being a matter for lawsuits. Workmen should receive certain and definite compensation for all accidents in industry irrespective of negligence. The employer is the agent of the public and on his own responsibility and for his own profit he serves the public. When he starts in motion agencies which create risks for others, he should take all the ordinary and extraordinary risks involved; and the risk he thus at the moment assumes will ultimately be assumed, as it ought to be, by the general public. Only in this way can the shock of the accident be diffused, instead of falling upon the man or woman least able to bear it, as is now the case. The community at large should share the burdens as well as the benefits of industry. By the proposed law, employers would gain a desirable certainty of obligation and get rid of litigation to determine it, while the workman and his family would be relieved from a crushing load. With such a policy would come increased care, and accidents would be reduced in number. The national laws providing for employers' liability on railroads engaged in interstate commerce and for safety appliances, as well as for diminishing the hours any employee of a railroad should be permitted to work, should all be strengthened wherever in actual practice they have shown weakness; they should be kept on the statute-books in thoroughgoing form.

The constitutionality of the employers' liability act passed by the preceding Congress has been carried before the courts. In two jurisdictions the law has been declared unconstitutional, and in three jurisdictions its constitutionality has been affirmed. The question has been carried to the Supreme Court, the case has been heard by that tribunal, and a decision is expected at an early date. In the event that the court should affirm the constitutionality of the act, I urge further legislation along the lines advocated in my message to the preceding Congress. The practice of putting the entire burden of loss of life or limb upon the victim or the victim's family is a form of social injustice in which the United States stands in unenviable prominence. In both our Federal and State legislation we have, with few exceptions, scarcely gone farther than the repeal of the fellow-servant principle of the old law of liability, and in some of our States even this slight modification of a completely outgrown principle has not yet been secured. The legislation of the rest of the industrial world stands out in striking contrast to our backwardness in this respect. Since 1895 practically every country of Europe, together with Great Britain, New Zealand, Australia, British Columbia, and the Cape of

Good Hope has enacted legislation embodying in one form or another the complete recognition of the principle which places upon the employer the entire trade risk in the various lines of industry. I urge upon the Congress the enactment of a law which will at the same time bring Federal legislation up to the standard already established by all the European countries, and which will serve as a stimulus to the various States to perfect their legislation in this regard.

32. · A DEFENSE OF VETERANS' PENSIONS

Roosevelt's deepening understanding of the need for employers' liability laws was paralleled by a growing awareness of the problems faced by superannuated manual and clerical workers. Although he did not recommend a general social security system until several years after he left the presidency, he did give the matter attention while still in office. The document printed below, an excerpt from a letter defending his partly political inspired expansion of pensions for Union veterans of the Civil War, reveals the state of his thought in 1904.

Washington, May 28, 1904

My dear Whitridge:

. . . Most of our friends who live softly do not understand that the great majority of people who live by hard manual labor have begun to find their wage-earning capacity seriously impaired by the time they are sixty. The man of sixty-two has on the average great difficulty in getting a new job anywhere if he is dependent upon the labor of his hands. Where there are old-age pensions, as in New Zealand for instance, some such

Letter to Frederick W. Whitridge, May 28, 1904. *The Letters*, IV, 808–10.

age as in New Zealand, sixty-five is usually selected as the age when a man's physical ability to earn a livelihood is supposed to have ceased, and he receives the full old-age pension, which in New Zealand corresponds almost exactly to our twelve dollars. It is I think an understatement to say that the average man of sixty-two has lost his capacity to do manual labor to the extent of one-half of what he did in his prime. At seventy on the average it has stopped entirely. Of course there are men at sixty-two to seventy who are all right; but there are a much greater number who before these ages have become half or entirely crippled so far as doing manual labor is concerned. As a matter of fact, in the Departments in Washington we find this is true, not merely of physical labor but of clerical labor. It is the rarest thing in the world for us to have a clerk over sixty whose usefulness is not greatly impaired, and by seventy he is as a rule kept merely from motives of mercy. Now the average wageworker does not lay by enough money to keep him in his old age, and when he has fought in the Civil War I am entirely willing that he shall be cared for to the extent indicated in my order. Personally I believe that this order will remove the necessity for any further pension legislation, and I have so treated it.

Now is there anything you would like to question me about concerning this pension order or anything else, my dear fellow? Of course write me freely.

33. · FOR A BROADER PENSION SYSTEM

After repeating calls for an inheritance tax, and child labor and employers' liability legislation in his last Annual Message, Roose-

From Roosevelt's Annual Message to Congress, 1908. *Messages and Papers*, XI, 1364–65.

velt focused briefly on old-age pensions. He was still hopeful at that time that private industry could resolve the problem, and the intent of these remarks was to encourage it to do so.

. . . There should no longer be any paltering with the question of taking care of the wage-workers who, under our present industrial system, become killed, crippled, or worn out as part of the regular incidents of a given business. The majority of wage-workers must have their rights secured for them by State action; but the National Government should legislate in thoroughgoing and far-reaching fashion not only for all employees of the National Government, but for all persons engaged in interstate commerce. The object sought for could be achieved to a measurable degree, as far as those killed or crippled are concerned, by proper employers' liability laws. As far as concerns those who have been worn out, I call your attention to the fact that definite steps toward providing old-age pensions have been taken in many of our private industries. These may be indefinitely extended through voluntary association and contributory schemes, or through the agency of savings-banks, as under the recent Massachusetts plan. To strengthen these practical measures should be our immediate duty; it is not at present necessary to consider the larger and more general governmental schemes that most European governments have found themselves obliged to adopt. . . .

34. · "THE PROBLEM OF UNEMPLOYMENT"

The failure of the Progressive party to establish itself in the Congressional elections of 1914 along with the outbreak of World

An address at the Metropolitan Opera House, New York, January 26, 1915. *New York Times,* January 27, 1915, pp. 1, 4.

War I drove Roosevelt in new directions in 1915. From then until his death in 1919 the burden of his energy went into issues raised by the war. Nevertheless, he continued to give some thought to domestic problems and even to embrace new solutions. He pressed for a democratic conscription program. He fought vigorously for a democratic tax structure after the United States entered the war. And he came out for farm subsidies and a general social security program at the end of the war. Meanwhile, in a speech that relegated most of the vestiges of his early Calvinism to limbo, he contended that the industrial system, rather than lack of initiative by workers, was responsible for the burden of unemployment. He proposed among other things to resolve the problem by creating a permanent, yet flexible, public works administration roughly similar to the one later established by the New Deal. This address was made at a meeting to raise funds for the unemployed. Roosevelt contributed $10,000.

A month ago I made a visit to certain places downtown where any one can see for himself some evidences of what the conditions of unemployment and of suffering in this city are at this time. There is no need of my describing, even in outline, what I saw. This can be done by many men more competent than I am. But I saw enough to enable me to check statements that had been made me. I was very painfully impressed by finding places where hundreds of men, many of them eager for employment, were sleeping on dirty floors, or on newspapers spread out on these floors, or on the sawdust of bar-rooms, because they had nowhere else to sleep, and many of these men had not for days eaten anything not given them by charity and had no prospect ahead of them of meals on any other basis.

In one place where I stopped—two or three bare rooms in a cheap private employment agency—over a hundred men were passing the night. This represented unhealthy crowding, considering the lack of ventilation; but on one very cold night I was informed that over four hundred men came to pass the night. There were no bunks or beds, nothing but the floor and two or three benches. These four hundred men jammed the rooms so full that they could neither sit down nor lie down. They stood throughout the night wedged together so close that they could not fall, and therefore could sleep only standing. What shape do you think those men were in to hunt jobs next day? . . .

. . . Our object must be to meet two different situations. The immediate need is to get funds for the destitute unemployed here in our big city and to devise plans by which private individuals and associations co-operating with and working under the municipal government will try to meet the present situation—a situation due to the fact that this winter, owing to the general hard times, the unemployment and the misery and suffering are vastly greater than in any ordinary winter.

This is the immediate relief that we have in view, but in addition to that we should consider practicable ways and try to develop long-time projects for the purpose of tackling the permanent industrial problem of unemployment in this country.

As for the first matter, let me urge that we keep clear of the two besetting sins, hardness of heart and softness of head. Just at the moment hardness of the heart, or at least callous and careless indifference to the dreadful misery around us, is the prime difficulty to be overcome; but when we come to long-time projects and permanent plans we must remember all the innumerable evils that flow from softness of head.

The municipality must of course take the lead in securing immediate relief measures. But the city government cannot do more than a certain amount. In addition, the decent citizens who have jobs, the decent citizens who have money, are bound to try in practical fashion to show their belief in the doctrine that each man and each woman must be in some sort the keeper of his or her less fortunate brothers and sisters. What we really need just at this moment is to be good neighbors to our neighbors who are badly off.

Let us by all means work through the charitable associations and arrange to pay a month's rent here and there or give grocery tickets here and there, but above all let us remember the skilled working man and woman who are out of jobs, who have never before asked aid, and who starve and freeze silently. . . .

. . . Take up the matter of evictions. Of course, care must be exercised not to pauperize people, not to make men dependents and drones, and not to encourage people whose wits are devoted to devising methods of living on others. I do not wonder that magistrates sometimes grow to feel a distrust of foolish philanthropy; but it does seem to me that before a court order for eviction is signed, where the family has children, the case should be reported to the City Department of Charities; the report of the Department of Charities in such a case should be on the judge's desk when he takes action.

As for the permanent work to be done here in New York and in the nation at large, there is not time for me to do more than just speak of it; for the question represents not one but a great variety of problems, which must be dealt with in many different ways.

The Municipal Lodging House should be further developed; it should be equipped so as to give discriminating attention to each one of the groups of people who apply to the city for help; it should be made a great human repair-shop.

The segregation, of which I have above spoken, between the unemployed and the unemployable, and among the different grades of unemployed and unemployable, must surely be carried out. . . .

. . . One of the essentials is vastly to increase the work of the public employment bureaus. The present method by which a man or a woman finds a job is about as primitive as an ox-team, and is expensive in waste, in time, and in the very life of the workers. The available work and the available workers in the community should be registered at some point where both can meet. Public employment bureaus should handle not merely common labor and the near-unemployable, but also the highest kinds of labor . . .

. . . I earnestly wish the National Government would at once start work through the Reclamation Service, and through the River and Harbor Service, in such ways as to relieve unemployment. To approach the subject of rivers and harbors from this standpoint instead of from the usual pork-barrel standpoint, would be a welcome change. On some matters work could be begun within thirty days. Investigation is needed; full knowledge is needed; but do let our representatives in public life and our organizers of work realize not only that talk is worthless unless ultimately translated into action, but that there ought to be some immediate translation of words into action, in any case like the present. . . .

. . . If, for example, the machinery no longer needed at Panama were at once used on a great scheme of flood control in the Mississippi basin, including the Ohio and Missouri, much would be accomplished; and there are works at Mobile, for instance, at the mouth of the Columbia, and in connection with Boston Harbor and the Hudson which every one admits to be needed. The work at such points would do immense good. By all means have a comprehensive study and assemble complete data; but let the actual beginning, the actual putting men to work, go hand in hand with the study and the collection of the data.

Let us establish a Federal Employment Bureau to act as a clearing-house for State and municipal bureaus and to handle the reserve labor supply and intercity and interstate employment, and to begin classification of employables and unemployables and to make investigations. Let us eliminate the padrone and the boarding boss as labor agents; and have the government regulate and oversee private agencies in addition to establishing public agencies.

All kinds of things must be done. Efforts must be made to get businesses to combine different types of activities, one conducted at one season and one at another, in order to prevent seasonal unemployment, and to distribute the work through the year; and efforts ought to be made to establish businesses in which winter work is done near farming communities where the tremendous demand is for summer work. It may be that the direction of children into industry should be a recognized feature of our public-school system. The Federal Government should at once do all it can as an immediate emergency measure to help in getting settlers on the land; and all the varied fields of national activity should be opened so far as the government has the power, work on needed public highways should be pushed at once; and in Alaska the government should not delay a day longer than necessary in pushing the building of railroads to open the coal-fields.

What I thus say about a permanent labor policy of course represents nothing but the mere effort to call attention by the sketchiest kind of an outline to the way in which the problem should be approached from the permanent standpoint. The immediate need is to deal with the misery under which our fellow men and fellow women here in this city and in the neighborhood roundabout are weighed down. That need must be met through the action of the government authorities, of the churches, of the organized charities, and, above all, by each of us individually. It is a good thing to come here and to assemble elsewhere and talk of what should be done, but only on condition that this very week we start in actually to do it. Friends, words are good only when they are translated into deeds. Let us show our faith by our works, each of us individually and all of us collectively.

Federal Aid to Education

35. · THE NATIONAL BUREAU OF EDUCATION

Federal aid to education on a massive scale was not seriously considered in Roosevelt's time. As his letter on agricultural high schools (see Document 21) and this extract from his Annual Message of 1908 suggest, however, he believed that the federal government should expand its operations. In particular, he felt that it should collect and collate information for dissemination to state and local governments.

The share that the National Government should take in the broad work of education has not received the attention and the care it rightly deserves. The immediate responsibility for the support and improvement of our educational systems and institutions rests and should always rest with the people of the several States acting through their State and local governments, but the nation has an opportunity in educational work which must not be lost and a duty which should no longer be neglected.

The National Bureau of Education was established more than forty years ago. Its purpose is to collect and diffuse such information "as shall aid the people of the United States in the establishment and maintenance of efficient school systems and otherwise promote the cause of education throughout the country." This purpose in no way conflicts with the educational work of the States, but may be made of great advantage to the States by giving them the fullest, most accurate, and hence

From the Annual Message to Congress, 1908. *Messages and Papers*, XI, 1385–86.

the most helpful information and suggestion regarding the best educational systems. The nation, through its broader field of activities, its wider opportunity for obtaining information from all the States and from foreign countries, is able to do that which not even the richest States can do, and with the distinct additional advantage that the information thus obtained is used for the immediate benefit of all our people.

With the limited means hitherto provided, the Bureau of Education has rendered efficient service, but the Congress has neglected to adequately supply the bureau with means to meet the educational growth of the country. The appropriations for the general work of the bureau, outside education in Alaska, for the year 1909 are but $87,500—an amount less than they were ten years ago, and some of the important items in these appropriations are less than they were thirty years ago. It is an inexcusable waste of public money to appropriate an amount which is so inadequate as to make it impossible properly to do the work authorized, and it is unfair to the great educational interests of the country to deprive them of the value of the results which can be obtained by proper appropriations.

I earnestly recommend that this unfortunate state of affairs as regards the national educational office be remedied by adequate appropriations. This recommendation is urged by the representatives of our common schools and great State universities and the leading educators, who all unite in requesting favorable consideration and action by the Congress upon this subject.

VIII · RACE AND NATIONALITY

The Force of Environment

36. · HAITIAN AND AFRICAN NEGROES *a sexist, racist snob*

Although Roosevelt has often been classified as a racist, his attitude toward racial groups was governed more by cultural than by
genetic considerations. He believed that the real measure of superiority was a people's ability to industrialize and to form responsible
governments; and he consequently held the Japanese in higher
regard than the Chinese or, indeed, the Russians. "What nonsense
it is to speak of the Chinese and the Japanese as of the same race,"
he wrote in 1905. "I should hang my head in shame if I were
capable of discriminating against a Japanese general or admiral,
Could statesman, philanthropist or artist, because he and I have different
discriminate shades of skin." The following letter to one of Great Britain's most
against a distinguished and enlightened colonial administrators is especially
Jap revealing of Roosevelt's scholarly approach to the racial question
peon and his strongly environmentalist orientation. Obviously, he had
not dismissed the possibility that Negroes might be inherently inferior to whites. But, as his contention that Haitian culture should
be compared to African tribal culture implies, he was open to, and
actively sought, evidence to the contrary.

Oyster Bay, July 11, 1908
My dear Sir Harry: I was greatly interested in your letter and
it makes me very sincerely desirous that you should come to
the United States while I am President. If you do, I hope it

Letter to Sir Harry Hamilton Johnston, July 11, 1908. *The Letters,* VI,
1125–27.

195

will be after September 25th, and that you will give me the pleasure of spending a night at The White House. . . .

. . . What I am seriously concerned with is the great problem which you discuss; the problem, or rather the group of many complex problems, which we mean when we speak of the Negro question. I do wish I could hear from you at length, of course best of all in personal conversation, about Liberia; and I very earnestly hope that if you get over here you will visit the other Negro Republic—Haiti. I should like a more sympathetic interpretation of Haiti than that of St. John's[1] book. It may be that he tells fundamentally the truth, but yet that he does not give this truth its proper relative value. That Haiti stands behind the ordinary tropical American republic, low tho some of these tropical American republics are, is, I believe, beyond question. But what I would like to know is, whether the falling back has literally been to the old West African level. It seems to me that if St. John had compared Haiti, not with its pretensions, not with civilized or semicivilized states, but with the savage states or low-grade barbaric states from which the ancestors of most of the Haitian Negroes originally came, we would have had better material on which to base judgment. I know no one who by experience, training, temperament and ability is better able to make such a comparison than you are. I will of course help you in every way to look into the Negro problem here, and I think I could tell you a good deal about it and put you in the way of learning much for yourself . . . . I do not know whether you are familiar with South Africa or not. In connection therewith, I am struck by how little this problem has to do, after all, with the question of the black—just as little as the existence of anti-Japanese feeling, for instance, has to do with whether its location is Vancouver or San Francisco. Thus the information I have would certainly go to show that Negroes are better treated in Jamaica than in most of the black-belt districts of the United

[1] Spenser Buckingham St. John, author of *Hayti; or, The Black Republic* (London, 1884) [Ed.].

States. On the other hand, at Johannesburg and Kimberly the Negroes are certainly treated worse. I never had a complaint from an American Negro who goes to Jamaica. On the contrary, we commonly hear from such Negro that the British treat his people better than the Americans. But the American Negroes who go to South Africa write volumes of complaints about such indignities, for instance, as being forced to walk in the middle of the street and not on the sidewalk; or being herded in with savage kaffirs in the . . . , and so forth, and so forth.

On the one hand I very firmly believe in granting to Negroes and to all other races the largest amount of self-government which they can exercise. On the other hand, I have the impatient contempt that I suppose all practical men must have for the ridiculous theorists who decline to face facts and who wish to give even to the most utterly undeveloped races of mankind a degree of self-government which only the very highest races have been able to exercise with any advantage. An even more noxious type, by the way, is the man who panders to these theorists so far as advocating treatment of races that are far away, but promptly repudiates their theories when the application is sought nearer home. Usually such sentimentalists play into the hands of the excessively unsentimental individuals who are occupied in nothing whatever but in exploiting inferior races for their own benefit.

[margin note: COULDN'T COMPREHEND THAT BLAX HAD THEIR OWN GOVT.]

Indeed, if you are kind enough to send me your new book on the Congo you may feel sure that among all its readers there will be none more interested than I am. I do hope that you will get over here. . . .

37. · RACE, PROSTITUTION, AND ENVIRONMENT

Because Roosevelt used the terms *race* and *nationality* interchangeably, many of his harsh judgments about ethnic groups have

Autobiography, pp. 198–99.

been incorrectly characterized as racist. His strictures against the Irish are a case in point. As a freshman state legislator in 1882, Roosevelt wrote in his diary that "the average Catholic Irishman of the first generation as represented in this Assembly, is a low, venal, corrupt and unintelligent brute." At the same time, however, he demonstrated his ability to rise above the predispositions that sometimes formed his generalizations by adding that two Irish-American farmers were "among the best members of the house." The following selection from his *Autobiography* is informative both for its refusal to link prostitution with "permanent race characteristics" and its assertion that the moral or cultural environment was a more critical determinant of prostitution than the economic environment.

. . . Any man who knows the wide variation in the proportions of the different races and nationalities engaged in prostitution must come to the conclusion that it is out of the question to treat economic conditions as the sole conditions or even as the chief conditions that determine this question. There are certain races—the Irish are honorably conspicuous among them—which, no matter what the economic pressure, furnish relatively few inmates of houses of ill-fame. I do not believe that the differences are due to permanent race characteristics; this is shown by the fact that the best settlement houses find that practically all their "long-term graduates," so to speak, all the girls that come for a long period under their influence, no matter what their race or national origin, remain pure. In every race there are some naturally vicious individuals and some weak individuals who readily succumb under economic pressure. A girl who is lazy and hates hard work, a girl whose mind is rather feeble, who is of "subnormal intelligence," as the phrase now goes, or a girl who craves cheap finery and vapid pleasure, is always in danger. A high ideal of personal purity is essential. Where the same pressure under the same economic conditions has tenfold the effect on one set of people that it has on another, it is evident that the question of moral

CAUSES OF PROSTITUTION

standards is even more important than the question of economic standards, very important though this question is. It is
important for us to remember that the girl ought to have the
chance, not only for the necessaries of life, but for innocent
pleasure; and that even more than the man she must not be
broken by overwork, by excessive toil. Moreover, public opinion and the law should combine to hunt down the "flagrant
man swine" who himself hunts down poor or silly or unprotected girls. But we must not, in foolish sentimentality, excuse
the girl from her duty to keep herself pure. Our duty to
achieve the same moral level for the two sexes must be performed by raising the level for the man, not by lowering it
for the woman; and the fact that society must recognize its
duty in no shape or way relieves, not even to the smallest
degree, the individual from doing his or her duty. Sentimentality which grows maudlin on behalf of the wilful prostitute is
a curse; to confound her with the entrapped or coerced girl,
the real white slave, is both foolish and wicked. There are evil
women just as there are evil men, naturally depraved girls
just as there are naturally depraved young men; and the right
and wise thing, the just thing, to them, and the generous
thing to innocent girls and decent men, is to wage stern war
against the evil creatures of both sexes. . . .

The Negro Problem

38. · "THE EDUCATION OF THE NEGRO"

Whatever the theoretical sub-structure of Roosevelt's views on
race, a strong sense of gradualism governed his attitude toward

An address at Tuskegee Institute, October 24, 1905. *Presidential Addresses,* IV, 521–27.

Negroes in practice. Based largely on the belief that it would take longer than sociologists now think for Negroes to acquire professional and managerial skills, it also reflected his hypersensitivity to the mores and prejudices of Southern whites. Both the strengths and weaknesses of this approach are implicit in the speech that follows. Roosevelt's enthusiastic endorsement of Booker T. Washington's program of vocational education was salutary as far as it went; but its implied rejection of higher education suggests a failure to realize the importance of developing an informed and sophisticated Negro leadership such as W. E. B. DuBois was urging at the time.

To the white population as well as to the black, it is of the utmost importance that the negro be encouraged to make himself a citizen of the highest type of usefulness. It is to the interest of the white people that this policy be conscientiously pursued, and to the interest of the colored people that they clearly realize that they have opportunities for economic development here in the South not now offered elsewhere. Within in the last twenty years the industrial operations of the South have increased so tremendously that there is a scarcity of labor almost everywhere; so that it is the part of wisdom for all who wish the prosperity of the South to help the negro to become in the highest degree useful to himself, and therefore to the community in which he lives. The South has always depended, and now depends, chiefly upon her native population for her work. Therefore in view of the scarcity not only of common labor, but of skilled labor, it becomes doubly important to train every available man to be of the utmost use, by developing his intelligence, his skill, and his capacity for conscientious effort. Hence the work of the Tuskegee Normal and Industrial Institute is a matter of the highest practical importance to both the white man and the black man, and well worth the support of both races alike in the South and in the North. Your fifteen hundred students are not only being educated in head and heart, but also trained to industrial efficiency, for from the beginning Tuskegee has placed especial emphasis upon the training of men and women in agriculture, mechanics, and household duties. Training in these three fundamental directions does not embrace all that the negro, or any other race, needs, but it does cover in a very large degree the field in which the negro can at present do most for himself and be most helpful to his white neighbors. Every black man who leaves this institute better able to do mechanical or industrial work adds by so much to the wealth of the whole community and benefits all people in the community. The professional and mercantile avenues to success are overcrowded; for the present the best chance of success awaits the intelligent worker at some mechanical trade or on a farm; for this man will almost certainly achieve industrial independence. I am pleased, but not in the least surprised, to learn that many among the men and women trained at Tuskegee find immediate employment as leaders and workers among their own people, and that their services are eagerly sought by white people for various kinds of industrial work, the demand being much greater than the supply. Viewed from any angle, ignorance is the costliest crop that can be raised in any part of this Union. Every dollar put into the education of either white man or black man, in head, in hand, and in heart, yields rich dividends to the entire community. Merely from the economic standpoint it is of the utmost consequence to all our citizens that institutions such as this at Tuskegee should be a success. But there are other and even higher reasons that entitle it to our support. In the interest of humanity, of justice, and of self-protection, every white man in America, no matter where he lives, should try to help the negro to help himself. It is in the interest and for the protection of the white man to see that the negro is educated. It is not only the duty of the white man, but it is to his interest, to see that the negro is protected in property, in life, and in all his legal rights. Every time a law is broken, every in-

dividual in the community has the moral tone of his life lowered. Lawlessness in the United States is not confined to any
one section; lynching is not confined to any one section; and
there is perhaps no body of American citizens who have deserved so well of the entire American people as the public
men, the publicists, the clergymen, the countless thousands
of high-minded private citizens, who have done such heroic
work in the South in arousing public opinion against lawlessness in all its forms, and especially against lynching. I very
earnestly hope that their example will count in the North as
well as in the South, for there are just as great evils to be
warred against in one region of our country as in another,
though they are not in all places the same evils. And when
any body of men in any community stands bravely for what
is right, these men not merely serve a useful purpose in doing
the particular task to which they set themselves, but give a
lift to the cause of good citizenship throughout the Union.
I heartily appreciate what you have done at Tuskegee; and
I am sure you will not grudge my saying that it could not
possibly have been done save for the loyal support you have
received from the white people roundabout; for during the
twenty-five years of effort to educate the black man here in
the midst of a white community of intelligence and culture,
there has never been an outbreak between the races, or any
difficulty of any kind. All honor is due to the white men of
Alabama, to the white men of Tuskegee, for what they have
done. And right here let me say that if in any community a
misunderstanding between the races arises, over any matter,
infinitely the best way out is to have a prompt, frank, and full
conference and consultation between representatives of the
wise, decent, cool-headed men among the whites and the wise,
decent, cool-headed colored men. Such a conference will always tend to bring about a better understanding, and will be
a great help all round.

Hitherto I have spoken chiefly of the obligations existing

on the part of the white man. Now remember on the other
hand that no help can permanently avail you save as you
yourselves develop capacity for self-help. You young colored
men and women educated at Tuskegee must by precept and
example lead your fellows toward sober, industrious, law-
abiding lives. You are in honor bound to join hands in favor
of law and order and to war against all crime, and especially
against all crime by men of your own race; for the heaviest
wrong done by the criminal is the wrong to his own race. You
must teach the people of your race that they must scrupulously observe any contract into which they in good faith
enter, no matter whether it is hard to keep or not. If you save
money, secure homes, become taxpayers, and lead clean, decent, modest lives, you will win the respect of your neighbors
of both races. Let each man strive to excel his fellows only
by rendering substantial service to the community in which
he lives. The colored people have many difficulties to pass
through, but these difficulties will be surmounted if only the
policy of reason and common sense is pursued. You have
made real and great progress. According to the census the
colored people of this country own and pay taxes upon something like three hundred million dollars' worth of property,
and have blotted out over fifty per cent of their illiteracy.
What you have done in the past is an indication of what you
will be able to accomplish in the future under wise leadership. Moral and industrial education is what is most needed,
in order that this progress may continue. The race cannot expect to get everything at once. It must learn to wait and bide
its time; to prove itself worthy by showing its possession of
perseverance, of thrift, of self-control. The destiny of the race
is chiefly in its own hands, and must be worked out patiently
and persistently along these lines. Remember also that the
white man who can be of most use to the colored man is that
colored man's neighbor. It is the Southern people themselves
who must and can solve the difficulties that exist in the South;

of course what help the people of the rest of the Union can give them must and will be gladly and cheerfully given. The hope of advancement for the colored man in the South lies in his steady, common-sense effort to improve his moral and material condition, and to work in harmony with the white man in upbuilding the Commonwealth. The future of the South now depends upon the people of both races living up to the spirit and letter of the laws of their several States and working out the destinies of both races, not as races, but as law-abiding American citizens.

39. · LYNCHING AND MOB VIOLENCE

Actually, Roosevelt had few illusions about white Southerners and race. He once complained to the novelist, Owen Wister, about Charleston aristocrats who "shriek in public about miscegenation, but . . . leer as they talk to me privately of the colored mistresses and colored children of white men whom they know." And he clearly perceived the implications of the Southern tradition of violence. His commitment to national unity was so strong, however, that even when he attacked lynching he carefully deferred to Southern prejudices and sensibilities. Thus the statement on lynching in his Annual Message of 1906 starts by accepting the Southern contention that most lynchings were incited by rape, follows with comments by prominent Southerners modifying the allegation, and closes with a vigorous and unqualified condemnation of lynching.

In connection with the delays of the law, I call your attention and the attention of the nation to the prevalence of crime among us, and above all to the epidemic of lynching and mob

From Roosevelt's Annual Message to Congress, 1906. *Messages and Papers*, XI, 1187–89.

violence that springs up, now in one part of our country, now in another. Each section, North, South, East, or West, has its own faults; no section can with wisdom spend its time jeering at the faults of another section; it should be busy trying to amend its own shortcomings. To deal with the crime of corruption it is necessary to have an awakened public conscience, and to supplement this by whatever legislation will add speed and certainty in the execution of the law. When we deal with lynching even more is necessary. A great many white men are lynched, but the crime is peculiarly frequent in respect to black men. The greatest existing cause of lynching is the perpetration, especially by black men, of the hideous crime of rape—the most abominable in all the category of crimes, even worse than murder. Mobs frequently avenge the commission of this crime by themselves torturing to death the man committing it; thus avenging in bestial fashion a bestial deed, and reducing themselves to a level with the criminal.

Lawlessness grows by what it feeds upon; and when mobs begin to lynch for rape they speedily extend the sphere of their operations and lynch for many other kinds of crimes, so that two-thirds of the lynchings are not for rape at all; while a considerable proportion of the individuals lynched are innocent of all crime. Governor Candler, of Georgia, stated on one occasion some years ago: "I can say of a verity that I have, within the last month, saved the lives of half a dozen innocent negroes who were pursued by the mob, and brought them to trial in a court of law in which they were acquitted." As Bishop Galloway, of Mississippi, has finely said: "When the rule of a mob obtains, that which distinguishes a high civilization is surrendered. The mob which lynches a negro charged with rape will in a little while lynch a white man suspected of crime. Every Christian patriot in America needs to lift up his voice in loud and eternal protest against the mob spirit that is threatening the integrity of this Republic." Governor Jelks, of Alabama, has recently spoken as follows: "The lynching of any person for whatever crime is inexcusable anywhere—it is a defiance of orderly government; but the killing of innocent people under any provocation is infinitely more horrible; and yet innocent people are likely to die when a mob's terrible lust is once aroused. The lesson is this: No good citizen can afford to countenance a defiance of the statutes, no matter what the provocation. The innocent frequently suffer, and, it is my observation, more usually suffer than the guilty. The white people of the South indict the whole colored race on the ground that even the better elements lend no assistance whatever in ferreting out criminals of their own color. The respectable colored people must learn not to harbor their criminals, but to assist the officers in bringing them to justice. This is the larger crime, and it provokes such atrocious offenses as the one at Atlanta. The two races can never get on until there is an understanding on the part of both to make common cause with the law-abiding against criminals of any color." USUALLY BLACK.

Moreover, where any crime committed by a member of one race against a member of another race is avenged in such fashion that it seems as if not the individual criminal, but the whole race, is attacked, the result is to exasperate to the highest degree race feeling. There is but one safe rule in dealing with black men as with white men; it is the same rule that must be applied in dealing with rich men and poor men; that is, to treat each man, whatever his color, his creed, or his social position, with even-handed justice on his real worth as a man. White people owe it quite as much to themselves as to the colored race to treat well the colored man who shows by his life that he deserves such treatment; for it is surely the highest wisdom to encourage in the colored race all those individuals who are honest, industrious, law-abiding, and who therefore make good and safe neighbors and citizens. Reward or punish the individual on his merits as an individual.

Evil will surely come in the end to both races if we substitute for this just rule the habit of treating all the members of the race, good and bad, alike. There is no question of "social equality" or "negro domination" involved; only the question of relentlessly punishing bad men, and of securing to the good man the right to his life, his liberty, and the pursuit of his happiness as his own qualities of heart, head, and hand enable him to achieve it.

Every colored man should realize that the worst enemy of his race is the negro criminal, and above all the negro criminal who commits the dreadful crime of rape; and it should be felt as in the highest degree an offense against the whole country, and against the colored race in particular, for a colored man to fail to help the officers of the law in hunting down with all possible earnestness and zeal every such infamous offender. Moreover, in my judgment, the crime of rape should always be punished with death, as is the case with murder; assault with intent to commit rape should be made a capital crime, at least in the discretion of the court; and provision should be made by which the punishment may follow immediately upon the heels of the offense; while the trial should be so conducted that the victim need not be wantonly shamed while giving testimony, and that the least possible publicity shall be given to the details.

The members of the white race on the other hand should understand that every lynching represents by just so much a loosening of the bands of civilization; that the spirit of lynching inevitably throws into prominence in the community all the foul and evil creatures who dwell therein. No man can take part in the torture of a human being without having his own moral nature permanently lowered. Every lynching means just so much moral deterioration in all the children who have any knowledge of it, and therefore just so much additional trouble for the next generation of Americans.

Let justice be both sure and swift; but let it be justice

under the law, and not the wild and crooked savagery of a mob.

40. · A LILY-WHITE SOUTHERN PROGRESSIVE DELEGATION

Few actions have more tarnished Roosevelt's image as a progressive than his decision to seat all-white, rather than mixed Negro and white, delegations from Florida, Mississippi, and Georgia to the Progressive National Convention of 1912. Not only did it alienate the Negro community, including Booker T. Washington, but it also opened Roosevelt to charges of opportunism and insincerity. Neither charge was accurate. The wisdom of the decision was surely dubious; but as this letter to the son of the author of *Uncle Remus* shows, it was a logical outgrowth of Roosevelt's basic views as well as of his belief that a progressive government would best serve Negro interests in the long run. *THE VERY LONG RUN.*

[handwritten margin note: WHY WOULDN'T HE ADMIT BLAX?]

[handwritten margin note: A GOOD NEGRO QUALITY]

Oyster Bay, August 1, 1912

My dear Mr. Harris: In pursuance of our conversation I write you this letter. There is a peculiar fitness in writing it to the son of the man whose work made all Americans his debtors. Your father possessed genius; and moreover he possessed that gentleness of soul, that broad and tender sympathy with his fellows, for the lack of which genius cannot atone. His life and his work tended to bring his fellow countrymen, North and South, into ever closer relations of good will and understanding; and surely it should be needless to say that the author of *Uncle Remus* and of "Free Joe and the Rest of the

Letter to Julian La Rose Harris, August 1, 1912. *The Letters,* VII, 584–90.

World" felt a deep and most kindly interest in the welfare of the negro.

Many letters dealing with the subject of which you spoke to me have been sent to me within the last few days. These letters, from equally worthy citizens, take diametrically opposite positions. Those written by men living in the North usually ask me to insist that we get from the South colored Delegates to the National Progressive Convention. Those written by citizens of the South ask that I declare that the new party shall be a white man's party. I am not able to agree to either proposal.

In this country we cannot permanently succeed except upon the basis of treating each man on his worth as a man. We can fulfill our high mission among the nations of the earth, we can do lasting good to ourselves and to all mankind, only if we so act that the humblest among us, so long as he behaves in straight and decent fashion, has guaranteed to him under the law his right to life, to liberty, to protection from injustice, his right to enjoy the fruits of his own honest labor, and his right of the pursuit of happiness in his own way, so long as he does not trespass on the rights of others. Our only safe motto is "All men up" and not "Some men down." For us to oppress any class of our fellow citizens is not only wrong to others but hurtful to ourselves; for in the long run such action is no more detrimental to the oppressed than to those who think that they temporarily benefit by the oppression. Surely no man can quarrel with these principles. Exactly as they should be applied among white men without regard to their difference of creed, or birthplace, or social station, without regard to whether they are rich men or poor men, men who work with their hands or men who work with their brains; so they should be applied among all men without regard to the color of their skins.

These are the principles to which I think our countrymen should adhere, the objects which I think they should have steadily in mind. There is need not merely of all our high purpose, but of all our wisdom and patience in striving to realize them. Above all, it is essential that we should not in such a way as to make believe that we are achieving these objects, and yet by our actions indefinitely postpone the time when it will become even measurably possible to achieve them. For this reason I cannot adopt either of the two diametrically opposite suggestions made to me in the letters of which I have spoken.

I believe that the Progressive Movement should be made from the beginning one in the interest of every honest, industrious, law-abiding colored man, just as it is in the interest of every honest, industrious, law-abiding white man. I further believe that the surest way to render the movement impotent to help either the white man or the colored man in those regions of the South where the colored man is most numerous, would be to try to repeat the course that has been followed by the Republican Party in those districts for so many years, or to endeavor in the States in question to build up a Progressive Party by the same methods which in those States have resulted in making the Republican Party worse than impotent.

Henry Ward Beecher once said that the worst enemy of the colored man was the man who stirred up enmity between the white and colored men who have to live as neighbors. In the South the Democratic machine has sought to keep itself paramount by encouraging the hatred of the white man for the black; the Republican machine has sought to perpetuate itself by stirring up the black man against the white; and surely the time has come when we should understand the mischief in both courses, and should abandon both.

We have made the Progressive issue a moral, not a racial issue. I believe that wherever the racial issue is permitted to become dominant in our politics, it always works harm to both races, but immeasurably most harm to the weaker race. I believe that in this movement only damage will come if we either

abandon our ideals on the one hand, or, on the other, fail resolutely to look facts in the face, however unpleasant these facts
may be. Therefore I feel that we have to adapt our actions to
the actual conditions and actual needs and feelings of each
community; not abandoning our principles, but not in one
community endeavoring to realize them in ways which will
simply cause disaster in that community, although they may
work well in another community. Our object must be the same
everywhere, but the methods by which we strive to attain it
must be adapted to the needs of the several states, or it will
never be attained at all.

In many of the States of the Union where there is a considerable colored population we are able in very fact and at the
present moment to bring the best colored men into the movement on the same terms as the white man. In Rhode Island
and Maryland, in New York and Indiana, in Ohio and Illinois,
in New Jersey and Pennsylvania, to speak only of States of
which I have personal knowledge, this is now being done, and
from some or all of these states colored delegates will be sent
to the National Progressive Convention in Chicago. Let me
point out that the Progressive Party is already, at its very
birth, endeavoring in these States, in its own home, to act with
fuller recognition of the rights of the colored man than ever
the Republican party did. Until I was President the white Republicans of the North, although they had loudly insisted that
the colored man should have office with even greater firmness
insisted that he should have office only in the South, or at any
rate, not in the North. When, for instance, I tried to appoint a
colored man to office in Ohio I was wholly unable to get the
necessary assent from the white Republican leaders of Ohio,
and had to appoint the man in Washington; and in appointing
a colored man to a high position in New York I was obliged
to do it by main force and against the wish of the entire party
organization. In the Republican National Conventions the colored members have been almost exclusively from the South,

and the great majority of them have been men of such character that their political activities were merely a source of harm, and of very grave harm, to their own race. We, on the contrary, are hoping to see in the National Progressive Convention colored delegates from the very places where we expect to develop our greatest strength, and we hope to see these men of such character that their activities shall be of benefit not only to the people at large but especially to their own race. So much for the course we are able to follow in these States; and the citizens of these States can best help the negro race by doing justice to these negroes who are their own neighbors. In many Northern States there have been lynchings and race riots with sad and revolting accompaniments; in many of these States there has been failure to punish such outrageous conduct and what is even more important, failure to deal in advance wisely and firmly with the evil conditions, among both black man and the white, which has caused the outrages.

There are other States, including the majority of the Southern States, where the conditions are wholly different. Much is to be said for the men who forty-five years ago, with motives which were for the most part and among most of their number of a lofty and disinterested type, attempted a course of action in those States which in actual practice has lamentably failed to justify itself and I make no attempt at this time to strive to apportion the blame for the failure. It is unwise to revive bitterness by dwelling on the errors and shortcomings of the past. Let us profit by them, but reproach no man because of them. We are now starting a new movement for the betterment of our people, a movement for social and industrial justice which shall be nationwide, a movement which is to strive to accomplish actual results and not to accept high-sounding phrases as a substitute for deeds. Therefore we are not to be pardoned if at the outset, with the knowledge gained by forty-five years' experience of failure, we repeat the course that has led to such failure, and abandon the effort to make the movement for social and industrial justice really nation-wide.

For forty-five years the Republican Party has striven to build up in the Southern States in question a party based on the theory that the pyramid will unsupported stand perma-nently on its apex instead of on its base. For forty-five years the Republican Party has endeavored in these States to build up a party in which the negro should be dominant, a party consisting almost exclusively of negroes. Those who took the lead in this experiment were actuated by high motives, and no one should now blame them because of what, with the knowledge they then had and under the then existing circum-stances, they strove to do. But in actual practice the result has been lamentable from every standpoint. It has been productive of evil to the colored men themselves; it has been productive only of evil to the white men of the South; and it has worked the gravest injury to, and finally the disruption and destruc-tion of, the great Republican Party itself. In the States in ques-tion where the negro predominates in numbers, and in the sections of other states in which he predominates in numbers, the Republican Party has in actual fact become practically non-existent in so far as votes at the polls are concerned. The number of votes cast in these states and districts for the Re-publican ticket on Election Day has become negligible. It has long been recognized that these states will never give a Re-publican electoral vote; that these states or districts will never send a Republican or a colored man to Congress. The num-ber of colored men in them who hold any elective office of the slightest importance is negligible. In these states and dis-tricts the Republic Party, in actual practice, and disregarding individual exceptions, exists only to serve the purposes of a small group of politicians, for the most part white, but in-cluding some colored men, who have not the slightest interest in elections, and whose political activities are confined to securing offices by sending to National Conventions delegations which are controlled by the promise of office or by means even more questionable. Once in four years they send to the National Conventions delegates who represent absolutely nothing in the way of voting strength, and in consideration of the votes of the delegates thus delivered they endeavor to secure their local offices from any National Republican Administration.

The progress that has been made among the negroes of the South during these forty-five years has not been made as a result of political effort of the kind I have mentioned. It has been made as the result of effort along industrial and educational lines. Again allowing for the inevitable exception, it remains true, as one of the wisest leaders of the colored race has himself said, that the only white man who in the long run, can effectively help the colored man is that colored man's neighbor. There are innumerable white men in the South sincerely desirous of doing justice to the colored man, of helping him upward on his difficult path, of securing him just treatment before the law; white men who set their faces sternly against lynch law and mob violence, who attack all such abuses as peonage, who fight to keep the school funds equitably divided between white and colored schools, who endeavor to help the colored man to become a self-supporting and useful member of the community. The white men who live elsewhere can best help the colored man in the South by upholding the hands of those white men of the South who are thus endeavoring to benefit and to act honestly by the colored men with whom they dwell in community neighborhood and with whose children their children will continue to dwell in community neighborhood. Actual experience for nearly half a century has shown that it is futile to endeavor to substitute for such action by the white man to his colored neighbor, action by outside white men, action which painful experience has shown to be impotent to help the colored man, but which

[handwritten marginalia:] XCLUDES THE BLACK FROM POLITICAL POWER — SENDS HIM BACK TO THE STEPPIN FETCH STAGE.

[handwritten marginalia:] WHO FIGHT TO KEEP THE WHITE SEPARATED FROM THE BLACK.

[handwritten note at bottom:] ↳ WHAT HE IS SAYING IS THAT INTEGRATION IS THE TOUGHEST ROW TO HOE + IMPLICITLY? THAT SEGREGATION IS NECESSARY

does irritate the white man whom nevertheless it cannot control. We are not facing theories, we are facing actual facts, and it is well for us to remember Emerson's statement that in the long run the most unpleasant truth is a safer traveling companion than the pleasantest falsehood.

The action of the Republican machine in the South, then, in endeavoring to keep alive a party based only on negro votes, where, with few exceptions, the white leaders are in it only to gain reward for themselves by trafficking in negro votes, has been bad for the white men of the South, whom it has kept solidified in an unhealthy and unnatural political bond, to their great detriment and to the detriment of the whole Union; and it has been bad for the colored men of the South. The effect on the Republican Party has long been disastrous, and has finally proved fatal. There has in the past been much venality in Republican National Conventions in which there was an active contest for the nomination for President, and this venality has been almost exclusively among the rotten-borough delegates, and for the most part among the negro delegates from these Southern States in which there was no real Republican Party. Finally, in the Convention at Chicago last June, the breakup of the Republican Party was forced by those rotten-borough delegates from the South. In the Primary States of the North the colored men in most places voted substantially as their white neighbors voted. But in the Southern States, where there was no real Republican Party, and where colored men, or whites selected purely by colored men, were sent to the convention, representing nothing but their own greed for money or office the majority was overwhelmingly antiprogressive. Seven eighths of the colored men from these rotten-borough districts upheld by their votes the fraudulent actions of the men who in that Convention defied and betrayed the will of the mass of the plain people of the party. In spite of the hand-picked delegates chosen by the bosses in certain northern states, in spite of the scores of delegates deliberately stolen from the rank and file of the party by the corrupt political machine which dominated the National Committee and the Convention itself, there would yet have been no hope of reversing in the National Convention the action demanded by the overwhelming majority of the Republicans who had a chance to speak for themselves in their primaries, had it not been for the two hundred and fifty votes or thereabouts sent from the states in which there is no Republican Party. For forty-five years everything has been sacrificed to the effort to build up in these states a Republican Party which should be predominantly and overwhelmingly negro, and now those for whom the effort has been made turned and betrayed that party itself. It would be not merely foolish but criminal to disregard the teachings of such a lesson. The disruption and destruction of the Republican Party, and the fact that it has been rendered absolutely impotent as an instrument for anything but mischief in the country at large has been brought about in large part by the effort to pretend that in the Southern States a sham is a fact, by the insistence upon treating the ghost party in the Southern States as a real party, by refusing to face the truth, which is that under existing conditions there is not and cannot be in the Southern States a party based primarily upon the negro vote and under negro leadership or the leadership of white men who derive their power solely from negroes. With these forty-five years of failure of this policy in the South before our eyes, and with catastrophe thereby caused to a great National Party not yet six weeks distant from us, it would be criminal for the Progressives to repeat the course of action responsible for such disaster, such failure, such catastrophe. The loss of instant representation by southern colored delegates is due to the fact that the sentiment of the Southern negro collectively has been prostituted by dishonest professional politicians both white and black, and the

[handwritten margin note: BY NOT ALLOWING BLAX TO RUN.]

[handwritten margin note: REAL REASON FOR NOT INVITING BLAX.]

[handwritten note at bottom: ⌐ SAYS (IMP.) PRO. PARTY WILL BE AS BAD.]

machinery does not exist (and can never be created as long as present political conditions are continued) which can secure what a future of real justice will undoubtedly develop, namely, the right of political expression by the negro who shows that he possesses the intelligence, integrity and self-respect which justify such right of political expression in his white neighbor.

We face certain actual facts, sad and unpleasant facts, but facts which must be faced if we are to dwell in the world of realities and not of shams, and if we are to try to make things better by deeds and not merely to delude ourselves by empty words. It would be much worse than useless to try to build up the Progressive Party in these Southern States where there is no real Republican Party, by appealing to the negroes or to the men who in the past have derived their sole standing from leading and manipulating the negroes. As a matter of fact and not of theory all that could possibly result from such action would be to create another impotent little corrupt faction of would-be officeholders, of delegates whose expenses to conventions had to be paid, and whose votes sometimes had to be bought. No real good could come from such action to any man, black or white; the negro would be hurt and not helped throughout the Union; the white man would be hurt in the South, the Progressive Party would be damaged irreparably at the beginning. I earnestly believe that by appealing to the best white men in the South, the men of justice and of vision as well as of strength and leadership, and by frankly putting the movement in their hands from the outset we shall create a situation by which the colored men of the South will ultimately get justice as it is not possible for them to get justice if we are to continue and perpetuate the present conditions. The men to whom we appeal are the men who have stood for securing the colored man in his rights before the law, and they can do for him what neither the Northern white man nor the colored men themselves can do. Our only wise course from the

standpoint of the colored man himself is to follow the course
that we are following toward him in the North and to follow
the course we are following toward him in the South.

WANT MEN WHO WILL GIVE BLAX RIGHTS — IT NEVER
OCCURRED TO HIM TO SELECT BLACK MEN WHO MAY
BE ABLE TO STRENGTHEN THE PARTY 1 THE BLACK CAUSE.

Cultural Nationalism Versus Cultural Pluralism

EVEN TO SET EXAMPLE BY MEMBERSHIP.

41. · ASSIMILATION OF AMERICAN INDIANS

Although Roosevelt's reluctance to offend the South caused him
to move cautiously, he was actually a mild integrationist. During his
governorship he had signed with approval a bill banning race discrimination in the public schools of New York, and while president
he occasionally indicated a desire to bring Negroes into the main-
stream of American life. As a cultural nationalist, Roosevelt believed zealously that unity, not diversity, was the ultimate ideal;
and just as he deplored the divisive influence of states' rights, so
did he disdain the modern concept of cultural pluralism. One of
the clearest demonstrations of this was his policy toward American
Indians. He felt that they should be assimilated rather than perpetuated as distinct tribal groups; and though he regarded them
as less advanced than Negroes, he pushed a program designed to
create an environment—social, moral, economic, and educational—
that would gradually prepare them to fulfill the responsibilities of
citizenship in an industrialized society.

IN N.Y.
NOT IN
N.C.

HOW CAN
HE JUSTIFY
P-PINE
XPANSION —
MOVE TOWARD
TAKING
THEM ON
A COMMER.
BASIS.

< ECONOMICALLY PROFITABLE

IN A WHITE IND.
SOCIETY WHICH
WILL ALWAYS
SUBORDINATE
THE
INTRUDER.

a. From the Annual Message to Congress, 1901.

In my judgment the time has arrived when we should definitely make up our minds to recognize the Indian as an individual and not as a member of a tribe. The General Allotment
Act is a mighty pulverizing engine to break up the tribal mass.

Messages and Papers, X, 450–51.

It acts directly upon the family and the individual. Under its provisions some 60,000 Indians have already become citizens of the United States. We should now break up the tribal funds, doing for them what allotment does for the tribal lands; that is, they should be divided into individual holdings. There will be a transition period during which the funds will in many cases have to be held in trust. This is the case also with the lands. A stop should be put upon the indiscriminate permission to Indians to lease their allotments. The effort should be steadily to make the Indian work like any other man on his own ground. The marriage laws of the Indians should be made the same as those of the whites.

In the schools the education should be elementary and largely industrial. The need of higher education among the Indians is very, very limited. On the reservations care should be taken to try to suit the teaching to the needs of the particular Indian. There is no use in attempting to induce agriculture in a country suited only for cattle-raising where the Indian should be made a stock-grower. The ration system, which is merely the corral and the reservation system, is highly detrimental to the Indians. It promotes beggary, perpetuates pauperism, and stifles industry. It is an effectual barrier to progress. It must continue to a greater or less degree as long as tribes are herded on reservations and have everything in common. The Indian should be treated as an individual—like the white man. During the change of treatment inevitable hardships will occur; every effort should be made to minimize these hardships; but we should not because of them hesitate to make the change. There should be a continuous reduction in the number of agencies.

In dealing with the aboriginal races few things are more important than to preserve them from the terrible physical and moral degradation resulting from the liquor traffic. We are doing all we can to save our own Indian tribes from this evil. Wherever by international agreement this same end can be attained as regards races where we do not possess exclusive control, every effort should be made to bring it about.

b. From the Annual Message to Congress, 1902.

In dealing with the Indians our aim should be their ultimate absorption into the body of our people. But in many cases this absorption must and should be very slow. In portions of the Indian Territory the mixture of blood has gone on at the same time with progress in wealth and education, so that there are plenty of men with varying degrees of purity of Indian blood who are absolutely indistinguishable in point of social, political, and economic ability from their white associates. There are other tribes which have as yet made no perceptible advance toward such equality. To try to force such tribes too fast is to prevent their going forward at all. Moreover, the tribes live under widely different conditions. Where a tribe has made considerable advance and lives on fertile farming soil it is possible to allot the members lands in severalty much as is the case with white settlers. There are other tribes where such a course is not desirable. On the arid prairie-lands the effort should be to induce the Indians to lead pastoral rather than agricultural lives, and to permit them to settle in villages rather than to force them into isolation.

The large Indian schools situated remote from any Indian reservation do a special and peculiar work of great importance. But, excellent though these are, an immense amount of additional work must be done on the reservations themselves among the old, and above all among the young, Indians.

The first and most important step toward the absorption of the Indian is to teach him to earn his living; yet it is not necessarily to be assumed that in each community all Indians must become either tillers of the soil or stock-raisers. Their industries may properly be diversified, and those who show

Messages and Papers, X, 544–45.

special desire or adaptability for industrial or even commercial pursuits should be encouraged so far as practicable to follow out each his own bent.

Every effort should be made to develop the Indian along the lines of natural aptitude, and to encourage the existing native industries peculiar to certain tribes, such as the various kinds of basket-weaving, canoe-building, smith work, and blanket work. Above all, the Indian boys and girls should be given confident command of colloquial English, and should ordinarily be prepared for a vigorous struggle with the conditions under which their people live, rather than for immediate absorption into some more highly developed community. *DON'T RUSH IT.*

The officials who represent the government in dealing with the Indians work under hard conditions, and also under conditions which render it easy to do wrong and very difficult to detect wrong. Consequently they should be amply paid on the one hand, and on the other hand a particularly high standard of conduct should be demanded from them, and where misconduct can be proved the punishment should be exemplary. *DEAL IN BOOZE.*

ROUGH TASK DEALING W/. DRUNKEN INDIANS

42. · CULTURAL DYNAMISM AND HYPHENATED AMERICANISM

Both in theory and in practice, Roosevelt's concept of cultural unity was dynamic and open-ended rather than static or closed. As the first of the two selections printed below, a letter to the eminent psychologist and German apologist, Hugo Münsterberg, suggests, he wanted the United States to absorb those foreign ideals and institutions that were desirable and reject those that were not. Yet, as the second selection, a passage from one of Roosevelt's World War I essays, makes equally clear, there could be no divided loyalty, whether by citizens of Revolutionary War stock or by the sons of recent immigrants.

a. From a letter to Hugo Münsterberg, February 8, 1916.

New York, February 8, 1916

To Hugo Münsterberg
Private not for publication

My dear Professor Münsterberg . . . Now, as for what you say about the Americans of German descent. With most of what you say I entirely agree. I do not for a moment believe that the Americanism of today should be a mere submission to the American ideals of the period of the Declaration of Independence. Such action would be not only to stand still, but to go back. American democracy, of course, must mean an opportunity for everyone to contribute his own ideas to the working out of the future. But I will go further than you have done. I have actively fought in favor of grafting on our social life, no less than on our industrial life, many of the German ideals. For instance, I like the German type of club much more than I like the American type of club. In the German clubs in this country women were admitted long before that was the case in American clubs. Of course, I suppose I shall never again be received in the Milwaukee clubs; but of all the clubs I have ever been in, that Milwaukee German Club is the one where I really enjoyed myself most! It has often puzzled me to find out why it has been impossible to spread these clubs and have them the recognized type of American club, just as much as of German-American club. I think that one explanation lies in the fact that they have been unconsciously used to keep their members away from American life. If with entire frankness, those handling them had treated them as American clubs, to develop every kind of ideal that was found good, including those that they had brought over from Germany, I think most of the difficulty would have been averted and that they would have spread everywhere. This is only an example; I am certain

I have tried to graft German ideals and habits a dozen times, for every single English ideal or habit, on American life. One word about preparedness! The Illinois *Staats-Zeitung* is an example. It is fighting preparedness tooth and nail. It is backing up David Starr Jordan[1] and people like him; and I think this pretty bad. Many of the Milwaukee German-Americans have been advocating the same pacifist position for America, at the same time that they defend German militarism.

With real thanks for your letter,

b. "International Duty and Hyphenated Americanism."

I stand for the American citizen of German birth or descent, precisely as I stand for any other American. But I do not stand at all for the German-American, or any other kind of hyphenated American. When I was President I was brought into close contact with many officers of the army and navy. Colonel George Washington Goethals has done the best work done by any American of recent years. He is of Dutch parentage. But he is no more a Dutch-American than I am. He is just plain American. Among my military and naval aides were Lee, Grant, Sheridan, and Osterhaus, all descended from generals who fought in the Union or Confederate armies. Two of them were of old Revolutionary stock, Scotch or English. The grandfather of the third was born in Ireland, and the grandfather of the fourth in Germany. But they were all Americans and nothing else. General Wood, of Revolutionary stock, started Cuba on the road to self-government; General Barry, of Irish parentage, commanded the army that rescued Cuba from revolution; and one was exactly as good an American as the other. Among the admirals upon whom I leaned were Dewey, Evans, Taylor, and Cameron Winslow, of Revolutionary stock; and

An essay in *Fear God and Take Your Own Part* (New York, George H. Doran Co., 1916), pp. 141–5. Printed in *The Works*, XX, 456–59.

[1] Chancellor of Stanford University, 1913–1916 [Ed.].

NONE OF BLACK OR LATIN DESCENT.

O'Neil and Schroeder, one of Irish and the other of German descent; and the last two were exactly as good Americans as the other four. It would have been a crime as well as a calamity to endeavor to divide all these and all the other fine and gallant officers of our army and navy on lines of birth or national origin or creed. It is no less a crime and a calamity to attempt to divide our citizens as a whole along such lines.

There was never a better American than Jacob Riis, who was born in Denmark and whom I always thought about the best American I ever knew. The Americans in whom I believe include Jews and Catholics and Protestants. They include men of old native American descent and other men of recent German, English, French, Irish, Italian, Scandinavian, Magyar, and Slavonic descent; but all are Americans entitled to be treated as such, and claiming to be nothing else. I as emphatically condemn opposition to a good American who happens to be of German birth or descent, because of that fact, as I condemn action by such a man designed to serve not the United States, but some foreign power. I speak against the German-American who seeks to use his American citizenship in the interest of a foreign power and who thereby shows himself an unworthy American. I should speak exactly as quickly against the American of English or French or Scandinavian or Irish descent who was guilty of similar conduct. The following letter which I recently wrote explains itself:

"—— I am very sorry but I cannot sign that appeal. I do not approve of it. You are asking Americans to proclaim themselves Anglo-Americans, and to sympathize with England on the ground that England is the motherland, and in order to make what you call 'hands across the sea' a matter of living policy. I do not believe that this is the right attitude for Americans to take. England is not my motherland any more than Germany is my fatherland. My motherland and fatherland and my own land are all three of them the United States. I am among those Americans whose ancestors include men and

TRUE
REFORMER.

women from many different European countries. The propor-
tion of Americans of this type will steadily increase. I do not
believe in hyphenated Americans. I do not believe in German-
Americans or Irish-Americans; and I believe just as little in
English-Americans. I do not approve of American citizens of
German descent forming organizations to force the United
States into practical alliance with Germany because their ancestors came from Germany. Just as little do I believe in
American citizens of English descent forming leagues to force
the United States into an alliance with England because their
ancestors came from England. We Americans are a separate
people. We are separated from, although akin to, many European peoples. The old Revolutionary stock was predominantly
English, but by no means exclusively so; for many of the descendants of the Revolutionary New Yorkers, Pennsylvanians,
and Georgians have, like myself, strains of Dutch, French,
Scotch, Irish, Welsh, and German blood in their veins. During
the century and a quarter that has elapsed since we became a
nation, there has been far more immigration from Germany
and Ireland and probably from Scandinavia than there has
been from England. We have a right to ask all of these immigrants and the sons of these immigrants that they become
Americans and nothing else; but we have no right to ask that
they become transplanted or second-rate Englishmen. Most
emphatically I myself am not an Englishman-once-removed! I
am straight United States!" . . .

43. · THE OPEN SOCIETY

Roosevelt's commitment to both social justice and cultural unity
made him a vigorous proponent of the open society. He recognized,

Letter to Lyman Abbott, May 29, 1908. *The Letters*, VI, 1041–43 as many old-stock Americans did not, that the channels of social and economic advancement would have to be opened if the newer immigrants were to be assimilated, and as president he appointed the first Jew in history, Oscar Straus, to a cabinet position. Roosevelt's intensely personal feelings on the matter are faithfully represented in this letter to the publisher of *The Outlook*, one of the most influential Protestant, middle-class magazines of the period.

Washington, May 29, 1908

My dear Dr. Abbott: . . . I grow extremely indignant at the attitude of coarse hostility to the immigrant taken by so many natives of the type he describes. I have never had much chance to deal with the Slav, Magyar, or Italian; but wherever I have had the chance I have tried to do with them as with the German and the Irishman, the Catholic and the Jew, and that is, treat them so as to appeal to their self-respect and make it easy for them to become enthusiastically loyal Americans as well as good citizens. I have one Catholic in my Cabinet and have had another, and I now have a Jew in the Cabinet; and part of my object in each appointment was to implant in the minds of our fellow-Americans of Catholic or of Jewish faith, or of foreign ancestry or birth, the knowledge that they have in this country just the same rights and opportunities as everyone else, just the same chance of reward for doing the highest kind of service; and therefore just the same ideals as a standard toward which to strive. I want the Jewish young man who is born in this country to feel that Straus stands for his ideal of the successful man rather than some crooked Jew money-maker. I want the young Catholic of Irish or French descent to feel that if he acts as a good American should, he can become a Cabinet minister like Bonaparte or Wynne; a Governor of the Philippines, like Smith; a judge, like Tracey; in short, that the right chance is open to him and the right ideals before him. In my Cabinet there sit together Meyer,

[handwritten margin note: HE IS BEING TRULY NOBLE IN ELEVATING A #-MAKER TO HIS CABINET]

whose granduncle was a colonel under Blucher at Waterloo; and Bonaparte, whose great grandfather was Napoleon's brother and a king whom Meyer's granduncle helped to overthrow. That they are both good Americans and nothing else is all that we think of; (and it is not considered) nobody asks whether any member of my Cabinet is of English, or Scotch, or Dutch, or German, or Irish descent; whether he is Protestant, Catholic or Jew. In short, we have acted on principles of straight Americanism; and I am glad that before I end my term I shall have in my Cabinet Luke Wright, a representative of the South, a man who fought in the Confederate service, and who is just as loyal an American today as the best veterans of the Grand Army. It was the one thing which I felt was wanted to (point out) emphasize the entire Americanism of the Cabinet, to give it from the national standpoint an absolutely representative character.

So give my regards to Steiner. I wish I could help in some striking fashion to do justice to, and get justice for, the Slav! (just as I hope I have succeeded in doing any good for representatives of other races)—and our other recent immigrants just as has finally been done for the sons of those who came here a generation ago.

Religious Pluralism

44. · RELIGION AND POLITICS

Roosevelt's conception of cultural unity, or, as he called it, "sane nationalism," permitted religious diversity. Though he had no interest in theology, he did regard religion as a powerful moral force;

Letter to J. C. Martin, November 6, 1908. *The Letters*, VI, 1333–35.

and for this reason he was as respectful of Catholicism and Judaism as of his own Protestantism. His religious tolerance was further strengthened by his appreciation of the values of the Founding Fathers, by his hostility toward irrational forms of discrimination, and, most decisively, by his realization that "second-class" citizenship made cultural unity impossible to attain. In 1904 he publicly expressed the wish that a Catholic would someday be elected President. And in 1908 he reacted against the whispering campaign inspired by William Howard Taft's Unitarianism and the false reports that his wife and brother were Catholic by writing this public letter to a Dayton, Ohio, piano dealer.

Washington, November 6, 1908

My dear Sir: I have received your letter running in part as follows:

While it is claimed almost universally that religion should not enter into politics, yet there is no denying that it does, and the mass of the voters that are not Catholics will not support a man for office, especially for President of the United States, who is a Roman Catholic.

Since Taft has been nominated for President by the Republican party, it is being circulated and is constantly urged as a reason for not voting for Taft that he is an infidel (Unitarian) and his wife and brother Roman Catholics. ° ° ° If his feelings are in sympathy with the Roman Catholic church on account of his wife and brother being Catholics, that would be objectionable to a sufficient number of voters to defeat him. On the other hand if he is an infidel, that would be sure to mean defeat. ° ° ° I am writing this letter for the sole purpose of giving Mr. Taft an opportunity to let the world know what his religious belief is.

I received many such letters as yours during the campaign, expressing dissatisfaction with Mr. Taft on religious grounds; some of them on the ground that he was a Unitarian, and others on the ground that he was suspected to be in sympathy with Catholics. I did not answer any of these letters during the campaign because I regarded it as an outrage even to agitate such a question as a man's religious convictions, with the purpose of influencing a political election. But now that the campaign is over, when there is opportunity for men calmly to consider whither such propositions as those you make in your letter would lead, I wish to invite them to consider them, and I have selected your letter to answer because you advance both the objections commonly urged against Mr. Taft, namely: that he is a Unitarian, and also that he is suspected of sympathy with the Catholics.

You ask that Mr. Taft shall "let the world know what his religious belief is." This is purely his own private concern; it is a matter between him and his Maker, a matter for his own conscience; and to require it to be made public under penalty of political discrimination is to negative the first principles of our Government, which guarantee complete religious liberty, and the right to each man to act in religious affairs as his own conscience dictates. Mr. Taft never asked my advice in the matter, but if he had asked it, I should have emphatically advised him against thus stating publicly his religious belief. The demand for a statement of a candidate's religious belief can have no meaning except that there may be discrimination for or against him because of that belief. Discrimination against the holder of one faith means retaliatory discrimination against men of other faiths. The inevitable result of entering upon such a practice would be an abandonment of our real freedom of conscience and a reversion to the dreadful conditions of religious dissension which in so many lands have proved fatal to true liberty, to true religion, and to all advance in civilization.

To discriminate against a thoroly upright citizen because he belongs to some particular church, or because, like Abraham Lincoln, he has not avowed his allegiance to any church, is an outrage against that liberty of conscience which is one of the foundations of American life. You are entitled to know whether a man seeking your suffrages is a man of clean and upright life, honorable in all his dealings with his fellows, and fit by qualification and purpose to do well in the great office for which he is a candidate; but you are not entitled to know matters which lie purely between himself and his Maker. If it is proper or legitimate to oppose a man for being a Unitarian, as was John Quincy Adams, for instance, as is the Rev. Edward Everett Hale, at the present moment Chaplain of the Senate, and an American of whose life all good Americans are proud—then it would be equally proper to support or oppose a man because of his views on justification by faith, or the method of administering the sacrament, or the gospel of salvation by works. If you once enter on such a career there is absolutely no limit at which you can legitimately stop.

So much for your objections to Mr. Taft because he is a Unitarian. Now, for your objections to him because you think his wife and brother to be Roman Catholics. As it happens, they are not; but if they were, or if he were a Roman Catholic himself, it ought not to affect in the slightest degree any man's supporting him for the position of President. You say that "the mass of the voters that are not Catholics will not support a man for any office, especially for President of the United States, who is a Roman Catholic." I believe that when you say this you foully slander your fellow countrymen. I do not for one moment believe that the mass of our fellow citizens, or that any considerable number of our fellow citizens, can be influenced by such narrow bigotry as to refuse to vote for any thoroly upright and fit man because he happens to have a particular religious creed. Such a consideration should never be treated as a reason for either supporting or opposing a candidate for political office. Are you aware that there are several States in this Union where the majority of the people are now Catholics? I should reprobate in the severest terms the Catholics who in those States (or in any other States) refused to vote for the most fit man because he happened to be a Protestant; and my condemnation would be exactly as severe for Protestants who, under reversed circumstances, refused to vote for a Catholic. In public life I am happy to say that I have known many men who were elected, and constantly re-elected, to office in districts where the great majority of their constituents were of a different religious belief. I know Catholics who have for many years represented constituencies mainly Protestant, and Protestants who have for many years represented constituencies mainly Catholic; and among the Congressmen whom I knew particularly well was one man of Jewish faith who represented a district in which there were hardly any Jews at all. All of these men by their very existence in political life refute the slander you have uttered against your fellow Americans.

I believe that this Republic will endure for many centuries. If so there will doubtless be among its Presidents Protestants and Catholics, and, very probably at some time, Jews. I have consistently tried while President to act in relation to my fellow Americans of Catholic faith as I hope that any future President who happens to be a Catholic will act towards his fellow Americans of Protestant faith. Had I followed any other course I should have felt that I was unfit to represent the American people.

In my Cabinet at the present moment there sit side by side Catholic and Protestant, Christian and Jew, each man chosen because in my belief he is peculiarly fit to exercise on behalf of all our people the duties of the office to which I have appointed him. In no case does the man's religious belief in any way influence his discharge of his duties, save as it makes him more eager to act justly and uprightly in his relations to all men. The same principles that have obtained in appointing the members of my Cabinet, the highest officials under me, the officials to whom is entrusted the work of carrying out all the important policies of my administration, are the principles upon which all good Americans should act in choosing, whether by election or appointment, the man to fill any office from the highest to the lowest in the land.

45. · "RELIGION AND THE PUBLIC SCHOOLS"

Another reason for Roosevelt's religious tolerance was his belief that the public-school system would ultimately blunt religious differences. Accordingly, he supported public education warmly and constantly guarded against the infiltration of denominational influences. In this speech, delivered in a city where Catholic influence on the public-shool system was already strong, he warns, among other things, against public aid to religious schools.

It is a very real pleasure for me that I am able to speak tonight on such a subject in answer to a request made by such men as those who asked me to come, and it is always a pleasure to me to speak to a Massachusetts audience, for I can say with all sincerity that a man who addresses the people of your State is justified in feeling that he will meet a prompt and hearty response to any appeal on behalf of honesty, of fair play, of decent government, and of whole-hearted Americanism.

What I mean to dwell upon especially is the American side of the public-school question. There is no need for me to argue before an audience like this in favor of the public schools.

A speech at Boston, Massachusetts, November 1893. Reprinted in *Citizenship, Politics, and the Elemental Values, The Works,* XV, 32–40. Originally appeared in *American Ideals and Other Essays, Social and Political* (G. P. Putnam's Sons, 1897).

There is no need to say a word to the men and women of Massachusetts in behalf of a free system of non-sectarian education by the State, a system which guarantees an education to every boy and girl, without any more regard being paid to creed than to birthplace.

The public schools are the nurseries from which spring the future masters of the commonwealth; and, in making up the estimate of any State's real greatness, the efficiency of its public-school system and the extent to which it is successful in reaching all the children in the State count for a hundredfold more than railroads and manufactories, than shipping or farms, than anything which is symbolic of mere material prosperity, great though the importance of this mere material prosperity undoubtedly also is. Napoleon, in speaking of his soldiers, is reported to have said that in warfare the moral is to the physical as ten to one; and what is true in the army is no less true in civil life.

It is of the utmost importance that our people shall be well housed, well clothed, and well fed; but all this shall avail nothing if they have not well-trained minds and a sturdy and convinced morality, while if only they possess these last two attributes, if only they possess character and common sense, there is no fear whatsoever that they will lack those material things which they can "earn" by the labor of their hands.

Because we are unqualifiedly and without reservation against any system of denominational schools maintained by the adherents of any creed with the help of State aid, therefore we as strenuously insist that the public schools shall be free from sectarian influences, and, above all, free from any attitude of hostility to the adherents of any particular creed; and we denounce as the worst foes of the public schools those who, under the pretense of friendship for them, stir up hostility toward them by seeking to discriminate in their name against those people who hold a given religious belief. Exactly as we welcome to them alike the children of Jew and Gentile, of Catholic and Protestant, so we insist that in their management no one creed shall have any special jurisdiction, but the professors of all creeds be treated alike, in order that every American citizen, without regard to what his own private religious belief may be, shall feel that he has as much voice as any other man, whether of his own faith or of some different faith, in the management of the schools to which his children go.

In other words, our plea is simply that in your treatment of the common school you act as every man should act in American public life, as a whole. We have a right to demand that every man, native born or foreign born, shall in American public life act merely as an American. To quote a phrase I have used more than once before, we don't wish any hyphenated Americans; we do not wish you to act as Irish-Americans or British-Americans or native-Americans; but as Americans pure and simple.

Permit me to give you a small illustration out of my own recent experience. The other day, in choosing a civil-service board in a northwestern post-office, I was in doubt as to which of two equally good men to take for a certain vacancy. Then I was informed, through some self-constituted spokesman of the town, that one of these men was a Protestant and one a Catholic, and that the latter must not be appointed, as the town was controlled by an organization which objected to any but Protestants holding such positions. That settled it; my doubts were resolved at once; and I immediately appointed the Catholic, exactly as, had the situation been reversed, and similar objection been raised against the Protestant, I would have appointed him. As far as the sphere of my official action extends I can guarantee that any manifestation of such feeling will be checked in short order.

The Know-nothing Movement in every form is entirely repugnant to true Americanism and this is, perhaps, especially the case when it is directed not merely against American citizens of foreign origin, but also against even native-born Americans of a different creed. We Americans give to men of all races equal and exact justice. That has been our boast as a nation ever since the day when the Puritan of Massachusetts and the Catholic of Maryland sat in the same hall and signed the same Declaration of Independence. On the roll of honor where we have engraved the names of the nation's statesmen and soldiers, patriots and commonwealth-builders, no distinction is known of creed or of race origin, nor even of birthplace. What man with a particle of patriotic spirit would be capable of paying heed to the fact that Albert Gallatin, the secretary of the treasury, came from Switzerland, any more than of paying heed to the fact that Carl Schurz, the secretary of the interior, came from Germany? What man who reveres our flag and holds precious its honor and glory cares whether the soldiers who followed Sherman in his great march to the sea followed a Protestant, or the soldiers who were rallied by Sheridan after his great ride from Winchester were rallied by a Catholic? . . .

. . . Moreover, exactly as all Americans have a common right to be proud of American statesmen and soldiers and writers, utterly regardless of what their religious convictions may have been, so long as they did all that in them lay for America, so all Americans, without distinction of faith, have a right to be proud of those great men who stand as the exponents of the different creeds on American soil, who stand as the leaders in our religious thought. The country is better, every man in it, Protestant or Catholic, is better, because of the life of Bishop Brooks; and in the same way, every true American, Catholic or Protestant, should be glad that there lives in the United States so stout a champion of Americanism as Archbishop Ireland— the only bishop, by the way, in existence, who is entitled to wear that badge of nobility, the button of the Loyal Legion.

What I have said about Americanism in connection with our whole political life applies with peculiar force to the public schools. We should set our faces like a rock against any attempt to allow State aid to be given to any sectarian system of education; and on the other hand, we should set our faces like a rock against any attempt to exclude any set of men from their full and proper share in the government of the public schools because of their religion. There should, of course, be frank and vigorous condemnation of any attempt to put in control of the public schools men hostile to them, just as there should be of any attempt to coerce children from being sent to them; but remember to be just in your condemnation, and to condemn individuals and not classes unless the classes really deserve it.

There are Lutherans and Episcopalians who are hostile to the public schools as well as Catholics; and there are plenty of others who vie with one another in eager and intelligent support of the schools. Only yesterday I was reading an account of a very interesting ceremony in Father Corrigan's Catholic church in Hoboken. In his address Father Corrigan emphasized the fact that a very large section of his church in America favored the public schools, and insisted that to abandon that position would be the greatest calamity that could befall the church in America; and the draping of our national flag and the singing of the national anthem were the most prominent features in the exercises. Certainly it would be difficult to wish for more thoroughgoing Americanism than this.

I am a pretty good party man, and do not leave my party on any issue, unless I think that I really ought to, yet I should most certainly refuse to support a school ticket made up by any party if it was made up avowedly in the interests of the professors of one creed—whether it was my own creed or not—and with the purpose of discriminating against those who hold a different religious belief. If I found that Catholics were attempting to establish Catholic control over the public schools, I should certainly fight them for all that was in me, and if I found that Protestants were trying to do the same thing, I should fight them every whit as hard.

One of the very greatest benefits arising from the public

schools is that Catholics and Protestants, Americans of every origin and faith, brought up in them, inevitably in after-life have kindlier feelings toward their old school-fellows of different creeds, and look at them with a wiser and manlier charity, than could possibly be the case had they never had a chance to mingle together in their youth; thus the possibility for the growth on American soil of the savage sectarian hatreds of Europe is minimized. But this kindly feeling can never exist if one side has legitimate cause for the belief that it is being discriminated against by the other, and especially if, in the name of toleration, intolerance comes to the fore.

The bigots who advocate and try to bring about such discrimination are really playing into the hands of the upholders of sectarian schools.

When I was in the New York legislature, on two or three different occasions, bills were introduced appropriating money to Roman Catholic institutions, and I opposed them on the broad ground that it was against the American idea to give money for any sectarian purpose, and though I was denounced, of course, by certain bigots for my attitude, yet I received the hearty and cordial support of the bulk of my many Catholic friends and associates, social and political, and of all those for whose opinion I most cared; and there were Catholic votes cast as mine were in the New York legislature.

So if there were any tendency to try to control the public schools in a Know-nothing spirit, to try to discriminate against Catholics, whether as trustees or as teachers, because they were Catholics, any desire not to give them, when it was deserved, the same ample and cordial recognition that good trustees and teachers ought to have, then I am sure that I can appeal to every right-thinking American, whatever his religion, to stand up against so utterly un-American a doctrine, and to do his best to see that full justice is done to the Catholic, as much as to the Protestant.

Exactly as in our public schools the lessons should be conducted in no language but in English, neither in German, French, Spanish, or any other, exactly as the children should be taught to speak United States and to think United States, and to be United States, so we have a right to demand that the voters, in settling about the public schools, should vote as Americans merely, and should realize that it is utterly abhorrent to and unworthy of real Americanism to discriminate for or against any American because of his birthplace or because of his creed.

Immigration Restriction

46. · TOWARD MORE SCIENTIFIC ADMISSIONS STANDARDS

Despite his enlightened attitude toward first-generation Americans, Roosevelt believed that immigration should be controlled. His Annual Messages repeatedly adverted to the need for comprehensive revision of admissions policy, and in 1907 Congress responded by creating the Dillingham Commission. Although the Commission was later charged with racism, Roosevelt and most of the Commission's members were more concerned with the economics than the eugenics of immigration. In common with labor leaders and many of the nation's leading economists and sociologists, Roosevelt feared that the unrestricted influx of unskilled laborers was holding down wages; and like many of these same sociologists, he also believed that too many morally, mentally, or physically unfit immigrants were being admitted. But as his assertion that "we cannot afford to pay heed to whether . . . [the immigrant] is of one creed or another, of one nation or another" implies, he had little sympathy with racist views of the Immigration Restriction League or many of the country's leading intellectuals.

From the Annual Message to Congress, 1905. *Messages and Papers,* XI, 1165–66.

The question of immigration is of vital interest to this country. In the year ending June 30, 1905, there came to the United States 1,026,000 alien immigrants. In other words, in the single year that has just elapsed there came to this country a greater number of people than came here during the 169 years of our colonial life which intervened between the first landing at Jamestown and the Declaration of Independence. It is clearly shown in the report of the commissioner-general of immigration that while much of this enormous immigration is undoubtedly healthy and natural, a considerable proportion is undesirable from one reason or another; moreover, a considerable proportion of it, probably a very large proportion, including most of the undesirable class, does not come here of its own initiative, but because of the activity of the agents of the great transportation companies. These agents are distributed throughout Europe, and by the offer of all kinds of inducements they wheedle and cajole many immigrants, often against their best interest, to come here. The most serious obstacle we have to encounter in the effort to secure a proper regulation of the immigration to these shores arises from the determined opposition of the foreign steam-ship lines who have no interest whatever in the matter save to increase the returns on their capital by carrying masses of immigrants hither in the steerage quarters of their ships.

As I said in my last message to the Congress, we cannot have too much immigration of the right sort and we should have none whatever of the wrong sort. Of course, it is desirable that even the right kind of immigration should be properly distributed in this country. We need more of such immigration for the South; and special effort should be made to secure it. Perhaps it would be possible to limit the number of immigrants allowed to come in any one year to New York and other Northern cities, while leaving unlimited the number allowed to come to the South; always provided, however, that a stricter effort is made to see that only immigrants of the right kind come to our country anywhere. In actual practice it has proved so difficult to enforce the immigration laws where long stretches of frontier marked by an imaginary line alone intervene between us and our neighbors that I recommend that no immigrants be allowed to come in from Canada and Mexico save natives of the two countries themselves. As much as possible should be done to distribute the immigrants upon the land and keep them away from the congested tenement-house districts of the great cities. But distribution is a palliative, not a cure. The prime need is to keep out all immigrants who will not make good American citizens. The laws now existing for the exclusion of undesirable immigrants should be strengthened. Adequate means should be adopted, enforced by sufficient penalties, to compel steamship companies engaged in the passenger business to observe in good faith the law which forbids them to encourage or solicit immigration to the United States. Moreover, there should be a sharp limitation imposed upon all vessels coming to our ports as to the number of immigrants in ratio to the tonnage which each vessel can carry. This ratio should be high enough to insure the coming hither of as good a class of aliens as possible. Provision should be made for the surer punishment of those who induce aliens to come to this country under promise or assurance of employment. It should be made possible to inflict a sufficiently heavy penalty on any employer violating this law to deter him from taking the risk. It seems to me wise that there should be an international conference held to deal with this question of immigration, which has more than a merely national significance; such a conference could, among other things, enter at length into the methods for securing a thorough inspection of would-be immigrants at the ports from which they desire to embark before permitting them to embark.

In dealing with this question it is unwise to depart from the old American tradition and to discriminate for or against any man who desires to come here and become a citizen, save on the ground of that man's fitness for citizenship. It is our right and duty to consider his moral and social quality. His standard of living should be such that he will not, by pressure of competition, lower the standard of living of our own wage-workers; for it must ever be a prime object of our legislation to keep high their standard of living. If the man who seeks to come here is from the moral and social standpoint of such a character as to bid fair to add value to the community he should be heartily welcomed. We cannot afford to pay heed to whether he is of one creed or another, of one nation or another. We cannot afford to consider whether he is Catholic or Protestant, Jew or Gentile; whether he is Englishman or Irishman, Frenchman or German, Japanese, Italian, Scandinavian, Slav, or Magyar. What we should desire to find out is the individual quality of the individual man. In my judgment, with this end in view, we shall have to prepare through our own agents a far more rigid inspection in the countries from which the immigrants come. It will be a great deal better to have fewer immigrants, but all of the right kind, than a great number of immigrants, many of whom are necessarily of the wrong kind. As far as possible we wish to limit the immigration to this country to persons who propose to become citizens of this country, and we can well afford to insist upon adequate scrutiny of the character of those who are thus proposed for future citizenship. There should be an increase in the stringency of the laws to keep out insane, idiotic, epileptic, and pauper immigrants. But this is by no means enough. Not merely the anarchist, but every man of anarchistic tendencies, all violent and disorderly people, all people of bad character, the incompetent, the lazy, the vicious, the physically unfit, defective, or degenerate should be kept out. The stocks out of which American citizenship is to be built should be strong and healthy, sound in body, mind, and character. If it be objected that the government agents would not always select well, the answer is that they would certainly select better than do the agents and brokers of foreign steamship companies, the people who now do whatever selection is done.

IX · THE SCIENCE OF
GOVERNMENT

Civil Service Reform

47. · "THE SPOILS SYSTEM IN OPERATION"

In no cause except national defense was Roosevelt's interest deeper and his support more sustained than in civil service reform. He concluded early in life that republican government would rise or fall on the integrity and efficiency of its office holders, and from the beginning to the end of his political career he fought vigorously to improve and expand the merit principle. Appointed to the United States Civil Service Commission in the spring of 1889, Roosevelt energized, and in a very real sense, institutionalized, what had been to then a precarious and ill-supported experiment. The speech printed below is graphically revealing of the values and experiences he brought to his new office.

I was asked down here distinctly on the understanding that I was to be the tail of the kite. That was put first in writing, and for fear I should mistake it and think I was a part of the kite, it was afterward told me personally. Now I am perfectly willing to be the tail, but I think it very hard that the body of the kite should make fun of me.

I am not a mere theorist; I have been a practical Republican politician, and as such I have fallen under the displeasure of

Address before the Civil Service Reform Association, Baltimore, Maryland, February 23, 1889. *Civil Service Reformer*, V (March 1889), 40–1.

some of you, and I came down simply, as our Methodist friends say, "to bear testimony." I want the Republican party to keep the pledges in victory which it made in adversity, and I want to do my small share in making the party keep those promises. It is always easy for an individual or a party to make promises; the strain comes when the party or individual has to make them good. Now the Republican party has committed itself definitely against the spoils system. On that point its platform leaves no room for doubt. President-elect Harrison's letter leaves no room for doubt as to his position. I feel sure that, from a merely selfish standpoint, it will inure to the benefit of the Republican party to keep its pledge; but whether it does or does not so inure, I wish to see that pledge kept. I feel that this is a true reform. For that reason I not only admire and honor Senators Hoar and Hawley, Congressmen Lodge, of Massachusetts, Hitt, of Illinois, and your own able representative, Mr. McComas, as citizens, but I regard them as loyally keeping faith with the party, by the stand they have taken in Congress. On the other hand, when Senator Ingalls sees fit to appear as the mouthpiece and champion of the spoilsman, not only do I feel outraged as a citizen at his appearing in this guise, making himself a part of all that is most evil and most degrading in our politics, but I feel that he is a traitor to his party. I do not think there can be doubt about my position on this question.

I think it is mere idle chatter to talk of the merit system as being undemocratic and un-American. The spoils system is emphatically undemocratic, for the spoils system means the establishing and perpetuation of a grasping and ignorant oligarchy. The merit system is essentially democratic and essentially American, and in line with the utterances and deeds of our forefathers of the days of Washington and Madison. If you will pardon me, I will give a personal experience of mine in New York to prove the corruption of the spoils system. Without expressing too much local pride, I doubt if even

Baltimore offers more fertile object-lessons of this sort than New York.

I remember when I was first elected to the legislature receiving several applications for appointment on the police force. One applicant said he wished to be a policeman because he unfortunately had the habit of getting drunk and so could not get any other work. Another wrote me, and I have the letter now, that he wanted me to get a friend of his appointed a policeman because the friend had promised him two hundred dollars to get him appointed, and he knew I would rather have that money go to a Republican than to a Democrat. Another instance occurred during the course of an investigation which, as chairman of a legislative committee, I conducted, into the working of some of the departments in New York. I cannot be absolutely certain as to the details of the figures at this distance of time, but what I shall say is in substance correct. We had under examination the county clerk, Mr. Keenan.

He was one of the most delightful witnesses that was ever before a legislative committee. Not having engaged counsel, he held back nothing and told us the literal truth. We asked him what was the amount of his fees in a year. He said eighty-two thousand dollars a year. Now, that is about a quarter of a million dollars for his three years' term. We asked him what he had contributed to the campaign fund of his party. Well, he didn't know. We pressed him, and finally he replied he could not say whether it was over or under fifty thousand dollars. Then came a question which was asked perfunctorily and to which an entirely perfunctory answer was expected. I asked him if he attended to the duties of his office. He rather electrified the committee by saying very promptly that he did not. I said: "Mr. Keenan, I doubt if you have understood the point of what I have asked you; I mean, do you do your official duties?" He answered: "Yes, when they don't interfere with my political duties." "Now," I said, "will you kindly explain to me what you mean by political duties?" That he evidently regarded as a piece of hypocrisy on my part, for he said to me reproachfully: "Mr. Roosevelt, you are a member of a political organization yourself." He then told us, by way of illustration of the pressure of his political duties, that he was unable to come down earlier in the morning than twelve o'clock, as he had to spend a good part of the morning "bailing out his 'constituents'!"

I use this illustration merely to point out to you what is a spoilsman's theory of duty. He represented, I believe, the better class of spoilsmen, because there is a worse class—the class that steals. We had at that time a prominent member of the board of aldermen who in his leisure hours was a burglar. In his youth he had followed that trade, and though rather an old man, and one who had risen in the world, he would still resume it occasionally for amusement. We had another very prominent politician who was a "fence," a receiver of stolen goods. Mr. Keenan was a perfectly honest man as far as I know. It never occurred to him that that was not the right way to run a public office. He told us another fact which illustrates the wastefulness of the spoils system. I asked Keenan how he did his duties, and he said he paid his deputy extra to do them. This deputy was paid three thousand dollars a year by the city to do his own work as deputy, but Keenan, out of his eighty-two thousand dollars, paid one thousand five hundred dollars more to his deputy to do Keenan's work. So that gives you the exact market value of the work Keenan had to do. This immense sum of eighty-two thousand dollars was regarded partly as a reward for Keenan's political services, and partly as a fund to defray campaign expenses for his party. A state of affairs like that will inevitably produce corruption in the ballot. In New York City I don't believe there is as much actual buying of votes, although there is a good deal, as there is in the country districts, but corruption is generally effected by buying the district leaders or the district organizations. These would be powerless but for the spoils system.

Pardon me one more personal reminiscence. The last time I appeared before my people for office, a gentleman told me that whatever party I belonged to before the election, after the election I belonged to the party of "the extreme left." Possibly this story will explain my misfortune as well as illustrate my point.

I was at our headquarters one day, when a card was brought in from O'Donovan Rossa. I went out to see him, and he was not a prepossessing-looking gentleman. He came down straight and square and instantly to work. He said I was running for mayor and he would like to help me, and would guarantee me his influence in his journal and in his local dynamite societies for the sum of two hundred and fifty dollars. I told him that I was much obliged for his courtesy in thinking of me, but I would not close with his offer. "I see," he said, "you are running this canvass for your health; I thought you wanted to win." Then I told him there were very few people in New York whom I could afford to insult at that time, but he was one of them, and I would thank him to get out.

These are not exceptional cases, but are the habitual, invariable accompaniment and product of the spoils system in great cities.

I think that, of all people who are harmed by the spoils system, the poor suffer most. The rich man who wishes to corrupt a legislature, or the rich company which wishes to buy franchises from a board of aldermen and pay a big price for it, do not suffer so much as the poor from the results of the system. I dare say that in New York we see the system at its worst, but at its best it is thoroughly rotten, and a disgrace to every community enjoying the right of suffrage.

I am from my heart a Republican. I honor Benjamin Harrison, and I believe the Republican party and the Republican President will have the best chance to do a great work that they have ever had since the close of the Civil War. If they can rise to the height of it, they will confer an immense advantage on the party and an inestimable advantage on the country. I expect from the President an extension of the classified service, and I wish to see Congress repeal the four-years-term act, and make such appropriations that the Civil Service Commission's work shall be unhampered.

48. · "THE MERIT SYSTEM VERSUS THE PATRONAGE SYSTEM"

As most men who knew him agree, Roosevelt was above all else a moralist. Here, in a characteristic effort to marshal public support for civil service reform, the values that made him the conscience of the nation for hundreds of thousands of men and women are intersticed with a classic statement of the case for the merit system. What emerges is a sense of fairmindedness, a deep commitment to democracy, the open society, and the good of the whole; also, undisguised contempt for those unmoved by higher considerations than self-interest. Even more than the cult of efficiency, these were the values behind Roosevelt's consuming interest in a strong civil service system based on merit.

In American politics there obtain at the present moment two systems in accordance with which appointments to minor governmental positions are made—the spoils or patronage system, and the merit or reformed system. The underlying principle of the former is that set forth in the pithy and now famous sentence of one of its founders, "To the victors belong

Theodore Roosevelt, "The Merit System Versus the Patronage System," *The Century*, XXXIX (February 1890), 628–33.

the spoils." It treats all offices as fit objects wherewith to reward partisan service, as prizes to be scrambled for by the smirched victors in a contemptible struggle for political plunder, as bribes to be parcelled out among the most active and influential henchmen of the various party leaders. The upholders of the merit system, on the other hand, maintain that offices should be held for the benefit of the whole public, and not for the benefit of that particular section of the public which enters into politics as a lucrative, though rather dirty, game; they believe that the multitude of small government positions, of which the duties are wholly unconnected with political questions, should be filled by candidates selected, not for political reasons, but solely with reference to their special fitness for the duty they seek to perform; and, furthermore, they believe that the truly American and democratic way of filling these offices is by an open and manly rivalry, into which every American citizen has a right to enter, without any more regard being paid to his political than to his religious creed, and without being required to render degrading service to any party boss, or do aught save show by common-sense, practical tests that he is the man best fitted to perform the particular service needed.

This is a perfectly fair and moderate statement of the two contrasted systems; and when the question is thus resolved into its simplest terms it is, of course, impossible for any honest and intelligent citizen to hesitate in his choice. Unfortunately, however, it is almost impossible to get the average voter to realize that the above really is a true statement of the question, when stripped of verbiage, and put in the language of naked truth. He is apt to be misled by the unceasing clamor of the interested advocates of the old spoils system; and their name is legion, for they include every place-mongering big politician and every place-hunting small politician in the land, not to speak of the malodorous tribe of political hangers-on, who are too lazy to do honest work, and who know very well that if tried by the standard of merit alone they would no longer have the faintest chance of getting easy jobs at the public expense. These people are naturally ferocious foes of a reform which would deprive them of their exceedingly noxious influence in public affairs; and in their opposition they receive powerful aid from the cynicism of many intelligent men, who do not believe it possible to better political conditions; from the puzzle-headed inability of many honest, but prejudiced and narrow-minded, people to understand what the question really is, and from the good nature, the indifference, the selfishness, the timidity, and the conservatism of that large number of citizens who never bestir themselves to do away with any evil that is not brought sharply home to their pockets.

One great trouble is that, thanks to having lived under the spoils system for sixty years, a great many people have come to accept it as being inevitably incident to our system of politics; and they grumble at it only as they grumble at droughts or freshets. Besides, they know there are in every party plenty of men competent to fill the offices; and they vaguely believe that it is merely a question as to which set of competent men is chosen. But this is not the case at all. If a party victory meant that all offices already filled by the most competent members of the defeated party were to be thereafter filled by the most competent members of the victorious party, the system would still be absurd, but it would not be particularly baneful. In reality, however, this is not what the system of partisan appointments means at all. Wherever it is adopted it is inevitable that the degree of party service, or more often of service to some particular leader, and not merit, shall ultimately determine the appointment, even as among the different party candidates themselves. Once admit that it is proper to turn out an efficient Republican clerk in order to replace him by an efficient Democratic clerk, or *vice versa,* and the inevitable next step is to consider solely Republicanism or Democracy, and not efficiency, in making the appointment;

while the equally inevitable third step is to consider only that peculiar species of Republicanism or Democracy which is implied in adroit and unscrupulous service rendered to the most influential local boss. Of course, both boss and henchman are often—perhaps generally—very good fellows, anxious to make good records and serve the public well; but it is at least safe to say that this is not necessarily the case.

The evil of the spoils system consists much less in the monopolizing of the offices by one party than in the monopolizing of the offices by the politicians at the expense of the people. Yet we have become so wedded to the vicious theory of party appointments that many men in public life are not even able to understand what is really the evil of which we complain; and hence some sapient gentlemen have recently been advocating a plan to divide all the offices among the adherents of both parties, by distributing them among the congressmen. . . .

. . . It is therefore perfectly plain that the remedy lies in changing the system. For honest politicians to refrain from meddling with patronage, while leaving dishonest politicians full liberty to do so, is in the long run to work harm rather than good. The offices must be taken out of reach of all politicians, good or bad, by some permanent system of law.

The civil-service law accomplishes this end wherever it applies and is enforced; and in consequence the government employees protected by it, over twenty-eight thousand in all—nearly a fourth of the total number in the service of the United States—are now withdrawn from the degrading influences of the spoils system; and, as a direct result, in these offices the public business is performed more honestly and efficiently than ever before, while the offices themselves no longer form part of the vast bribery fund which is what the official patronage has become. The adherents of the old system naturally detest the new one, because of the good which it has done; and when, for very shame, they dare not openly defend the abuses by which they and their kind profit, they strive to do it indirectly by attacking the proposed remedy. They admit that the patronage system is evil; but try to delay real reform by proposing some foolish measure that would accomplish nothing but harm, or else confine themselves to clamorous misrepresentations of the purpose and scope of the only genuine measure of relief that has yet been proposed. . . .

As a rule, however, the opponents of the reform neither argue intelligently against it nor propose any substitute, but confine themselves strictly to simple misrepresentation and abuse. It is, of course, the kind of measure which especially arouses the ire of the cheaper variety of demagogue—the man who naturally opposes any measure to promote honest and decent government. Such a one has not morality enough to be ashamed of avowing that he wishes to pay off his private political debts by bribes, at the public expense, in the shape of offices, and is both too coarse-minded and too dull-witted to feel the scorn with which he and his antics are regarded by all upright and honorable thinking men. No argument is too flimsy or too contemptible for him to try. He takes great delight in calling the merit system "Chinese," apparently because one of its adjuncts is the competitive examination, while in China there has long existed a clumsy and overgrown system of such examinations. As well might he inveigh against our alphabet because the Chinese have long had a cumbersome alphabet of their own, or against the use of gunpowder because it was first used in China, or decline to carry a Winchester rifle because jingals have long been known in the East. Again, he rails at the system as "English," and as tending to produce an "office-holding aristocracy." Of course he does not believe these arguments; he can't, and retain his sanity. While England was a purely aristocratic community the spoils system flourished there far more rankly than ever it did here; and it is only since England has begun to take giant strides toward democracy that she has introduced the merit system, which the founders of our own Republic regarded as the only one worthy of a

free and high-minded nation. A system which opens the public
service to all men, of whatever rank in life, who prove themselves most worthy to enter it, and which retains them in office
only so long as they serve the public with honesty, efficiency,
and courtesy, is in its very essence democratic; whereas, on
the contrary, the spoils system—which still obtains in most
European kingdoms, and reaches its fullest development under
the despotic government of Russia—is essentially undemocratic, in that it treats the public service not as the property
of the whole people, to be administered solely in their interest,
but as a bribery chest for the benefit of a few powerful individuals, or groups of individuals, who use it purely in the spirit
of personal or political favoritism. It is among the most potent
of the many forces which combine to produce the ward boss,
the district heeler, the boodle alderman, and all their base and
obscure kindred who in our great cities are ever striving to
change the government from an honest democracy into a corrupt and ignorant oligarchy, wherein only the vile and the dishonest shall rule and hold office.

When a man is ashamed to use such merely demagogic arguments, he commonly, as a last resort, assails the methods by
which it is attempted to put theory into practice, and especially
the competitive examinations. Of course in introducing a radi-
cally new system there is bound to be friction. In extending the
limits of the classified service inevitably from time to time mis-
takes are made, which the commission strive forthwith to correct; and in preparing a multitude of examination-papers they
occasionally ask questions which it would be wise to leave
unasked, or try to test a man's capacity in some way which
experience shows will not work satisfactorily. Any fault of this
character should of course be pointed out and immediately
remedied; but, equally of course, it furnishes no serious argument against the system. . . .

One of these assertions is that the examinations favor "boys
fresh from school," instead of men with experience of the

world. This is simply untrue. The average age of successful candidates for the ordinary positions, such as those of clerk and letter-carrier, is about twenty-eight years. The boy fresh from school evidently stands less chance than the man who has left his school-days at least ten years behind him.

But the favorite assertion is, that "irrelevant" and "impractical" questions are asked. This again is simply false. The commission strongly object to asking irrelevant questions. Surely no questions can be so irrelevant to a man's duties as copyist or railway-mail clerk as are questions about his political backing and about how he voted at the last election; and these are the very questions which those who thus prate about the examinations are themselves desirous of asking. As a matter of fact the questions are strictly pertinent to the positions for which the candidates are examined. The commission has not yet tried to introduce a merit test for laborers, although this must in the end be done (probably on the lines indicated by the Massachusetts State law, which provides for a system of registration of laborers). As yet the great bulk of the examinations, probably ninety per cent, are held to fill positions as clerk, copyist, letter-carrier, and the like. In all these cases plain, common-sense questions are asked, such as appeal to the average intelligence as being suitable for testing the applicant's fitness for the special position he seeks to fill. . . .

Finally, we who believe in the reform refer to that best of tests, experience, as demonstrating, beyond all question, that the merit system is not only practical, but produces the most admirable results. Wherever a public officer has taken office, believing in the law, or, even if not believing in it, willing to give it a fair and honest trial, it has invariably been found to work well. The public offices which have furnished the most conspicuous examples of honest and efficient administration of the public business have been precisely those in which the civil-service law has been most rigidly and scrupulously obeyed. . . .

The merit system is the system of fair play, of common sense, and of common honesty; and therefore it is essentially American and essentially democratic.

49. · "FAIR PLAY IN THE CIVIL SERVICE: AN OPEN LETTER"

The policies described in this open letter were typical of those Roosevelt pursued during his six years on the Civil Service Commission. He often lectured Congress on the need to improve the existing law. He called Southern Democratic congressmen into his office to explain how their constituents could win federal jobs by competitive examination. And he firmly refused to jump names on the lists. As he once admonished a job-seeker who had the temerity to discuss his connections, "No political influence will help you in the least. Not both your Senators and all your Representatives in Congress together could avail to have you certified from our registers."

I am informed by the local board of examiners of the Baltimore Post-Office that at present few but Republicans apply to be examined for the positions of carriers and clerks in that office. In view of the approaching August examinations I wish to make through your columns a statement to all Democrats, and to all citizens generally, without regard to party affiliations, who may think of applying for such positions. On behalf of the Civil Service Commission I desire to extend an earnest invitation to all who wish to enter the classified service at the Baltimore Post-Office to come forward and be examined. The commission will do all in its power to see that they are treated with perfect fairness, irrespective of their party affiliations, and will guarantee that their papers will be marked and their

Letter to the Editor of the Baltimore *Sun,* June 1890. Printed in the *Civil Service Reformer,* VI (July 1890), 73.

names listed and certified for appointment exactly according to the averages they make for themselves in the examination. It is illegal for the postmaster or any appointing officer to refuse to appoint, or to discriminate in any way against, any candidate for a place in the classified service because of his politics. The law is designed expressly to secure an equal chance to Republicans and Democrats. Democrats have exactly the same right that Republicans have to examination and certification by the commission and to appointment by the postmaster or other appointing officer. Under the law affecting the classified service it is an offense, punishable by removal from office, for the postmaster or any similar officer to try to find out a man's politics, or to take politics into account in any way in making appointments.

I sincerely hope that every young man, whatever his politics, Democratic or otherwise, who desires to enter the government service as a clerk or carrier in the Baltimore Post-Office will come forward at the next examination. We guarantee him fair play as far as we are concerned. It is our especial desire to get Democrats to enter these examinations as freely as Republicans, and we shall do all in our power to see that political considerations are given no weight in making appointments, and that all applicants, Democrats and Republicans, are treated alike.

The Art of Administration

50. · THE EXECUTIVE DIRECTS HIS SUBORDINATES

Among the reasons for Roosevelt's success as an administrator were his continuous attention to detail, his readiness to compromise constructively, and his capacity for growth. The following letter to the Interstate Commerce Commission bears on all three. During the debate on the Hepburn railroad rate regulation bill in 1906, Roosevelt had rejected Senator Robert M. La Follette's proposal that he fight for a physical evaluation clause on the realistic grounds that Congress would refuse to approve it and possibly turn down the bill as a whole. Events proved the President right; he won as much as it was possible to win at that time and from that Congress. Characteristically, however, he then marshaled opinion behind physical evaluation in preparation for the next test.

Washington, March 15, 1907

Gentlemen: In view of certain facts that have been brought out in connection with your recent investigation concerning the consolidation and combination of the Union Pacific, Southern Pacific and other roads, and in view of certain complaints and inquiries addrest to me concerning the large issues of stock of various other roads, it seems to me that the time is ripe for your body to report to me specific recommendations on various points where I think the powers of the Government, acting thru your Commission, should be greatly increased.

In the first place, I feel that the time has come when there should be in the possession of the Government full knowledge of the real value or worth of and the indebtedness of the various railroads of the country. I wish to know the physical valuation of the roads, in addition of course to their nominal valuation. In this connection it is, I suppose, almost unnecessary to point out that the valuation of the terminals must not be divorced from the valuation of the other railroad property, tho it should be separately stated. The knowledge as to the real and nominal valuation will not only be of worth in dealing with the question of rates, but also in dealing with the next point as to which I desire your specific advice.

Letter to the Interstate Commerce Commission, March 15, 1907. *The Letters*, V, 622–23.

The next point is as to what specific measure should be recommended by me to the Congress for the purpose of securing supervision and control by action thru your body of the capitalization of the stock and bond issues of the various railroads. Of the great issues of stocks and bonds now going on, some doubtless are for entirely legitimate purposes; others may be for trading or speculative purposes. This should no longer be allowed. Exactly as the developments in the insurance investigations a year ago showed the necessity of a far more rigid governmental control of insurance companies, so your investigations have proved the necessity of a far more rigid governmental control of railroad companies. I do not believe in the sweeping and indiscriminate prohibition of all combinations which has been so marked and as I think so mischievous a feature of our anti-trust legislation. I believe that certain combinations are necessary to the proper conduct of business. But I believe that they should be entered into only subject to the approval of your Commission and subject to their publication in detail. With these two conditions fulfilled it would be out of the question for the combination to do hurt, and as your body has pointed out in its report it is impossible to carry on the business of the country save by certain of the traffic combinations which the law condemns. In other words I should make the approval of your Commission a condition precedent to the establishment of the combination instead of permitting the combination to be entered into and then action to be taken to test its propriety.

I should like from your further careful study of the question a fairly comprehensive outline of some system of national incorporation or national license which would give the national government far-reaching control over all railroads engaged in interstate commerce. I desire from you on this point as well as upon the others that I raise information in such detail as will enable me definitely to indicate to the Congress the exact kind of law demanded by the situation.

I desire to know the relations of the big railway corporations to the smaller corporations they control and also to the water transportation companies which they control. I also desire to know as far as you are able to furnish the information, the ownership of the great industrial enterprises along the lines of the great railroads, in so far as these great railroads have interest in or ownership of these industrial enterprises—mining, manufacturing or others. It may be that in certain cases no harm comes from such ownership just as in certain cases it may be that no harm comes from the ownership or control of the smaller railroad corporations by the larger ones. But I desire to get from your Commission its judgment on these points and any recommendations it may desire to make as to specific legislation which will give to the government a sufficient power of supervision and control to prevent the acquisition for improper purposes or by improper means or the management in an improper manner by any great railroad corporation of any lesser railroad corporation or industrial enterprise. I desire to know how far it is advisable to go in forbidding outright such holdings and how far our aim can best be met by permitting such holdings subject to the previous approval of the Commission and to the fact of the holding being made public.

I also desire from you a report as to what specific legislation should be past [sic] to minimize the terrible loss of life now constantly occurring thru accidents upon the railroads and furthermore what changes, if any, should be made in the legislation now on the statute books or which may be put on the statute books as regards the liability of employers for accidents to their employees and limiting the hours of labor of such employees on the railroads of the country engaged in interstate commerce.

In short, I desire from you recommendations definite and precise in character to secure a far more thoro-going supervision and control than we now have over the great agencies of interstate transportation.

Delegated Power and Direct Democracy

51. · THE COMMISSION IDEAL

One of the inconsistencies in Roosevelt's thought was his attitude toward democratic representation and delegated power. He believed strongly that the people should have a powerful voice in government, and he consequently favored direct primaries and the recall of state judicial decisions. (See Document 52.) On the other hand, as he states in the following editorial, he also believed that Congressmen responded too readily to the special interests of their constituents. He proposed, therefore, to create commissions of experts empowered to make recommendations that Congress could accept or reject, but not amend.

The August number of the *World's Work* contains an article which is of interest to all who are concerned in the vital subject to which we give the somewhat foggy title of "Political Reform." The article, for obvious reasons anonymous, is written by a member of Congress who, the editors of the *World's Work* say, has served for more than ten years in the House of Representatives, has acted on many important committees, and has been successful in "getting things" for his constituency. The article is described as "showing the reason why the 'pork-barrel,' special tariff favors, and private pension bills become

Theodore Roosevelt, "A Remedy for Some Forms of Selfish Legislation," *The Outlook*, XCV (August 6, 1910), 759–63.

law," the reason being, to quote the words of the author, that "the dictum of the constituency to the Congressmen is, 'Get all you can for US.' There are no restrictions placed upon his method of getting it. . . . Until the American people themselves become more National and less local, until constituencies cease to regard their Congressmen as solicitors at the National Treasury, Congress will continue to enact iniquitous groups of local favors into National legislation."

This serious charge against the American people—for which there is unquestionably altogether too much justification—the author proceeds to substantiate by relating some of his own experiences with constituents which, however surprising they may seem to the general reader, will seem almost commonplace to all who know how the average constituency does in actual practice treat its congressman.

The writer sets forth the fact that, in the first place, ninety per cent of the letters which a congressman receives are requests for special favors to be obtained in some way or other, directly or indirectly, from the United States Treasury. For instance, while the Payne-Aldrich tariff law was under discussion, this particular congressman received in May, 1909, the following letter from the secretary of a powerful commercial association in his district:

"I have been instructed by the board of directors of this association to advise you that at special meeting May 20, a resolution, copy of which is enclosed, was unanimously adopted, urging our Representatives in Congress to use every endeavor to have the present tariff on [mentioning three of the products of the industries referred to] increased one cent per pound and the present tariff on [mentioning the other two products] increased half a cent per pound. I wish to further advise you that we have heard from Senator ———— and he informs us that he will take care of this matter in the Senate."

When the bill was finally passed, the congressman succeeded in adding half a cent a pound to the duty on two of these products and in preventing any reduction on the others. A year later, when the popular clamor against the bill had become acute, the same association that had asked him to vote for increases wrote to the congressman denouncing the bill as "the most iniquitous measure ever enacted by Congress" and requesting him to explain by letter why he had voted with "the Reactionaries" to pass the bill. When it was pointed out to the association that it had urged the congressman to obtain an increase of duty on the products in which it was interested, it dropped its demand for an explanation. An influential newspaper published in his district editorially commended him while the bill was under debate for his "intelligent efforts" to increase the duty on manufactured articles in which the district was interested, and a year later the same newspaper in the same editorial column denounced him as one of "the legislative banditti responsible for the Payne-Aldrich measure."

As with the tariff, so with pensions; the congressman is urged to obtain local favors without regard to national interests. . . .

. . . River and harbor legislation is another field in which local selfishness busies itself, to the exclusion of national needs. In this case requests are not made by letter but by delegations which come to Washington besieging their senators and representatives. "There is," says the frank writer of this article, "figuratively speaking, between $50,000,000 and $60,-000,000 on the table to be divided. The Committee divides it so that every one is satisfied, at least to a reasonable extent." Every one, that is, but the people at large, the people who have no special interest to serve, and who feel keenly indignant that the rivers and harbors of the United States are developed in a fashion so inferior to that of Europe.

Nor are all the requests for legislation merely. One constituent desired to have this particular congressman put his name on the free mailing-list for all public documents. That this would be impossible, because it would mean delivering to the applicant several tons of documents every month, does not in the slightest detract from the interest of the fact elicited by an investigation that the applicant was the manufacturer of an article made from waste paper, and the public documents would afford a very useful source of raw material.

Is there a remedy for such a state of things? The answer is, Yes; and, moreover, it is a remedy which Congress can itself immediately provide.

There is no complete remedy, of course. No scheme can be devised which can prevent such a request as that of the constituent last named who wished public documents to use in his private paper business. Requests like this merely mean that in every district individuals will always be found who will request improper favors. As regards these people, all that can be done is to create a vigorous public opinion—an opinion which shall not only make it uncomfortable for any man to demand such favors, but which shall cordially support the congressman in refusing them and hold him accountable for granting them. We must trust to individual integrity to resist such individual and sporadic attempts to corrupt it.

The case is entirely different when we come to the other favors mentioned. These favors are those which the congressman describes as being improperly, habitually, and insistently demanded by large portions of a given constituency, with at least the acquiescence of the constituency as a whole. It is futile to expect to cure this type of evil merely by solemnly saying that each congressman ought to be good. It is futile to ask the average congressman to cut his own throat by disregarding the requests of his own constituents for special and improper favors in the matter of tariff legislation, river and harbor legislation, and pension legislation; even though these same constituents adopt the beautifully illogical position of expressing a great—and, curiously enough, often a sincere—indignation that their congressman, as the only means of securing for them what they insist he shall secure, joins with other congressmen in granting for all other constituencies the same improper favors which are eagerly demanded by his own individual constituency. Moreover, under the present system, the small man, when he asks for something in which his own district is keenly interested, is told by the big man who represents the big interest that he can't have his little favor granted unless he agrees to stand by those who wish to grant the big favor—and the small man may be remorselessly "held up" in this fashion, even though the small favor he asks is proper, and the big favor he is required to grant entirely improper. When such is the pressure upon the average representative, there is certain to be more or less yielding on his part, in the great majority of cases. It is idle to hope that reform will come through mere denunciation of the average congressman, or by merely beseeching him to reach the height of courage, wisdom, and disinterestedness achieved only by the exceptional man; by the man who is so brave and far-seeing and high-minded that he really will think only of the interests of the country as a whole.

On the other hand, it is just as idle for congressmen to seek to excuse themselves as a body by uttering jeremiads as to the improper way in which their constituents press them to do things that ought not to be done. The individual congressman can be excused only by frankly admitting that the fault lies with the congressmen taken collectively. The remedy is simple and easy of application.

Congress has now, and has long had, the power to rid its members of almost all the improper pressure brought to bear upon the individual by special interests—great and small, local and metropolitan—on such subjects as tariff legislation, river and harbor legislation, and pension legislation. . . .

In the case of the tariff and the river and harbor legislation, what is needed in each case is ample provision for a commission of the highest possible grade, composed of men who thoroughly know the subject, and who possess every attribute required for the performance of the great and difficult task of framing in outline the legislation that the country, as distinguished from special interests, really needs. These men, from the very nature of the case, will be wholly free from the local pressure of special interests so keenly felt by every man who is dependent upon the vote of a particular district every two years for his continuance in public life. Such a river and harbor commission could report, and probably would report, a great and comprehensive national scheme for river and harbor improvements fit to be considered by the people as a whole upon its merits, and not dependent for enactment into law upon a system of log-rolling designed to placate special interests which are powerful in each of many score congressional districts. Such a tariff commission could get at the facts of labor cost here and abroad by expert inquiry, and not by the acceptance of interested testimony; such a commission could consider dispassionately the probable effect upon the entire social and economic body of all changes in any given branch of the tariff, and its recommendations would represent the exercise of careful judgment from a disinterested standpoint. Such a commission could work in harmony with the commissioner of labor, so as to insure that the laborers for whom the tariff is passed get the full benefit of it; for the major part of the benefit of a protective tariff should unquestionably go to the wage-workers.

Even under such conditions of tariff-making errors might be committed, but they would be merely those errors of disinterested judgment incidental to every kind of public or, for the matter of that, private effort, and the work would not be hampered from the beginning by the need of gratifying private selfishness. . . .

. . . As soon as business becomes at all complex—and nothing can be more complex than the business of a nation of a hundred million people—it can only be performed by delegating to experts the duty of dealing with all that can properly be delegated. It is only by such delegation that it is possible to secure the proper consideration of the exceedingly important business which cannot properly be delegated. The voters, as a whole, for instance, must necessarily declare directly upon all really vital issues, and they should do this when the issue is a man just as much as when the issue is one of legislation. Indeed, in my judgment, there are certain matters, as to which the voters do not at present have the chance of thus acting directly, where it is important that the chance be given them. But they can only exercise such choice with wisdom and benefit where it is vitally necessary to exercise it, on condition of not being confused by the requirement of exercising it in the great multitude of cases where there is no such necessity, and where they can with advantage delegate the duty to the man they deem most fit to do the business.

What is true of the voters is equally true of legislators and administrators the moment that their tasks become sufficiently complex. The village constable in a small community can do all his work directly. But the President of the United States can do his work at all only by delegating the enormous mass of it to his appointees, and by confining his own share of the purely administrative work largely to supervision and direction of these employees. When a President appoints a commission to investigate such a vital matter as, for instance, country life, or the conservation of natural resources, he does not abdicate his own authority; he merely faces the fact that by no possibility can he himself do this important piece of work as well as experts whom he appoints to devote their whole time to that purpose. Now, Congress can with wisdom act in such matters of prime legislative importance as the tariff and river and harbor improvement, in the same way that the President acts in such matters of prime administrative importance as country life and conservation. It no more represents abdication of power on the part of Congress to appoint a first-class tariff commission than it represents abdication of power on the part of the President to appoint a first-class country life or conservation commission, or than it represents abdication of power on the part of voters to elect as governor a man to whom they give all possible power to do his work well. In each case the body delegating the authority, so far from abdicating the power, has secured its wise use by intrusting it to a man or men especially equipped to use it well, and this man, or these men, can in turn be held to the most rigid accountability if it is not well used, in the exclusive service of the people as a whole.

52. · "THE RECALL OF JUDICIAL DECISIONS"

For more than a quarter of a century prior to the Bull Moose Campaign of 1912 Roosevelt had been disturbed by the property-consciousness of federal and state courts. He had first become conscious of the problem in 1885 when the New York Court of Appeals nullified a tenement workshop law he had sponsored as an assemblyman. In 1902, partly because he wanted to leaven the conservatism of the Supreme Court, he appointed Oliver Wendell Holmes, Jr. associate justice. Thereafter he gave increasing attention to the abuse of the labor injunction, and in 1907 and 1908 he assailed the courts in phrases that presaged his sweeping indictments in the Progressive Era. Finally, on February 21, 1912, at Columbus, Ohio, he came out for the recall of judicial decisions on the state level. There had been "foolish and iniquitous decisions" in a number of states, he thundered, and they had "almost always been rendered at the expense of the weak" and of the "wage-workers." The result was "a monstrous perversion of the Constitution into an instrument

Address at Philadelphia, Pennsylvania, April 10, 1912. *Progressive Principles,* ed. Elmer H. Youngman (New York: Progressive National Service, 1913), pp. 84–101.

for the perpetuation of social and industrial wrong and for the oppression of the weak and helpless." The following speech shows how Roosevelt held to that position in the face of a heavy counter-attack by conservatives and many progressives.

In the New York *World* of Thursday appears a detailed statement that some very eminent lawyers of New York have undertaken the formation of what they style the "Independent Judiciary Association." They propose, to use their own words, "to combat the spread of two ideas," namely, the recall of judges, and the referendum to the people of a certain class of cases of judicial decisions; and they assert, in President Taft's words, that these ideas "lay the axe at the root of the tree of well-ordered freedom." Many of the signers are distinguished men, standing high in their community; but we can gain a clew as to just what kind of well-ordered freedom they have in mind, the kind of "freedom" to the defense of which they are rushing, when we see among the signers of this call the names of attorneys for a number of corporations not distinguished for a high-keyed sense of civic duty, or for their disinterested conduct toward the public; such as, for instance, the Standard Oil Company, the Sugar Trust, the American Tobacco Company, the Metropolitan Traction Company of New York, and certain defunct corporations, the looting of which has passed into the history of financial and stock-jobbing scandal, and forms one of its blackest chapters. I find also the name of one of the attorneys for the Northern Securities Company, which some years ago was dissolved at the suit of the government, instituted by my direction; I notice the name of the attorney for the New York Stock Exchange; and I do not overlook that of a member of the bar of New York who some years ago was denounced by the very papers now applauding him and his associates, as a retained accelerator of public opinion in favor of certain measures of the Metropolitan Street Railway Company, which at the time were under general denunciation in New York as "traction grabs." The head of the association is announced to be Mr. Choate; and one of the members is Mr. Milburn, who in 1904 was the head of the Parker Constitution Club, a similar body, with a similar purpose, namely, to uphold privilege and sustain the special interests against the cause of justice and against the interest of the people as a whole.

I hold absolutely to my conviction that some basis of accommodation must be found between the declared policy of the States on matters of social justice within the proper scope of regulation in the interest of health, of decent living and working conditions, and of morals, and the attempt of the courts to substitute their own ideas on these subjects for the declarations of the people, made through their elected representatives in the several States. . . .

. . . My proposal is for the exercise of the referendum by the people themselves in a certain class of decisions of constitutional questions in which the courts decide against the power of the people to do elementary justice. When men of trained intelligence call this "putting the axe to the tree of well-ordered freedom," it is quite impossible to reconcile their statements both with good faith and with even reasonably full knowledge of the facts.

All that is necessary to do in order to prove the absolute correctness of the statement I have just made is to call your attention to the plain and obvious facts in the case. In the first place, consider the present practice in various countries in which there is substantially the same well-ordered freedom as in our own land. For instance, take the republic of France and the great English-speaking commonwealths of the British Empire, England, Canada, Australia, all of which are governed by the Parliaments in substantially the same manner that we are governed. In every country I have named the decision of the legislature on constitutional questions is absolute and not subject to action by the judiciary; and whenever the courts make a decision which the legislature regards as establishing a construction of the constitution which is unwarranted, the legislature, if it chooses, can by law override that construction and establish its own construction of the constitution. Not long ago this very method was adopted in England. On that occasion the courts held that labor-unions could be treated as corporations and sued and money taken from them by process of law. Parliament at once passed a law overriding the decision and summarily declared that the constitution should thereafter be construed by the courts in the directly opposite sense to the construction which they had adopted.

Now, Mr. Milburn is by birth an Englishman, and Mr. Choate has been ambassador to England, and it is quite impossible that they can be sincere in asserting that "well-ordered freedom" would be destroyed in this country by adopting a practice by no means as extreme (from the standpoint of giving the people instead of the courts the ultimate power to decide certain constitutional questions) as the practice which now obtains, and which always has obtained in England, in France since it was a republic, and just across our own border in Canada and in every province of Canada.

Either Messrs. Choate and Milburn hold that there is no "well-ordered freedom" in England, Scotland, in Australia, in Ontario, New Brunswick, or Manitoba, which is preposterous, or else they must admit that they are talking nonsense when they say that the adoption of my proposal would mean the destruction of "well-ordered freedom" in this country. There is no other alternative. If I could truthfully use less harsh language about the attitude of these gentlemen upon this question I would; the language I do use is merely descriptive.

Now, consider my proposal itself; and I shall illustrate it by two or three concrete cases which will show just what the attitude of these great corporation lawyers is on questions of fundamental justice as against special privilege. My proposal is merely to secure to the people the right which the Supreme Court, speaking through Mr. Justice Holmes, in the Oklahoma Bank Cases, say they undoubtedly should possess. My proposal is that the people shall have the power to decide for themselves, in the last resort, what legislation is necessary in exercising the police powers, the general welfare powers, so as to give expression to the general morality, the general opinion, of the people. In England, Canada, and the other countries I have mentioned, no one dreams that the court has a right to express an opinion in such matters as against the will of the people shown by the action of the legislature. I do not propose to go as far as this. I do not propose to do in these matters what England, Canada, Australia, and France have always done, that is, make the legislature supreme over the courts in these cases. I merely propose to make legislature and court alike responsible to the sober and deliberate judgment of the people, who are masters of both legislature and courts.

This proposal is precisely and exactly in line with Lincoln's attitude toward the Supreme Court in the Dred Scott case, and with the doctrines he laid down for the rule of the people in his first inaugural as President. Messrs. Choate and Milburn well know that this is true; they well know that my position in no essential way differs from the principles laid down and acted upon by Abraham Lincoln in this matter. I am not dealing with any case of justice as between man and man, nor am I speaking of the Federal courts, which, because of the peculiar features of our Constitution, must be treated by themselves. Nor am I speaking of the recall of judges, a measure which I do not wish to see adopted in any community unless it proves impossible in any other way to get the judges to do justice—and I will add that nothing will so tend to strengthen the movement for the recall as action like this of Messrs. Choate and Milburn, and their associates, in seeking to buttress special privilege in the courts and to make them the bulwark of injustice instead of justice. I am seeking to introduce a system which will obviate the need of such a drastic measure as the recall. If in any case the legislature has passed a law under the police power for the purpose of promoting social and industrial justice and the courts declare it in conflict with the fundamental law of the State, the constitution as laid down by the people, then I propose that after due deliberation —for a period which could not be for less than two years after the passage of the original law—the people shall themselves have the right to declare whether or not the proposed law is to be treated as constitutional.

It is a matter of mere terminology whether this is called a method of construing or applying the Constitution, or a quicker method of getting the Constitution amended. It is certainly far superior to the ordinary method of getting the Constitution amended, because it will apply merely to the case at issue, and therefore would be definite and clear in its action; whereas, actual experience with the Fourteenth Amendment to the National Constitution, for instance, has shown us that an amendment passed by the people with one purpose may be given by the courts a construction which makes it apply to wholly different purposes and in a wholly different manner. The Fourteenth Amendment has been construed by the courts to apply to a multitude of cases to which it is positive the people who passed the amendment had not the remotest idea of applying it.

Some of my opponents say that under my proposal there would be conflicting interpretations by the people of the Constitution. In the first place, this is mere guesswork on the part of our opponents. In the next place, the people could not decide in more conflicting fashion, could not possibly make their decisions conflict with one another to a greater degree, than has actually been the case with the courts. No popular vote could reverse an earlier popular vote more completely than was the case with the decisions of the Supreme Court in the Legal Tender Cases and the Income Tax Cases. At this moment the courts of Massachusetts, Iowa, and Washington, and the Supreme Court of the nation, construe clauses of the Constitution to permit one thing and the court of appeals in New York construes identically the same language to mean the direct reverse, and this not as regards unimportant matters, but as regards matters of vital importance to the welfare of hundreds of thousands of citizens, in cases like the Workmen's Compensation Act and the act limiting the hours of labor for women in factories.

The best way to test the merits of my proposal is to consider a few specimen cases to which it would apply. Within the last thirty years the court of appeals of New York has been one of the most formidable obstacles to social reform, one of the most formidable obstacles in the way of getting industrial justice, which men who strive for justice have had to encounter. Among very many other laws which this court has made abortive, or decided not to be laws on the ground that they conflicted with the Constitution, are the following:

1. The law for preventing the manufacture of tobacco in tenement-houses; the decision of the court in this case retarded by at least twenty years the work of tenement-house reform, and was directly responsible for causing hundreds of thousands of American citizens now alive to be brought up under conditions of reeking filth and squalor, which immeasurably decreased their chance of turning out to be good citizens. Yet this decision was rendered by perfectly well-meaning men who knew law, but who did not know life, and who, forsooth, based their decision on the ground that they would not permit legislation to interfere with the "sanctity of the home"—the home in question in many cases having precisely the "sanctity" that attaches to one room in which two large families, one with a boarder, live and work day and night, the tobacco they manufacture being surrounded with every kind of filth.

2. The courts held unconstitutional the law under which a girl was endeavoring to recover damages for the loss of her arm, taken off because dangerous machinery was not guarded. In this case the judges announced that they were "protecting the girl's liberty" to work where she would endanger life and limb if she chose! Of course, as the girl had no liberty save the "liberty" of starving or else of working under the dangerous conditions, the courts were merely protecting the liberty of her employer to endanger the lives of his employees, or kill or cripple them, with immunity to himself. I do not believe that in our entire history there is an instance in which a majority of the voters have showed such tyranny and such callous indifference to the suffering of a minority as were shown by these doubtless well-meaning judges in this case.

3. When the legislature of New York passed a law limiting the hours of labor of women in factories to ten hours a day for six days a week, and forbade their being employed after nine in the evening and before six in the morning, the New York court of appeals declared it unconstitutional, and a malign inspiration induced them to state in their opinion that the time had come for courts "fearlessly" to interpose a barrier against such legislation. Fearlessly! The court fearlessly condemned helpless women to be worked at inhuman toil for hours so long as to make it impossible that they should retain health or strength; and "fearlessly" upheld the right of big factory owners and small sweatshop owners to coin money out of the blood of the wretched women and girls whom they worked haggard for their own profit. To protect such wrong-doers was of course an outrage upon the decent and high-minded factory owners who did not wish to work the women and girls to an excessive degree, but who were forced to do so by the competition of the callous factory owners whom the court, by this decision, deliberately aided and abetted in their wrong-doing. Court after court in other States, including as conservative a State as Massachusetts, have declared such a

law as this constitutional, yet the court of appeals in New York declared it unconstitutional. No popular majority vote could ever be more inconsistent with another popular majority vote than is the record of the court of appeals of New York in this matter when compared with the record of other courts in other States.

4. The Workmen's Compensation Act, but a year or two ago, was declared unconstitutional by the court of appeals of New York, although a directly reverse decision in precisely similar language had been rendered not only by the State courts of Iowa and Washington, but by the Supreme Court of the United States. Here again it is worth while to point out that no vote by popular majority could render the Constitution more uncertain of construction than the court of appeals of New York rendered it by making the decision it did in the teeth of the decision of the Supreme Court and of other State courts; and throughout our history no decision by a majority of the people in any State has shown more flagrant disregard of the elementary rights of a minority, no popular vote has ever in any State more flagrantly denied justice, than was the case in this decision by the highest court of the State of New York, but a year or two ago.

Now, in these cases in New York under the plan I propose, the people of the State of New York, after due deliberation, would have had an opportunity to decide for themselves whether the constitution which they themselves made should or should not be so construed as to prevent them from doing elementary justice in these matters. Remember also that in this case the conflict was not only between the New York legislature and the New York court. The New York court also took square issue, in its construction of constitutional provisions, with the position taken by State courts elsewhere in the Union, and with the position taken by the Supreme Court of the United States.

It would be an absolute physical impossibility for the people of the State, voting at the polls, to have interpreted the constitution more mischievously than the court of appeals has repeatedly interpreted it during the last quarter of a century, as regards the class of cases which I am now considering.

My proposal is merely to give the people an effective constitutional weapon for use against wrong and injustice. Messrs. Choate and Milburn and their allies, in taking the position they do, nakedly champion vested wrong. They appear as the champions and apologists of privilege as against the mass of our people—the farmers, the working men, the small shopkeeper, the decent hard-working citizens of every grade. They defend the courts because the courts in these cases I have mentioned have done injustice, have decided against the people, have decided in favor of the special interests and in favor of privilege. I do not question the good intentions of most of the great lawyers who take this attitude. But the only alternative to questioning their good intentions is to admit that their life-long association with corporations, the habits they have contracted by acting as highly paid special pleaders for privilege, for special interests and for vested wrong, and their utter ignorance of real life and of the needs of the people as a whole, have rendered them unfit to act as advisers of the public, unfit to know what justice is.

Messrs. Choate and Milburn and their associates in effect take the position that the people have not the right to secure workmen's compensation laws, or laws limiting the hours of labor for women in factories, or laws protecting workers from dangerous machinery, or laws making conditions decent in tenement-houses. It is a mere sham for any man to say that he approves of such laws so long as he upholds the courts in declaring them unconstitutional, so long as he fails to approve thoroughgoing action which will give the people power, with reasonable speed, to upset such court decision and to secure real and substantial justice. Messrs. Choate and Milburn say that we are "putting the axe to the root of the tree of well-ordered freedom," when we ask that New York—and every other State where there is need—take effective steps to provide such legislation as many other States of the Union already possess, and as almost every other civilized country outside of the United States has on the statute-books. A more absurd plea was never made than this plea that "well-ordered freedom" will be destroyed by doing justice to men, women, and children who are ground down by excessive toil under conditions ruinous to life and limb; and this, and precisely this, and nothing but this, is what our opponents say when their statement is stripped of verbiage. In this matter Messrs. Choate and Milburn and their associates appear as the attorneys of privilege, as special pleaders for special interests, and as the representatives of those great corporations that deny justice to small competitors and to their employees and their customers; and they appear against the people as a whole, and are hostile to the essentials of justice.

Vermont is a State in which "well-ordered freedom" certainly obtains. Are Messrs. Choate and Milburn aware that in Vermont the actual practice about the judges is that they are appointed practically for life, but subject to recall, and therefore to a referendum on their actions, every two years? In that State the judges are elected by the legislature, and in practice the legislature always re-elects the judge as long as he wishes to serve, unless he proves unfaithful, when the principle of the recall is applied by the simple process of not re-electing him. In the last twenty or thirty years this has been done in but one case. In Vermont the judges are as upright and independent as any judges in the Union; but in constitutional cases such as those I have mentioned they do really represent, and not misrepresent, the people.

In short, Messrs. Choate and Milburn and their associates, if their language is to be accepted as sincere, know nothing of the position taken by courts and legislatures in other lands as regards these constitutional questions, know little as to what has been done in certain of our own States thereon, and know practically nothing about the needs of the immense bulk of their countrymen. They do not even know what is elementary knowledge among the men specially trained in constitutional law in their country; men like Dean Lewis, of the University of Pennsylvania Law School, and Professor Scofield, professor of law at the Northwestern Law School. In a recent article Professor Scofield has shown that the State courts of Illinois have behaved no better than the State courts of New York in these matters. He quotes the emphatic criticisms of these decisions of which I complain by the late Dean Thayer, of the Harvard Law School. He says that these decisions make of the law a weapon with which the strong can strike down the weak, that they make of the law not a shield to protect the people, but a sword to smite down the people; that they are arbitrary, and that our protest against them represents one phase of the struggle against arbitrary power and in favor of the law of the land, and he sees that my proposal is merely to use a constitutional method to restore to the State lawmaking bodies the power which the Supreme Court of this nation says belongs to them.

There are sincere and well-meaning men of timid nature who are frightened by the talk of tyranny of the majority. Those worthy gentlemen are nearly a century behind the times. It is true that De Tocqueville, writing about eighty years ago, said that in this country there was great tyranny by the majority. His statement may have been true then, although certainly not to the degree he insisted, but it is not true now. That profound and keen thinker, Mr. James Bryce, in "The American Commonwealth" treats of this in his chapter on the "Tyranny of the Majority" by saying that it does not exist. His own words are that:

"It is no longer a blemish on the American system, and the charges against democracy from the supposed example of America are groundless. The fact that the danger once dreaded has now disappeared is no small evidence of the recuperative forces of the American Government, and the healthy tone of the American people."

I wish that our opponents, Mr. Taft, Mr. Choate, Mr. Milburn, Mr. Penrose, Mr. Guggenheim, Mr. Lorimer, and the rest of their companions, who so dread and distrust the American people, would in this matter copy the good faith and sanity of the learned and able ambassador from Great Britain.

I shall protest against the tyranny of the majority whenever it arises, just as I shall protest against every other form of tyranny. But at present we are not suffering in any way from the tyranny of the majority. We suffer from the tyranny of the bosses and of the special interests, that is, from the tyranny of minorities. Mr. Choate, Mr. Milburn, and their allies are acting as the servants and spokesmen of the special interests and are standing cheek by jowl with the worst representatives of politics when they seek to keep the courts in the grasp of privilege and of the politicians; for this is all they accomplish when they prevent them from being responsible in proper fashion to the people. These worthy gentlemen speak as if the judges were somehow imposed on us by Heaven, and were responsible only to Heaven. As a matter of fact judges are human just like other people, and in this country they will either be chosen by the people and responsible to the people, or they will be chosen by, and responsible to, the bosses and the special interests and the political and financial beneficiaries of privilege. It is this last system which Mr. Choate and Mr. Milburn and their allies are by their actions upholding. In the course they are taking, they and the respectable men associated with them, are, in some cases certainly unconsciously, and in other cases I fear consciously, acting on behalf of the special interests, political and financial, and in favor of privilege, and against the interest of the plain people and against the cause of justice and of human right. In the long run this

country will not be a good place for any of us to live in unless
it is a reasonably good place for all of us to live in; and it will
neither become nor remain a good place for all of us to live in
if we permit our government to be turned aside from its original purpose and to become a government such as Mr. Taft,
Mr. Choate, Mr. Lorimer, Mr. Milburn, Mr. Penrose, Mr. Guggenheim, and their allies wish to make it—a government by
corporation attorneys on the bench and off the bench; and this
without regard to whether particular individuals among these
corporation attorneys mean well or mean ill, without regard to
whether they are or are not conscious of the fact that they are
really serving the cause of special privilege and not the cause
of the people.

States' Rights Versus the National Interest

53. · A BLIND FOR VESTED INTERESTS

Roosevelt's disdain for "pork-barreling" was matched by his in-
tolerence of states' rights. On this, as on so many other issues, his
attitude was formed by his concern for efficiency and social justice;
and on this, no less than on the others, his policy was governed
more by historical realities than by philosophical abstractions. In
this excerpt from a 1907 speech at Harvard, he expands on how
special business interests were using states' rights to rationalize
their opposition to federal action.

. . . So it is with the great questions which group themselves
round the control of corporations in the interest of the public.

From a speech at the Harvard Union, February 23, 1907. *Presidential
Addresses,* VI, 1175.

There has been a curious revival of the doctrine of States' rights in connection with these questions, by the people who know that the States cannot with justice to both sides practically control the corporations, and who therefore advocate such control because they do not venture to express their real wish, which is that there shall be no control at all. Honest and fair dealing railway corporations will gain and not lose by adequate Federal control; most emphatically, it is both the duty and the interest of our people to deal fairly with such corporations, and to see that a premium is put upon the honest management of them, and that those who invest in them are amply protected. But those who invoke the doctrine of States' rights to protect State corporate creations in predatory activities extended through other States are as short-sighted as those who once invoked the same doctrine to protect the special slaveholding interest. The States have shown that they have not the ability to curb the power of syndicated wealth, and, therefore, in the interest of the people, it must be done by national action. Our present warfare is against special privilege. . . .

54 · THE LIMITATIONS OF THE STATE GOVERNMENTS

Roosevelt's crusade for conservation while president had further convinced him of the often reactionary and generally inefficient quality of state governments. In this letter to an Oregon Congressman-elect, he first dilates on Oregon's inability to administer its own forests, then declares that even if Oregon were capable of

Letter to Abraham Walter Lafferty, December 20, 1910. *The Letters*, VII, 187–89.

handling additional forest lands, the National Forests belonged to the nation as a whole and should be administered by the National Forest Service.

Oyster Bay, December 20, 1910

Dear Sir: I shall be very glad indeed to confer with you concerning public land and forest laws which you contemplate urging in Congress, in accordance with your letter of November 26. I am in hearty sympathy with the prompt restoration to homestead entry of all agricultural lands in the National Forests. . . . But I am . . . strongly opposed to the conveyance of the National Forests in trust to the States wherein they are located. My attitude on . . . this question has been perfectly clear; . . . and no adequate reason has been advanced, of which I am aware, that would warrant my changing my position. At this very moment we are endeavoring to get the United States Government to take over from the Eastern states the Appalachian and White Mountain reserves, just because the States have not done as well as the Nation is doing or can do.

There are two reasons why the National Forests, in Oregon for example, should not be turned over in trust to the State. The first and more important one is that the forest question is necessarily, through its connection with the rivers and in other ways, an interstate question, and that the National Forests can be handled far better for the general welfare by the Federal Government than by any State. Belonging as they do to the people of all the States, although conferring the major part of their benefits upon the States in which they lie, the forests are naturally, and in my belief will permanently remain, better adapted to Federal than to State control.

The only reason which could seriously be urged against National care of the National forest property would be that it could be better handled through some other agency. Now, the second reason against transferring the National Forests in

Oregon to the care of the State is that Oregon is wholly unprepared to do the work. We may not unfairly judge of what
Oregon would do in comparison with the Federal Government by what it has done already. I quote from the report of
the Oregon Conservation Commission, dated eleven days before your letter was written:

. . . The Federal Forest Service is the only public agency
doing anything to take care of the Oregon forests. Its expenditures for protection alone in 1910 will exceed $200,000. Of
this approximately half is for patrol and half for trail and
telephone building and additional fire fighting labor. . . .
Ordinarily the Forest Service confines its fire work to the National Forests, but this year the menace to homes and property
outside led it to disregard official boundaries in many instances. In either case the benefit accrues to the State for
National Forest timber is a State asset in all but stumpage
returns and twenty-five per cent of these also are paid to the
counties. As adequately as Congressional appropriations permit, the Forest Service takes care of about a third of the timber in the State. It has also begun reforestation.

The State Board of Forestry, created in 1907 by a statute
that also provided an excellent forest code, remains practically
powerless because it is not supplied with any machinery for
active work. It is thus shorn of any real function except to
make recommendations to the legislature, and has not the
means of collecting information to make these effective. Its
appropriation is only $250 a year. This insignificant sum is
Oregon's total contribution, as a State to the cause of forest
preservation. It is the least appropriated by any state in the
Union that has any forest system at all.

To sum up, although Oregon is trying to bring about wise
use of its fish, its game, and its agricultural resources, and
spends money to this end, it absolutely neglects its most vulnerable resource—its forests.

It is perfectly obvious from these official statements in a
report not yet thirty days old that the State of Oregon, having

failed to meet its responsibility as to forest protection within its own undisputed sphere, is in no position either to demand or accept still further responsibility. This seems to me conclusive for the present. But it must be clearly understood that even if the State of Oregon were on a par with the Federal Government in its equipment and capacity to handle the National Forests, I should still be strongly opposed to the transfer of these forests to the care of the State. They belong to the Nation, and the Nation is responsible for their care and protection. That responsibility it can discharge through the Forest Service better than it can possibly be discharged through separate forest organizations in a number of individual States.

For these reasons I am for National control of the National Forests.

55. · "LIMITATION OF GOVERNMENTAL POWER"

States' rights became a critical issue early in the presidential campaign of 1912 when Woodrow Wilson refused to endorse the Progressive Party's child-labor and other social-justice planks on the grounds that the federal government should not legislate such matters. Although Wilson had actually qualified the statement Roosevelt quotes below ("The history of liberty is a history of the limitation of governmental power, not the increase of it"), his predilection for states' rights consistently compromised his progressivism. But in spite of Roosevelt's hammer-like blows in this and other speeches, it was not until late in his first administration that Wilson recognized the validity of Roosevelt's contention that it was impossible to achieve social justice without weakening states' rights.

Address at San Francisco, California, September 14, 1912. *New York Times*, September 15, 1912, p. 8.

In one of his campaign speeches Mr. Wilson made a sweeping assault on the Progressive platform and programme and defined his own position as to social and industrial justice. According to the stenographic report of his speech, Mr. Wilson stated that there is no hope for social reform through the platform of the Progressive party, saying: "In the very platform itself is supplied the demonstration that it is not a serviceable instrument. They do propose to serve civilization and humanity but they cannot serve civilization and humanity with that kind of government. . . . The history of liberty is a history of the limitation of governmental power, not the increase of it."

And he then continues to uphold what he calls "representative" government and "representative" assemblies as against the platform that we propose, and also to uphold the Democratic proposals for dealing with labor and the trusts as against the Progressive proposals.

Mr. Wilson is fond of asserting his platonic devotion to the purposes of the Progressive party. But such platonic devotion is utterly worthless from a practical standpoint, because he antagonizes the only means by which those purposes can be made effective. It is idle to profess devotion to Progressive principles and at the same time to antagonize the only methods by which they can be realized in actual fact.

The key to Mr. Wilson's position is found in the statement I have just quoted, when he says that "The history of liberty is a history of the limitation of governmental power, not the increase of it."

This is a bit of outworn academic doctrine which was kept in the schoolroom and the professorial study for a generation after it had been abandoned by all who had experience of actual life. It is simply the *laissez-faire* doctrine of the English political economists three-quarters of a century ago. It can be applied with profit, if anywhere at all, only in a primitive community under primitive conditions, in a community such as the United States at the end of the eighteenth century, a community before the days of Fulton, Morse, and Edison. To apply it now in the United States at the beginning of the twentieth century, with its highly organized industries, with its railways, telegraphs, and telephones, means literally and absolutely to refuse to make a single effort to better any one of our social or industrial conditions.

Moreover, Mr. Wilson is absolutely in error in his statement, from the historical standpoint.

So long as governmental power existed exclusively for the king and not at all for the people, then the history of liberty was a history of the limitation of governmental power. But now the governmental power rests in the people, and the kings who enjoy privilege are the kings of the financial and industrial world; and what they clamor for is the limitation of governmental power, and what the people sorely need is the extension of governmental power.

If Mr. Wilson's statement means nothing, then he ought not to have made it.

If it means anything, it means that every law for the promotion of social and industrial justice which has been put upon the statute-books ought to be repealed, and every law proposed should be abandoned, for without exception every such law represents an increase of governmental power. Does Mr. Wilson mean to repeal the interstate commerce commission law? If not, does he deny that it represents a great increase of governmental power over the railroads? Let him take whichever horn of the dilemma he chooses. Either his statement is not in accordance with the facts or else he is bound, if it is in accordance with the facts as he sees them, to include in his programme the repeal of the Interstate Commerce Commission Act.

Again, every Progressive State in the Union has passed laws for factory inspection; every such law means an increase of governmental power. Is Mr. Wilson in favor of repealing those laws? If he is not, then what does he mean by saying that the history of liberty is the history of the limitation of governmental power?

The fact is that his statement is a mere bit of professorial rhetoric, which has not one particle of foundation in the facts of the present day.

Again, we propose to limit the hours of working girls to eight hours a day; we propose to limit the hours of working men in continuous industries to eight hours a day, and to give them one day's rest a week. Both of these proposals represent an increase in the exercise of governmental power, an extension of governmental power. Does Mr. Wilson mean that he is against this extension? If not, then his sentence which I have just quoted and which represents the key-note of his speech, means nothing whatever.

In other words, Mr. Wilson's promise is either a promise that is not to be kept or else it means the undoing of every particle of social and industrial advance we have made and the refusal to go forward along the lines of industrial and social progress.

He stands for a policy which necessarily means, if that policy is honestly put into effect, that he must be against every single progressive measure, for every progressive measure means an extension, instead of a limitation, of governmental control.

We propose to do away with occupational disease. Is he against this proposition? He must be if he believes in limitation of government control.

We propose a workman's compensation act. Is he against this proposition? He must be if he sincerely means that he is in favor of the limitation of governmental control.

We propose to regulate the conditions of work in factories, the conditions of life in tenement-houses, the conditions of life and work in construction camps—every one of these proposals means an extension of governmental control. Is he against them?

Either he is against his own principle or he is against these reforms. He can choose either horn of the dilemma he wishes; but one or the other he must choose.

He has definitely committed himself to the use of the taxing power only for the purpose of raising revenue. In that case he is against its use to put out of existence the poisonous-match industry. He is against its use for the purpose of preventing opium coming into this country. He is against its use for preventing wildcat banking. In short, he is against its use in every case where we now use it to tax out of existence dangers and abuses.

The trouble with Mr. Wilson is that he is following an outworn philosophy and that the history of which he is thinking is the history of absolute monarchies and Oriental despotisms. He is thinking of government as embodied in an absolute king or in an oligarchy or aristocracy. He is not thinking of our government, which is a government by the people themselves.

The only way in which our people can increase their power over the big corporation that does wrong, the only way in which they can protect the working man in his conditions of work and life, the only way in which the people can prevent children working in industry or secure women an eight-hour day in industry, or secure compensation for men killed or crippled in industry, is by extending, instead of limiting, the powers of government.

There is no analogy whatever, from the standpoint of real liberty, and of real popular need, between the limitations imposed by the people on the power of an irresponsible monarch or a dominant aristocracy, and the limitations sought to be imposed by big financiers, by big corporation lawyers, and by well-meaning students of a dead-and-gone system of political economy on the power of the people to right social wrongs and limit social abuses, and to secure for the humble what, unless there is an extension of the powers of government, the arrogant and the powerful will certainly take from the humble.

If Mr. Wilson really believes what he has said, then Mr. Wilson has no idea of our government in its actual working. He is not thinking of modern American history or of present-day American needs. He is thinking of *Magna Carta*, which limited the power of the English king, because his power over the people had before been absolute. He is thinking of the Bill of Rights, which limited the power of the governing class in the interest of the people, who could not control that governing class.

Our proposal is to increase the power of the people themselves and to make the people in reality the governing class. Therefore Mr. Wilson's proposal is really to limit the power of the people and thereby to leave unchecked the colossal embodied privileges of the present day.

Now, you can adopt one philosophy or the other. You can adopt the philosophy of *laissez-faire*, of the limitation of governmental power, and turn the industrial life of this country into a chaotic scramble of selfish interests, each bent on plundering the other and all bent on oppressing the wage-worker. This is precisely and exactly what Mr. Wilson's proposal means; and it can mean nothing else. Under such limitations of governmental power as he praises, every railroad must be left unchecked, every great industrial concern can do as it chooses with its employees and with the general public; women must be permitted to work as many hours a day as their taskmasters bid them; great corporations must be left unshackled to put down wages to a starvation limit and to raise the price of their products as high as monopolistic control will permit.

The reverse policy means an extension, instead of a limitation, of governmental power; and for that extension we Progressives stand.

We propose to handle the colossal industrial concerns engaged in interstate business as we are handling the great railways engaged in interstate business; and we propose to go forward in the control of both, doing justice to each but exacting justice from each; and we propose to work for justice to the farmer and the wage-worker in the same fashion. . . .

. . . The people of the United States have but one instrument which they can efficiently use against the colossal combinations of business—and that instrument is the government of the United States (and of course in the several States the governments of the States where they can be utilized). Mr. Wilson's proposal is that the people of the United States shall throw away this, the one great instrument, the one great weapon they have with which to secure themselves against wrong. He proposes to limit the governmental action of the people and therefore to leave unlimited and unchecked the action of the great corporations whose enormous power constitutes so serious a problem in modern industrial life. Remember that it is absolutely impossible to limit the power of these great corporations whose enormous power constitutes so serious a problem in modern industrial life except by extending the power of the government. All that these great corporations ask is that the power of the government shall be limited. No wonder they are supporting Mr. Wilson, for he is advocating for them what they hardly dare venture to advocate for themselves. These great corporations rarely want anything from the government except to be let alone and to be permitted to work their will unchecked by the government. All that they really want is that governmental action shall be limited. In every great corporation suit the corporation lawyer will be found protesting against extension of governmental power. Every court decision favoring a corporation takes the form of declaring unconstitutional some extension of governmental power. Every corporation magnate in the country who is not dealing honestly and fairly by his fellows asks nothing better than that Mr. Wilson's programme be carried out and that there be stringent limitations of governmental power.

There once was a time in history when the limitation of governmental power meant increasing liberty for the people.

In the present day the limitation of governmental power, of governmental action, means the enslavement of the people by the great corporations who can only be held in check through the extension of governmental power. . . .

. . . Mr. Wilson's attitude toward the tariff is exactly in keeping with his attitude toward social and industrial reforms. He is against the minimum wage for women exactly as he is against a protective tariff. His principles would prevent us either effectually helping labor or effectually regulating and controlling big business.

He is against using the power of the government to help the people to whom the government belongs.

We take flat issue with him. We propose to use the government as the most efficient instrument for the uplift of our people as a whole; we propose to give a fair chance to the workers and strengthen their rights. We propose to use the whole power of the government to protect all those who, under Mr. Wilson's *laissez-faire* system, are trodden down in the ferocious, scrambling rush of an unregulated and purely individualistic industrialism.

X · PROGRESSIVE REFORM

Responsible and Constructive Criticism

56. · "THE MAN WITH THE MUCK-RAKE"

Roosevelt's memorable indictment of "muck-raking" in the spring of 1906 was a logical outgrowth of several of his basic values. His fair-mindedness, along with his fear of revolution and his faith in welfare capitalism, had always caused him to disapprove of essentially negative social criticism. Although he realized that he could hardly have pushed his program through Congress without the public support whipped up by journalists like Ray Stannard Baker, he was nonetheless repelled by the one-sided criticisms of American institutions that reached a crescendo during the middle years of his presidency. Hence, in part, the decision to castigate purveyors of half-truths and deliberate distortions as "muck-rakers." Even as he thus indicted them, however, he underscored his standing endorsement of constructive criticism; he also recommended two far-reaching reforms—a graduated inheritance tax and federal supervision of all big business.

Over a century ago Washington laid the cornerstone of the Capitol in what was then little more than a tract of wooded wilderness here beside the Potomac. We now find it necessary

Address at Washington, D. C., April 14, 1906. *Presidential Addresses*, V, 712–24.

to provide by great additional buildings for the business of the government. This growth in the need for the housing of the government is but a proof and example of the way in which the nation has grown and the sphere of action of the National Government has grown. We now administer the affairs of a nation in which the extraordinary growth of population has been outstripped by the growth of wealth and the growth in complex interests. The material problems that face us to-day are not such as they were in Washington's time, but the underlying facts of human nature are the same now as they were then. Under altered external form we war with the same tendencies toward evil that were evident in Washington's time, and are helped by the same tendencies for good. It is about some of these that I wish to say a word to-day.

In Bunyan's "Pilgrim's Progress" you may recall the description of the Man with the Muck-rake, the man who could look no way but downward, with the muck-rake in his hand; who was offered a celestial crown for his muck-rake, but who would neither look up nor regard the crown he was offered, but continued to rake to himself the filth of the floor.

In "Pilgrim's Progress" the Man with the Muck-rake is set forth as the example of him whose vision is fixed on carnal instead of on spiritual things. Yet he also typifies the man who in this life consistently refuses to see aught that is lofty, and fixes his eyes with solemn intentness only on that which is vile and debasing. Now, it is very necessary that we should not flinch from seeing what is vile and debasing. There is filth on the floor, and it must be scraped up with the muck-rake; and there are times and places where this service is the most needed of all the services that can be performed. But the man who never does anything else, who never thinks or speaks or writes, save of his feats with the muck-rake, speedily becomes, not a help to society, not an incitement to good, but one of the most potent forces for evil.

There are, in the body politic, economic and social, many

and grave evils, and there is urgent necessity for the sternest war upon them. There should be relentless exposure of and attack upon every evil man whether politician or business man, every evil practice, whether in politics, in business, or in social life. I hail as a benefactor every writer or speaker, every man who, on the platform, or in book, magazine, or newspaper, with merciless severity makes such attack, provided always that he in his turn remembers that the attack is of use only if it is absolutely truthful. The liar is no whit better than the thief, and if his mendacity takes the form of slander, he may be worse than most thieves. It puts a premium upon knavery untruthfully to attack an honest man, or even with hysterical exaggeration to assail a bad man with untruth. An epidemic of indiscriminate assault upon character does not good, but very great harm. The soul of every scoundrel is gladdened whenever an honest man is assailed, or even when a scoundrel is untruthfully assailed.

Now, it is easy to twist out of shape what I have just said, easy to affect to misunderstand it, and, if it is slurred over in repetition, not difficult really to misunderstand it. Some persons are sincerely incapable of understanding that to denounce mud-slinging does not mean the indorsement of whitewashing; and both the interested individuals who need whitewashing, and those others who practise mud-slinging, like to encourage such confusion of ideas. One of the chief counts against those who make indiscriminate assault upon men in business or men in public life, is that they invite a reaction which is sure to tell powerfully in favor of the unscrupulous scoundrel who really ought to be attacked, who ought to be exposed, who ought, if possible, to be put in the penitentiary. If Aristides is praised overmuch as just, people get tired of hearing it; and overcensure of the unjust finally and from similar reasons results in their favor.

Any excess is almost sure to invite a reaction; and, unfortunately, the reaction, instead of taking the form of punishment of those guilty of the excess, is very apt to take the form either of punishment of the unoffending or of giving immunity, and even strength, to offenders. The effort to make financial or political profit out of the destruction of character can only result in public calamity. Gross and reckless assaults on character, whether on the stump or in newspaper, magazine, or book, create a morbid and vicious public sentiment, and at the same time act as a profound deterrent to able men of normal sensitiveness and tend to prevent them from entering the public service at any price. As an instance in point, I may mention that one serious difficulty encountered in getting the right type of men to dig the Panama Canal is the certainty that they will be exposed, both without, and, I am sorry to say, sometimes within, Congress, to utterly reckless assaults on their character and capacity.

At the risk of repetition let me say again that my plea is, not for immunity to but for the most unsparing exposure of the politician who betrays his trust, of the big business man who makes or spends his fortune in illegitimate or corrupt ways. There should be a resolute effort to hunt every such man out of the position he has disgraced. Expose the crime, and hunt down the criminal; but remember that even in the case of crime, if it is attacked in sensational, lurid, and untruthful fashion, the attack may do more damage to the public mind than the crime itself. It is because I feel that there should be no rest in the endless war against the forces of evil that I ask that the war be conducted with sanity as well as with resolution. The men with the muck-rakes are often indispensable to the well-being of society; but only if they know when to stop raking the muck, and to look upward to the celestial crown above them, to the crown of worthy endeavor. There are beautiful things above and roundabout them; and if they gradually grow to feel that the whole world is nothing but muck, their power of usefulness is gone. If the whole picture is painted black there remains no hue whereby to single out the rascals for distinction from their fellows. Such painting finally induces a kind of moral color-blindness; and people affected by it come to the conclusion that no man is really black, and no man really white, but they are all gray. In other words, they neither believe in the truth of the attack, nor in the honesty of the man who is attacked; they grow as suspicious of the accusation as of the offense; it becomes well-nigh hopeless to stir them either to wrath against wrong-doing or to enthusiasm for what is right; and such a mental attitude in the public gives hope to every knave, and is the despair of honest men.

To assail the great and admitted evils of our political and industrial life with such crude and sweeping generalizations as to include decent men in the general condemnation means the searing of the public conscience. There results a general attitude either of cynical belief in and indifference to public corruption or else of a distrustful inability to discriminate between the good and the bad. Either attitude is fraught with untold damage to the country as a whole. The fool who has not sense to discriminate between what is good and what is bad is well-nigh as dangerous as the man who does discriminate and yet chooses the bad. There is nothing more distressing to every good patriot, to every good American, than the hard, scoffing spirit which treats the allegation of dishonesty in a public man as a cause for laughter. Such laughter is worse than the crackling of thorns under a pot, for it denotes not merely the vacant mind, but the heart in which high emotions have been choked before they could grow to fruition.

There is any amount of good in the world, and there never was a time when loftier and more disinterested work for the betterment of mankind was being done than now. The forces that tend for evil are great and terrible, but the forces of truth and love and courage and honesty and generosity and sympathy are also stronger than ever before. It is a foolish and timid, no less than a wicked, thing to blink the fact that the forces of evil are strong, but it is even worse to fail to take into account the strength of the forces that tell for good. Hysterical sensationalism is the very poorest weapon wherewith to fight for lasting righteousness. The men who with stern sobriety and truth assail the many evils of our time, whether in the public press, or in magazines, or in books, are the leaders and allies of all engaged in the work for social and political betterment. But if they give good reason for distrust of what they say, if they chill the ardor of those who demand truth as a primary virtue, they thereby betray the good cause, and play into the hands of the very men against whom they are nominally at war.

In his "Ecclesiastical Polity" that fine old Elizabethan divine, Bishop Hooker, wrote:

"He that goeth about to persuade a multitude that they are not so well governed as they ought to be, shall never want attentive and favorable hearers; because they know the manifold defects whereunto every kind of regimen is subject, but the secret lets and difficulties, which in public proceedings are innumerable and inevitable, they have not ordinarily the judgment to consider."

This truth should be kept constantly in mind by every free people desiring to preserve the sanity and poise indispensable to the permanent success of self-government. Yet, on the other hand, it is vital not to permit this spirit of sanity and self-command to degenerate into mere mental stagnation. Bad though a state of hysterical excitement is, and evil though the results are which come from the violent oscillations such excitement invariably produces, yet a sodden acquiescence in evil is even worse. At this moment we are passing through a period of great unrest—social, political, and industrial unrest. It is of the utmost importance for our future that this should prove to be not the unrest of mere rebelliousness against life, of mere dissatisfaction with the inevitable inequality of conditions, but the unrest of a resolute and eager ambition to secure the betterment of the individual and the nation. So far as this movement of agitation throughout the country takes the form of a fierce discontent with evil, of a determination to punish the authors of evil, whether in industry or politics, the feeling is to be heartily welcomed as a sign of healthy life.

If, on the other hand, it turns into a mere crusade of appetite against appetite, of a contest between the brutal greed of the "have-nots" and the brutal greed of the "haves," then it has no significance for good, but only for evil. If it seeks to establish a line of cleavage, not along the line which divides good men from bad, but along that other line, running at right angles thereto, which divides those who are well off from those who are less well off, then it will be fraught with immeasurable harm to the body politic.

We can no more and no less afford to condone evil in the man of capital than evil in the man of no capital. The wealthy man who exults because there is a failure of justice in the effort to bring some trust magnate to an account for his misdeeds is as bad as, and no worse than, the so-called labor leader who clamorously strives to excite a foul class feeling on behalf of some other labor leader who is implicated in murder. One attitude is as bad as the other, and no worse; in each case the accused is entitled to exact justice; and in neither case is there need of action by others which can be construed into an expression of sympathy for crime.

It is a prime necessity that if the present unrest is to result in permanent good the emotion shall be translated into action, and that the action shall be marked by honesty, sanity, and self-restraint. There is mighty little good in a mere spasm of reform. The reform that counts is that which comes through steady, continuous growth; violent emotionalism leads to exhaustion.

It is important to this people to grapple with the problems connected with the amassing of enormous fortunes, and the use of those fortunes, both corporate and individual, in business. We should discriminate in the sharpest way between fortunes well-won and fortunes ill-won; between those gained as an incident to performing great services to the community as a whole, and those gained in evil fashion by keeping just within the limits of mere law-honesty. Of course no amount of charity in spending such fortunes in any way compensates for misconduct in making them. As a matter of personal conviction, and without pretending to discuss the details or formulate the system, I feel that we shall ultimately have to consider the adoption of some such scheme as that of a progressive tax on all fortunes, beyond a certain amount, either given in life or devised or bequeathed upon death to any individual—a tax so framed as to put it out of the power of the owner of one of these enormous fortunes to hand on more than a certain amount to any one individual; the tax, of course, to be imposed by the National and not the State Government. Such taxation should, of course, be aimed merely at the inheritance or transmission in their entirety of those fortunes swollen beyond all healthy limits.

Again, the National Government must in some form exercise supervision over corporations engaged in interstate business—and all large corporations are engaged in interstate business—whether by license or otherwise, so as to permit us to deal with the far-reaching evils of overcapitalization. This year we are making a beginning in the direction of serious effort to settle some of these economic problems by the railway-rate legislation. Such legislation, if so framed, as I am sure it will be, as to secure definite and tangible results, will amount to something of itself; and it will amount to a great deal more in so far as it is taken as a first step in the direction of a policy of superintendence and control over corporate wealth engaged in interstate commerce, this superintendence and control not to be exercised in a spirit of malevolence toward the men who have created the wealth, but with the firm purpose both to do justice to them and to see that they in their turn do justice to the public at large.

The first requisite in the public servants who are to deal in this shape with corporations, whether as legislators or as executives, is honesty. This honesty can be no respecter of persons. There can be no such thing as unilateral honesty. The danger is not really from corrupt corporations; it springs from the corruption itself, whether exercised for or against corporations.

The eighth commandment reads: "Thou shalt not steal." It does not read: "Thou shalt not steal from the rich man." It does not read: "Thou shalt not steal from the poor man." It reads simply and plainly: "Thou shalt not steal." No good whatever will come from that warped and mock morality which denounces the misdeeds of men of wealth and forgets the misdeeds practised at their expense; which denounces bribery, but blinds itself to blackmail; which foams with rage if a corporation secures favors by improper methods, and merely leers with hideous mirth if the corporation is itself wronged. The only public servant who can be trusted honestly to protect the rights of the public against the misdeed of a corporation is that public man who will just as surely protect the corporation itself from wrongful aggression. If a public man is willing to yield to popular clamor and do wrong to the men of wealth or to rich corporations, it may be set down as certain that if the opportunity comes he will secretly and furtively do wrong to the public in the interest of a corporation.

But, in addition to honesty, we need sanity. No honesty will make a public man useful if that man is timid or foolish, if he is a hot-headed zealot or an impracticable visionary. As we strive for reform we find that it is not at all merely the case of a long up-hill pull. On the contrary, there is almost as much of breeching work as of collar work; to depend only on traces means that there will soon be a runaway and an upset. The men of wealth who to-day are trying to prevent the regulation and control of their business in the interest of the public by the proper government authorities will not succeed, in my judgment, in checking the progress of the movement. But if they did succeed they would find that they had sown the wind and would surely reap the whirlwind, for they would ultimately provoke the violent excesses which accompany a reform coming by convulsion instead of by steady and natural growth.

On the other hand, the wild preachers of unrest and discontent, the wild agitators against the entire existing order, the men who act crookedly, whether because of sinister design or from mere puzzle-headedness, the men who preach destruction without proposing any substitute for what they intend to destroy, or who propose a substitute which would be far worse than the existing evils—all these men are the most dangerous opponents of real reform. If they get their way they will lead the people into a deeper pit than any into which they could fall under the present system. If they fail to get their way they will still do incalculable harm by provoking the kind of reaction which, in its revolt against the senseless evil of their teaching, would enthrone more securely than ever the very evils which their misguided followers believe they are attacking.

More important than aught else is the development of the broadest sympathy of man for man. The welfare of the wageworker, the welfare of the tiller of the soil, upon these depend the welfare of the entire country; their good is not to be sought in pulling down others; but their good must be the prime object of all our statesmanship.

Materially we must strive to secure a broader economic opportunity for all men, so that each shall have a better chance to show the stuff of which he is made. Spiritually and ethically we must strive to bring about clean living and right thinking. We appreciate that the things of the body are important; but we appreciate also that the things of the soul are immeasurably more important. The foundation-stone of national life is, and ever must be, the high individual character of the average citizen.

Socialism

57. · TWO VIEWS OF SOCIALISM

Even during Roosevelt's most progressive phase his concern for character—for personal honesty, morality, and initiative—caused him to eschew doctrinaire interpretations of man and society. He believed, as he wrote Upton Sinclair in 1906, that "there are many, many men who lack any intelligence or character and who therefore cannot . . . raise themselves." And he was quite convinced, as he told Lincoln Steffens in 1908, that "under government ownership corruption can flourish just as rankly as under private ownership." Thus he regarded scientific materialism as ill-founded, socialist proposals for "free love" as immoral, and the Marxian ideal of remuneration according to need as absurd. What is most revealing in the two articles printed below, however, is Roosevelt's insight into the causes of social unrest, his appreciation of the moral commitment of many marginal socialists, his open acceptance of numerous socialist reforms, and his rejection of socialist-baiting.

a. ". . . Where We Cannot Work With Socialists"

It is always difficult to discuss a question when it proves impossible to define the terms in which that question is to be discussed. Therefore there is not much to be gained by a discussion of Socialism *versus* Individualism in the abstract. Neither absolute Individualism nor absolute Socialism would be compatible with civilization at all; and among the arguments of the extremists of either side the only unanswerable ones are those which show the absurdity of the position of the other. Not so much as the first step toward real civilization

The Outlook, XCI (March 20, 1909), 619–23.

can be taken until there arises some development of the right of private property; that is, until men pass out of the stage of savage socialism in which the violent and the thriftless forcibly constitute themselves co-heirs with the industrious and the intelligent in what the labor of the latter produces. But it is equally true that every step toward civilization is marked by a check on individualism. The ages that have passed have fettered the individualism which found expression in physical violence, and we are now endeavoring to put shackles on that kind of individualism which finds expression in craft and greed. There is growth in all such matters. The individualism of the Tweed Ring type would have seemed both commonplace and meritorious to the Merovingian Franks, where it was not entirely beyond their comprehension; and so in future ages, if the world progresses as we hope and believe it will progress, the standards of conduct which permit individuals to make money out of pestilential tenements or by the manipulation of stocks, or to refuse to share with their employees the dreadful burdens laid upon the latter by the inevitable physical risks in a given business, will seem as amazing to our descendants as we now find the standards of a society which regarded Clovis and his immediate successors as pre-eminently fit for leadership. . . .

. . . The immorality and absurdity of the doctrines of Socialism . . . are quite as great as those of the advocates, if such there be, of an unlimited individualism. As an academic matter there is more need of refutation of the creed of absolute Socialism than of the creed of absolute individualism; for it happens that at the present time a greater number of visionaries, both sinister and merely dreamy, believe in the former than in the latter. One difficulty in arguing with professed Socialists of the extreme, or indeed of the opportunist, type, however, is that those of them who are sincere almost invariably suffer from great looseness of thought; for if they did not keep their faith nebulous, it would at once become abhorrent in the eyes of any upright and sensible man. The doctrinaire Socialists, the extremists, the men who represent the doctrine in its most advanced form, are, and must necessarily be, not only convinced opponents of private property, but also bitterly hostile to religion and morality; in short, they must be opposed to all those principles through which, and through which alone, even an imperfect civilization can be built up by slow advances through the ages.

Indeed, these thoroughgoing Socialists occupy, in relation to all morality, and especially to domestic morality, a position so revolting—and I choose my words carefully—that it is difficult even to discuss it in a reputable paper. In America the leaders even of this type have usually been cautious about stating frankly that they proposed to substitute free love for married and family life as we have it, although many of them do in a roundabout way uphold this position. In places on the Continent of Europe, however, they are more straightforward, their attitude being that of one of the extreme French Socialist writers, M. Gabriel Deville, who announces that the Socialists intend to do away with both prostitution and marriage, which he regards as equally wicked—his method of doing away with prostitution being to make unchastity universal. Professor Carl Pearson, a leading English Socialist, states their position exactly: "The sex relation of the future will not be regarded as a union for the birth of children, but as the closest form of friendship between man and woman. It will be accompanied by no child-bearing or rearing, or by this in a much more limited number than at present. With the sex relationship, so long as it does not result in children, we hold that the State in the future will in nowise interfere, but when it does result in children, then the State will have a right to interfere." He then goes on to point out that in order to save the woman from "economic dependence" upon the father of her children, the children will be raised at the expense of the State; the usual plan being to have huge buildings like foundling asylums.

Mr. Pearson is a scientific man . . . ; and the above quotation states in naked form just what logical scientific Socialism would really come to. Aside from its thoroughly repulsive quality, it ought not to be necessary to point out that the condition of affairs aimed at would in actual practice bring about the destruction of the race within, at most, a couple of generations; and such destruction is heartily to be desired for any race of such infamous character as to tolerate such a system. . . .

These same Socialist leaders, with a curious effrontery, at times deny that the exponents of "scientific Socialism" assume a position as regards industry which in condensed form may be stated as, that each man is to do what work he can, or, in other words, chooses, and in return is to take out from the common fund whatever he needs; or, what amounts to the same thing, that each man shall have equal remuneration with every other man, no matter what work is done. . . . In our own country, in "Socialism Made Plain," a book officially circulated by the Milwaukee division of the Socialist party, the statement is explicit: "Under the labor time-check medium of exchange proposed by Socialists, any laborer could exchange the wealth he produced in any given number of hours for the wealth produced by any other laborer in the same number of hours." It is unnecessary to point out that the pleasing idea of these writers could be realized only if the State undertook the duty of taskmaster, for otherwise it is not conceivable that anybody whose work would be worth anything would work at all under such conditions. Under this type of Socialism, therefore, or communism, the government would have to be the most drastic possible despotism; a despotism so drastic that its realization would only be an ideal. . . .

In other words, on the social and domestic side doctrinaire Socialism would replace the family and home life by a glorified state free-lunch counter and state foundling asylum, deliberately enthroning self-indulgence as the ideal, with, on its

darker side, the absolute abandonment of all morality as between man and woman; while in place of what Socialists are
pleased to call "wage slavery" there would be created a system which would necessitate either the prompt dying out of
the community through sheer starvation, or an iron despotism
over all workers, compared to which any slave system of the
past would seem beneficent, because less utterly hopeless.

"Advanced" Socialist leaders are fond of declaiming against
patriotism, of announcing their movement as international, and
of claiming to treat all men alike; but on this point, as on all
others, their system would not stand for one moment the test
of actual experiment. If the leaders of the Socialist party in
America should to-day endeavor to force their followers to
admit all negroes and Chinamen to a real equality, their party
would promptly disband, and, rather than submit to such
putting into effect of their avowed purpose, would, as a literal
fact, follow any capitalistic organization as an alternative. . . .

. . . We need have but scant patience with those who assert
that modern conditions are all that they should be, or that
they cannot be improved. . . . There are dreadful woes in
modern life, dreadful suffering among some of those who toil,
brutal wrong-doing among some of those who make colossal
fortunes by exploiting the toilers. It is the duty of every honest
and upright man, of every man who holds within his breast
the capacity for righteous indignation, to recognize these
wrongs, and to strive with all his might to bring about a better
condition of things. But he will never bring about this better
condition by misstating facts and advocating remedies which
are not merely false, but fatal.

Take, for instance, the doctrine of the extreme Socialists,
that all wealth is produced by manual workers, that the entire
product of labor should be handed over every day to the
laborer, that wealth is criminal in itself. Of course wealth is
no more criminal than labor. Human society could not exist
without both; and if all wealth were abolished this week, the

majority of laborers would starve next week. . . . A great industry could no more be managed by a mass-meeting of manual laborers than a battle could be won in such fashion, than a painters' union could paint a Rembrandt, or a typographical union write one of Shakespeare's plays.

The fact is that this kind of Socialism represents an effort to enthrone privilege in its crudest form. Much of what we are fighting against in modern civilization is privilege. We fight against privilege when it takes the form of a franchise to a street-railway company to enjoy the use of the streets of a great city without paying an adequate return; when it takes the form of a great business combination which grows rich by rebates which are denied to other shippers; when it takes the form of a stock-gambling operation which results in the watering of railway securities so that certain inside men get an enormous profit out of a swindle on the public. All these represent various forms of illegal, or, if not illegal, then anti-social, privilege. But there can be no greater abuse, no greater example of corrupt and destructive privilege, than that advocated by those who say that each man should put into a common store what he can and take out what he needs. This is merely another way of saying that the thriftless and the vicious, who could or would put in but little, should be entitled to take out the earnings of the intelligent, the foresighted, and the industrious. Such a proposition is morally base. To choose to live by theft or by charity means in each case degradation, a rapid lowering of self-respect and self-reliance. The worst wrongs that capitalism can commit upon labor would sink into insignificance when compared with the hideous wrong done by those who would degrade labor by sapping the foundations of self-respect and self-reliance. . . .

In short, it is simply common sense to recognize that there is the widest inequality of service, and that therefore there must be an equally wide inequality of reward, if our society is to rest upon the basis of justice and wisdom. Service is the true test by which a man's worth should be judged. We are against privilege in any form: privilege to the capitalist who exploits the poor man, and privilege to the shiftless or vicious poor man who would rob his thrifty brother of what he has earned. Certain exceedingly valuable forms of service are rendered wholly without capital. On the other hand, there are exceedingly valuable forms of service which can be rendered only by means of great accumulations of capital, and not to recognize this fact would be to deprive our whole people of one of the great agencies for their betterment. The test of a man's worth to the community is the service he renders to it, and we cannot afford to make this test by material considerations alone. One of the main vices of the Socialism which was propounded by Proudhon, Lassalle, and Marx, and which is preached by their disciples and imitators, is that it is blind to everything except the merely material side of life. It is not only indifferent, but at bottom hostile, to the intellectual, the religious, the domestic and moral life; it is a form of communism with no moral foundation, but essentially based on the immediate annihilation of personal ownership of capital, and, in the near future, the annihilation of the family, and ultimately the annihilation of civilization.

b. ". . . *Where We Can Work With Socialists*"

It is true that the doctrines of communistic Socialism, if consistently followed, mean the ultimate annihilation of civilization. Yet the converse is also true. Ruin faces us if we decline steadily to try to reshape our whole civilization in accordance with the law of service, and if we permit ourselves to be misled by any empirical or academic consideration into refusing to exert the common power of the community where

The Outlook, XCI (March 27, 1909), 662–64.

only collective action can do what individualism has left un-done, or can remedy the wrongs done by an unrestricted and ill-regulated individualism. There is any amount of evil in our social ind industrial conditions of to-day, and unless we recognize this fact and try resolutely to do what we can to remedy the evil, we run great risk of seeing men in their misery turn to the false teachers whose doctrines would indeed lead them to greater misery, but who do at least recognize the fact that they are now miserable. At the present time there are scores of laws in the interest of labor—laws putting a stop to child labor, decreasing the hours of labor where they are excessive, putting a stop to unsanitary crowding and living, securing employers' liability, doing away with unhealthy conditions in various trades, and the like—which should be passed by the national and the various State legislatures; and those who wish to do effective work against Socialism would do well to turn their energies into securing the enactment of these laws.

Moreover, we should always remember that Socialism is both a wide and a loose term, and that the self-styled Social-ists are of many and utterly different types. If we should study only the professed apostles of radical Socialism, of what these men themselves like to call "scientific Socialism," or if we should study only what active leaders of Socialism in this country have usually done, or read only the papers in which they have usually expressed themselves, we would gain an utterly wrong impression of very many men who call them-selves Socialists. There are many peculiarly high-minded men and women who like to speak of themselves as Socialists, whose attitude, conscious or unconscious, is really merely an indignant recognition of the evil of present conditions and an ardent wish to remedy it, and whose Socialism is really only an advanced form of liberalism. Many of these men and women in actual fact take a large part in the advancement of moral ideas, and in practice wholly repudiate the purely materialistic, and therefore sordid, doctrines of those Socialists whose creed really is in sharp antagonism to every principle of public and domestic morality, who war on private property with a bitterness but little greater than that with which they war against the institutions of the home and the family, and against every form of religion, Catholic or Protestant. The Socialists of this moral type may in practice be very good citizens indeed, with whom we can at many points co-operate. They are often joined temporarily with what are called the "opportunist Socialists"—those who may advocate an impossible and highly undesirable Utopia as a matter of abstract faith, but who in practice try to secure the adoption only of some given principle which will do away with some phase of existing wrong. With these two groups of Socialists it is often possible for all far-sighted men to join heartily in the effort to secure a given reform or do away with a given abuse. Probably, in practice, wherever and whenever Socialists of these two types are able to form themselves into a party, they will disappoint both their own expectations and the fears of others by acting very much like other parties, like other aggregations of men; and it will be safe to adopt whatever they advance that is wise, and to reject whatever they advance that is foolish, just as we have to do as regards countless other groups who on one issue or set of issues come together to strive for a change in the political or social conditions of the world we live in. The important thing is generally the next step. We ought not to take it unless we are sure that it is advisable; but we should not hesitate to take it when once we are sure; and we can safely join with others who also wish to take it, without bothering our heads overmuch as to any somewhat fantastic theories they may have concerning, say, the two hundredth step, which is not yet in sight.

There are many schemes proposed which their enemies, and a few of their friends, are pleased to call Socialistic, or which are indorsed and favored by men who call themselves Socialists, but which are entitled each to be considered on its merits with regard only to the practical advantage which each would confer. Every public man, every reformer, is bound to refuse to dismiss these schemes with the shallow statement that they are "Socialistic"; for such an attitude is one of mere mischievous dogmatism. There are communities in which our system of State education is still resisted and condemned as Socialism; and we have seen within the past two years in this country men who were themselves directors in national banks, which were supervised by the government, object to such supervision of railways by the government on the ground that it was "Socialistic." An employers' liability law is no more Socialistic than a fire department; the regulation of railway rates is by no means as Socialistic as the digging and enlarging of the Erie Canal at the expense of the State. A proper compensation law would merely distribute over the entire industry the shock of accident or disease, instead of limiting it to the unfortunate individual on whom, through no fault of his, it happened to fall. As communities become more thickly settled and their lives more complex, it grows ever more and more necessary for some of the work formerly performed by individuals, each for himself, to be performed by the community for the community as a whole. Isolated farms need no complicated system of sewerage; but this does not mean that public control of sewerage in a great city should be resisted on the ground that it tends toward Socialism. Let each proposition be treated on its own merits, soberly and cautiously, but without any of that rigidity of mind which fears all reform. If, for instance, the question arises as to the establishment of day nurseries for the children of mothers who work in factories, the obvious thing to do is to approach it with an open mind, listen to the arguments for and against, and, if necessary, try the experiment in actual practice. If it is alleged that small groups of farmers have prospered by doing much of their work in common, and by a kind of mutual insurance and supervision, why of course we should look into the matter with an open mind, and try to find out, not what we want the facts to be, but what the facts really are.

We cannot afford to subscribe to the doctrine, equally hard and foolish, that the welfare of the children in the tenement-house district is no concern of the community as a whole. If the child of the thronged city cannot live in decent surroundings, have teaching, have room to play, have good water and clean air, then not only will he suffer, but in the next generation the whole community will to a greater or less degree share his suffering. . . .

. . . Socialism strives to remedy what is evil alike in domestic and in economic life, and its tendency is to insist that the economic remedy is all-sufficient in every case. We should all join in the effort to do away with the evil; but we should refuse to have anything to do with remedies which are either absurd or mischievous, for such, of course, would merely aggravate the present suffering. The first thing to recognize is that, while economic reform is often vital, it is never all-sufficient. The moral reform, the change of character—in which law can sometimes play a large, but never the largest, part—is the most necessary of all. . . .

So with our industrial system. In many respects the wage system can be bettered; but screaming about "wage slavery" is largely absurd; at this moment, for instance, I am a "wage slave" of *The Outlook*. Under certain conditions and in certain cases the co-operative system can to a greater or less degree be substituted with advantage for, or, more often, can be used to supplement, the wage system; but only on condition of recognizing the widely different needs occasioned by different conditions, which needs are so diverse that they must sometimes be met in totally different ways.

We should do everything that can be done, by law or otherwise, to keep the avenues of occupation, of employment, of work, of interest, so open that there shall be, so far as it is humanly possible to achieve it, a measurable equality of opportunity; an equality of opportunity for each man to show the stuff that is in him. When it comes to reward, let each man, within the limits set by a sound and far-sighted morality, get what, by his energy, intelligence, thrift, courage, he is able to get, with the opportunity open. We must set our faces against privilege; just as much against the kind of privilege which would let the shiftless and lazy laborer take what his brother has earned as against the privilege which allows the huge capitalist to take toll to which he is not entitled. We stand for equality of opportunity, but not for equality of reward unless there is also equality of service. If the service is equal, let the reward be equal; but let the reward depend on the service; and, mankind being composed as it is, there will be inequality of service for a long time to come, no matter how great the equality of opportunity may be and just so long as there is inequality of service it is eminently desirable that there should be inequality of reward.

We recognize, and are bound to war against, the evils of to-day. The remedies are partly economic and partly spiritual, partly to be obtained by laws, and in greater part to be obtained by individual and associated effort; for character is the vital matter, and character cannot be created by law. These remedies include a religious and moral teaching which shall increase the spirit of human brotherhood; an educational system which shall train men for every form of useful service —and which shall train us to prize common sense no less than morality; such a division of the profits of industry as shall tend to encourage intelligent and thrifty tool-users to become tool-owners; and a government so strong, just, wise, and democratic that, neither lagging too far behind nor pushing heedlessly in advance, it may do its full share in promoting these ends.

The Progressive Synthesis

58. · "THE NEW NATIONALISM"

Long before he left the White House and long before he read Herbert Croly's *The Promise of American Life* (1909), Roosevelt had become an advanced progressive. Almost every plank in the Progressive party platform of 1912 had been foreshadowed in his messages and speeches of 1907 and 1908; and in his final Annual Message he had envisioned such a comprehensive reform program that the New York *Commercial and Financial Chronicle* had complained that if a fraction of its recommendations were put into law "they would commit the country to a course of new experiments and make over the face of social creation." In one sense, therefore, Roosevelt's famed "New Nationalism" speech was more a political than an ideological testament. As such, it signified his continuing commitment to progressivism and his determination to force the Taft administration to follow his policies or suffer the consequences. Yet the speech was also notable for its synthesis of Roosevelt's mature progressivism, a progressivism based, as he put it, on the proposition that "the object of government is the welfare of the people."

We come here to-day to commemorate one of the epoch-making events of the long struggle for the rights of man—the

A speech at Osawatomie, Kansas, August 31, 1910. Theodore Roosevelt, *The New Nationalism* (New York: The Outlook Company, 1910), pp. 3–33.

long struggle for the uplift of humanity. Our country—this great Republic—means nothing unless it means the triumph of a real democracy, the triumph of popular government, and, in the long run, of an economic system under which each man shall be guaranteed the opportunity to show the best that there is in him. That is why the history of America is now the central feature of the history of the world; for the world has set its face hopefully toward our democracy; and, O my fellow citizens, each one of you carries on your shoulders not only the burden of doing well for the sake of your own country, but the burden of doing well and of seeing that this nation does well for the sake of mankind.

There have been two great crises in our country's history: first, when it was formed, and then, again, when it was perpetuated; and, in the second of these great crises—in the time of stress and strain which culminated in the Civil War, on the outcome of which depended the justification of what had been done earlier, you men of the Grand Army, you men who fought through the Civil War, not only did you justify your generation, not only did you render life worth living for our generation, but you justified the wisdom of Washington and Washington's colleagues. If this Republic had been founded by them only to be split asunder into fragments when the strain came, then the judgment of the world would have been that Washington's work was not worth doing. It was you who crowned Washington's work, as you carried to achievement the high purpose of Abraham Lincoln.

Now, with this second period of our history the name of John Brown will be forever associated; and Kansas was the theatre upon which the first act of the second of our great national life dramas was played. It was the result of the struggle in Kansas which determined that our country should be in deed as well as in name devoted to both union and freedom; that the great experiment of democratic government on a national scale should succeed and not fail. In name we had the

Declaration of Independence in 1776; but we gave the lie by our acts to the words of the Declaration of Independence until 1865; and words count for nothing except in so far as they represent acts. This is true everywhere; but, O my friends, it should be truest of all in political life. A broken promise is bad enough in private life. It is worse in the field of politics. No man is worth his salt in public life who makes on the stump a pledge which he does not keep after election; and, if he makes such a pledge and does not keep it, hunt him out of public life. I care for the great deeds of the past chiefly as spurs to drive us onward in the present. I speak of the men of the past partly that they may be honored by our praise of them, but more that they may serve as examples for the future.

It was a heroic struggle; and, as is inevitable with all such struggles, it had also a dark and terrible side. Very much was done of good, and much also of evil; and, as was inevitable in such a period of revolution, often the same man did both good and evil. For our great good fortune as a nation, we, the people of the United States as a whole, can now afford to forget the evil, or, at least, to remember it without bitterness, and to fix our eyes with pride only on the good that was accomplished. Even in ordinary times there are very few of us who do not see the problems of life as through a glass, darkly; and when the glass is clouded by the murk of furious popular passion, the vision of the best and the bravest is dimmed. Looking back, we are all of us now able to do justice to the valor and the disinterestedness and the love of the right, as to each it was given to see the right, shown both by the men of the North and the men of the South in that contest which was finally decided by the attitude of the West. We can admire the heroic valor, the sincerity, the self-devotion shown alike by the men who wore the blue and the men who wore the gray; and our sadness that such men should have had to fight one another is tempered by the glad knowledge that ever hereafter their descendants shall be found fighting side by side, struggling in peace as well as in war for the uplift of their common country, all alike resolute to raise to the highest pitch of honor and usefulness the nation to which they all belong. As for the veterans of the Grand Army of the Republic, they deserve honor and recognition such as is paid to no other citizens of the Republic; for to them the republic owes its all; for to them it owes its very existence. It is because of what you and your comrades did in the dark years that we of to-day walk, each of us, head erect, and proud that we belong, not to one of a dozen little squabbling contemptible commonwealths, but to the mightiest nation upon which the sun shines.

I do not speak of this struggle of the past merely from the historic standpoint. Our interest is primarily in the application to-day of the lessons taught by the contest of half a century ago. It is of little use for us to pay lip-loyalty to the mighty men of the past unless we sincerely endeavor to apply to the problems of the present precisely the qualities which in other crises enabled the men of that day to meet those crises. It is half melancholy and half amusing to see the way in which well-meaning people gather to do honor to the men who, in company with John Brown, and under the lead of Abraham Lincoln, faced and solved the great problems of the nineteenth century, while, at the same time, these same good people nervously shrink from, or frantically denounce, those who are trying to meet the problems of the twentieth century in the spirit which was accountable for the successful solution of the problems of Lincoln's time.

Of that generation of men to whom we owe so much, the man to whom we owe most is, of course, Lincoln. Part of our debt to him is because he forecast our present struggle and saw the way out. He said:

"I hold that while man exists it is his duty to improve not only his own condition, but to assist in ameliorating mankind."

And again:

"Labor is prior to, and independent of, capital. Capital is

only the fruit of labor, and could never have existed if labor had not first existed. Labor is the superior of capital, and deserves much the higher consideration."

If that remark was original with me, I should be even more strongly denounced as a Communist agitator than I shall be anyhow. It is Lincoln's. I am only quoting it; and that is one side; that is the side the capitalist should hear. Now, let the working man hear his side.

"Capital has its rights, which are as worthy of protection as any other rights. . . . Nor should this lead to a war upon the owners of property. Property is the fruit of labor; . . . property is desirable; is a positive good in the world."

And then comes a thoroughly Lincolnlike sentence:

"Let not him who is houseless pull down the house of another, but let him work diligently and build one for himself, thus by example assuring that his own shall be safe from violence when built."

It seems to me that, in these words, Lincoln took substantially the attitude that we ought to take; he showed the proper sense of proportion in his relative estimates of capital and labor, of human rights and property rights. Above all, in this speech, as in many others, he taught a lesson in wise kindliness and charity; an indispensable lesson to us of to-day. But this wise kindliness and charity never weakened his arm or numbed his heart. We cannot afford weakly to blind ourselves to the actual conflict which faces us to-day. The issue is joined, and we must fight or fail.

In every wise struggle for human betterment one of the main objects, and often the only object, has been to achieve in large measure equality of opportunity. In the struggle for this great end, nations rise from barbarism to civilization, and through it people press forward from one stage of enlightenment to the next. One of the chief factors in progress is the destruction of special privilege. The essence of any struggle for healthy liberty has always been, and must always be, to take from some one man or class of men the right to enjoy power, or wealth, or position, or immunity, which has not been earned by service to his or their fellows. That is what you fought for in the Civil War, and that is what we strive for now.

At many stages in the advance of humanity, this conflict between the men who possess more than they have earned and the men who have earned more than they possess is the central condition of progress. In our day it appears as the struggle of freemen to gain and hold the right of self-government as against the special interests, who twist the methods of free government into machinery for defeating the popular will. At every stage, and under all circumstances, the essence of the struggle is to equalize opportunity, destroy privilege, and give to the life and citizenship of every individual the highest possible value both to himself and to the commonwealth. That is nothing new. All I ask in civil life is what you fought for in the Civil War. I ask that civil life be carried on according to the spirit in which the army was carried on. You never get perfect justice, but the effort in handling the army was to bring to the front the men who could do the job. Nobody grudged promotion to Grant, or Sherman, or Thomas, or Sheridan, because they earned it. The only complaint was when a man got promotion which he did not earn.

Practical equality of opportunity for all citizens, when we achieve it, will have two great results. First, every man will have a fair chance to make of himself all that in him lies; to reach the highest point to which his capacities, unassisted by special privilege of his own and unhampered by the special privilege of others, can carry him, and to get for himself and his family substantially what he has earned. Second, equality of opportunity means that the commonwealth will get from every citizen the highest service of which he is capable. No man who carries the burden of the special privileges of another can give to the commonwealth that service to which it is fairly entitled.

I stand for the square deal. But when I say that I am for the square deal, I mean not merely that I stand for fair play under the present rules of the game, but that I stand for having those rules changed so as to work for a more substantial equality of opportunity and of reward for equally good service. One word of warning, which, I think, is hardly necessary in Kansas. When I say I want a square deal for the poor man, I do not mean that I want a square deal for the man who remains poor because he has not got the energy to work for himself. If a man who has had a chance will not make good, then he has got to quit. And you men of the Grand Army, you want justice for the brave man who fought, and punishment for the coward who shirked his work. Is not that so?

Now, this means that our government, National and State, must be freed from the sinister influence or control of special interests. Exactly as the special interests of cotton and slavery threatened our political integrity before the Civil War, so now the great special business interests too often control and corrupt the men and methods of government for their own profit. We must drive the special interests out of politics. That is one of our tasks to-day. Every special interest is entitled to justice —full, fair, and complete—and, now, mind you, if there were any attempt by mob-violence to plunder and work harm to the special interest, whatever it may be, that I most dislike, and the wealthy man, whomsoever he may be, for whom I have the greatest contempt, I would fight for him, and you would if you were worth your salt. He should have justice. For every special interest is entitled to justice, but not one is entitled to a vote in Congress, to a voice on the bench, or to representation in any public office. The Constitution guarantees protection to property, and we must make that promise good. But it does not give the right of suffrage to any corporation.

The true friend of property, the true conservative, is he who insists that property shall be the servant and not the master of the commonwealth; who insists that the creature of man's making shall be the servant and not the master of the man who made it. The citizens of the United States must effectively control the mighty commercial forces which they have themselves called into being.

There can be no effective control of corporations while their political activity remains. To put an end to it will be neither a short nor an easy task, but it can be done.

We must have complete and effective publicity of corporate affairs, so that the people may know beyond peradventure whether the corporations obey the law and whether their management entitles them to the confidence of the public. It is necessary that laws should be passed to prohibit the use of corporate funds directly or indirectly for political purposes; it is still more necessary that such laws should be thoroughly enforced. Corporate expenditures for political purposes, and especially such expenditures by public-service corporations, have supplied one of the principal sources of corruption in our political affairs.

It has become entirely clear that we must have government supervision of the capitalization, not only of public-service corporations, including, particularly, railways, but of all corporations doing an interstate business. I do not wish to see the nation forced into the ownership of the railways if it can possibly be avoided, and the only alternative is thoroughgoing and effective regulation, which shall be based on a full knowledge of all the facts, including a physical valuation of property. This physical valuation is not needed, or, at least, is very rarely needed, for fixing rates; but it is needed as the basis of honest capitalization.

We have come to recognize that franchises should never be granted except for a limited time, and never without proper provision for compensation to the public. It is my personal belief that the same kind and degree of control and supervision which should be exercised over public-service corporations should be extended also to combinations which control necessaries of life, such as meat, oil, and coal, or which deal in them on an important scale. I have no doubt that the ordinary man who has control of them is much like ourselves. I have no doubt he would like to do well, but I want to have enough supervision to help him realize that desire to do well.

I believe that the officers, and, especially, the directors, of corporations should be held personally responsible when any corporation breaks the law.

Combinations in industry are the result of an imperative economic law which cannot be repealed by political legislation. The effort at prohibiting all combination has substantially failed. The way out lies, not in attempting to prevent such combinations, but in completely controlling them in the interest of the public welfare. For that purpose the Federal Bureau of Corporations is an agency of first importance. Its powers, and, therefore, its efficiency, as well as that of the Interstate Commerce Commission, should be largely increased. We have a right to expect from the Bureau of Corporations and from the Interstate Commerce Commission a very high grade of public service. We should be as sure of the proper conduct of the interstate railways and the proper management of interstate business as we are now sure of the conduct and management of the national banks, and we should have as effective supervision in one case as in the other. The Hepburn Act, and the amendment to the act in the shape in which it finally passed Congress at the last session, represent a long step in advance, and we must go yet further.

There is a wide-spread belief among our people that, under the methods of making tariffs which have hitherto obtained, the special interests are too influential. Probably this is true of both the big special interests and the little special interests. These methods have put a premium on selfishness, and, naturally, the selfish big interests have gotten more than their smaller, though equally selfish, brothers. The duty of Congress is to provide a method by which the interest of the whole people shall be all that receives consideration. To this end there must be an expert tariff commission, wholly removed from the possibility of political pressure or of improper business influence. Such a commission can find the real difference between cost of production, which is mainly the difference of labor cost here and abroad. As fast as its recommendations are made, I believe in revising one schedule at a time. A general revision of the tariff almost inevitably leads to logrolling and the subordination of the general public interest to local and special interests.

The absence of effective State, and, especially, national, restraint upon unfair money-getting has tended to create a small class of enormously wealthy and economically powerful men, whose chief object is to hold and increase their power. The prime need is to change the conditions which enable these men to accumulate power which it is not for the general welfare that they should hold or exercise. We grudge no man a fortune which represents his own power and sagacity, when exercised with entire regard to the welfare of his fellows. Again, comrades over there, take the lesson from your own experience. Not only did you not grudge, but you gloried in the promotion of the great generals who gained their promotion by leading the army to victory. So it is with us. We grudge no man a fortune in civil life if it is honorably obtained and well used. It is not even enough that it should have been gained without doing damage to the community. We should permit it to be gained only so long as the gaining represents benefit to the community. This, I know, implies a policy of a far more active governmental interference with social and economic conditions in this country than we have yet had, but I think we have got to face the fact that such an increase in governmental control is now necessary.

No man should receive a dollar unless that dollar has been fairly earned. Every dollar received should represent a dollar's worth of service rendered—not gambling in stocks, but service rendered. The really big fortune, the swollen fortune, by the mere fact of its size acquires qualities which differentiate it in kind as well as in degree from what is possessed by men of relatively small means. Therefore, I believe in a graduated income tax on big fortunes, and in another tax which is far more easily collected and far more effective—a graduated inheritance tax on big fortunes, properly safeguarded against evasion and increasing rapidly in amount with the size of the estate.

The people of the United States suffer from periodical financial panics to a degree substantially unknown among the other nations which approach us in financial strength. There is no reason why we should suffer what they escape. It is of profound importance that our financial system should be promptly investigated, and so thoroughly and effectively revised as to make it certain that hereafter our currency will no longer fail at critical times to meet our needs.

It is hardly necessary for me to repeat that I believe in an efficient army and a navy large enough to secure for us abroad that respect which is the surest guaranty of peace. A word of special warning to my fellow citizens who are as progressive as I hope I am. I want them to keep up their interest in our internal affairs; and I want them also continually to remember Uncle Sam's interests abroad. Justice and fair dealing among nations rest upon principles identical with those which control justice and fair dealing among the individuals of which nations are composed, with the vital exception that each nation must do its own part in international police work. If you get into trouble here, you can call for the police; but if Uncle Sam gets into trouble, he has got to be his own policeman, and I want to see him strong enough to encourage the peaceful aspirations of other peoples in connection with us. I believe in national friendships and heartiest good-will to all nations; but national friendships, like those between men, must be founded on respect as well as on liking, on forbearance as well as upon trust. I should be heartily ashamed of any American who did not try to make the American Government act as justly toward the other nations in international relations as he himself would act toward any individual in private relations. I should be heartily ashamed to see us wrong a weaker power, and I should hang my head forever if we tamely suffered wrong from a stronger power.

Of conservation I shall speak more at length elsewhere. Conservation means development as much as it does protection. I recognize the right and duty of this generation to develop and use the natural resources of our land; but I do not recognize the right to waste them, or to rob, by wasteful use, the generations that come after us. I ask nothing of the nation except that it so behave as each farmer here behaves with reference to his own children. That farmer is a poor creature who skins the land and leaves it worthless to his children. The farmer is a good farmer who, having enabled the land to support himself and to provide for the education of his children, leaves it to them a little better than he found it himself. I believe the same thing of a nation.

Moreover, I believe that the natural resources must be used for the benefit of all our people, and not monopolized for the benefit of the few, and here again is another case in which I am accused of taking a revolutionary attitude. People forget now that one hundred years ago there were public men of good character who advocated the nation selling its public lands in great quantities, so that the nation could get the most money out of it, and giving it to the men who could cultivate it for their own uses. We took the proper democratic ground that the land should be granted in small sections to the men who were actually to till it and live on it. Now, with the water-power, with the forests, with the mines, we are brought face to face with the fact that there are many people who will go with us in conserving the resources only if they are to be allowed to exploit them for their benefit. That is one of the fundamental reasons why the special interests should be driven out of politics. Of all the questions which can come before this nation, short of the actual preservation of its existence in a great war, there is none which compares in importance with the great central task of leaving this land even a better land for our descendants than it is for us, and training them into a better race to inhabit the land and pass it on. Conservation is a great moral issue, for it involves the patriotic duty of insuring the safety and continuance of the nation. Let me add that the health and vitality of our people are at least as well worth conserving as their forests, waters, lands, and minerals, and in this great work the national government must bear a most important part.

I have spoken elsewhere also of the great task which lies before the farmers of the country to get for themselves and their wives and children not only the benefits of better farming, but also those of better business methods and better conditions of life on the farm. The burden of this great task will fall, as it should, mainly upon the great organizations of the farmers themselves. I am glad it will, for I believe they are all well able to handle it. In particular, there are strong reasons why the Departments of Agriculture of the various States, the United States Department of Agriculture, and the agricultural colleges and experiment stations should extend their work to cover all phases of farm life, instead of limiting themselves, as they have far too often limited themselves in the past, solely to the question of the production of crops. And now a special word to the farmer. I want to see him make the farm as fine a farm as it can be made; and let him remember to see that the improvement goes on indoors as well as out; let him remember that the farmer's wife should have her share of thought and attention just as much as the farmer himself.

Nothing is more true than that excess of every kind is followed by reaction; a fact which should be pondered by reformer and reactionary alike. We are face to face with new conceptions of the relations of property to human welfare, chiefly because certain advocates of the rights of property as against the rights of men have been pushing their claims too far. The man who wrongly holds that every human right is secondary to his profit must now give way to the advocate of human welfare, who rightly maintains that every man holds his property subject to the general right of the community to regulate its use to whatever degree the public welfare may require it.

But I think we may go still further. The right to regulate the use of wealth in the public interest is universally admitted. Let us admit also the right to regulate the terms and conditions of labor, which is the chief element of wealth, directly in the interest of the common good. The fundamental thing to do for every man is to give him a chance to reach a place in which he will make the greatest possible contribution to the public welfare. Understand what I say there. Give him a chance, not push him up if he will not be pushed. Help any man who stumbles; if he lies down, it is a poor job to try to carry him; but if he is a worthy man, try your best to see that he gets a chance to show the worth that is in him. No man can be a good citizen unless he has a wage more than sufficient to cover the bare cost of living, and hours of labor short enough so that after his day's work is done he will have time and energy to bear his share in the management of the community, to help in carrying the general load. We keep countless men from being good citizens by the conditions of life with which we surround them. We need comprehensive workmen's compensation acts, both State and national laws to regulate child labor and work for women, and, especially, we need in our common schools not merely education in book-learning, but also practical training for daily life and work. We need to enforce better sanitary conditions for our workers and to extend the use of safety appliances for our workers in industry and commerce, both within and between the States. Also, friends, in the interest of the working man himself we need to set our faces like flint against mob-violence just as against corporate greed; against violence and injustice and lawlessness by wage-workers just as much as against lawless cunning and greed and selfish arrogance of employers. If I could ask but one thing of my fellow countrymen, my request would be that, whenever they go in for reform, they remember the two sides, and that they always exact justice from one side as much as from the other. I have small use for the public servant who can always see and denounce the corruption of the capitalist, but who cannot persuade himself, especially before election, to say a word about lawless mob-violence. And I have equally small use for the man, be he a judge on the bench, or editor of a great paper, or wealthy and influential private citizen, who can see clearly enough and denounce the lawlessness of mob-violence, but whose eyes are closed so that he is blind when the question is one of corruption in business on a gigantic scale. Also remember what I said about excess in reformer and reactionary alike. If the reactionary man, who thinks of nothing but the rights of property, could have his way, he would bring about a revolution; and one of my chief fears in connection with progress comes because I do not want to see our people, for lack of proper leadership, compelled to follow men whose intentions are excellent, but whose eyes are a little too wild to make it really safe to trust them. Here in Kansas there is one paper which habitually denounces me as the tool of Wall Street, and at the same time frantically repudiates the statement that I am a Socialist on the ground that that is an unwarranted slander of the Socalists.

National efficiency has many factors. It is a necessary result of the principle of conservation widely applied. In the end it will determine our failure or success as a nation. National efficiency has to do, not only with natural resources and with men, but it is equally concerned with institutions. The State must be made efficient for the work which concerns only the people of the State; and the nation for that which concerns all the people. There must remain no neutral ground to serve as a refuge for lawbreakers, and especially for lawbreakers of great wealth, who can hire the vulpine legal cunning which will teach them how to avoid both jurisdictions. It is a misfortune when the national legislature fails to do its duty in providing a national remedy, so that the only national activity is the purely negative activity of the judiciary in forbidding the State to exercise power in the premises.

I do not ask for overcentralization; but I do ask that we work in a spirit of broad and far-reaching nationalism when we work for what concerns our people as a whole. We are all Americans. Our common interests are as broad as the continent. I speak to you here in Kansas exactly as I would speak in New York or Georgia, for the most vital problems are those which affect us all alike. The National Government belongs to the whole American people, and where the whole American people are interested, that interest can be guarded effectively only by the National Government. The betterment which we seek must be accomplished, I believe, mainly through the National Government.

The American people are right in demanding that New Nationalism, without which we cannot hope to deal with new problems. The New Nationalism puts the national need before sectional or personal advantage. It is impatient of the utter confusion that results from local legislatures attempting to treat national issues as local issues. It is still more impatient of the impotence which springs from overdivision of governmental powers, the impotence which makes it possible for local selfishness or for legal cunning, hired by wealthy special interests, to bring national activities to a deadlock. This New Nationalism regards the executive power as the steward of the public welfare. It demands of the judiciary that it shall be interested primarily in human welfare rather than in property, just as it demands that the representative body shall represent all the people rather than any one class or section of the people.

I believe in shaping the ends of government to protect

property as well as human welfare. Normally, and in the long run, the ends are the same; but whenever the alternative must be faced, I am for men and not for property, as you were in the Civil War. I am far from underestimating the importance of dividends; but I rank dividends below human character. Again, I do not have any sympathy with the reformer who says he does not care for dividends. Of course, economic welfare is necessary, for a man must pull his own weight and be able to support his family. I know well that the reformers must not bring upon the people economic ruin, or the reforms themselves will go down in the ruin. But we must be ready to face temporary disaster, whether or not brought on by those who will war against us to the knife. Those who oppose all reform will do well to remember that ruin in its worst form is inevitable if our national life brings us nothing better than swollen fortunes for the few and the triumph in both politics and business of a sordid and selfish materialism.

If our political institutions were perfect, they would absolutely prevent the political domination of money in any part of our affairs. We need to make our political representatives more quickly and sensitively responsive to the people whose servants they are. More direct action by the people in their own affairs under proper safeguards is vitally necessary. The direct primary is a step in this direction, if it is associated with a corrupt-practices act effective to prevent the advantage of the man willing recklessly and unscrupulously to spend money over his more honest competitor. It is particularly important that all moneys received or expended for campaign purposes should be publicly accounted for, not only after election, but before election as well. Political action must be made simpler, easier, and freer from confusion for every citizen. I believe that the prompt removal of unfaithful or incompetent public servants should be made easy and sure in whatever way experience shall show to be most expedient in any given class of cases.

One of the fundamental necessities in a representative government such as ours is to make certain that the men to whom the people delegate their power shall serve the people by whom they are elected, and not the special interests. I believe that every national officer, elected or appointed, should be forbidden to perform any service or receive any compensation, directly or indirectly, from interstate corporations; and a similar provision could not fail to be useful within the States.

The object of government is the welfare of the people. The material progress and prosperity of a nation are desirable chiefly so far as they lead to the moral and material welfare of all good citizens. Just in proportion as the average man and woman are honest, capable of sound judgment and high ideals, active in public affairs—but, first of all, sound in their home life, and the father and mother of healthy children whom they bring up well—just so far, and no farther, we may count our civilization a success. We must have—I believe we have already—a genuine and permanent moral awakening, without which no wisdom of legislation or administration really means anything; and, on the other hand, we must try to secure the social and economic legislation without which any improvement due to purely moral agitation is necessarily evanescent. Let me again illustrate by a reference to the Grand Army. You could not have won simply as a disorderly and disorganized mob. You needed generals; you needed careful administration of the most advanced type; and a good commissary—the cracker line. You well remember that success was necessary in many different lines in order to bring about general success. You had to have the administration at Washington good, just as you had to have the administration in the field; and you had to have the work of the generals good. You could not have triumphed without that administration and leadership; but it would all have been worthless if the average soldier had not had the right stuff in him. He had to have the right stuff in him, or you could not get it out of him. In the last analysis, therefore, vitally necessary though it was to have the right kind of organization and the right kind of generalship, it was even more vitally necessary that the average soldier should have the fighting edge, the right character. So it is in our civil life. No matter how honest and decent we are in our private lives, if we do not have the right kind of law and the right kind of administration of the law, we cannot go forward as a nation. That is imperative; but it must be an addition to, and not a substitution for, the qualities that make us good citizens. In the last analysis, the most important elements in any man's career must be the sum of those qualities which, in the aggregate, we speak of as character. If he has not got it, then no law that the wit of man can devise, no administration of the law by the boldest and strongest executive, will avail to help him. We must have the right kind of character—character that makes a man, first of all, a good man in the home, a good father, a good husband—that makes a man a good neighbor. You must have that, and, then, in addition, you must have the kind of law and the kind of administration of the law which will give to those qualities in the private citizen the best possible chance for development. The prime problem of our nation is to get the right type of good citizenship, and, to get it, we must have progress, and our public men must be genuinely progressive.

59. · THE CAUSE IS GREATER THAN ITS LEADER

On October 14, 1912, just as the Bull Moose Campaign was moving into its climax, Roosevelt was shot in the chest by a de-

A speech at Milwaukee, Wisconsin, October 14, 1912. *Progressive Principles*, ed. Elmer H. Youngman (New York: Progressive National Service, 1913), pp. 102–14.

mented young man as he stepped into an automobile in Milwaukee. The bullet pierced his manuscript, fractured a rib, and lodged a little short of his right lung. Roosevelt fell backward on impact, coughed in his hand to ascertain if his lung was punctured, and then insisted that he be driven to the Milwaukee Auditorium to deliver his speech. The following stenographic account of his remarks, which departed considerably from his prepared text, testifies to the depth and intensity of his belief in social justice and the open society.

Friends, I shall ask you to be as quiet as possible. I don't know whether you fully understand that I have just been shot; but it takes more than that to kill a Bull Moose. But fortunately I had my manuscript, so you see I was going to make a long speech, and there is a bullet—there is where the bullet went through—and it probably saved me from it going into my heart. The bullet is in me now, so that I cannot make a very long speech, but I will try my best.

And now, friends, I want to take advantage of this incident and say a word of solemn warning to my fellow countrymen. First of all, I want to say this about myself: I have altogether too important things to think of to feel any concern over my own death; and now I cannot speak to you insincerely within five minutes of being shot. I am telling you the literal truth when I say that my concern is for many other things. It is not in the least for my own life. I want you to understand that I am ahead of the game, anyway. No man has had a happier life than I have led; a happier life in every way. I have been able to do certain things that I greatly wished to do, and I am interested in doing other things. I can tell you with absolute truthfulness that I am very much uninterested in whether I am shot or not. It was just as when I was colonel of my regiment. I always felt that a private was to be excused for feeling at times some pangs of anxiety about his personal safety, but I cannot understand a man fit to be a colonel who can pay any heed to his personal safety when he is occupied as he ought to be occupied with the absorbing desire to do his duty.

I am in this cause with my whole heart and soul. I believe that the Progressive movement is for making life a little easier for all our people; a movement to try to take the burdens off the men and especially the women and children of this country. I am absorbed in the success of that movement.

Friends, I ask you now this evening to accept what I am saying as absolutely true, when I tell you I am not thinking of my own success. I am not thinking of my life or of anything connected with me personally. I am thinking of the movement. I say this by way of introduction, because I want to say something very serious to our people and especially to the newspapers. I don't know anything about who the man was who shot me to-night. He was seized at once by one of the stenographers in my party, Mr. Martin, and I suppose is now in the hands of the police. He shot to kill. He shot—the shot, the bullet went in here—I will show you.

I am going to ask you to be as quiet as possible for I am not able to give the challenge of the bull moose quite as loudly. Now, I do not know who he was or what party he represented. He was a coward. He stood in the darkness in the crowd around the automobile and when they cheered me, and I got up to bow, he stepped forward and shot me in the darkness.

Now, friends, of course, I do not know, as I say, anything about him; but it is a very natural thing that weak and vicious minds should be inflamed to acts of violence by the kind of awful mendacity and abuse that have been heaped upon me for the last three months by the papers in the interest of not only Mr. Debs but of Mr. Wilson and Mr. Taft.

Friends, I will disown and repudiate any man of my party who attacks with such foul slander and abuse any opponent of any other party; and now I wish to say seriously to all the daily newspapers, to the Republican, the Democratic, and the Socialist parties, that they cannot, month in and month out and year in and year out, make the kind of untruthful, of bitter assault that they have made and not expect that brutal, violent natures, or brutal and violent characters, especially when the brutality is accompanied by a not very strong mind; they cannot expect that such natures will be unaffected by it.

Now, friends, I am not speaking for myself at all. I give you my word, I do not care a rap about being shot; not a rap.

I have had a good many experiences in my time and this is one of them. What I care for is my country. I wish I were able to impress upon my people—our people, the duty to feel strongly but to speak the truth of their opponents. I say now, I have never said one word on the stump against any opponent that I cannot defend. I have said nothing that I could not substantiate and nothing that I ought not to have said—nothing that I—nothing that, looking back at, I would not say again.

Now, friends, it ought not to be too much to ask that our opponents—[*speaking to some one on the stage*]—I am not sick at all. I am all right. I cannot tell you of what infinitesimal importance I regard this incident as compared with the great issues at stake in this campaign, and I ask it not for my sake, not the least in the world, but for the sake of our common country, that they make up their minds to speak only the truth, and not to use the kind of slander and mendacity which if taken seriously must incite weak and violent natures to crimes of violence. Don't you make any mistake. Don't you pity me. I am all right. I am all right and you cannot escape listening to the speech either.

And now, friends, this incident that has just occurred—this effort to assassinate me—emphasizes to a peculiar degree the need of this Progressive movement. Friends, every good citizen ought to do everything in his or her power to prevent the coming of the day when we shall see in this country two recognized creeds fighting one another, when we shall see the creed of the "Havenots" arraigned against the creed of the "Haves." When that day comes then such incidents as this to-night will

be commonplace in our history. When you make poor men—
when you permit the conditions to grow such that the poor
man as such will be swayed by his sense of injury against the
men who try to hold what they improperly have won, when
that day comes, the most awful passions will be let loose and
it will be an ill day for our country.

Now, friends, what we who are in this movement are endeavoring to do is to forestall any such movement by making
this a movement for justice now—a movement in which we
ask all just men of generous hearts to join with the men who
feel in their souls that lift upward which bids them refuse to
be satisfied themselves while their countrymen and country-
women suffer from avoidable misery. Now, friends, what we
Progressives are trying to do is to enroll rich or poor, whatever
their social or industrial position, to stand together for the
most elementary rights of good citizenship, those elementary
rights which are the foundation of good citizenship in this
great Republic of ours.

(*At this point a renewed effort was made to persuade
Mr. Roosevelt to conclude his speech.*)

My friends are a little more nervous than I am. Don't you
waste any sympathy on me. I have had an A-1 time in life and
I am having it now.

I never in my life was in any movement in which I was able
to serve with such whole-hearted devotion as in this; in which
I was able to feel as I do in this that common weal. I have
fought for the good of our common country.

And now, friends, I shall have to cut short much of the
speech that I meant to give you, but I want to touch on just
two or three of the points.

In the first place, speaking to you here in Milwaukee, I wish
to say that the Progressive party is making its appeal to all our
fellow citizens without any regard to their creed or to their
birthplace. We do not regard as essential the way in which a
man worships his God or as being affected by where he was

born. We regard it as a matter of spirit and purpose. In New York, while I was police commissioner, the two men from whom I got the most assistance were Jacob Riis, who was born in Denmark, and Arthur von Briesen, who was born in Germany—both of them as fine examples of the best and highest American citizenship as you could find in any part of this country.

I have just been introduced by one of your own men here—Henry Cochems. His grandfather, his father, and that father's seven brothers, all served in the United States army, and they entered it four years after they had come to this country from Germany. Two of them left their lives, spent their lives, on the field of battle. I am all right—I am a little sore. Anybody has a right to be sore with a bullet in him. You would find that if I was in battle now I would be leading my men just the same. Just the same way I am going to make this speech.

At one time I promoted five men for gallantry on the field of battle. Afterward in making some inquiries about them I found it happened that two of them were Protestants, two Catholics, and one a Jew. One Protestant came from Germany and one was born in Ireland. I did not promote them because of their religion. It just happened that way. If all five of them had been Jews I would have promoted them, or if all five had been Protestants I would have promoted them; or if they had been Catholics. In that regiment I had a man born in Italy who distinguished himself by gallantry; there was a young fellow, a son of Polish parents, and another who came here when he was a child from Bohemia, who likewise distinguished themselves; and friends, I assure you, that I was incapable of considering any question whatever, but the worth of each individual as a fighting man. If he was a good fighting man, then I saw that Uncle Sam got the benefit from it. That is all.

I make the same appeal in our citizenship. I ask in our civic life that we in the same way pay heed only to the man's quality of citizenship, to repudiate as the worst enemy that we can have whoever tries to get us to discriminate for or against any man because of his creed or his birthplace.

Now, friends, in the same way I want our people to stand by one another without regard to differences or class or occupation. I have always stood by the labor unions. I am going to make one omission to-night. I have prepared my speech because Mr. Wilson has seen fit to attack me by showing up his record in comparison with mine. But I am not going to do that to-night. I am going to simply speak of what I myself have done and of what I think ought to be done in this country of ours.

It is essential that there should be organizations of labor. This is an era of organization. Capital organizes and therefore labor must organize. My appeal for organized labor is twofold; to the outsider and the capitalist I make my appeal to treat the laborer fairly, to recognize the fact that he must organize, that there must be such organization, that the laboring man must organize for his own protection, and that it is the duty of the rest of us to help him and not hinder him in organizing. That is one-half of the appeal that I make.

Now, the other half is to the labor man himself. My appeal to him is to remember that as he wants justice, so he must do justice. I want every labor man, every labor leader, every organized union man, to take the lead in denouncing crime or violence. I want them to take the lead in denouncing disorder and in denouncing the inciting of riot; that in this country we shall proceed under the protection of our laws and with all respect to the laws, and I want the labor men to feel in their turn that exactly as justice must be done them so they must do justice. That they must bear their duty as citizens, their duty to this great country of ours, and that they must not rest content unless they do that duty to the fullest degree.

I know these doctors, when they get hold of me, will never let me go back, and there are just a few things more that I want to say to you.

And here I have got to make one comparison between Mr. Wilson and myself, simply because he has invited it and I cannot shrink from it. Mr. Wilson has seen fit to attack me, to say that I did not do much against the trusts when I was President. I have got two answers to make to that. In the first place what I did, and then I want to compare what I did while I was President with what Mr. Wilson did not do while he was governor.

When I took office the antitrust law was practically a dead letter and the interstate commerce law in as poor a condition. I had to revive both laws. I did. I enforced both. It will be easy enough to do now what I did then, but the reason that it is easy now is because I did it when it was hard.

Nobody was doing anything. I found speedily that the interstate commerce law by being made more perfect could be made a most useful instrument for helping solve some of our industrial problems. So with the antitrust law. I speedily found that almost the only positive good achieved by such a successful lawsuit as the Northern Securities suit, for instance, was in establishing the principle that the government was supreme over the big corporation, but that by itself that law did not accomplish any of the things that we ought to have accomplished; and so I began to fight for the amendment of the law along the lines of the interstate commerce law, and now we propose, we Progressives, to establish an interstate commission having the same power over industrial concerns that the Interstate Commerce Commission has over railroads, so that whenever there is in the future a decision rendered in such important matters as the recent suits against the Standard Oil, the Sugar—no, not that—Tobacco—Tobacco Trust—we will have a commission which will see that the decree of the court is really made effective; that it is not made a merely nominal decree.

Our opponents have said that we intend to legalize monopoly. Nonsense. They have legalized monopoly. At this moment the Standard Oil and Tobacco Trust monopolies are legalized; they are being carried on under the decree of the Supreme Court. Our proposal is really to break up monopoly. Our proposal is to lay down certain requirements, and then require the commerce commission—the industrial commission—to see that the trusts live up to those requirements. Our opponents have spoken as if we were going to let the commission declare what the requirements should be. Not at all. We are going to put the requirements in the law and then see that the commission requires them to obey the law.

And now, friends, as Mr. Wilson has invited the comparison, I only want to say this: Mr. Wilson has said that the States are the proper authorities to deal with the trusts. Well, about eighty per cent of the trusts are organized in New Jersey. The Standard Oil, the Tobacco, the Sugar, the Beef, all those trusts are organized in New Jersey and the laws of New Jersey say that their charters can at any time be amended or repealed if they misbehave themselves and give the government ample power to act about those laws, and Mr. Wilson has been governor a year and nine months and he has not opened his lips. The chapter describing what Mr. Wilson has done about the trusts in New Jersey would read precisely like a chapter describing the snakes in Ireland, which ran: "There are no snakes in Ireland." Mr. Wilson has done precisely and exactly nothing about the trusts.

I tell you, and I told you at the beginning, I do not say anything on the stump that I do not believe. I do not say anything I do not know. Let any of Mr. Wilson's friends on Tuesday point out one thing or let Mr. Wilson point out one thing he has done about the trusts as governor of New Jersey.

And now, friends, there is one thing I want to say especially to you people here in Wisconsin. All that I have said so far is what I would say in any part of this Union. I have a peculiar right to ask that in this great contest you men and women of Wisconsin shall stand with us. You have taken the lead in progressive movements here in Wisconsin. You have taught the rest of us to look to you for inspiration and leadership. Now, friends, you have made that movement here locally. You will be doing a dreadful injustice to yourselves; you will be doing a dreadful injustice to the rest of us throughout the Union, if you fail to stand with us now that we are making this national movement. What I am about to say now I want you to understand. If I speak of Mr. Wilson I speak with no mind of bitterness. I merely want to discuss the difference of policy between the Progressive and the Democratic party and to ask you to think for yourselves which party you will follow. I will say that, friends, because the Republican party is beaten. Nobody needs to have any idea that anything can be done with the Republican party.

When the Republican party—not the Republican party—when the bosses in the control of the Republican party, the Barneses and Penroses, last June stole the nomination and wrecked the Republican party for good and all—I want to point out to you nominally they stole that nomination from me, but really it was from you. They did not like me, and the longer they live the less cause they will have to like me. But while they do not like me, they dread you. You are the people that they dread. They dread the people themselves, and those bosses and the big special interests behind them made up their mind that they would rather see the Republican party wrecked than see it come under the control of the people themselves. So I am not dealing with the Republican party. There are only two ways you can vote this year. You can be progressive or reactionary. Whether you vote Republican or Democratic it does not make any difference, you are voting reactionary.

Now, the Democratic party in its platform and through the utterances of Mr. Wilson has distinctly committed itself to the old flintlock, muzzle-loaded doctrine of States' rights, and I have said distinctly that we are for the people's rights. We are for the rights of the people. If they can be obtained best through the National Government, then we are for national rights. We are for the people's rights however it is necessary to secure them.

Mr. Wilson has made a long essay against Senator Beveridge's bill to abolish child labor. It is the same kind of an argument that would be made against our bill to prohibit women from working more than eight hours a day in industry. It is the same kind of argument that would have to be made; if it is true, it would apply equally against our proposal to insist that in continuous industries there shall be by law one day's rest in seven and a three-shift eight-hour day. You have labor laws here in Wisconsin, and any chamber of commerce will tell you that because of that fact there are industries that will not come into Wisconsin. They prefer to stay outside where they can work children of tender years, where they can work women fourteen and sixteen hours a day, where, if it is a continuous industry, they can work men twelve hours a day and seven days a week.

Now, friends, I know that you of Wisconsin would never repeal those laws even if they are to your commercial hurt, just as I am trying to get New York to adopt such laws even though it will be to New York's commercial hurt. But if possible I want to arrange it so that we can have justice without commercial hurt, and you can only get that if you have justice enforced nationally. You won't be burdened in Wisconsin with industries not coming to the State if the same good laws are extended all over the other States. Do you see what I mean? The States all compete in a common market; and it is not justice to the employers of a State that has enforced just and proper laws to have them exposed to the competition of another State where no such laws are enforced. Now, the Democratic platform, and their speakers, declare that we shall not have such laws. Mr. Wilson has distinctly declared that you shall not have a national law to prohibit the labor of children, to prohibit child labor. He has distinctly declared that we shall not have a law to establish a minimum wage for women.

I ask you to look at our declaration and hear and read our

platform about social and industrial justice and then, friends, vote for the Progressive ticket without regard to me, without regard to my personality, for only by voting for that platform can you be true to the cause of progress throughout this Union.

60. · "TWO NOTEWORTHY BOOKS ON DEMOCRACY"

The outbreak of World War I, coupled with the failure of the Bull Moosers to establish themselves in the Congressional elections of 1914, caused Roosevelt to lose interest in the Progressive Party as a political organization. Nevertheless, his commitment to progressive ideology continued. Here he endorses new books by two of the progressive movement's foremost intellectuals, Herbert Croly and Walter Lippmann, both of whom had been profoundly influenced by his own presidential policies. He is especially impressed by Croly's brief for moderate collectivism and a strong executive, and by Lippmann's case for vigorous labor unions and constructive revision of the anti-trust laws. What is most significant about the review, however, is Roosevelt's sharp assertion that reformers must recognize the need for, and adjust their programs to, economic productivity.

There are books of which it is impossible to make an epitome, and which therefore it is impossible to review save in the way of calling attention to their excellence. Bryce's "American Commonwealth," Lowell's "Study of Representative Government in Europe," Thayer's "Study of Cavour," illustrate what is meant by this statement. Two new volumes, "Progressive

A review of Herbert Croly's *Progressive Democracy* (1914) and Walter Lippmann's *Drift and Mastery* (1914). *The Outlook,* CVIII (November 18, 1914), 648–51.

Democracy," by Herbert Croly, and "Drift and Mastery," by Walter Lippmann, come in this category. No man who wishes seriously to study our present social, industrial, and political life with the view of guiding his thought and action so as to work for national betterment in the future can afford not to read these books through and through and to ponder and digest them. They worthily carry forward the argument contained in the authors' previous works—"The Promise of American Life," by Mr. Croly, and "A Preface to Politics," by Mr. Lippmann.

Both of these writers stand foremost among those of our thinkers who recognize the grave abuses of our present system and the need of breaking the shackles which the interested beneficiaries and the disinterested but fanatical devotees of the past would impose upon us. Both thoroughly realize the absolute need that we shall move forward toward a definite goal unless we are willing to see misfortune come to our people. But each is as far as possible from those unwise reformers who denounce everything that smacks of the past as vicious, and who consider all change of any kind as in itself beneficial. Both of them—and Mr. Lippmann especially so—are believers in a great increase in the application of the principle of collective action. But neither of them makes a fetich of ultracollectivism any more than of ultraindividualism, and each is entirely fearless in opposing mischievous action, even although it is now or has been recently supported by the great majority of our people.

Mr. Croly explicitly points out that the position which American conservatism has elected to defend arouses on the part of its defenders a sincere and admirable loyalty of conviction. He recognizes that our traditional constitutional system has had a long and honorable career, and has contributed enormously to American political and social prosperity, giving stability, order, and security to a new political experiment undertaken in a new country under peculiarly hazardous and trying conditions.

He also gives the wise warning that in order to attack the old system progressivism must not occupy a position of mere nihilism, of mere destruction; that it must not represent wild-eyed and unbalanced seeking after an impossible millennium; and, furthermore, that it must be constructive rather than restorative. In his book he poses the two questions: (1) Whether any substitute is needed for the traditional system, and (2) whether the progressive creed offers what can fairly be considered such a working substitute. He answers both questions in the affirmative; but the value of his book, although it consists partly in the working out of the definite conclusions he reaches, consists even more in the spirit in which he has attempted to reach these conclusions.

Mr. Croly strikes at the root of the difficulties encountered by men who seriously strive for a juster economic and social life when he points out that the chief obstacles to securing the needed betterment are found in the legalism with which we have permitted our whole government to be affected, and in the extreme difficulty of amending the Constitution. As for the latter point, objection to an easier method of amending the Constitution can be reasonably advanced only by those who sincerely and frankly disbelieve in the fitness of the people for self-government. Government under a Constitution which in actual practice can be amended only on the terms which formerly permitted the Polish Parliament to legislate, and under a system of court procedure which makes the courts the ultimate irresponsible interpreters of the Constitution, and therefore ultimately the irresponsible makers of the law under the Constitution—such government really represents a system as emphatically undemocratic as government by a hereditary aristocracy. As Mr. Croly says, what is needed is not to increase the power of Congress at the expense of the judiciary, or to conserve the power of the judiciary at the expense of Congress or of the Executive, but to increase popular control over all the organs of government; and this can be accomplished only by the increase of direct popular power over the Constitution.

No less admirable is Mr. Croly's showing of the damage done to justice and to the whole democratic ideal by the saturation of our government with legalism. As he points out, the final outcome of this effort was to make the paralyzing of administration by law an everyday spectacle. Under such conditions the ship of state merely drifted round and round. In practice the public welfare was sedulously sacrificed to this theory of government by litigation. The law continually prevented the correction of abuses and continually shielded officials who had gone wrong, but it never helped to make things go right. Corruption increased and special privilege was fostered. In practice the equal protection of the laws meant very unequal opportunity to bring lawsuits, and government by law was turned into government by corporations and political bosses. This continued until observers of vision finally became convinced that democracy and legalism were incompatible.

The great corporation, the great corporation lawyer, and the boss are now merged together as representing rule over the people, and the demagogue, whose revolt occasionally tempers this far from beneficent despotism, often aggravates as many ills as he remedies. Mr. Croly points out how direct government by the people themselves, entered into with wisdom and caution, offers, on the whole, not only the best but the only real remedy for these abuses. He shows that to call pure democracy "retrogressive" or a "return to old forms" is a mere play upon words, of no more account than it would be to stigmatize in similar fashion the attempt to recover classic humanism after its eclipse in the Middle Ages. The adoption of direct government may in the end accomplish most of its purposes by reinvigorating representative government; and not the least interesting part of Mr. Croly's book is a study of the method proposed in Oregon for achieving this result. Mr. Croly emphatically believes in nationalizing our democracy, but this does not in the least mean mere centralization of power. On the contrary, he no more makes a fetich of centralization than of particularism. It is eminently desirable that we should keep in State and in city vigorous forms of local self-government. What is meant by the nationalization of the democratic method is the giving to the whole people themselves the power to do those things that are essential in the interest of the whole people.

The dominant note of Mr. Lippmann's book is the insistence that in the present unrest there is altogether too much aimless drift, aimless beating of the waves to and fro, and that what is needed is a mastery of the movement; which can come in a democracy only if the people, or at least the leaders of the people, have the courage to face the facts and the wisdom and vision to think rationally about them. Mr. Lippmann, with caustic humor, shows the folly alike of the persons who believe in the non-existent virtues of a non-existent golden past and of the persons who merely dream of a golden future without making any sane effort to better conditions in the present. Too many of the dreamers of the last type refuse to confront the uncomfortable fact that in life retrogression is almost, and at times quite, as common as progress, and that there is no necessary truth whatever in the proposition that whatever is later in time is better in fact. He shows that no liberty worth having can come from a mere happy-go-lucky breaking of chains. "It is with emancipation that real tasks begin, and liberty is a searching challenge, for it takes away the guardianship of the master and the comfort of the priest."

Two of the most fundamental and admirable chapters in Mr. Lippmann's book are those entitled "A Key to the Labor Movement" and "A Nation of Villagers." In the former he makes the point, which cannot be too much insisted upon, that strong labor organizations are indispensable to progress. They not only benefit the persons who are thus organized, but they benefit society as a whole. It is the economic weakness and wretchedness of those who constitute the Industrial Workers of the World which make the Industrial Workers of the World so potent a source of aimless, of merely destructive, unrest. It is the strength and economic power of the great brotherhoods of railway employees and of similar effective labor organizations which have given, not merely dignity and strength to the labor movement, but also additional solidity to our social structure.

Nowhere is Mr. Lippmann's clear sight and courage better shown than in his treatment of the trusts. During the past quarter of a century probably more mischief has been done, and is now being done, by our treatment of the trusts than by any other one phase of our governmental activity. He points out that the Sherman Antitrust Law has, on the whole, worked very great evil. Indeed, almost the only good that has been accomplished under it has been accomplished by the Northern Securities suit, and this merely by establishing the power of the National Government to deal with corporations engaged in interstate business, a power secured by getting the Supreme Court to reverse a previous most unwise and improper decision. The Sherman Antitrust Law should only remain as applicable to corporations which refuse to obey the decrees of an adequate, powerful administrative body in the nature of an interstate business commission. Mr. Lippmann is, with justice, equally severe upon those who have organized the "trusts" that do evil and upon the professional antitrust leaders who have endeavored merely to break up big business corporations and to secure the "new freedom" by bringing us back to an era of unlimited and ruthless competition between small business concerns. He says, quite justly, that "the stupid hostility of antitrust laws" has perverted all real constructive policy on the part of the nation and the States, has concentrated the thinking of our people on inessentials, has driven creative business men to underhand methods, and has put a high money value on intrigue and legal cunning, demagoguery, and waste. "The trusts have survived it all, but in mutilated form, the battered makeshifts of a trampled promise. They have learned every art of evasion—the only art reformers allowed them to learn."

Of course our policy as regards the trusts should be frankly to accept in its essentials the doctrine laid down by President Van Hise[1] in his book entitled "Combination and Control."

Mr. Lippmann sees clearly, as does Mr. Croly, that democracy cannot possibly be achieved save among a people fit for democracy. There can be no real political democracy unless there is something approaching an economic democracy. A democracy must consist of men who are intellectually, morally, and materially fit to be their own masters. There can be neither political nor industrial democracy unless people are reasonably well-to-do, and also reasonably able to achieve the difficult task of self-mastery. As Mr. Lippmann says, the first item in any rational programme for a democratic State must be the insistence on a reasonably high minimum standard of life, and therefore of pay, for the average worker.

It is not possible even for reformers of lofty vision and fine and sane judgment to treat of everything. Neither of these two books dwells sufficiently upon, although both of them hint at, certain vital facts which are connected with a further fundamental fact, that there must be ample prosperity in the nation. Public welfare depends upon general public prosperity, and the reformer whose reforms interfere with the general prosperity will accomplish little.

We cannot pay for what the highest type of democracy demands unless there is a great abundance of prosperity. A business that does not make money necessarily pays bad wages and renders poor service. Merely to change the ownership of the business without making it yield increased profits will achieve nothing. In practice this means that when the nation suffers from hard times wage-workers will concern themselves, and must concern themselves, primarily with a return to good times, and not with any plan for securing social and industrial

[1] Charles Richard Van Hise, president of the University of Wisconsin, 1903–1918, and scholarly advocate of regulation of trusts [Ed.].

justice. If women cannot get any work, and nevertheless have
to live, they will be far more concerned with seeing a factory
opened in which they can work at night or work twelve hours
every day than they are concerned with the abolition of night-
work or the limitation of hours of labor. Exactly the same is
true of men. In the recent election in Pennsylvania the majority
of the miners and wage-workers generally voted for the Republican machine, although this Republican machine had just
defeated a workmen's compensation act, a child-labor law, a
minimum wage for women law, and various other bits of very
desirable labor legislation. The attitude of the wage-workers
was perfectly simple. They wished employment. They wished
a chance to get a job. They believed that they had more chance
if the candidates of the Republican machine were elected than
they would otherwise have. Personally I very strongly believe
that they were in error; but it was their belief that counted.
The average voter usually sees what he is voting about in very
simple form. He does not regard the political picture as an
etching and follow out the delicate tracery. He treats it as a
circus poster, in which the colors are in very vivid contrast and
are laid on with a broad brush. When the average man feels
the pinch of poverty, the only things he sees in the political
picture are the broad, vivid colors which in his mind deal with
that particular matter. He wishes to have his material condition improved at the present time or in the immediate future;
and for the moment questions of ultimate betterment, and
especially of moral betterment, sink into abeyance. This attitude is in no way peculiar to the laboring man or the farmer.
It is just as evident in the big business man and in his college-
bred son, and in the wealthy clubs of which these two make
up most of the membership.

Finally, it is imperative to count the cost of all reforms, and
therefore to remember that only a wealthy state can spend
money sufficient to embody the reform into law. There is no
point in having prosperity unless there can be an equitable

division of prosperity. But there can be no equitable division of prosperity until the prosperity is there to divide. All reformers with any wisdom will keep this fact steadily in mind, and will realize that it is their duty in all legislation to work for the general prosperity of the community; and this in spite of the further fact that no good comes from the performance of this first duty unless some system of equity and justice is built upon the prosperity thus secured.

XI · WAR AND PEACE

The Case for Military Preparedness

61. · "WARLIKE POWER—THE PREREQUISITE FOR THE
PRESERVATION OF SOCIAL VALUES"

Was Roosevelt a militarist? There was a sense, surely, in which
he was. No man who went to war with his exhilaration in 1898 or
who sought a command as desperately as he did in 1917 can escape
the taint. Yet, as the following essay and numerous other writings
and actions suggest, he was not a true philosophical militarist. As
president he opposed creation of a large standing army—the hallmark of militarism—and worked conscientiously on a variety of
fronts to promote general peace. After he modified his aspirations
for commercial supremacy in the Far East, moreover, he thought
in terms of retrenchment rather than expansion. Nevertheless, his
interpretation of history—he viewed it as a struggle between the
barbaric and the civilized, the unjust and the just—convinced him
that military power and the will to use it if necessary were the
first requisite for peaceful existence. For that reason he persistently
exalted the soldierly virtues.

In December last I was asked to address the American Sociological Congress on "the effect of war and militarism on
social values." In sending my answer I pointed out that infi-

A paper delivered before the American Sociological Congress, Washington, D. C., December 28–31, 1914. American Sociological Society,
Papers and Proceedings, X (1915), 12–21.

GERMANY
VS.

U. S.

nitely the most important fact to remember in connection with the subject in question is that if an unscrupulous, warlike, and militaristic nation is not held in check by the warlike ability of a neighboring non-militaristic and well-behaved nation, then the latter will be spared the necessity of dealing with its own "moral and social values" because it won't be allowed to deal with anything. Until this fact is thoroughly recognized, and the duty of national preparedness by justice-loving nations explicitly acknowledged, there is very little use of solemnly debating such questions as the one which the sociological congress assigned me—which, in detail, was "'How war and militarism affect such social values as the sense of the preciousness of human life; care for child welfare; the conservation of human resources; upper-class concern for the lot of the masses; interest in popular education; appreciation of truth-telling and truth-printing; respect for personality and regard for personal rights." It seems to me positively comic to fail to appreciate, with the example of Belgium before our eyes, that the real question which modern peace-loving nations have to face is not how the militaristic or warlike spirit within their own borders will affect these "values," but how failure on their part to be able to resist the militarism of an unscrupulous neighbor will affect them. Belgium had a very keen sense of the "preciousness of human life" and of "the need for the care of child welfare and the conservation of human resources," and there was much "concern" by the Belgian "upper classes for the lot of the masses," great "interest in popular education and appreciation of truth-telling and truth-printing and a high respect for personality and regard for personal rights." But all these "social values" existed in Belgium only up to the end of July, 1914. Not a vestige of them remained in 1915. To discuss them as regards present-day Belgium is sheer prattle, simply because on August 4, 1914, Belgium had not prepared her military strength so that she could put on her frontiers at least half a million thoroughly armed and trained men of fighting spirit.

In similar fashion the question of the internal reformation of China at this moment is wholly secondary to the question whether any China will remain to be reformed internally. A Chinese gentleman wrote me the other day that he had formerly been absorbed in plans for bringing China abreast of the modern movement, but that the events of the past year had shown him that what he really ought to be absorbed in was the question whether or not China would be able by military preparation to save itself from the fate of Korea. Korean "social values" now have to be studied exclusively through a Japanese medium. At this moment the Armenians, who for some centuries have sedulously avoided militarism and war, and have practically applied advanced pacifist principles, are suffering a fate, if possible, worse than that of the Belgians; and they are so suffering precisely and exactly because they have been pacifists, whereas their neighbors, the Turks, have not been pacifists but militarists. They haven't the vestige of a "social value" left, to be "affected" by militarism or by anything else. *A WILDLY SPECIOUS ARGUMENT.*

In the thirteenth century Persia had become a highly civilized nation, with a cultivated class of literary men and philosophers, with universities, and with great mercantile interests. These literary men and merchants took toward the realities of war much the same attitude that is taken in our own country by gentlemen of the stamp of Messrs. David Starr Jordan and Henry Ford. Unfortunately for these predecessors of the modern pacifists, they were within striking distance of Genghis Khan and his Mongols; and, as of course invariably happens in such a case, when the onrush came, the pacifists' theories were worth just about what a tissue-paper barrier would amount to against a tidal wave. Russia at that time was slowly struggling upward toward civilization. She had become Christian. She was developing industry and she was struggling toward individual freedom. In other words, she was in halting fashion developing the "social values" of which the foregoing extract speaks. But she had not developed military efficiency; she had not developed efficiency in war. The Mongols overwhelmed her as fire overwhelms stubble. For two centuries the Russians were trodden under foot by an alien dominion so ruthless, so brutal, that when they finally shook it off, all popular freedom had been lost and the soul of the nation seared by torment and degradation; and to this day the scars remain on the national life and character. The chief difficulties against which Russia has had to struggle in modern times are due ultimately to the one all-essential fact that in the early part of the thirteenth century she had not developed the warlike strength to enable her to hold her own against a militaristic neighbor. The Russian Jew of to-day is oppressed by the Russian Christian because that Christian's ancestor in the thirteenth century had not learned efficiency in war.

There are well-meaning people, utterly incapable of learning any lesson taught by history, utterly incapable even of understanding aright what has gone on before their very eyes during the past year or two, who nevertheless wish to turn this country into an Occidental China—the kind of China which every intelligent Chinaman of the present day is seeking to abolish. There are plenty of politicians, by no means as well-meaning, who find it to their profit to pander to the desire common to most men to live softly and easily and avoid risk and effort. Timid and lazy men, men absorbed in money-getting, men absorbed in ease and luxury, and all soft and slothful people naturally hail with delight anybody who will give them high-sounding names behind which to cloak their unwillingness to run risks or to toil and endure. Emotional philanthropists to whom thinking is a distasteful form of mental exercise enthusiastically champion this attitude. The faults of all these men and women are of a highly non-militaristic and unwarlike type; and naturally they feel great satisfaction in condemning misdeeds which are incident to lives that they would themselves be wholly unable to lead without an amount of toil and effort that they are wholly unwilling to undergo. These men and women are delighted to pass resolutions in favor of anything with a lofty name, provided always that no demand is ever made upon them to pay with their bodies to even the smallest degree in order to give effect to these lofty sentiments. It is questionable whether in the long run they do not form a less desirable national type than is formed by the men who are guilty of the downright iniquities of life; for the latter at least have in them elements of strength which, if guided aright, could be used to good purpose.

Now, it is probably hopeless ever to convince the majority of these men except by actual disaster that the course they follow is not merely wicked, because of its subordination of duty to ease, but from their own standpoint utterly short-sighted—as the fate of the Armenians and the Chinese of the present day shows. But I believe that the bulk of our people are willing to follow duty, even though it be rather unpleasant and rather hard, if it can be made clearly evident to them; and, moreover, I believe that they are capable of looking ahead, and of considering the ultimate interest of themselves and their children, if only they can be waked up to vital national needs. The members of sociological societies and kindred organizations, and philanthropists, and clergymen, and educators, and all other leading men, should pride themselves on furnishing leadership in the right direction to these men and women who wish to do what is right.

The first thing to do is to make these citizens understand that war and militarism are terms whose values depend wholly upon the sense in which they are used. The second thing is to make them understand that there is a real analogy between the use of force in international and the use of force in intranational or civil matters; although of course this analogy must not be pushed too far.

In the first place, we are dealing with a matter of definition. A war can be defined as violence between nations, as the use of force between nations. It is analogous to violence between individuals within a nation—using violence in a large sense as equivalent to the use of force. When this fact is clearly grasped, the average citizen will be spared the mental confusion he now suffers because he thinks of war as *in itself* wrong. War, like peace, is properly a means to an end—righteousness. Neither war nor peace is in itself righteous, and neither should be treated as of itself the end to be aimed at. Righteousness is the end. Righteousness when triumphant brings peace; but peace may not bring righteousness. Whether war is right or wrong depends purely upon the purpose for which, and the spirit in which, it is waged. Here the analogy with what takes place in civil life is perfect. The exertion of force or violence by which one man masters another may be illustrated by the case of a black-hander who kidnaps a child, knocking down the nurse or guardian; and it may also be illustrated by the case of the guardian who by violence withstands and thwarts the blackhander in his efforts to kidnap the child, or by the case of the policeman who by force arrests the black-hander or white-slaver or whoever it is and takes his victim away from him. There are, of course, persons who believe that all force is immoral, that it is always immoral to resist wrong-doing by force. I have never taken much interest in the individuals who profess this kind of twisted morality; and I do not know the extent to which they practically apply it. But if they are right in their theory, then it is wrong for a man to endeavor by force to save his wife or sister or daughter from rape or other abuse, or to save his children from abduction and torture. It is a waste of time to discuss with any man a position of such folly, wickedness, and poltroonery. But unless a man is willing to take this position, he cannot honestly condemn the use of force or violence in war—for the policeman who risks and perhaps loses or takes life in dealing with an anarchist or white-slaver or black-hander or burglar or highwayman must be justified or condemned on precisely the same principles which require us to differentiate among wars and to condemn unstintedly certain nations in certain wars and equally without stint to praise other nations in certain other wars.

If the man who objects to war also objects to the use of force in civil life as above outlined, his position is logical, although both absurd and wicked. If the college presidents, politicians, automobile manufacturers, and the like, who during the past year or two have preached pacifism in its most ignoble and degrading form are willing to think out the subject and are both sincere and fairly intelligent, they must necessarily condemn a police force or a posse comitatus just as much as they condemn armies; and they must regard the activities of the sheriff and the constable as being essentially militaristic and therefore to be abolished.

There are small communities with which I am personally acquainted where the general progress has been such as really to permit of this abolition of the policeman. In these communities—and I have in mind specifically one in New England and one in the Province of Quebec—the constable and sheriff have no duties whatever to perform, so far as crimes or deeds of violence are concerned. The "social values" in these communities are not in any way affected by either the international militarism of the soldier or by the civil militarism of the policeman, and on the whole good results; although I regret to say that in each of the two communities I have in mind there have been some social developments that were not pleasant.

We ought all of us to endeavor to shape our action with a view to extending so far as possible the area in which such conditions can be made to obtain. But at present the area cannot, as a matter of plain fact, be extended to most populous communities, or even to ordinary scantily peopled communities; and to make believe that it can be thus extended is a proof, not of goodness of heart, but of softness of head.

As a matter of practical common sense it is not worth while

spending much time at this moment in discussing whether we ought to take steps to abolish the police force in New York, Chicago, San Francisco, or Montreal, because no police force is needed in a certain Vermont town or a certain Quebec village. Such a discussion would not help us in the least toward an appreciation and development of the "social values" of any one of the big cities in question.

Exactly the same principle, only a fortiori, applies as regards war. On the whole, there is a much greater equality of intellectual and moral status among the individuals in a great civilized community than there is between the various nations and peoples of the earth. The task of getting all the policemen, all the college professors, all the business men and mechanics, and also all the professional crooks, in New York to abandon the reign of force and to live together in harmony without any police force would be undoubtedly very much easier than to secure a similar working agreement among the various peoples of Europe, America, Asia, and Africa. One of the commonest failings of mankind is to try to make amends for failure to perform the duty at hand by grandiloquent talk about something that is afar off. Most of our worthy pacifist friends adopt in this matter the attitude Mrs. Jellyby took toward foreign missions when compared with her own domestic and neighborhood duties. Instead of meeting together and passing resolutions to affect the whole world, let them deal with the much easier task of regulating their own localities. When we have discovered a method by which right living may be spread so universally in Chicago and New York that the two cities can with safety abolish their police forces, then, and not till then, it will be worth while to talk about "the abolition of war." Until that time the discussion will not possess even academic value.

The really essential things for men to remember, therefore, in connection with war are, first, that neither war nor peace is immoral in itself, and, secondly, that in order to preserve the

"social values" which were enumerated in the quotation with
which I began this chapter it is absolutely essential to prevent
the dominance in our country of the one form of militarism
which is surely and completely fatal—that is, the military dominion of an alien enemy. *W. W. I. UNDERWAY—*

It is utterly impossible to appreciate social values at all or to
discriminate between what is socially good and socially bad
unless we appreciate the utterly different social values of different wars. The Greeks who triumphed at Marathon and
Salamis did a work without which the world would have been
deprived of the social value of Plato and Aristotle, of Aeschy-
lus, Herodotus, and Thucydides. The civilization of Europe,
America, and Australia exists to-day at all only because of the
victories of civilized man over the enemies of civilization, because of victories stretching through the centuries from the
days of Miltiades and Themistocles to those of Charles Martel
in the eighth century and those of John Sobieski in the seven-
teenth century. During the thousand years that included the
careers of the Frankish soldier and the Polish king, the Christians of Asia and Africa proved unable to wage successful war
with the Moslem conquerors; and in consequence Christianity
practically vanished from the two continents; and to-day nobody can find in them any "social values" whatever, in the
sense in which we use the words, so far as the sphere of
Mohammedan influence and the decaying native Christian
churches are concerned. There are such "social values" to-day
in Europe, America, and Australia only because during those
thousand years the Christians of Europe possessed the warlike
power to do what the Christians of Asia and Africa had failed
to do—that is, to beat back the Moslem invader. It is of course
worth while for sociologists to discuss the effect of this European militarism on "social values," but only if they first clearly
realize and formulate the fact that if the European militarism
had not been able to defend itself against and to overcome the
militarism of Asia and Africa, there would have been no "social

values" of any kind in our world to-day, and no sociologists to discuss them.

The Sociological Society meets at Washington this year only because the man after whom the city was named was willing to go to war. If he and his associates had not gone to war, there would have been no possibility of discussing "social values" in the United States, for the excellent reason that there would have been no United States. If Lincoln had not been willing to go to war, to appeal to the sword, to introduce militarism on a tremendous scale throughout the United States, the sociologists who listened to this chapter, when it was read to them, if they existed at all, would not be considering the "social values" enumerated above, but the "social values" of slavery and of such governmental and industrial problems as can now be studied in the Central American republics.

It is a curious fact that during the thirty years prior to the Civil War the men who in the Northern and especially the Northeastern States gradually grew to take most interest in the antislavery agitation were almost equally interested in anti-militaristic and peace movements. Even a casual glance at the poems of Longfellow and Whittier will show this. They were strong against slavery and they were strong against war. They did not take the trouble to think out the truth, which was that in actual fact slavery could be abolished only by war; and when the time came they had to choose between, on the one hand, the "social values" of freedom and of union and, on the other hand, the "social value" of peace, for peace proved incompatible with freedom and union. Being men fit to live in a free country, they of course chose freedom and union rather than peace. I say men; of course I mean women also. I am speaking of Julia Ward Howe and Harriet Beecher Stowe just exactly as I am speaking of Longfellow and Lowell and Whittier.

Now, during the thirty years preceding the Civil War these men and women often debated and occasionally in verse or

prose wrote about the effect of war on what we now call
"social values." I think that academically they were a unit in
saying that this effect was bad; but when the real crisis came,
when they were faced by the actual event, they realized that
this academic discussion as to the effect of war on "social
values" was of no consequence whatever. They did not want
war. Nobody wants war who has any sense. But when they
moved out of a world of dreams into a world of realities they
realized that now, as always in the past has been the case, and
as undoubtedly will be the case for a long time in the future,
war may be the only alternative to losing, not merely certain
"social values," but the national life which means the sum of
all "social values." They realized that as the world is now it is
a wicked thing to use might against right, and an unspeakably
silly, and therefore in the long run also a wicked thing, to
chatter about right without preparing to put might back of
right. They abhorred a wanton or an unjust war and condemned those responsible for it as they ought always to be
condemned; and, on the other hand, they realized that righteous war for a lofty ideal may and often does offer the only
path by which it is possible to move upward and onward.
There are unquestionably real national dangers connected
even with a successful war for righteousness; but equally without question there are real national dangers connected even
with times of righteous peace. There are dangers attendant on
every course, dangers to be fought against in every kind of life,
whether of an individual or of a nation. But it is not merely
danger, it is death, the death of the soul even more than the
death of the body, which surely awaits the nation that does
not both cultivate the lofty morality which will forbid it to do
wrong to others, and at the same time spiritually, intellectually, and physically prepare itself, by the development of the
stern and high qualities of the soul and the will no less than in
things material, to defend by its own strength its own existence; and, as I at least hope some time will be the case, also

to fit itself to defend other nations that are weak and wronged, when in helpless misery they are ground beneath the feet of the successful militarism which serves evil. At present, in this world, and for the immediate future, it is certain that the only way successfully to oppose the might which is the servant of wrong is by means of the might which is the servant of right.

Nothing is gained by debate on non-debatable subjects. No intelligent man desires war. But neither can any intelligent man who is willing to think fail to realize that we live in a great and free country only because our forefathers were willing to wage war rather than accept the peace that spells destruction. No nation can permanently retain any "social values" worth having unless it develops the warlike strength necessary for its own defense.

Toward a World Order

62. · THE SECOND HAGUE CONFERENCE

Roosevelt's support of international agreements and agencies to maintain peace further modifies his image as a militarist. To be sure, he regarded the arbitration treaties sponsored by William Howard Taft and William Jennings Bryan as unrealistic, and he refused to associate unqualifiedly with the ultra-idealistic peace movement led by Andrew Carnegie. He also insisted at the end of World War I that a formal alliance between the United States, Great Britain, and France would be a more effective guarantor of peace than the League of Nations. Yet he himself issued a call for a second Hague Conference in 1904; and as the conference prepared to convene in 1907 he wrote that he would do his best "to get this Government to agree to any feasible scheme which will

Letter to Andrew Carnegie, April 5, 1907. *The Letters,* V, 638–42.

tend to minimize the chances of war occurring without previous efforts to secure mediation or arbitration." In the letter printed below Roosevelt reiterates his opinion that, although righteousness must take precedence over peace, a limitation on armaments and the adoption of a general (but not all-inclusive) arbitration treaty would be desirable.

Washington, April 5, 1907

My dear Mr. Carnegie: I much regret my inability to be present with you. Mr. Root will speak to you at length, and no man in the country is better fitted than he to address you on the subject you have so much at heart; for no man has in keener or more practical fashion, or with a nobler disinterestedness of purpose, used the national power to further what I believe to be the national purpose of bringing nearer the day when the peace of righteousness, the peace of justice, shall obtain among nations.

In this letter of mine I can do little more than wish you and your association Godspeed in your efforts. My sympathy with the purposes you have at heart is both strong and real, and by right of it I shall make to you some suggestions as to the practical method for accomplishing the ends we all of us have in view. First and foremost, I beseech you to remember that tho it is our bounden duty to work for peace, yet it is even more our duty to work for righteousness and justice. It is "Righteousness that exalteth a nation," and tho normally peace is the handmaid of righteousness, yet, if they are ever at odds, it is righteousness whose cause we must espouse. In the second place, I again earnestly ask that all good and earnest men who believe strongly in this cause, but who have not themselves to bear the responsibility of upholding the nation's honor, shall not by insisting upon the impossible put off the day when the possible can be accomplished. The peoples of the world have advanced unequally along the road that leads to justice and

fair-dealing, one with another (exactly as there has been unequal progress in securing such justice by each within its own
borders); and the road stretches far ahead even of the most
advanced. Harm and not good would result if the most advanced nations, those in which most freedom for the individual
is combined with most efficiency in securing orderly justice as
between individuals, should by agreement disarm and place
themselves at the mercy of other peoples less advanced, of
other peoples still in the stage of military barbarism or military
despotism. Anything in the nature of general disarmament
would do harm and not good if it left the civilized and peace-
loving peoples, those with the highest standards of municipal
and international obligation and duty, unable to shock the
other peoples who have no such standards, who acknowledge
no such obligations.

Finally, it behooves all of us to remember, and especially
those of us who either make or listen to speeches, that there
are few more mischievous things than the custom of uttering
or applauding sentiments which represent mere oratory, and
which are not, and cannot be, and have not been, translated
from words into deeds. An impassioned oration about peace
which includes an impassioned demand for something which
the man who makes the demand either knows or ought to
know cannot, as a matter of fact, be done, represents not gain,
but loss, for the cause of peace; for even the noblest cause is
marred by advocacy which is either insincere or foolish.

These warnings that I have uttered do not mean that I believe we can do nothing to advance the cause of international
peace. On the contrary, I believe that we can do much to advance it, provided only we act with sanity, with self-restraint,
with power; which must be the prime qualities in the achievement of any reform. The nineteenth century saw, on the whole,
a real and great advance in the standard of international conduct, both as among civilized nations and by strong nations

CIVILIZATION
ABSOLU
PAX
CAN BE ACHIEVED

towards weaker and more backward peoples. The twentieth century will, I believe, witness a much greater advance in the same direction. The United States has a right to speak on behalf of such a cause, and to ask that its course during the half dozen opening years of the century be accepted as a guaranty of the truth of its professions. During these six years we can conscientiously say that without sacrificing our own rights we have yet scrupulously respected the rights of all other peoples. With the great military nations of the world, alike in Europe and in that newest Asia which is also the oldest, we have preserved a mutually self-respecting and kindly friendship. In the Philippine Islands we are training a people in the difficult art of self-government with more success than those best acquainted with the facts had dared to hope. We are doing this because we have acted in a spirit of genuine disinterestedness, of genuine and single-minded purpose to benefit the islanders—and I may add, in a spirit wholly untainted by that silly sentimentality which is often more dangerous to both the subject and the object than downright iniquity. In Panama we are successfully performing what is to be the greatest engineering feat of the ages, and while we are assuming the whole burden of the work, we have explicitly pledged ourselves that the use is to be free for all mankind. In the islands of the Caribbean we have interfered not as conquerors, but solely to avert the need of conquest. The United States army is at this moment in Cuba, not as an act of war, but to restore Cuba to the position of a self-governing republic. With Santo Domingo we have just negotiated a treaty especially designed to prevent the need of any interference either by us or by any foreign nation with the internal affairs of the island, while at the same time securing the honest creditors their debts and to the government of the island an assured income, and giving to the islanders themselves the chance, if only they will take advantage of it, to achieve the internal

BASIC AM. CLAIM

S. DOM INTO

1907

peace they so sorely need. Mr. Root's trip thru South America marked the knitting together in the bonds of self-respecting friendship of all the republics of this continent; it marked a step toward the creation among them of a community of public feeling which will tell for justice and peace thruout the western hemisphere. By the joint good offices of Mexico and ourselves we averted one war in Central America, and did what we could to avert another, altho we failed. We have more than once, while avoiding officious international meddling, shown our readiness to help other nations secure peace among themselves. A difficulty which we had with our friendly neighbor to the south of us, we solved by referring it to arbitration at The Hague. A difficulty which we had with our friendly neighbor to the north of us, we solved by the agreement of a joint commission composed of representatives of the two peoples in interest. We try to avoid meddling in affairs that are not our concern, and yet to have our views heard where they will avail on behalf of fair-dealing and against cruelty and oppression. We have concluded certain arbitration treaties. I only regret that we have not concluded a larger number.

Our representatives will go to the second peace conference at The Hague instructed to help in every practicable way to bring some steps nearer completion the great work which the first conference began. It is idle to expect that a task so tremendous can be settled by any one or two conferences, and those who demand the impossible from such a conference not only prepare acute disappointment for themselves, but by arousing exaggerated and baseless hopes which are certain to be disappointed, play the game of the very men who wish the conference to accomplish nothing. It is not possible that the conference should go more than a certain distance further in the right direction. Yet I believe that it can make real progress on the road towards international justice, peace and fair-dealing. One of the questions, altho not to my mind one of the most important, which will be brought before the conference, will be that of the limitation of armaments. The United States, owing to its peculiar position, has a regular army so small as to be infinitesimal when compared to that of any other first-class power. But the circumstances which enable this to be so are peculiar to our case, and do not warrant us in assuming the offensive attitude of schoolmaster towards other nations. We are no longer enlarging our navy. We are simply keeping up its strength, very moderate indeed when compared with our wealth, population and coast line; for the addition of one battleship a year barely enables us to make good the units which become obsolete. The most practicable step in diminishing the burden of expense caused by the increasing size of naval armaments would, I believe, be an agreement limiting the size of all ships hereafter to be built; but hitherto it has not proved possible to get other nations to agree with us on this point.

More important than reducing the expense of the implements of war is the question of reducing the possible causes of war, which can most effectually be done by substituting other methods than war for the settlement of disputes. Of those other methods the most important which is now attainable is arbitration. I do not believe that in the world as it actually is it is possible for any nation to agree to arbitrate all difficulties which may arise between itself and other nations; but I do believe that there can be at this time a very large increase in the classes of cases which it is agreed shall be arbitrated, and that provision can be made for greater facility and certainty of arbitration. I hope to see adopted a general arbitration treaty among the nations; and I hope to see The Hague Court greatly increased in power and permanency, and the judges in particular made permanent and given adequate salaries, so as to make it increasingly probable that in each case that may come before them they will decide between the nations, great or small, exactly as a judge within our own limits

IDEA OF A SUPREME COURT FOR ALL

NATIONS - ARBITRATION.

decides between the individuals, great or small, who come before him. Doubtless many other matters will be taken up at The Hague; but it seems to me that this of a general arbitration treaty is perhaps the most important.

Again wishing you all good fortune in your work,

63. · "INTERNATIONAL PEACE"

Roosevelt's mediation of the Russo-Japanese War of 1904-1905 earned him the Nobel Peace Prize, and on May 5, 1910, partly at the instance of Andrew Carnegie, he addressed the Nobel Committee. His address faithfully expressed his long-held views on both the limitations and possibilities of the peace movement, though it overemphasized the latter, presumably in deference to the sensibilities of his audience.

It is with peculiar pleasure that I stand here to-day to express the deep appreciation I feel of the high honor conferred upon me by the presentation of the Nobel Peace Prize. The gold medal which formed part of the prize I shall always keep, and I shall hand it on to my children as a precious heirloom. The sum of money provided as part of the prize by the wise generosity of the illustrious founder of this world-famous prize system I did not, under the peculiar circumstances of the case, feel at liberty to keep. I think it eminently just and proper that in most cases the recipient of the prize should keep for his own use the prize in its entirety. But in this case, while I did not act officially as President of the United States, it was nevertheless only because I was President that I was enabled to act

Address before the Nobel Prize Committee at Christiania, Norway, May 5, 1910. *The Works,* XVIII, 410–15.

at all; and I felt that the money must be considered as having been given me in trust for the United States. I therefore used it as a nucleus for a foundation to forward the cause of industrial peace as being well within the general purpose of your committee; for in our complex industrial civilization of to-day the peace of righteousness and justice, the only kind of peace worth having, is at least as necessary in the industrial world as it is among nations. There is at least as much need to curb the cruel greed and arrogance of part of the world of capital, to curb the cruel greed and violence of part of the world of labor, as to check a cruel and unhealthy militarism in international relationships.

We must ever bear in mind that the great end in view is righteousness, justice as between man and man, nation and nation, the chance to lead our lives on a somewhat higher level, with a broader spirit of brotherly good-will one for another. Peace is generally good in itself, but it is never the highest good unless it comes as the handmaid of righteousness; and it becomes a very evil thing if it serves merely as a mask for cowardice and sloth, or as an instrument to further the ends of despotism or anarchy. We despise and abhor the bully, the brawler, the oppressor, whether in private or public life; but we despise no less the coward and the voluptuary. No man is worth calling a man who will not fight rather than submit to infamy or see those that are dear to him suffer wrong. No nation deserves to exist if it permits itself to lose the stern and virile virtues; and this without regard to whether the loss is due to the growth of a heartless and all-absorbing commercialism, to prolonged indulgence in luxury and soft effortless ease, or to the deification of a warped and twisted sentimentality.

Moreover, and above all, let us remember that words count only when they give expression to deeds or are to be translated into them. The leaders of the Red Terror prattled of

peace while they steeped their hands in the blood of the innocent; and many a tyrant has called it peace when he has
scourged honest protest into silence. Our words must be
judged by our deeds; and in striving for a lofty ideal we must
use practical methods; and if we cannot attain all at one leap,
we must advance toward it step by step, reasonably content so
long as we do actually make some progress in the right direction.

Now, having freely admitted the limitations to our work,
and the qualifications to be borne in mind, I feel that I have
the right to have my words taken seriously when I point out
where, in my judgment, great advance can be made in the
cause of international peace. I speak as a practical man, and
whatever I now advocate I actually tried to do when I was
for the time being the head of a great nation, and keenly jeal-
ous of its honor and interest. I ask other nations to do only
what I should be glad to see my own nation do.

The advance can be made along several lines. First of all,
there can be treaties of arbitration. There are, of course, states
so backward that a civilized community ought not to enter
into an arbitration treaty with them, at least until we have
gone much farther than at present in securing some kind of
international police action. But all really civilized communities
should have effective arbitration treaties among themselves.
I believe that these treaties can cover almost all questions liable to arise between such nations, if they are drawn with the
explicit agreement that each contracting party will respect the
other's territory and its absolute sovereignty within that territory, and the equally explicit agreement that (aside from the
very rare cases where the nation's honor is vitally concerned)
all other possible subjects of controversy will be submitted to
arbitration. Such a treaty would insure peace unless one party
deliberately violated it. Of course, as yet there is no adequate
safeguard against such deliberate violation, but the establishment of a sufficient number of these treaties would go a long

way toward creating a world opinion which would finally find expression in the provision of methods to forbid or punish any such violation.

Secondly, there is the farther development of the Hague Tribunal, of the work of the conferences and courts at The Hague. It has been well said that the first Hague Conference framed a Magna Charta for the nations; it set before us an ideal which has already to some extent been realized, and toward the full realization of which we can all steadily strive. The second Conference made further progress; the third should do yet more. Meanwhile the American Government has more than once tentatively suggested methods for completing the Court of Arbitral Justice, constituted at the second Hague Conference, and for rendering it effective. It is earnestly to be hoped that the various governments of Europe, working with those of America and of Asia, shall set themselves seriously to the task of devising some method which shall accomplish this result. If I may venture the suggestion, it would be well for the statesmen of the world in planning for the erection of this world court, to study what has been done in the United States by the Supreme Court. I cannot help thinking that the Constitution of the United States, notably in the establishment of the Supreme Court and in the methods adopted for securing peace and good relations among and between the different States, offers certain valuable analogies to what should be striven for in order to secure, through The Hague courts and conferences, a species of world federation for international peace and justice. There are, of course, fundamental differences between what the United States Constitution does and what we should even attempt at this time to secure at The Hague; but the methods adopted in the American Constitution to prevent hostilities between the States, and to secure the supremacy of the Federal Court in certain classes of cases, are well worth the study of those who seek at The Hague to obtain the same results on a world scale.

In the third place, something should be done as soon as possible to check the growth of armaments, especially vital armaments, by international agreement. No one power could or should act by itself; for it is eminently undesirable, from the standpoint of the peace of righteousness, that a power which really does believe in peace should place itself at the mercy of some rival which may at bottom have no such belief and no intention of acting on it. But, granted sincerity of purpose, the great powers of the world should find no insurmountable difficulty in reaching an agreement which would put an end to the present costly and growing extravagance of expenditure on naval armaments. An agreement merely to limit the size of ships would have been very useful a few years ago, and would still be of use; but the agreement should go much further.

Finally, it would be a master stroke if those great powers honestly bent on peace would form a League of Peace, not only to keep the peace among themselves, but to prevent, by force if necessary, its being broken by others. The supreme difficulty in connection with developing the peace work of The Hague arises from the lack of any executive power, of any police power, to enforce the decrees of the court. In any community of any size the authority of the courts rests upon actual or potential force; on the existence of a police, or on the knowledge that the able-bodied men of the country are both ready and willing to see that the decrees of judicial and legislative bodies are put into effect. In new and wild communities where there is violence, an honest man must protect himself; and until other means of securing his safety are devised, it is both foolish and wicked to persuade him to surrender his arms while the men who are dangerous to the community retain theirs. He should not renounce the right to protect himself by his own efforts until the community is so organized that it can effectively relieve the individual of the duty of putting down violence. So it is with nations. Each nation must keep well prepared to defend itself until the establishment of some form of international police power, competent and willing to prevent violence as between nations. As things are now, such power to command peace throughout the world could best be assured by some combination between those great nations which sincerely desire peace and have no thought themselves of committing aggressions. The combination might at first be only to secure peace within certain definite limits and certain definite conditions; but the ruler or statesman who should bring about such a combination would have earned his place in history for all time and his title to the gratitude of all mankind.

XCLUSIVE POWERS

World War I

64. · THE UNITED STATES' STAKE IN THE WAR

After a brief period of indecision following the outbreak of World War I in the summer of 1914, Roosevelt concluded that a German victory would be inimical to American interests. This conclusion was strengthened by his aversion to the rape of Belgium and, later, by the destruction of the *Lusitania* and the violation of American "rights" on the high seas. Here Roosevelt calmly sets forth his position to the Harvard psychologist, Hugo Münsterberg, who was already emerging as one of the nation's leading German apologists.

Oyster Bay, October 3, 1914

My dear Professor Münsterberg: I have received your very interesting book and it impresses me very much. But, my dear

Letter to Hugo Münsterberg, October 3, 1914. *The Letters*, VIII, 822–25.

Münsterberg, there are two or three points that you leave out of calculation. The first and most essential is that when a nation faces immediate death or humiliation because of the deed of another nation, it cannot look to the future with lofty philosophy, see the possible resulting good of its own ruin, and disregard the moral question of the moment. I firmly believe that in 1812 it was an essential thing to overthrow Napoleonic France. I feel that the German movement against France and the English resistance to France represented the struggle for light. (Let me remind you that Russia, that Asia, as you call it, was then on the side of Germany and that Germany could have done nothing without Russia and would have acted inexcusably if she had remained under France's yoke because it could be truthfully said that France represented far more enlightenment than Russia.) At that time the United States made war on England and by just so much gave comfort and strength to the Napoleonic side in the European struggle. Yet the action of the United States was absolutely necessary. My criticism of the United States in 1812 is heavy but it is not because she went to war with England; it is because she did not prepare effectively in advance for the war and wage it effectively; and indeed, as far as I am concerned, I think she ought to have declared war on both France and England.

Now, this is the exact case with Belgium today. The more I have studied the case, the more keenly I have felt that there can be no satisfactory peace until Belgium's wrongs are redressed and until there is some kind of effective guaranty against the repetition of them as against her and others. I do not for a moment believe that the predominant German motive in this war was aggression. I regard the talk about the Kaiser "wishing a blood-bath" as preposterous. I am sure that nine tenths of the German people have acted primarily from fear—from an honorable fear, just as you phrase it, that German civilization would be wiped out if they did not strike their foes. But, my dear Münsterberg, there was a ten per cent remainder, including the bulk of the men high up, who have for fifty years cultivated a theory in international matters quite as aggressive, quite as regardless of the rights of others and of all questions of international morality, as that which the French and to an only less extent the English had cultivated in the preceding seventy years. This country was strongly anti-English for a generation after the Civil War, because of the attitude of England and (also France) during the Civil War. But you probably do not realize the deep impression made upon this country by the attitude of Germany toward us in the Spanish War, especially in connection with Admiral Diederichs[1] at Manila, and also by the attitude of Germany in South America.

Now, not for publication, but frankly between ourselves, do you not believe that if Germany won in this war, smashed the English Fleet and destroyed the British Empire, within a year or two she would insist upon taking the dominant position in South and Central America and upon treating the United States precisely as she treated Japan when she joined with Russia and France against Japan twenty years ago and took Kiaochow as her share? I believe so. Indeed I know so. For the great Germans with whom I have talked, when once we could talk intimately, accepted this view with a frankness that bordered on the cynical; just exactly as the big Russians with whom I have talked took the view that international morality had no place where Russian interests were concerned.

I am under no illusions as to any friendship for the United States that England or France may entertain. It would be worthless to us in any crisis unless it was greatly to the interest of France and England to support us. But it does seem to me that England had to act as she did when Belgium was invaded; and that as regards Belgium there are no two sides to the question.

[1] German admiral in command of German fleet at time of Battle of Manila Bay [Ed.].

I am not much interested in trying to get at the truth about the, alleged outrages on individuals. The unquestioned fact is that Belgium has been ruined, that wonderful and beautiful old cities have been destroyed, that millions of entirely unoffending plain people have been reduced to the last pitch of misery, because Germany deemed it to its interest to inflict upon Belgium the greatest wrong one nation can inflict upon another. I grant you that Germany sincerely believed that this was necessary to her own existence; but surely we are not to be excused if we do not try to prevent the possibility of the recurrence of such incidents.

What the outcome of this war may be no human being can tell. At the moment it looks as if both sides might hammer themselves into a state of absolute exhaustion. If the allies should win and should then wish to dismember Germany and reduce her to impotence, whatever I could do would be done to prevent such a deed. I would regard it as a frightful calamity to civilization; and if Austria falls to pieces, I very earnestly hope that the German portion and all the other portions that are willing will join the Germanic body—the German Empire. But most emphatically I hope that ample reparation will be made to Belgium and that an effectual guarantee against the repetition of such wrongs as those that she has suffered will be arranged.

Now, as to the Russian. You speak very bitterly of him, and indeed of the Slav as a whole. I freely admit that the Russian is backward. They have a long way to go, those Russians, before they leave far enough behind them the days of Tartar dominion and the days when Tartar dominion was only overthrown through the upgrowth of a government such as that of Ivan the Terrible. The attitude of the Russian toward the Finn, the Caucasian, the Pole, the Jew and the Slavonian German in the past has too often been an evil attitude. But I think that liberal ideas are gaining in Russia. The gain is slow but on the whole it seems to me that it is evident. I do not believe the

Russian will become an Asiatic. I think he will in the long run be the most effective means of preventing a recrudescence of Asiatic rule over Europe. Down at bottom, my dear Münsterberg, the Russian is just about like you or like me. The Englishman thinks of the German as an alien by race and innate disposition. I know better, for I have some English and some German blood in me, not to speak of other strains. In exactly the same way I find that here in America the descendants of the Slavonic immigrants become men precisely like ourselves. Surely in the end we can aim for a better understanding between German, Englishman and Slav; and such an understanding must be based on justice and no one of them must feel for the others either fear or contempt.

You will not misunderstand me. I am not an ultrapacificist. I regard the Wilson-Bryan attitude of trusting to fantastic peace treaties, to impossible promises, to all kinds of scraps of paper without any backing in efficient force, as abhorrent. It is infinitely better for a nation and for the world to have the Frederick the Great and Bismarck tradition as regards foreign policy than to have the Bryan or Bryan-Wilson attitude as a permanent national attitude, for the Bryan-Wilson attitude is one that would Chinafy the country and would reduce us to the impotence of Spain when it was under the leadership of Godoy[2]—"The Prince of Peace," as he was officially entitled. A milk-and-water righteousness unbacked by force is to the full as wicked as and even more mischievous than force divorced from righteousness. But surely there is a goal different from either toward which we can strive. Surely we can strive for an international peace of justice, based on ability to guard ourselves from injustice, and determination not to do injustice to others, a peace in which some step shall have been taken toward putting international force behind an international de-

[2] Manuel de Godoy, Spanish statesman, who supported Napoleon against England [Ed.].

sire to secure at least a reasonable approximation toward justice and fair play.

65. · THE *LUSITANIA* CRISIS.

The prolongation of American neutrality caused Roosevelt to become more and more shrill in his denunciation of President Wilson and the peace forces. In this letter to his son, Archibald, he vents his feelings shortly after the *Lusitania* was torpedoed on May 7, 1915, with a loss of more than one thousand lives.

Syracuse, New York, May 19, 1915

Dear Archie: There is a chance of our going to war; but I don't think it is very much of a chance. Wilson and Bryan are cordially supported by all the hyphenated Americans, by the solid flubdub and pacifist vote. Every soft creature, every coward and weakling, every man who can't look more than six inches ahead, every man whose god is money, or pleasure, or ease, and every man who has not got in him both the sterner virtues and the power of seeking after an ideal, is enthusiastically in favor of Wilson; and at present the good citizens, as a whole, are puzzled and don't understand the situation, and so a majority of them also tend to be with him. This is not pardonable; but it is natural. As a nation, we have thought very little about foreign affairs; we don't realize that the murder of the thousand men, women and children on the *Lusitania* is due, solely, to Wilson's abject cowardice and weakness in failing to take energetic action when the *Gulflight* was sunk but a few days

Letter to Archibald B. Roosevelt, May 19, 1915. *The Letters,* VIII, 922–23.

previously. He and Bryan are morally responsible for the loss of the lives of those American women and children—and for the lives lost in Mexico, no less than for the lives lost on the high seas. They are both of them abject creatures and they won't go to war unless they are kicked into it, and they will consider nothing whatever but their own personal advantage in the matter. Nevertheless, there is a chance that Germany may behave in such fashion that they will have to go to war. Of course, I will notify you at once if war is declared; but I hope in any event, that it won't be until you and Quentin have had your month in camp. . . .

66. · TOWARD TOTAL PREPAREDNESS

Roosevelt's urgent calls for preparedness during the years of American neutrality in World War I sharpened his image as a militarist even as they served powerfully to mobilize public opinion in favor of building up the army and navy. In the following letter to the president of the National Security League, a conservative and predominantly Republican citizens' preparedness society, Roosevelt offers the familiar justifications for defense increases. The letter has special interest, however, because it faithfully represents Roosevelt's progressivism and sense of *noblesse oblige* no less than his flaming ultranationalism.

Oyster Bay, January 10, 1917

My dear Mr. Menken: As it is unfortunately impossible for me to be present in person, I desire in this letter to express my heartiest good wishes for the success of your meeting and my

Letter to S. Stanwood Menken, January 10, 1917. *The Letters,* VIII, 1143–48.

belief that the movement, in which you are engaged, is one of the really vital movements—indeed at the moment it is I think *the* really vital movement—for the ultimate honor and welfare of this country.

We need, more than anything else in this country, thorough-going Americanism,—for unless we are Americans and nothing else, we are not a nation at all—and thoroughgoing preparedness in time of peace against war,—for if we are not thus prepared, we shall remain a nation only until some more virile nation finds it worth while to conquer us.

The work of preparedness—spiritual and material, civic, industrial, and military—and the work of Americanization are simply the two paramount phases or elements of the work of constructive patriotism which your Congress has gathered to foster. There can be no real preparedness in this country unless this country is thoroughly Americanized; for only a patriotic people will prepare; and there can be no deep national feeling for America, until we are all of us Americans through and through.

Americanism means many things. It means equality of rights and therefore equality of duty and of obligation. It means service to our common country. It means loyalty to one flag, to our flag, the flag of all of us. It means on the part of each of us respect for the rights of the rest of us. It means that all of us guarantee the rights of each of us. It means free education, genuinely representative government, freedom of speech and thought, equality before the law for all men, genuine political and religious freedom, and the democratizing of industry so as to give at least a measurable quality of opportunity for all, and so as to place before us, as our ideal in all industries where this ideal is possible of attainment, the system of co-operative ownership and management, in order that the tool users may, so far as possible, become the tool owners. Everything is un-American that tends either to government by a plutocracy, or government by a mob. To divide along the lines of section or caste or creed is un-American. All privilege based on wealth, and all enmity to honest men merely because they are wealthy, are un-American—both of them equally so. Americanism means the virtues of courage, honor, justice, truth, sincerity, and hardihood—the virtues that made America. The things that will destroy America are prosperity-at-any-price, peace-at-any-price, safety-first instead of duty-first, the love of soft living, and the get-rich-quick theory of life.

Preparedness must be of the soul no less than of the body. We must keep lofty ideals steadily before us, and must train ourselves in practical fashion so that we may realize these ideals. Throughout our whole land we must have fundamental common purposes, to be achieved through education, through intelligent organization, and through the recognition of the great vital standards of life and living. We must make Americanism and Americanization mean the same thing to the native born and to the foreign born; to the men and to the women; to the rich and to the poor; to the employer and to the wage-worker. If we believe in American standards, we shall insist that all privileges springing from them be extended to immigrants, and that they in return accept these standards with wholehearted and entire loyalty. Either we must stand absolutely by our ideals and conceptions of duty, or else we are against them. There is no middle course, and if we attempt to find one, we insure for ourselves defeat and disaster.

Citizenship must mean an undivided loyalty to America; there can be no citizenship on the 50-50 basis; there can be no loyalty half to America and half to Germany, or England, or France, or Ireland, or any other country. Our citizens must be Americans, and nothing else, and if they try to be something else in addition, then they should be sent out of this country and back to the other country to which, in their hearts, they pay allegiance. We must have one American language; the language of the Declaration of Independence and the Constitution, of Lincoln's Gettysburg speech and Second Inaugural, and of Washington's farewell address. The American standard of living conditions, and the American standard of working conditions, both must be high. We must insist upon them for immigrants, as well as for the native born. We must insist that the people who work here, live here; that they are not mere birds of passage from abroad. We must insist upon industrial justice, and we cannot get it if we let ignorance and need be preyed upon either by vulpine cunning or by wolfish brutality, and if we do not train the ignorant and the needy up to self-reliance and efficiency.

Preparedness does not mean merely a man with a gun. It means that too; but it means a great deal more. It means that in this country we must secure conditions which will make the farmer and the workingman understand that it is in a special sense their country; that the work of preparedness is entered into for the defense of the country which belongs to them, to all of us, and the government of which is administered in their interest, in the interest of all of us. At this moment, Lloyd George is able to do more than any other man in rallying the people of Great Britain to the defense of that Empire, because the workingmen, the men who actually do the manual labor, know that he has their welfare at heart, that the national ideal for which he is fighting is that which will give them the best chance for self-development, and for that happiness which comes to the man who achieves his rights at the same time that he performs his duties. He is followed by the people as a whole because they know that he stands for the people as a whole. We in America who are striving for preparedness must make it evident that the preparedness is to serve the people as a whole. The war on the other side has shown that there can be no efficient army in the field unless the men behind are trained and efficient, and unless they are whole-heartedly loyal in their patriotic devotion to their country. Here in America we must do justice to the workers, or they will not feel that this is the country to which their devotion is due; and we must exact patriotic devotion to the flag from them, for if they fail to render it they are unfit to live in this country at all. I appeal to all Americans to join in the common effort for the common good. Any man who holds back, and refuses to serve his country with wholehearted devotion, on the ground that enough has not been done for him, will do well to remember that any such holding back, or lukewarmness of patriotism, is itself an admission of inferiority, an admission of personal unfitness for citizenship in a democracy, and ought to deprive him of the rights of citizenship. As for the men of means, from whom we have the right to expect a special quality of leadership, let them remember that as much has been given to them, so much will be expected of them, and that they have no moral right whatsoever to the enjoyment of the ease and the comforts of life beyond that their fellows enjoy, unless they render service beyond what their fellows render.

I advocate military preparedness not for the sake of war, but for the sake of safeguarding this nation against war, so long as that is possible, and of guaranteeing its honor and safety if war should nevertheless come. We hope ultimately the day will come on this earth when wars will cease. But at present the realization of that hope seems as far in the future as the realization of that other hope, that some day in the future all crime shall cease. By wise action, based equally on observed good faith and on thoroughly prepared strength— the precise characteristics which during the last few years we have failed to show—we may hope to limit the probable field of wars; but at present it is as certain as anything can be that every great nation will at some time or other, as generations follow generations, have to face war, and that ours will be no exception to the rule. It is therefore not merely folly, but criminal and unpatriotic folly, to fail to prepare, or to preach the ignoble cult of the professional pacifist, the peace-at-any-price man.

We need first and foremost a thoroughly efficient and large Navy; a navy kept under professional guidance; a navy trained at every point with the sole purpose of making it the most formidable possible instrument of war the moment that war comes; a navy, the mismanagement of which shall be treated as a capital offense against the nation. In the next place, we need a small but highly efficient regular army, of say a quarter million men; an army where provision is made for a certain proportion of the promotions to be by merit, instead of merely seniority; an army of short-term soldiers, better paid than at present; and an army which, like the navy, shall be under the guidance of a general staff. Moreover, every year there should be at one time field maneuvers of from fifty to one hundred thousand men, so that the Army Commander, the Corps Commanders, the Division, Brigade, and Regimental Commanders, who would have to face a foe at the outbreak of war, would all have had experience in performing their duties, under actual field conditions, in time of peace.

The events of the last summer have shown that the Hay bill[1] was as foolish and unpatriotic a bit of flintlock legislation as was ever put on the statute book. I have the greatest admiration and respect for the individual militiamen who went to the border. But the system under which they were sent worked rank injustice to most of them, rank favoritism for some of them, and was worse than ineffective from the national standpoint. It is folly, and worse than folly, to pretend that the National Guard is an efficient second line of defense. Remember also that the laws passed nominally for the betterment of the regular army and navy are producing almost no result. The delays in building the ships are extraordinary. The shortage of enlisted men in the navy and army is appalling, nor is it being made good. It cannot wholly be made good under the volun-

[1] The Hay bill proposed to increase the National Guard [Ed.].

teer system. But much could be done. Our first care should
be to make the navy and the regular army thoroughly efficient.
But this is not enough. To trust only to the Navy and the
regular Army amounts merely to preparing to let the other
men do it. If we ordinary citizens are fit to be citizens of
this country, we shall fit ourselves to defend this country. No
man has a right to citizenship in a democracy, if, for any cause
whatsoever, he is unwilling to fight, or is morally or mentally
incapable of fighting, for the defense of that democracy
against a powerful alien aggressor. If a man is physically unfit
but is right in his soul and in his head, then he can render
high service to the nation, although incapable of bearing arms.
But, if from any moral or mental causes he is unwilling to train
himself to bear arms, and to bear them if necessary in his
country's cause, then he has no moral right to vote.

Be it remembered that such a national armed force as that
for which I ask, while very powerful for defense, would be
almost useless for aggression. I wish to see our Navy second
only to that of Great Britain, because Great Britain is the only
power whose naval needs are greater than ours. I do not ask
that our Army become second, or anywhere near second, to
Germany's because Germany's military needs are far greater
than ours; but merely that relatively to our size our army be
made to correspond to that of Switzerland.

This would mean that for the last two or three years of
school, our boys would have some military training, substantially such as is given in the Swiss and Australian schools; and
that at about the age of nineteen they would spend six months
in actual service in the field (or at sea with the fleet) with
the colors, and would thereafter for three or four years be
required to spend a couple of weeks each year with the colors.
Each year, among those who had served well for the six
months, a number could be chosen to be trained as officers.
These would then be given by the nation for two years, free,

a training somewhat like that at West Point, although not as rigid or as thorough. They would be required to pay for this training by, for a certain number of months during each of the few following years, doing their part in drilling the recruits of that year. It would probably be necessary to pay the recruits a small minimum wage so as to be sure that the poorest family would not suffer hardship because of the absence of the young man for six months. No man would be allowed to purchase exemption. The sons of the richest men in the land would have to serve exactly like anyone else, and do exactly the same work—which incidently would be a bit of uncommon good fortune for them.

Side by side with this preparation of the manhood of the country must go the preparation of its resources. The Government should keep a record of every factory, or workshop, of any kind which would be called upon to render service in war, and of all the railroads. All the workers in such factories and railroads should be tabulated so that in the event of war they would not be sent to the front if they could do better service where they were—although as far as possible every strong man should be sent to the front, to the position of danger, while work done in safety should be done by women and old men. The transportation system should receive special study. Factories which would be needed in time of war, should be encouraged by the Government to keep themselves properly prepared in time of peace, and should be required to fill specimen orders, so that there would be no chance of their breaking down in the event of a sudden call at the outbreak of war. Industrial preparedness must go hand in hand with military preparedness.

Indeed, this military preparedness and the acceptance by the nation of the principle of universal, obligatory, military training in time of peace, as a basis of universal, obligatory service in time of war, would do more than anything else to help us solve our most pressing social and industrial problems in time of peace. It would Americanize and nationalize our people as nothing else could possibly do. It would teach our young men that there are other ideals besides making money. It would render them alert, energetic, self-reliant, capable of command, and willing to obey; respectful to others, and demanding respect from others for themselves. It would be the best possible way to teach us how to use our collective strength in order to accomplish those social and industrial tasks which must be done by all of us collectively if we are to do them well.

Just before this war began the male and female apostles of folly and fatuity were at their highest pitch of denunciation of preparedness, and were announcing at the tops of their voices that never again would there be a great war. These preachers of professional pacifism, of peace-at-any-price, of peace put before righteousness and honor and duty, temporarily lead astray many good and earnest men and women. These good, honest intelligent men and women can be shown the facts and when shown the facts will ultimately see the profound immorality as well as the utter folly of the professional pacifist or peace-at-any-price policy. There is, however, little to hope for as regards the professional pacifists themselves. The antics of their brethren in England have shown that even although brayed in a mortar their folly shall not depart from them. At the moment their clamor is drowned by the thunder of the great war. But when this war comes to an end, their voices will be as loud as ever on behalf of folly and wickedness, and their brazen effrontery will be proof against all shame, as well as against all wisdom. They will unblushingly repeat every prophecy that has just been falsified by the merciless march of events; they will reiterate all the promises that have always been broken in the past and will always be broken in the future. They are in the majority of cases primarily concerned for the safety of their own wretched bodies, and they are physically safe in the course they follow, for if the disaster they court should come upon this nation, they would themselves instantly flee to safety, while their folly and wrongdoing would be atoned for by the blood of better and braver men. It is useless to appeal to these persons. But it is necessary to warn our people against them. If our people fail to prepare, whatever the real reason may be, and whatever the reason is which they allege, their fate in the end will be the same. Sooner or later, in such case, either we ourselves or our children will tread the stony path of disaster, and eat the bitter bread of shame.

67. · WAR AIMS AND PEACE PROPOSALS

Roosevelt's fierce partisanship, the emotions inflamed by the war, and the ill-will resulting from President Wilson's refusal to permit Roosevelt to organize a volunteer division in 1917 reinforced Roosevelt's animus toward Wilson and all that he represented. To assume, however, that these factors formed his basic attitude toward the Fourteen Points and the League of Nations is to overlook the assumptions that Roosevelt had consistently held. Indeed, the strictures against Wilson's peace program, as expressed in these articles published in the Kansas City *Star* during October and November of 1918, were almost predictable.

"UNCONDITIONAL SURRENDER"*

When the American people speak for unconditional surrender, it means that Germany must accept whatever terms the United States and its allies think necessary in order to right the

The Works, XXI, 418–30.

* Kansas City *Star,* October 26, 1918.

dreadful wrongs that have been committed and to safeguard the world for at least a generation to come from another attempt by Germany to secure world dominion. Unconditional surrender is the reverse of a negotiated peace. The interchange of notes, which has been going on between our government and the governments of Germany and Austria during the last three weeks, means, of course, if persisted in, a negotiated peace. It is the abandonment of force and the substitution of negotiation. This fact should be clearly and truthfully stated by our leaders, so that the American people may decide with their eyes open which course they will follow.

Those of us who believe in unconditional surrender regard Germany's behavior during the last five years as having made her the outlaw among nations. In private life sensible men and women do not negotiate with an outlaw or grow sentimental about him, or ask for a peace with him on terms of equality if he will give up his booty. Still less do they propose to make a league with him for the future, and on the strength of this league to abolish the sheriff and take the constable. On the contrary, they expect the law-officers to take him by force and to have him tried and punished. They do not punish him out of revenge, but because all intelligent persons know punishment to be necessary in order to stop certain kinds of criminals from wrong-doing and to save the community from such wrong-doing.

We ought to treat Germany in precisely this manner. It is a sad and dreadful thing to have to face some months or a year or so of additional bloodshed, but it is a much worse thing to quit now and have the children now growing up obliged to do the job all over again, with ten times as much bloodshed and suffering, when their turn comes. The surest way to secure a peace as lasting as that which followed the downfall of Napoleon is to overthrow the Prussianized Germany of the Hohenzollerns as Napoleon was overthrown. If we enter into a league of peace with Germany and her vassal allies, we must expect them to treat the arrangement as a scrap of paper whenever it becomes to their interest to do so.

"What Are the Fourteen Points"*

The European nations have been told that the fourteen points enumerated in President Wilson's message of January last are to be the basis of peace. It is, therefore, possible that Americans may like to know what they are. It is even possible that they may like to guess what they mean, although I am not certain that such guessing is permitted by the postmaster-general and the attorney-general under the new theory of making democracy safe for all kinds of peoples abroad who have never heard of it by interpreting democracy at home as meaning that it is unlawful for the people to express any except favorable opinions of the way in which the public servants of the people transact the public business.

The first point forbids "all private international understandings of any kind," and says there must be "open covenants of peace, openly arrived at," and announces that "diplomacy shall always proceed frankly in the public view." The President has recently waged war on Haiti and San Domingo and rendered democracy within these two small former republics not merely unsafe, but non-existent. He has kept all that he has done in the matter absolutely secret. If he means what he says, he will at once announce what open covenant of peace he has openly arrived at with these two little republics, which he has deprived of their right of self-determination. He will also announce what public international understanding, if any, he now has with these two republics, whose soil he is at present occupying with the armed forces of the United States and

* Kansas City *Star*, October 30, 1918.

hundreds of whose citizens have been killed by these armed forces. If he has no such public understanding, he will tell us why, and whether he has any private international understanding, or whether he invaded and conquered them and deprived them of the right of self-determination without any attempt to reach any understanding, either private or public. Moreover, he has just sent abroad on a diplomatic mission Mr. House, of Texas. Mr. House is not in the public service of the nation, but he is in the private service of Mr. Wilson. He is usually called Colonel House. In his official or semi-official biography, published in an ardently admiring New York paper, it is explained that he was once appointed colonel on a governor's staff, but carried his dislike of military ostentation to the point of giving his uniform to a negro servant to wear on social occasions. This attitude of respect for the uniform makes the President feel that he is peculiarly fit to negotiate on behalf of our fighting men abroad for whom the uniform is sacred. Associated with him is an editor of the New York *World*, which paper has recently been busy in denouncing as foolish the demand made by so many Americans for unconditional surrender by Germany.

I do not doubt that these two gentlemen possess charming social attributes and much private worth, but as they are sent over on a diplomatic mission, presumably vitally affecting the whole country, and as their instructions and purposes are shrouded in profound mystery, it seems permissible to ask President Wilson why in this particular instance diplomacy does not "proceed frankly in the public view"?

This first one of the fourteen points offers such an illuminating opportunity to test promise as to the future by performance in the present that I have considered it at some length. The other thirteen points and the subsequent points laid down as further requirements for peace I shall briefly take up in another article.

The second in the fourteen points deals with freedom of the

seas. It makes no distinction between freeing the seas from murder like that continually practised by Germany and freeing them from blockade of contraband merchandise, which is the practice of a right universally enjoyed by belligerents, and at this moment practised by the United States. Either this proposal is meaningless or it is a mischievous concession to Germany.

The third point promises free trade among all the nations, unless the words are designedly used to conceal President Wilson's true meaning. This would deny to our country the right to make a tariff to protect its citizens, and especially its working men, against Germany or China or any other country. Apparently this is desired on the ground that the incidental domestic disaster to this country will prevent other countries from feeling hostile to us. The supposition is foolish. England practised free trade and yet Germany hated England particularly, and Turkey practised free trade without deserving or obtaining friendship from any one except those who desired to exploit her.

The fourth point provides that this nation, like every other, is to reduce its armaments to the lowest limit consistent with domestic safety. Either this is language deliberately used to deceive or else it means that we are to scrap our army and navy and prevent riot by means of a national constabulary, like the State constabulary of New York or Pennsylvania.

Point five proposes that colonial claims shall all be treated on the same basis. Unless the language is deliberately used to deceive, this means that we are to restore to our brutal enemy the colonies taken by our allies while they were defending us from this enemy. The proposition is probably meaningless. If it is not, it is monstrous.

Point six deals with Russia. It probably means nothing, but if it means anything, it provides that America shall share on equal terms with other nations, including Germany, Austria, and Turkey, in giving Russia assistance. The whole proposition would not be particularly out of place in a college sophomore's exercise in rhetoric.

Point seven deals with Belgium and is entirely proper and commonplace.

Point eight deals with Alsace-Lorraine and is couched in language which betrays Mr. Wilson's besetting sin—his inability to speak in a straightforward manner. He may mean that Alsace and Lorraine must be restored to France, in which case he is right. He may mean that a plebiscite must be held, in which case he is playing Germany's evil game.

Point nine deals with Italy, and is right.

Point ten deals with the Austro-Hungarian Empire, and is so foolish that even President Wilson has since abandoned it.

Point eleven proposes that we, together with other nations, including apparently Germany, Austria, and Hungary, shall guarantee justice in the Balkan Peninsula. As this would also guarantee our being from time to time engaged in war over matters in which we had no interest whatever, it is worth while inquiring whether President Wilson proposes that we wage these wars with the national constabulary to which he desired to reduce our armed forces.

Point twelve proposes to perpetuate the infamy of Turkish rule in Europe, and as a sop to the conscience of humanity proposes to give the subject races autonomy, a slippery word which in a case like this is useful only for rhetorical purposes.

Point thirteen proposes an independent Poland, which is right; and then proposes that we guarantee its integrity in the event of future war, which is preposterous unless we intend to become a military nation more fit for overseas warfare than Germany is at present.

Point fourteen proposes a general association of nations to guarantee to great and small States alike political independence and territorial integrity. It is dishonorable to make this proposition so long as President Wilson continues to act as he is now acting in Haiti and San Domingo. In its essence

Mr. Wilson's proposition for a league of nations seems to be akin to the holy alliance of the nations of Europe a century ago, which worked such mischief that the Monroe Doctrine was called into being especially to combat it. If it is designed to do away with nationalism, it will work nothing but mischief. If it is devised in sane fashion as an addition to nationalism and as an addition to preparing our own strength for our own defense, it may do a small amount of good; but it will certainly accomplish nothing if more than a moderate amount is attempted and probably the best first step would be to make the existing league of the Allies a going concern.

As to the supplementary points or proposals, the four advanced or laid down in February were sound moral aphorisms of no value save as they may be defined in each particular case.

But the supplementary five proposals set forth by President Wilson last September were, on the whole, mischievous and were capable of a construction that would make them ruinous in their essence. They set forth the doctrine that there must be no discrimination between our friends and our enemies and no special economic or political alliances among friendly nations, but uniform treatment of all the league of nations; the said league, therefore, to include Germany, Austria, Turkey, and Russia upon a footing of equality of our allies. Either the words used mean nothing or they mean that we are to enter a league in which we make believe that our deadly enemies, stained with every kind of brutality and treachery, are as worthy of friendship as the Allies who have fought our battles for four years. No wonder that the proposal is enthusiastically applauded by Germany, Austria, and Turkey and by all our own pro-Germans and pacifists and Germanized Socialists and anti-American internationalists. It is the kind of proposition made by cold-blooded men who at least care nothing for the sufferings of others. It is eagerly championed by foolish and hysterical sentimentalists. It is accepted and used for sinister purposes by powerful and cynical wrong-doers. When the

President was making this proposition and during the subsequent month Germany was committing inhuman murders of the people on the *Ticonderoga* and *Leinster* at sea, and on shore was committing every species of murder, rape, enslavement, plunder, and outrage as her armies withdrew from France and Belgium.

President Wilson's announcement was a notice to the malefactors that they would not be punished for the murders. Let us treat the League of Nations only as an addition to, and not as a substitute for, thorough preparedness and intense nationalism on our part. Let none of the present international criminals be admitted until a sufficient number of years has passed to make us sure it has repented. Make conduct the test of admission to the league. In every crisis judge each nation by its conduct. Therefore, at the present time let us stand by our friends and against our enemies.

"Fourteen Scraps of Paper"*

In my article yesterday I discussed Mr. Wilson's fourteen peace points which had been accepted by Germany. After the article was sent in, Mr. Wilson explained one of the points by stating that it meant exactly the opposite of what it said. A New York paper has asked for the election of a Congress that shall see eye to eye with Mr. Wilson. But only a Congress of whirling dervishes could see eye to eye with Mr. Wilson for more than twenty-four hours at a time.

When Germany broke her treaty with Belgium, the German chancellor called it a scrap of paper. Any individual who proposes a treaty which plainly means one thing, and then, as soon as he finds it disagreeable to adhere to that obvious meaning, instantly interprets it as meaning exactly the oppo-

* Kansas City *Star*, October 31, 1918.

site, is treating it as a scrap of paper. Mr. Wilson's recent interpretation of what he meant in the point about economic barriers makes all the fourteen points scraps of paper unworthy of serious discussion by anybody, because no human being is supposed to say what any one of them means or to do more than guess whether to-morrow Mr. Wilson will not interpret each and all of them in a sense exactly the opposite to their meaning.

Mr. Wilson's language in the point in question was that he intended the removal "of all economic barriers and the estab- lishment of an equality of trade conditions among all the na- tions." By no honest construction of language can this be held to mean anything except that this nation, for example, could have no tariff of its own, but must live under exactly the same tariff, or no tariff, conditions with all other nations. But Mr. Wilson now notifies a Democratic senator that he did not mean any "restriction upon the free determination by any nation of its own economic policy." If he meant this, why did he not say it? Why did he say the exact opposite? His first statement is wholly incompatible with the interpretation he now puts on it. If anybody in private life entered into a con- tract in such manner and then sought to repudiate it by inter- preting it in such manner, there is not a court in Christendom that would not adjudge him guilty of having used language with deliberate intent to deceive.

Nor is this all. In his new interpretation of what he did not originally mean, the President now says that he proposes to prevent any nation, including the United States, from using its tariff to discriminate in favor of friendly nations and against hostile nations. This is what he now says and what he now means, but, of course, to-morrow he may say that in this new interpretation he again meant exactly the opposite of what he says. However this may be for the future, President Wilson at this moment says, for instance, we ought to abandon reci- procity treaties; that we ought to refuse to make such treaties with our friends, such as Cuba and Brazil, and ought to punish these friends by treating them on an exact equality with our embittered and malevolent enemy, Germany. I hold this to be thoroughly mischievous doctrine.

The great scientist, Huxley, who loved truth and abhorred falsehood, said that "the primary condition of honest literature is to leave the reader in no doubt as to the author's meaning." Evidently this primary condition is not fulfilled by Mr. Wilson's fourteen points. They should now be treated as scraps of paper and put where they belong, in the scrap-basket.

"THE FREEDOM OF THE SEAS AND THE ENSLAVEMENT OF MANKIND"[*]

The surest way to kill a great cause is to reduce it to a hard-and-fast formula and insist upon the application of the formula without regard to actual existing conditions.

It is announced in the press that the President is going to the Peace Conference especially to insist, among other things, on that one of his fourteen points dealing with the so-called "freedom of the seas." The President's position in the matter is, of course, eagerly championed by Germany, as it has been Germany's special position throughout the war. It is, of course, eagerly championed by the New York *World*, the Hearst papers, and all the rubber-stamp gentry. It is antagonized by England and France and by every anti-German in America who understands the situation.

It is utterly impossible, in view of the immense rapidity of the change in modern war conditions, to formulate abstract policies about such matters as contraband and blockades. These policies must be actually tested in order to see how they work. Both England and the United States have reversed

[*] Kansas City *Star*, November 22, 1918.

themselves in this matter on several different occasions. This is interesting as a matter of history, but from no other standpoint. If we are honorable and intelligent we will follow the course in this matter which, under existing conditions at this time, seems most likely to work justice in the immediate future.

Germany's position was that England had no right to blockade her so as to cut off her supplies from the outside world. President Wilson at the time accepted this view and talked a good deal about the freedom of the seas. Meanwhile Germany, through her submarines, began an unprecedented course of wholesale murder on the seas. President Wilson protested against this in language much more apologetic and tender than he had used in protesting against Great Britain blockading Germany in what was essentially the same manner in which we blockaded the South during the Civil War. He put the dollar above the man and incidentally above the women and the children. He protested more vigorously upon the interference with American goods than against the taking of American lives.

Then we finally went to war with Germany ourselves. We instantly adopted toward Germany and toward neutrals like Holland exactly the position which President Wilson had been denouncing England for adopting toward Germany and toward us. Our action in this case was quite right, whereas our protest against England's action had been entirely wrong.

President Wilson now proposes to accept the German view and provide a system which, if it had been in existence in 1914, would have meant the inevitable and rapid triumph of Germany.

If this particular one of the proposed fourteen points had been in treaty form and had been lived up to in 1914, Germany would have had free access to the outside world. England's fleet would not have enabled her to bring economic pressure to bear upon Germany and doubtless Germany would have

won an overwhelming victory within a couple of years. Therefore Mr. Wilson's proposal is that now, when no human being
can foretell whether Germany will feel chastened and morally
changed, we shall take steps which will mean that if the war
has to be fought over again, Germany's triumph will have been
secured in advance so far as we are able to secure it. All such
conditions, all merely academic questions as to the attitude of
America or of England before the outbreak of the Great War,
are insignificant. Whatever our views prior to the Great War,
we are fools, indeed, if we have not learned the lessons these
last four and a half terrible years have taught. The freedom
of the seas in the sense used by Germany and Mr. Wilson
would have meant the enslavement of mankind to Germany.
It would have meant that this country would at this time
either be lying prostrate under the feet of German invaders
or be purchasing peace by ransoms heavier than were paid by
Belgium. No patriotic American has the right to stand quiet
and see the President of the country, without any warrant from
the country, try to bring upon us such outrageous potential-
ities of disaster as would be implied in the general international adoption of the so-called "freedom of the seas." Such
freedom of the seas means the enslavement of mankind.

INDEX